Lecture Notes in Computer Scie

T0238404

Commenced Publication in 1973
Founding and Former Series Editors:
Gerhard Goos, Juris Hartmanis, and Jan van Leeuwen

Karen Yorav (Ed.)

Hardware and Software: Verification and Testing

Third International Haifa Verification Conference, HVC 2007
Haifa, Israel, October 23-25, 2007
Proceedings

 Springer

Volume Editor

Karen Yorav
IBM Haifa Labs
Haifa University Campus
Mount Carmel, Haifa, 31905, Israel
E-mail: yorav@il.ibm.com

Library of Congress Control Number: 2008920255

CR Subject Classification (1998): D.2.4-5, D.2, D.3, F.3

LNCS Sublibrary: SL 2 – Programming and Software Engineering

ISSN   0302-9743
ISBN-10   3-540-77964-7 Springer Berlin Heidelberg New York
ISBN-13   978-3-540-77964-3 Springer Berlin Heidelberg New York

Springer is a part of Springer Science+Business Media

springer.com

© Springer-Verlag Berlin Heidelberg 2008
Printed in Germany

Typesetting: Camera-ready by author, data conversion by Scientific Publishing Services, Chennai, India
Printed on acid-free paper   SPIN: 12225194   06/3180   5 4 3 2 1 0

Preface

This volume contains the proceedings of the 3rd Haifa Verification Conference (HVC 2007), which took place in Haifa during October 2007. HVC is a forum for researchers from both industry and academia to share and advance knowledge in the verification of hardware and software systems.

Academic research in verification is generally divided into two paradigms – formal verification and dynamic verification (testing). Within each paradigm, different algorithms and techniques are used for hardware and software systems. Yet, at their core, all of these techniques aim to achieve the same goal of ensuring the correct functionality of a complicated system. HVC is the only conference that brings together researchers from all four fields, thereby encouraging the migration of methods and ideas between domains.

With this goal in mind we established the HVC Award. This award recognizes a promising contribution to verification published in the last few years. It is aimed at developments that significantly advance the state of the art in verification technology and show potential for future impact on different verification paradigms. The winners of the HVC Award are chosen by an independent committee with experts from all fields of verification – both formal and dynamic, software and hardware. The winners of the 2007 HVC Award were Corina Păsăreanu and Willem Visser, for their work on combining static and dynamic analysis.

This year we received 32 submissions, out of which 15 were accepted after a thorough review conducted by the Program Committee (PC) and additional reviewers. Each paper was reviewed by at least three reviewers, sometimes more. PC members who submitted papers were not involved in any way in the review, discussion, or decision regarding their paper. The chosen papers were presented during the 3-day conference, along with keynote and invited presentations. These proceedings include reviewed papers as well as the extended abstracts of invited talks. In addition, we held a full-day tutorial titled: "Verification 101—The Basics of Hardware Verification and Software Testing." The tutorial was designed for non-experts who want to know what verification is all about and for people with knowledge in one aspect of verification (e.g., software testing) who wanted to become familiar with other aspects (e.g., formal verification). The goal was to supply the non-expert with the tools needed to better understand the talks that were later presented at the conference. The tutorial was hosted by our sponsor, the Caesarea Rothschild Institute (CRI) at the University of Haifa.

Attendance at the conference was very high, with more than 250 participants from 12 countries (Austria, Canada, Czech Republic, France, Germany, India, Israel, The Netherlands, Russia, Switzerland, UK, and USA). Thanks to sponsorship from Cadence Israel, we were able to offer student travel grants, thus enabling PhD students to travel to the conference to present their work.

I would like to thank the Organizing Committee, the HVC Award Committee, the Program Committee, and the authors of all submitted papers for their contribution to the high quality of this year's event. Thank you to the invited speakers who travelled from afar and made the conference that much more interesting: Bob Bentley, Aarti Gupta, Alan Hu, Bob Kurshan, Corina Păsăreanu, Wolfgang Roesner, and Andreas Zeller. Many thanks to Avi Ziv, Cindy Eisner, and Shmuel Ur for the excellent tutorial. Special thanks to Vered Aharon for doing an excellent job with the logistics of the conference and to all the people at IBM who put in time and energy to make this event a success: Tamar Dekel, Ephrat Elgarisi, Ruth Elnekave, Ettie Gilead, Yair Harry, Yael Hay-Karesenty, Chani Sacharen. Last but not least, I would like to thank our generous sponsors, and especially Amos Ziv from Cadence Israel and Martin Golumbic from CRI for all their help.

October 2007   Karen Yorav

Organization

Conference and Program Chair

Karen Yorav   IBM Haifa Research Lab, Israel

Organizing Committee

Sharon Barner   IBM Haifa Research Lab, Israel
David Bernstein   IBM Haifa Research Lab, Israel
Laurent Fournier   IBM Haifa Research Lab, Israel
Moshe Levinger   IBM Haifa Research Lab, Israel
Shmuel Ur   IBM Haifa Research Lab, Israel
Avi Ziv   IBM Haifa Research Lab, Israel

HVC Award Committee

Chair

Roderick Bloem, Graz University of Technology, Austria

Committee

Armin Biere   Johannes Kepler University, Linz, Austria
Ken McMillan   Cadence Berkeley Labs
Amos Noy   Cadence, Israel
Mauro Pezzè   Università degli Studi di Milano Bicocca,
                        University of Lugano, Italy
David Rosenblum   University College London, UK
Gil Shurek   IBM Haifa Research Lab, Israel

Program Committee

Sharon Barner   IBM Haifa Research Lab, Israel
Lyes Benalycherif   STMicroelectronics, France
Eyal Bin   IBM Haifa Research Lab, Israel
Roderick Bloem   Graz University of Technology, Austria
Jong-Deok Choi   Samsung Electronics, Korea
Alessandro Cimatti   IRST, Italy
Kerstin Eder   University of Bristol, UK
Bernd Finkbeiner   Universität des Saarlandes, Germany

Limor Fix	Intel, USA
Laurent Fournier	IBM Haifa Research Lab, Israel
Orna Grumberg	Technion, Israel
Aarti Gupta	NEC Labs America, USA
Klaus Havelund	NASA's Jet Propulsion Laboratory, Columbus Tech.
Alan Hu	Univ. of British Columbia, Canada
Warren Hunt	University of Texas, Austin, USA
Daniel Kroening	ETH Zürich, Switzerland
Tsvi Kuflik	University of Haifa, Israel
Orna Kupferman	Hebrew University, Israel
Mark Last	Ben-Gurion University of the Negev, Israel
João Lourenço	Universidade Nova de Lisboa, Portugal
Sharad Malik	Princeton University, USA
Erich Marschner	Cadence, USA
Ken McMillan	Cadence, USA
Amos Noy	Cadence, Israel
Viresh Paruthi	IBM, USA
Carl Pixley	Synopsys, USA
Andrew Piziali	USA
Wolfgang Roesner	IBM Austin, USA
Padmanabhan (Peter) Santhanam	IBM Hawthorne, USA
Fabio Somenzi	University of Colorado, USA
Scott D. Stoller	Stony Brook University, USA
Ofer Strichman	Technion, Israel
Paul Strooper	University of Queensland, Australia
Serdar Tasiran	Koc University, Turkey
Shmuel Ur	IBM Haifa Research Lab, Israel
Willem Visser	SEVEN Networks, USA
Tao Xie	North Carolina State University, USA
Karen Yorav	IBM Haifa Research Lab, Israel
Avi Ziv	IBM Haifa Research Lab, Israel

Additional Reviewers

Jason Baumgartner
Domagoj Babic
Nicolas Blanc
Angelo Brillout
Hana Chockler
Klaus Dräger
Steven German
Naghmeh Ghafari
Dan Goldwasser

John Havlicek
Robert L. Kanzelman
Jean Christophe Madre
Yehuda Naveh
Sergey Novikov
Rotem Oshman
Hans-Jörg Peter
Zvonimir Rakamaric
Smruti R. Sarangi
Sven Schewe
Avik Sinha
Jörn Guy Süß
Michael Veksler
Georg Weissenbacher
Christoph M. Wintersteiger
Margaret Wojcicki
Cemal Yilmaz

Sponsors

The Organizing Committee of HVC2007 gratefully acknowledges the generous financial support of:

IBM Haifa Research Lab

Cadence Israel

CRI—The Caesarea Edmond Benjamin de Rothschild Foundation Institute for Interdisciplinary Applications of Computer Science.

Table of Contents

Dynamic Hardware Verification

Merging Formal and Testing

Formal Verification for Software

Software Testing

Simulation vs. Formal:
Absorb What Is Useful; Reject What Is Useless

Alan J. Hu

Department of Computer Science
University of British Columbia

Abstract. This short paper is the result of the invited talk I gave at the 2007 Haifa Verification Conference. Its purpose is to briefly summarize the main points of my talk and to provide background references. The original talk abstract was, "Dynamic verification (simulation, emulation) and formal verification often live in separate worlds, with minimal interaction between the two camps, yet both have unique strengths that could complement the other. In this talk, I'll briefly enumerate what I believe are the best aspects of each verification style, and then explore some possibilities for drawing on the strengths of both camps."

1 The Bruce Lee Approach to Verification

> Absorb what is useful.
> Reject what is useless.
> — Bruce Lee

I was invited to give a talk based on my long-standing interest in both dynamic (simulation and emulation) as well as formal verification, and the interplay between them. As I contemplated what to talk about, I recalled Bruce Lee's famous slogan, quoted above. This led to Cindy Eisner suggesting that the talk be entitled "The Bruce Lee Approach to Verification."

Bruce Lee's quote was a reaction against the orthodoxy of traditional martial arts instruction. He was not the first to articulate such a challenge, nor the last, but he is perhaps the most famous.

Fig. 1 lists some general characteristics of traditional martial arts instruction. These characteristics are common to other traditional instructional systems, such as for monks, many traditional arts, or medieval guilds. Such a system is excellent for preserving the traditions of the group, and for deep study of the intricacies of a given tradition. Students develop strong bonds with their fellow students and great reverence for their teacher, their teacher's teacher, etc. For example, I trace my T'ai Chi Ch'uan lineage back to Cheng Man-Ch'ing, who founded the sub-style I practice, and from him back to the founder of the Yang style of T'ai Chi Ch'uan, and I hold great reverence and gratitude to my fellow students and my teachers for their abilities and what they have taught me. In some martial arts styles, this reverence is explicitly formalized. For example, in Aikido schools, every class begins and ends by bowing to a portrait of Morihei Ueshiba, the founder of Aikido.

The problem with the traditional style of instruction is that it can lead to group-think. The lack of communication with other styles slows the spread of good ideas and can lead

K. Yorav (Ed.): HVC 2007, LNCS 4899, pp. 1–7, 2008.

- Study is in a school led by the master or a group of affiliated masters.
- Introductory classes are in groups, taught by the master or senior students, with the syllabus set by the master(s).
- Advanced study is one-on-one with the master.
- Students interact almost exclusively with fellow students and the master.
- When students travel, they go to tournaments and workshops, where they interact and compete with others from the same style.
- Students read books, articles, and papers by the masters of their own style.
- Often, students and teachers denigrate other styles.

Fig. 1. Characteristics of Traditional Martial Arts Instruction

to stagnation. Worse, followers of a style can fail to notice their own assumptions and blind-spots. This causes problems when those assumptions don't hold. For example, in my talk, I showed a video clip of a challenge match, in which one fighter was repeatedly defeated by the other, because the losing fighter's training had not prepared him for the types of situations which tended to occur under the rules and conditions of the challenge match.[1] Bruce Lee's quote was a call to break out of the confines of one's style, to explore what other experts and masters have to offer, to challenge one's assumptions and seek out the best ideas from all sources.

How does this relate to verification? Fig. 2 lists some general characteristics of traditional martial arts instruction. Comparing and contrasting Figs. 1 and 2, one can notice some similarities. Although I do not bow to pictures of Ed Clarke and David Dill each morning when I go to work, I do hold great reverence for their expertise and gratitude for what they've taught me.

The problem, of course, is the same sorts of blind spots that result from spending most of one's time in one community. For example, I am from the formal verification community, but I believe I also have a good awareness of, and an open-mind toward, dynamic verification. Last year, I was giving a talk at the 2006 IEEE International Workshop on High-Level Design Validation and Test on some recent work by my student and myself on using formal verification to guide a commercial logic simulator [12]. I thought this work perfectly straddled the division between formal and simulation, but Gil Shurek and Eyal Bin pointed out that I was still stuck in a formal mind-set: I had assumed that "bad states" were specified declaratively, as a logical assertion, but in reality, bad states might only be identifiable by running a large and complex chunk of imperative software code that acts as a checker. I believe I have an approach to handling such checkers (via software model checking), but the fact that I had completely overlooked this issue illustrates a blind-spot I had acquired by my focus on formal verification.

In my talk, I showed examples of how almost any combination of good ideas from the dynamic and formal communities has produced interesting and useful research. This is not an exhaustive list! I am just giving some examples that come to mind, to illustrate the general value of breaking free of one's style and absorbing useful ideas from others.

---

[1] I'm being deliberately obscure, because I don't want to descend into a "My kung fu style is better than yours" debate. :-)

- Study is in a school led by the professor or a group of affiliated professors.
- Introductory classes are in groups, taught by the professor or graduate students, with the syllabus set by the professor(s).
- Advanced study is one-on-one with the professor.
- Students interact almost exclusively with fellow students and the professor.
- When students travel, they go to conferences and workshops, where they interact and compete with others from the same style.
- Students read books, articles, and papers by the masters of their own style.
- Often, students and teachers denigrate other styles.

Fig. 2. Characteristics of Traditional Computer Science and Electrical Engineering Education

2 Combining Simulation and Formal

2.1 Version 1.0

The most obvious strength of formal verification is its exhaustiveness, and the most obvious strength of simulation is its scalability. Some of the earliest efforts to derive the best of both worlds sought to use a bit of formal verification, to gain coverage, while relying on simulation to handle the size and complexity of real designs. For example, some leading companies combined the two approaches methodologically, using simulation and emulation as the workhorse for verification, but applying formal strategically to small, high-value areas (e.g., complex protocols or algorithms) that were deemed to be particularly bug-prone (e.g., [7]).

Other approaches combined some formal state-space exploration and random simulation into a single tool, using just a little bit of formal analysis to gain some coverage before the formal analysis exploded. Early examples of work along these lines include computing a few pre-images to enlarge target states for random simulation (e.g., [27,29]), under-approximate reachability through partial image computation (e.g., [25]), and more elaborate combinations (e.g., [18]).

These ideas continue to be valuable. However, I believe a finer-grained examination of the strengths of formal and simulation can yield many other valuable ideas.

2.2 Mix and Match: Good Ideas from Formal

At a slightly finer-grained level, what are the key good ideas to extract from the formal verification world?

1. *Exhaustive analysis is useful!* I believe this is a fundamental conceptual breakthrough from the formal verification community in the past 10–15 years. Previously, exhaustive, brute-force algorithms were typically discarded as impractical, but the formal verification community has repeatedly shown the value of exhaustive analysis for solving real problems. Enabling this breakthrough are two key supporting ideas:
   (a) *Smart, Brute Force:* For example, techniques like BDDs, SAT, SMT, and constraint solving are all brute-force techniques at their worst-case core, but considerable effort has made them efficient and practical for many real problems.

(b) *Abstraction:* This is the other Swiss Army Knife of formal verification. An exhaustive analysis can become tractable if we can group large (possibly infinite) sets of possibilities and analyze them all together.

2. *Machine-Readable Specifications.* This is a really good methodological idea that has long been advocated by the formal verification community and has been gaining broader acceptance. Unless "correctness" is specified unambiguously in a machine-readable form, advanced verification tool support is impossible.

Choosing any of the good ideas from the above list and applying them to simulation yields new, good ideas. For example, constrained test generation has been a major practical success, resulting from applying "smart, brute force" techniques like BDDs, SAT, constraint solving, and state-space traversal to the problem of generating input stimuli for simulation (e.g., [19,1,16]). Combining abstraction and simulation yields abstraction-guided simulation, where model-checking an abstracted version of a system yields information that can help a simulator reach a target state (e.g., [28,21,17,14,26,22,12,13]). And bringing formal, declarative, machine-readable specifications to simulation is the foundation behind assertion-based verification (ABV) (e.g., [6]).

2.3   Mix and Match: Good Ideas from Simulation

Similarly, we can try to extract the key good ideas that make simulation so effective. I have identified three:

1. *Compiled Code.* This was a major performance breakthrough for simulation and enables its continued scalability. The point is to execute the model as code, rather than interpreting it as data, resulting in far higher performance. Hardware accelerators for simulation, as well as emulation, are even more extreme versions of this idea.
2. *Metrics.* This is a major methodological contribution pioneered by the simulation community. Coverage metrics of some form are needed to measure and report verification progress.
3. *Domain Expertise.* I am not implying that formal verification engineers lack domain expertise. But as I look at the reported research in formal verification versus dynamic verification, the difference is striking: most papers on formal verification describe a general theory for a general class of systems to verify; most papers on dynamic verification are infused with vast amounts of detailed knowledge about the characteristics of the design. This domain expertise has allowed effective verification in practice, despite the theoretically execrable coverage provided by simulation.

As above, we can mix-and-match good ideas from formal and simulation to generate new, good ideas. Some arbitrary examples of domain-specificity being applied to "smart, brute force" include SAT solvers tuned for hardware bounded model checking (e.g., [15]) or automatically retuned for software verification [20]; applied to abstraction yields things like Burch-Dill pipelined processor verification [9]; applied to specification yields everything from broadly applicable, somewhat domain-specific specification languages like Sugar [5] and ForSpec [3] (the predecessors of PSL and SVA) all the way down to an obscure example from my own work [10], which allows specifying a cycle-accurate MIPS processor simulator in less than 300 lines of code that runs comparably fast to hand-crafted performance simulators.

Mixing-and-matching Simulation Item 2 (Metrics) produces good ideas like a notion of coverage for formal specifications [11], a coverage model based on predicate abstraction [4], and progress metrics for SAT solvers [2,8].

I am particularly fond of the compiled code idea, having started on this idea several years ago, but not having had the opportunity to explore it as much as I'd like. In the late 1990s, I was teaching computer architecture courses, and it was a fairly common observation that every unpredictable branch cost dozens of instructions, and every non-local memory access might cost hundreds or even thousands of instructions. Conversely, operations that could be done in parallel were essentially free. This led me to realize that formal verification algorithms and data structures were making particularly poor use of modern processors, whereas compiled simulation was particularly efficient. My student and I developed a SAT solver for bounded model checking that compiled the circuit into fast, straightline executable code, but also did some learning [8]. On certain examples, it could greatly outperform the leading SAT-solvers of the time. Combining the idea of exploiting compiled code with abstraction also led to interesting work. I have mentioned abstraction-guided simulation above. Some recent work in this area has sought to employ the idea with leading, commercial compiled-code simulators [26,12]. When we did this, we found that the speed advantage of compiled-code simulation was so great that it overwhelmed the effect of the abstraction-guidance, forcing us to develop a much more robust and effective guidance heuristic [13], which has worked well in extensive experiments on large designs. I do not have any good examples of the combination of compiled code and machine-readable, formal specifications, per se, but as mentioned earlier, it is important that formal tools be able to handle the operational, imperative specifications that are common in the simulation world, and for formal specifications to be compilable into an executable form for use with simulators and emulators (e.g., [24,23] are two of my favorite papers along these lines :-)).

3   The Future

We have only scratched the surface of the possible synergies between formal and simulation. For example, I believe there is a deep connection between abstraction and coverage.[2] The fundamental question is why anything works, given that formal verification is not universal in industrial practice, and the theoretical coverage of the set of all possible behaviors provided by simulation is some ε fraction of all possibilities. I believe the answer lies in a connection between the informal coverage matrices used to track simulation progress and the existence of a suitable abstraction for model-checking the design.

---

[2] Hana Chockler has looked at the question of abstraction versus her concept of coverage for formal specifications. Here, I am talking instead of the concept of coverage in the simulation sense — the fraction of the behavior space that has been exercised by the simulator.

Summing up, my advice (or Bruce Lee's advice) is:

– Train hard in your own style. Expertise and depth in your area are your foundation.
– Cross-Train: Friendly study and sparring with practitioners of other verification styles helps share good new ideas and illuminate blind spots.
– Learn from other masters, as well as your own.

This advice doesn't just apply to verification!

References

1. Aharon, A., Goodman, D., Levinger, M., Lichtenstein, Y., Malka, Y., Metzger, C., Molcho, M., Shurek, G.: Test program generation for functional verification of PowerPC processors in IBM. In: 32nd Design Automation Conference, pp. 279–285. ACM/IEEE (1995)
2. Aloul, F.A., Sierawski, B.D., Sakallah, K.A.: Satometer: How much have we searched. In: 39th Design Automation Conference, pp. 737–742. ACM/IEEE (2002)
3. Armoni, R., Fix, L., Flaisher, A., Gerth, R., Ginsburg, B., Kanza, T., Landver, A., Mador-Haim, S., Singerman, E., Tiemeyer, A., Vardi, M., Zbar, Y.: The ForSpec temporal logic: A new temporal property-specification language. In: Katoen, J.-P., Stevens, P. (eds.) TACAS 2002. LNCS, vol. 2280, pp. 296–311. Springer, Heidelberg (2002)
4. Ball, T.: A theory of predicate-complete test coverage and generation. Technical Report MSR-TR-2004-28, Microsoft Research, (April 2004)
5. Beer, I., Ben-David, S., Eisner, C., Fisman, D., Gringauze, A., Rodeh, Y.: The temporal logic sugar. In: Berry, G., Comon, H., Finkel, A. (eds.) CAV 2001. LNCS, vol. 2102, pp. 363–367. Springer, Heidelberg (2001)
6. Bening, L., Foster, H.: Principles of Verifiable RTL Design: A Functional Coding Style Supporting Verification Processes in Verilog, 2nd edn. Kluwer Academic Publishers, Dordrecht (2001)
7. Bentley, B.: High level validation of next generation microprocessors. In: International Workshop on High-Level Design, Validation, and Test, pp. 31–35. IEEE, Los Alamitos (2002)
8. Bingham, J.D., Hu, A.J.: Semi-formal bounded model checking. In: Brinksma, E., Larsen, K.G. (eds.) CAV 2002. LNCS, vol. 2404, pp. 280–294. Springer, Heidelberg (2002)
9. Burch, J.R., Dill, D.L.: Automatic verification of pipelined microprocessor control. In: Dill, D.L. (ed.) CAV 1994. LNCS, vol. 818, pp. 68–80. Springer, Heidelberg (1994)
10. Chang, F.S.-H., Hu, A.J.: Fast specification of cycle-accurate processor models. In: International Conference on Computer Design, pp. 488–492. IEEE, Los Alamitos (2001)
11. Chockler, H., Kupferman, O., Vardi, M.Y.: Coverage metrics for temporal logic model checking. In: Margaria, T., Yi, W. (eds.) TACAS 2001. LNCS, vol. 2031, pp. 528–542. Springer, Heidelberg (2001)
12. de Paula, F.M., Hu, A.J.: EverLost: A flexible platform for industrial-strength abstraction-guided simulation. In: Ball, T., Jones, R.B. (eds.) CAV 2006. LNCS, vol. 4144, pp. 282–285. Springer, Heidelberg (2006)
13. de Paula, F.M., Hu, A.J.: An effective guidance strategy for abstraction-guided simulation. In: 44th Design Automation Conference, pp. 63–68. ACM/IEEE (2007)
14. Edelkamp, S., Lluch-Lafuente, A.: Abstraction in directed model checking. In: Workshop on Connecting Planning Theory and Practice, pp. 7–13 (2004)
15. Ganai, M.K., Zhang, L., Ashar, P., Gupta, A., Malik, S.: Combining strengths of circuit-based and CNF-based algorithms for a high-performance SAT solver. In: 39th Design Automation Conference, pp. 747–750. ACM/IEEE (2002)

16. Geist, D., Farkas, M., Landver, A., Lichtenstein, Y., Ur, S., Wolfsthal, Y.: Coverage-directed test generation using symbolic techniques. In: Srivas, M., Camilleri, A. (eds.) FMCAD 1996. LNCS, vol. 1166, pp. 143–158. Springer, Heidelberg (1996)
17. Gupta, A., Casavant, A.E., Ashar, P. Liu, X.G. (Sean), Mukaiyama, A., Wakabayashi, K.: Property-specific testbench generation for guided simulation. In: 7th Asia and South Pacific Design Automation Conference and 15th International Conference on VLSI Design (VL-SID), pp. 524–531. IEEE, Los Alamitos (2002)
18. Ho, P.-H., Shiple, T., Harer, K., Kukula, J., Damiano, R., Bertacco, V., Taylor, J., Long, J.: Smart simulation using collaborative formal and simulation engines. In: International Conference on Computer-Aided Design, pp. 120–126. IEEE/ACM (2000)
19. Ho, R.C., Yang, C.H., Horowitz, M.A., Dill, D.L.: Architecture validation for processors. In: International Symposium on Computer Architecture (1995)
20. Hutter, F., Babić, D., Hoos, H.H., Hu, A.J.: Boosting verification by automatic tuning of decision procedures. In: Formal Methods in Computer-Aided Design, pp. 27–34. IEEE Computer Society Press, Los Alamitos (2007)
21. Kuehlmann, A., McMillan, K.L., Brayton, R.K.: Probabilistic state space search. In: International Conference on Computer-Aided Design, pp. 574–579. IEEE/ACM (1999)
22. Nanshi, K., Somenzi, F.: Guiding simulation with increasingly refined abstract traces. In: 43rd Design Automation Conference, pp. 737–742. ACM/IEEE (2006)
23. Ng, K., Hu, A.J., Yang, J.: Generating monitor circuits for simulation-friendly GSTE assertion graphs. In: International Conference on Computer Design, pp. 409–416. IEEE Computer Society Press, Los Alamitos (2004)
24. Oliveira, M.T., Hu, A.J.: High-level specification and automatic generation of IP interface monitors. In: 39th Design Automation Conference, pp. 129–134. ACM/IEEE (2002)
25. Ravi, K., Somenzi, F.: High-density reachability analysis. In: International Conference on Computer-Aided Design, pp. 154–158. IEEE/ACM (1995)
26. Shyam, S., Bertacco, V.: Distance-guided hybrid verification with GUIDO. In: Design Automation and Test in Europe, pp. 1211–1216 (2006)
27. Yang, C.H., Dill, D.L.: SpotLight: Best-first search of FSM state space. In: IEEE International High-Level Design Validation and Test Workshops (HLDVT) (1996)
28. Yang, C.H., Dill, D.L.: Validation with guided search of the state space. In: 35th Design Automation Conference, pp. 599–604. ACM/IEEE (1998)
29. Yuan, J., Shen, J., Abraham, J., Aziz, A.: On combining formal and informal verification. In: Grumberg, O. (ed.) CAV 1997. LNCS, vol. 1254, pp. 376–387. Springer, Heidelberg (1997)

Scaling Commercial Verification to Larger Systems

Robert Kurshan

Cadence Design Systems

Abstract. Simulation test coverage does not scale gracefully with growing system design size. Component interactions grow exponentially with the number of system components, while conventional system test at best can increase coverage as a linear function of allotted test time.

Likewise, capacity limitations are commonly cited as the essential gating factor that restricts the application of automatic formal verification (model checking) to at most a few design blocks.

Nonetheless, abstraction has long been used successfully in pilot projects to apply model checking to entire systems. Abstraction in conjunction with guided-random simulation can be used in the same way to increase coverage for conventional test.

While academic use of abstraction is old, its use in the EDA industry's commercial tool sets has been very limited, due to a perception that its use entails an unacceptably disruptive methodology change. It is shown here how quite general data-path abstraction incorporated into a hierarchical design flow can be introduced with only a modest change in methodology. This hierarchical design flow supports verification based on either simulation or model checking that can scale gracefully with increasing design complexity.

1 Introduction

Today, less than 50% of integrated circuit design cost is attributed to synthesis and layout. The major cost of design is debug and verification, amounting to 50% to 80% of the total. Moreover, the relative and absolute costs of debug and verification are growing, as a result of increasing design complexity.

There are two predominant sources of this increasing complexity: the increasing use of embedded software that is so tightly integrated into the hardware that it is hard or impossible to test the hardware and embedded software separately; and an exponential growth in design complexity.

These two sources of complexity offer quite different verification challenges. Verification in the presence of embedded software requires new algorithms, flows and methodologies, as well as abstraction to handle the greater functional complexity introduced by the large additional software design component.

As a design grows in complexity, it gains additional components that function largely in parallel. Since n parallel components of size m leads to m^n system states, and the complexity of verification grows in proportion to the size of the design state space, it thus grows exponentially with increasing design size.

K. Yorav (Ed.): HVC 2007, LNCS 4899, pp. 8–13, 2008.

The challenge of dealing with this complexity growth – both from embedded software and generally increasing design complexity – is what is addressed here.

As a related matter, it is widely held that the cost of fixing a bug grows exponentially with the stage of development at which it is detected and fixed. This is on account of the increasing interactions with other components, as the design is developed. These other components may be required to reflect changes from such fixes. Additionally, over time a developer may forget the details of a design, or may be unavailable to fix a bug, again increasing the cost of debugging as the design matures.

The hierarchical design flow proposed here addresses both the exponentially increasing verification challenge and the ambition to perform debug and verification earlier in the design flow.

Through the use of abstraction, the intractability of design verification is mitigated. Through use of an abstraction-based top-down stepwise refinement hierarchy, design components can be debugged and verified as soon as they are coded, which is at the earliest possible point in the design development flow.

Although a conventional view is that simulation test is not bound by the capacity limitations of model checking, this leaves a wrong impression. The fact that an arbitrarily large design can be fed into the compiler front-end of a simulation tool does not speak to the quality of the simulation that ensues. In fact, both simulation and model checking are equally compromised by design size. In the case of simulation, this is manifest by diminished coverage; in the case of model checking, it is limited capacity. They are two sides of the same coin.

Through hierarchical design, both coverage for simulation and capacity for model checking can be enhanced.

2   Abstraction as Divide-and-Conquer

The age-old strategy for dealing with an intractable task is divide-and-conquer. To build the 6M ton virtual monolith that was the Great Pyramid, the task was divided into the assembly of 2.3M blocks, each small enough to handle. Likewise, the key to verifying a large design is to divide it into blocks small enough to verify. To build the virtual pyramid, its component blocks needed to be assembled with great precision. Likewise, to stitch together verified design blocks into a virtual verification of a large design, mathematical precision is required. Otherwise, there is just a jumble of partial verifications that cannot speak to the behavior of the entire design.

Since the verification of large designs is provably intractable, our only hope lies with some form of divide-and-conquer, and that requires mathematical precision. Thus it is fair to say that whatever the future of verification, it necessarily will be based on formal methods. Design components may be verified through model checking or they may be tested with conventional (informal) simulation test. However, the stitching together of these component results into a virtual result for the entire design must be mediated by a formal method.

Compositional verification implements a sort of "horizontal" divide-and-conquer wherein the design is partitioned into its component blocks, abstractions of some blocks are used to verify local properties of other blocks, and then these local properties are used to deduce global properties of the large design. This second part: to deduce global properties of the large design from local properties can be very challenging, and many research papers have resulted from tour-de-force deductions of this type. The difficulties involved preclude this sort of "horizontal" verification from entering the routine commercial design flow.

However, there is another sort of divide-and-conquer that can be viewed as "vertical". This is where the design evolves in a top-down fashion that follows a precise stepwise refinement methodology. With "vertical" divide-and-conquer, one begins with certain components together with abstractions of others, as in the "horizontal" case. However, in the "vertical" flow, the abstractions are refined into their ultimate implementations, whereas in the "horizontal" flow, the implementations come first and are then abstracted.

The "vertical" flow cannot in fact be a pure top-down process, as it must end up with a target architecture. In fact, it's a combination top-down/bottom-up flow. One starts with the architecture, floor plan, block diagrams, functional specification, etc. as now, and begins coding the design as now, but in a different order.

The "vertical" flow proceeds through stepwise refinement, so that properties may be verified at a high level of abstraction after which they are guaranteed to hold at all subsequent levels of refinement. This facilitates early verification: as soon as a block is coded, it may be verified.

In the "vertical" flow, global properties are verified first, when the design is relatively simple, unencumbered by its low-level implementational details. Properties with greater locality are verified as the relevant blocks are coded, later in the flow. Since they may be verified locally, they do not require large portions of the design to participate in the verification. This flow can maintain a constant-sized granularity for verification, so that coverage and capacity issues are avoided.

3 Vertical (Hierarchical) Decomposition

There seems little choice but to code *data before control*: in order to define a controller, the data objects it controls must have been defined – after all, the controller must refer to the objects it controls. Therefore, today's design flow begins with a coding of the data structures that define data and data paths. Only once these data structures are completely coded may the designer begin to code the finite state machines and other control structures used to control the data.

However, there is something deeply dissatisfying about this order. After all, the controllers define the functional behavior of the design. One would like to define (and debug) them first, and only then code the design infrastructure defined by the data and data paths. It's as if you were required to build a house by first installing the plumbing and wiring, and only after this build the walls and floors.

Coding first the data structures that define data and data paths also leads to design instabilities. Once these data structures are defined, several designers may code controllers against them. However, in coding a controller it is not uncommon for a designer to find the previously coded data structures are insufficient. Perhaps a tag bit required by a controller to store its state in the data path was overlooked. Then the data structures need to be redefined. This may impact several designers and set back the design.

Thus, "data before control" is backward both for the interests of the design process and design stability.

In fact, it is possible to reverse this order for hardware designs and code *control before data*. This reversal is the key to the "vertical" flow proposed here.

The way to achieve this reversal is to use **stubs** to serve as place-holders for data and data paths. The developer begins the design by coding the controllers, which point to and manipulate these stubs.

These stubs have a semantics, and their refinement into the ultimate data structures that define the data and the data paths is precisely controlled to ensure that the refinement is conservative.

Some stubs are oracles. For example, a controller that needs to move a packet from one buffer to another, conditional on a CRC check of the packet, can be implemented using a stub for the ALU that will perform the CRC check. This stub ALU can be implemented as an oracle that nondeterministically emits a "yes" (CRC passed) or a "no". At a high level of abstraction the packet is also abstracted ("stubbed") as a token, so there is in fact no actual packet to check. At this high level of abstraction, what can be verified is that the controller does the correct action if the answer is "yes" and the correct action if the answer is "no".

Later, the packet stub and the ALU stub will be refined into their actual implementations. At that level it can be checked that the CRC is correct – a local verification independent of the controller. The controller need not be reverified at this lower level, since its correctness is inherited by the conservative refinement process.

Since the controller can be verified as soon as it is coded, it is fresh in the mind of the designer and thus easier to debug. At the same time, the design is simple since much is abstracted (stubbed out), so again debugging is easier. At lower levels of abstraction, debugging is likewise simpler, as at the lower levels the verification is more local, and thus entails smaller portions of the design.

Coding *control before data* is not an enormous methodology shift: in the end of the design flow, essentially the same RTL code is written as in the present-day flow. The shift is that the design is coded in a different order. All the same considerations of architecture, floor plan and function mediate this new flow just the same as in the old flow. Code must be written in some order; the change proposed here is only that order, not the code itself.

4 A Methodology for Hierarchical Design

The crux of the design method proposed here is to code control before data. But which controllers and in what order? The answer lies with a new wrinkle in the design process.

Although most will agree that it is important to define a test plan before design begins, all too often testing is the bastard child of design, left only to the end, to a "verification team" that lies low in the pecking order of the design elite. Leaving testing to the end has been the down-fall of great designs. This is widely understood, and yet astonishingly much less widely accommodated.

The catalyst of the *control before data* hierarchical design flow is a movement of verification to the top of the development elite. In this flow, the "verification team" gets promoted to become a "specification/verification team". This team works with the same design specifications as the designers, *before* design coding commences. They derive a complete formal specification of the design using, say, a standardized specification language (PSL, OVL, SVA). These design properties will be used as monitors for simulation test and as assertions and constraints for model checking.

It is important that this design specification be complete, in the sense that collectively the specified properties account for all required design functionality. While there are several criteria for checking "completeness" of a set of design properties that are currently in vogue, such as mutation checks or finite-state machine completeness, each of these have their short-comings.

A better means may be based on the old-fashioned (but time-honored) process of *review*. Just as with a code review where experts analyze a piece of code line-by-line, in a *specification review* the architects, designers and "specification/verification team" review drafts of design properties for correctness and completeness.

Once the specification is complete and deemed correct, the "specification/verification team" establishes a taxonomy of properties, from more global to more local. This taxonomy will drive the order of controller design.

The "specification/verification team" will work hand-in-hand with the designer to establish the order of design coding. Initially, the designer is given a high-level property. The designer codes the controllers required to verify this property, stubbing out the associated data and data paths. The "specification/verification team" will assist the designer in verifying these controllers for the designated property through simulation, model checking or a combination of the two. This way, the controller gets debugged as soon as it is written.

This process continues for other high-level properties, until all the global controllers have been coded and debugged.

Then the stubs are refined (possibly into some data path, some lower-level "local" controllers and new stubs for the remaining data path). The refinements are then verified in their more local context. The locality increases with decreasing granulatity of data. This balance tends to hold the verification complexity constant.

This process continues until all stubs are refined into their ultimate RTL. At this point the design is not only complete, but at the same time, completely verified.

This description serves to give an intuitive understanding of the process that is proposed. In fact, it cannot work as simply as the above description suggests. The refinement flow will not be so neatly linear (top-to-bottom) as this discussion may imply, but will involve imbalanced abstractions at various design levels and non-linear refinement flows. A more detailed description that addresses these realities is beyond the scope of this extended abstract. However, the simplistic linear flow conveys the correct intuition concerning intent and essence of the method.

From Hardware Verification to Software Verification: Re-use and Re-learn

Aarti Gupta

NEC Laboratories America
4 Independence Way
Princeton, NJ 08540, U.S.A.

Extended Abstract

With the growing maturity in hardware verification methods, there has been great interest in applying them to verification of software programs. Aside from issues of scale and complexity, there are many differences between the two domains in the underlying problem of searching for bugs. In this talk, I will describe our experiences with this transition, with emphasis on methods that worked and those that did not.

Verification methods based on Boolean Satisfiability (SAT) have emerged as a promising alternative to BDD-based symbolic model checking methods [8]. We have developed an efficient platform for SAT-based model checking [4], called VERISOL, which has been used successfully in industry practice to verify large hardware designs. It uses an efficient circuit representation with on-the-fly simplification algorithms, an incremental hybrid SAT solver, and utilizes several SAT-based engines for finding bugs (bounded model checking) and proofs (proof-based abstraction, SAT-based induction).

Inspired by its success on hardware designs, we attempted to re-use VERISOL for performing model checking in the back-end of F-SOFT [6], which is targeted for verifying C programs. We first derive a control flow graph (CFG) representation of the program, use static code analyses (program slicing, range analysis, constant folding) to simplify and reduce the CFG, and then derive a symbolic circuit model (under assumptions of finite data and finite recursion). The resulting bit-accurate circuit model of the program is then verified by VERISOL.

Our direct attempt at using hardware verification methods for verifying software models did not lead immediately to success. The two main problems were that the number of variables was too high, and BMC needed to go too deep. We therefore proposed several customized SAT-based heuristics to exploit the high-level structure in CFG models, which greatly improve SAT solver performance [5]. We have also proposed path balancing transformations on the CFG model, which enable additional on-the-fly simplification during BMC to improve performance [3]. To reduce the burden on the model checker, we use program analysis methods for static invariant generation [9] to find proofs more cheaply for array buffer overflow and pointer dereference errors. In our experience, a combination of these methods with SAT-based BMC works much better than predicate abstraction refinement for these checks, since the number of predicates and the number of refinement iterations tend to blow up.

To address the problem of bugs being too deep (when starting from the main function in a C program), we start verification from some intermediate function by

K. Yorav (Ed.): HVC 2007, LNCS 4899, pp. 14–15, 2008.

considering a default abstract environment at its interface. This re-uses the idea of a localization reduction [7]. A counterexample reported by the model checker may be spurious due to missing environment information. We use these counterexamples to guide *environment* refinement (*CEGER*). This is similar to standard CEGAR [2] or predicate abstraction refinement [1], except that we use it to refine only the environment, not the model of the program. The CEGER loop is not completely automated – we require help from the user to identify the spurious behavior and guide the refinement. However, the model checker assists the user by providing a concrete error trace, and a weakest precondition as a suggestion for the interface constraint. In practice, users find it much easier to modify a suggested constraint, than to create one.

With these techniques to scale up and supplement model checking for software programs, the F-SOFT platform has recently been used to start an in-house verification service within NEC. To date, it has found more than 450 likely bugs (many confirmed by developers) in four projects totalling 1.1 MLOC (with one 600 kLOC project).

Acknowledgements. I would like to thank the current and past members of the NEC Labs Verification Group – Pranav Ashar, Malay Ganai, Franjo Ivančič, Vineet Kahlon, Weihong Li, Nadia Papakonstantinou, Sriram Sankaranarayanan, Ilya Shlyakhter, Chao Wang, and James Yang – for their numerous contributions to these projects. I would also like to thank Y. Hashimoto, K. Ikeda, S. Iwasaki, A. Mukaiyama, K. Wakabayashi, and the SWED Group from NEC Corp. (Japan) for their support in the development and application of F-SOFT and VERISOL.

References

1. Ball, T., Majumdar, R., Millstein, T.D., Rajamani, S.K.: Automatic predicate abstraction of C programs. In: ACM SIGPLAN Conference on Programming Language Design and Implementation (2001)
2. Clarke, E.M., et al.: Counterexample-guided abstraction refinement. In: Emerson, E.A., Sistla, A.P. (eds.) CAV 2000. LNCS, vol. 1855, pp. 154–169. Springer, Heidelberg (2000)
3. Ganai, M.K., Gupta, A.: Accelerating high-level bounded model checking. In: IEEE International Conference on Computer-Aided Design (2006)
4. Ganai, M.K., Gupta, A., Ashar, P.: DiVer. In: Halbwachs, N., Zuck, L.D. (eds.) TACAS 2005. LNCS, vol. 3440, pp. 575–580. Springer, Heidelberg (2005)
5. Ivančič, F., Shlyakhter, I., Gupta, A., Ganai, M.K., Kahlon, V., Wang, C., Yang, Z.: Model checking C programs using F-SOFT. In: IEEE International Conference on Computer Design (2005)
6. Ivančič, F., et al.: F-Soft. In: Etessami, K., Rajamani, S.K. (eds.) CAV 2005. LNCS, vol. 3576, pp. 301–306. Springer, Heidelberg (2005)
7. Kurshan, R.P.: Computer-aided Verification of Coordinating Processes: the Automata-theoretic Approach. Princeton University Press, Princeton (1995)
8. Prasad, M.R., Biere, A., Gupta, A.: A survey of recent advances in SAT-based formal verification. STTT 7(2), 156–173 (2005)
9. Sankaranarayanan, S., et al.: Static analysis in disjunctive numerical domains. In: Yi, K. (ed.) SAS 2006. LNCS, vol. 4134, pp. 3–17. Springer, Heidelberg (2006)

Where Do Bugs Come from?
(Invited Talk)

Andreas Zeller

Saarland University, Germany

Abstract. A program fails. How can we locate the cause? A new generation of program analysis techniques automatically determines failure causes even in the absence of any specification - in the input, in the set of code changes, or in the program state: "GCC fails because of a cycle in the abstract syntax tree." Relying on automated tests and dynamic execution data is just one example of how future program analysis techniques will access and leverage data beyond specs and code; leveraging all available data will result in automated assistance for all developer decisions.

K. Yorav (Ed.): HVC 2007, LNCS 4899, p. 16, 2008.

Symbolic Execution and Model Checking for Testing

Corina S. Păsăreanu[1] and Willem Visser[2]

[1] Perot Systems Government Services/NASA Ames Research Center
Moffett Field, CA 94035, USA
Corina.S.Pasareanu@nasa.gov
[2] SEVEN Networks
Redwood City, CA 94063, USA
willem@gmail.com

Techniques for checking complex software range from model checking and static analysis to testing. We aim to use the power of exhaustive techniques, such as model checking and symbolic execution, to enable thorough testing of complex software. In particular, we have extended the Java PathFinder model checking tool (JPF) [3] with a symbolic execution capability [4,2] to enable test case generation for Java programs. Our techniques handle complex data structures, arrays, as well as multithreading, and generate optimized test suites that satisfy user-specified testing coverage criteria.

Programs are executed on symbolic, rather than concrete, inputs; the variable values are represented as expressions and constraints that reflect the code structure. JPF generates and analyzes different symbolic execution paths. The input constraints for one path are solved (using off-the-shelf constraint solvers) to generate tests that are guaranteed to execute that path. To bound the search space we put a limit on the model checking search depth, or on the number of constraints along one path. Alternatively, we use abstract state matching [1], which enables JPF to analyze an under-approximation of the program behavior.

Our techniques have been used in black box and white box fashion [5]. They have been applied to generate test sequences for object-oriented code [6] and test vectors for NASA software. Recently, we have also applied our techniques to (executable) models – using a JPF extension for UML Statecharts.

References

1. Anand, S., Păsăreanu, C.S., Visser, W.: Symbolic execution with abstract subsumption checking. In: Valmari, A. (ed.) SPIN 2006. LNCS, vol. 3925, Springer, Heidelberg (2006)
2. Anand, S., Păsăreanu, C.S., Visser, W.: A symbolic execution extension to Java PathFinder. In: Grumberg, O., Huth, M. (eds.) TACAS 2007. LNCS, vol. 4424, Springer, Heidelberg (2007)

K. Yorav (Ed.): HVC 2007, LNCS 4899, pp. 17–18, 2008.

3. Java PathFinder. http://javapathfinder.sourceforge.net
4. Khurshid, S., Păsăreanu, C.S., Visser, W.: Generalized symbolic execution for model checking and testing. In: Garavel, H., Hatcliff, J. (eds.) ETAPS 2003 and TACAS 2003. LNCS, vol. 2619, Springer, Heidelberg (2003)
5. Visser, W., Păsăreanu, C.S., Khurshid, S.: Test input generation with Java PathFinder. In: Proc. ISSTA (2004)
6. Visser, W., Păsăreanu, C.S., Pelánek, R.: Test input generation for Java containers using state matching. In: Proc. ISSTA (2006)

On the Characterization of Until as a Fixed Point Under Clocked Semantics

Dana Fisman[1,2]

[1] Hebrew University
[2] IBM Haifa Research Lab

Abstract. Modern hardware designs are typically based on multiple clocks. While a singly-clocked hardware design is easily described in standard temporal logics, describing a multiply-clocked design is cumbersome. Thus, it is desirable to have an easier way to formulate properties related to clocks in a temporal logic. In [6] a relatively simple solution built on top of the traditional LTL semantics was suggested and adopted by the IEEE standard temporal logic PSL. The suggested semantics was examined relative to a list of design goals, and it was shown that it answered all requirements except for preserving the least fixed point characterization of the until operator under multiple clocks. In this work we show that with a minor addition to the semantics of [6] this requirement is met as well.

1 Introduction

Synchronous hardware designs are based on a notion of discrete time, in which the flip-flop (or latch) takes the system from the current state to the next state. A flip-flop or latch is a memory element, which passes on some function of its inputs to its outputs, but only when its clock input is active. The signal that causes the flip-flop (or latch) to transition is termed the *clock*. In a singly-clocked hardware design, temporal operators in logics such as LTL [16,17] are interpreted with respect to the clock, so that the following LTL formula:

$$G(p \rightarrow Xq) \tag{1}$$

can be interpreted as "globally, if p then *at the next clock cycle*, q". Mapping between a state of a model for the temporal logic and a clock cycle of hardware can then be dealt with by the tool which builds a model from the source code (written in some hardware description language).

Modern hardware designs, however, are typically based on multiple clocks. In such a design, for instance, some flip-flops may be clocked with $clka$, while others are clocked with $clkb$. In this case, the mapping between temporal operators and clock cycles cannot be done automatically; rather, the formula itself must contain some indication of which clock to use. Thus, it is desirable to have an easier way to formulate properties related to clocks in a temporal logic. For example, the

K. Yorav (Ed.): HVC 2007, LNCS 4899, pp. 19–33, 2008.

linear temporal logic LTL can be extended with a clock operator, denoted @, so that the formula

$$(G(p \rightarrow Xq))@clka \tag{2}$$

stating that "globally, if p during a cycle of $clka$, then at the next cycle of $clka$, q" will be equivalent to the LTL formula

$$G((clka \land p) \rightarrow X(\neg clka \ W \ (clka \land q))) \tag{3}$$

In [6] a relatively simple solution built on top of the traditional LTL semantics is given. The underlying idea of this solution is that the only role of the clock operator should be to define a projection of the path onto those states where the clock "ticks", and it is its own dual. Actually, referring to a projection of the path is not precisely correct, as we allow access to states in between consecutive states of a projection in the event of a clock switch. However, the word "projection" conveys the intuitive function of the clock operator in the case that the formula is singly-clocked. Achieving this introduces a problem for paths on which the clock never ticks. This problem is solved in [6] by introducing a propositional strength operator that extends the semantics from non-empty paths to empty paths in the same way that the strong next operator [14,12] extends the semantics from infinite paths to finite paths.

The solution of [6] has been adopted by the standard temporal logic PSL [11,5] and extended to account for regular expression which are an important part of PSL. The definition of the clock operator in the standard temporal logic SVA [10] which is based on regular expressions and does not include LTL operators agrees with that of PSL.[1]

The logic given in [6], is measured against a list of design goals. It is shown that all design goals are met, but that the least fixed point characterization of until is not preserved when multiple clocks are involved. The characterization of until as a fixed point is not merely a theoretical issue — it has practical aspects as some tools (e.g. the ones built upon the automata theoretic approach [19]) rely on it. In this work we show that with a minor addition to the semantics of [6] the until operator preserves its least fixed point characterization (and the semantics preserves the other design goals as well).

The addition suggested herein can be thought of as *alignment* operators, such as those of [9], that takes you to the closest clock tick, when the current cycle is not a clock tick. Note that the next operators takes you to the *second* clock tick when the current cycle is not a clock tick. This is ok since on the projected path, the second clock tick is the second letter — exactly the place where the next operator will take you in standard LTL. The alignment operator comes in two version, weak and strong, in order to deal with the possibility the clock may stop ticking. The strong alignment operator demands the clock to tick at least once

---

[1] PSL stands for *Property Specification Language* and is defined IEEE Std 1850[TM]- 2005 [11]. Its formal syntax and semantics are defined in Annex B of this document. SVA stands for *System Verilog Assertions* and is defined in Annex E of IEEE Std 1800[TM]-2005 [10].

more, while the weak alignment operator makes no such requirement. On singly-clocked formulas there is no need for alignment operators, since a subformula is always evaluated on a clock tick (the clock operator causes the evaluation to consider the projected path, and all other operators keep the evaluation on this path). On multiply-clocked formulas, however, on the event of a clock switch a subformula may be evaluated on a cycle which is not a clock tick. The alignment operators, in this case, takes the evaluation to the closest relevant tick.

The remainder of the paper is organized as follows. In Section 2 we give the semantics of the logic, and explain the difference with [6]. In Section 3 we provide some simple observations on the semantics of the logic. In Section 4 we prove that the least fixed point characterization of until is preserved, as well as the other design goals of [6]. In Section 5 we conclude.

2   The Definition of LTL@

The semantics of [6] is defined with respect to a *clock context*. Evaluation of a formula of the form $\varphi@clk$ then sets clk to be the clock context. An unclocked formula can be seen as a formula working in clock context *true*. The temporal operators advance the evaluation according to the clock context. For example, the formula $\varphi U \psi$ requires that there would be a clock tick of the clock context where ψ holds and on every preceding tick of the clock φ holds.

The problem of finite paths introduced by the fact that the clock context may stop ticking is solved in [6] by defining two versions of the next operator as is done in LTL [14, pp.272-273] and the linear time μ-calculus [12]. The formula $X!\varphi$ of LTL holds on a word w if the length of w is at least two and φ holds on the second letter of w whereas the weak version holds also if the length of w is less than two. In LTL augmented with the clock operator as per [6] we get that $X!\varphi$ holds on a word w if the length of w projected onto the cycles where the clock context ticks is at least two (i.e. there are at least two clock ticks in w) and φ holds on the second tick whereas the weak version holds also if the are less than two ticks. The problem of empty paths introduced by the fact that the clock context may not tick at all is solved in [6] by providing a propositional strength operator. Given a proposition p, both $p!$ and p are formulas of the logic of [6], where the strong version $p!$ holds if on every non-empty word w, the first letter of w satisfies p; and the weak version holds also on the empty word.

In this work we solve the problem of finite and empty paths by augmenting the next operator with an *exponent*. That is, the next operators comes with a non-negative integer m, so that $X!^m\varphi$ holds if φ holds on the $(m+1)$-th future tick of the clock context (where future is understood to include the present). If the clock context is *true* the formula $X!^m\varphi$ requires φ to hold on the $(m+1)$-th letter of the given word. Similarly, $X^m\varphi$ holds if φ holds on the $m+1$-th future tick of the clock if there are $m+1$ future ticks. If the clock context is *true* the formula $X^m\varphi$ holds if φ holds on the $(m+1)$-th letter, or there are less than $m+1$ letters in the given word. The operators obtained by instantiating m with zero (i.e. $\mathsf{X}!^0$ and X^0) can be seen as alignment operators, similar to those of [9].[2] The formulas $\mathsf{X}!^0\varphi$ and $\mathsf{X}^0\varphi$ advance the evaluation to the closest clock tick, when the current cycle is not a clock tick, and evaluate φ there. If the current cycle is a clock tick φ is evaluated at the current cycle. Thus, if the clock context is *true* (or the formula is unclocked) φ is evaluated at the current letter. As expected the strong version requires that there would be at least one future clock tick while the next version holds also there are no clock ticks. If the clock context is *true* the strong version requires that the given word would not be empty whereas the weak version holds also if it is empty.

Remark 1. The alignment operators $\mathsf{X}!^0$ and X^0 move to the nearest concurrent or future clock tick. It might be practically useful to include also alignment operators that are strictly future. That is, while $\mathsf{X}!^0$ and X^0 do not advance when the current cycle is a clock tick, the strictly future alignment operators will advance to the next clock tick, when the current cycle is a clock tick (and to the closest clock tick when the current cycle is not a clock tick). These can be defined as syntactic sugaring by means of the existing operators, using T as the clock context.

2.1   Syntax

We define the syntax of $\mathrm{LTL}^@$ as follows, where we use the term *Boolean expression* to refer to any application of the standard Boolean operators to atomic propositions.

Definition 1 (Formulas of $\mathrm{LTL}^@$)

- *If b is a Boolean expression, then $b!$ and b are $\mathrm{LTL}^@$ formulas.*
- *If clk is a Boolean expression, m is a non-negative integer, and φ and ψ are $\mathrm{LTL}^@$ formulas, then the following are $\mathrm{LTL}^@$ formulas:*
  - $\neg\varphi$ • $\varphi \wedge \psi$ • $\mathsf{X}!^m\varphi$ • $\varphi U \psi$ • $\varphi @ clk$

Additional operators are derived from the basic operators defined above:

- $\varphi \vee \psi \overset{\text{def}}{=} \neg(\neg\varphi \wedge \neg\psi)$
- $\varphi \rightarrow \psi \overset{\text{def}}{=} \neg\varphi \vee \psi$
- $\mathsf{X}^m\varphi \overset{\text{def}}{=} \neg\mathsf{X}!^m\neg\varphi$
- $\mathsf{F}\varphi \overset{\text{def}}{=} \mathsf{T}U\varphi$
- $\mathsf{G}\varphi \overset{\text{def}}{=} \neg\mathsf{F}\neg\varphi$
- $\varphi W \psi \overset{\text{def}}{=} (\varphi U \psi) \vee \mathsf{G}\varphi$
- $\mathsf{X}\varphi \overset{\text{def}}{=} \mathsf{X}^1\varphi$
- $\mathsf{X}!\varphi \overset{\text{def}}{=} \mathsf{X}!^1\varphi$

where T is a Boolean expression that holds on every letter. In the sequel, we also use F, which is a Boolean expression that does not hold for any letter.

We refer to the subset of $\mathrm{LTL}^@$ consisting of the formulas that have no clock operator, by LTL. This subset is a slight generalization of the standard definition

---

[2] The operators $\mathsf{X}!^0$ and X^0 resemble the operator s_align @(c) and w_align @(c) of the assertion language ECBV [9]. The definition of the alignment operators here and there do not resemble since the language ECBV is defined by means of computations of an alternating automaton. The obtained semantics, however, does.

of LTL (as defined in [17]) – it consists of two version of Boolean expressions as well as the generalized version of the next operator. The important thing, however, is that it agrees with the standard semantics on the common operators (on non-empty paths, as the standard semantics is defined only over non-empty paths).

2.2   Semantics

We denote a letter by ℓ, and an empty, finite, or infinite word by u, v, or w. The *concatenation* of u and v is denoted by uv. If u is infinite, then $uv = u$. The empty word is denoted by ϵ, so that $w\epsilon = \epsilon w = w$. We denote the *length* of word v as $|v|$. The empty word ϵ has length 0, a finite word $v = (\ell_0\ell_1\cdots\ell_n)$ has length $n + 1$, and an infinite word has length ∞. We use i, j, and k to denote non-negative integers. For $i < |v|$ we use v^i to denote the $(i + 1)^{st}$ letter of v (since counting of letters starts at zero). We denote by $v^{i\cdots}$ the suffix of v starting at v^i.

The semantics of LTL$^@$ is defined inductively with respect to a word (which may be infinite, finite or empty) over the alphabet $\Sigma = 2^P$ where P is a given non-empty set of atomic propositions. We identify Boolean expression over P as elements of $B = 2^{2^P}$ (as they convey subset of possible valuations (assignments) to the set of propositions in P). For a Boolean expression $b \in B$ and a letter $\ell \in \Sigma$ we define the Boolean satisfaction relation $\Vdash$ by $\ell \Vdash b$ iff $\ell \in b$.

We first present the semantics of LTL over infinite, finite, and empty words (*unclocked semantics*). We then present the semantics of LTL$^@$ over infinite, finite, and empty words (*clocked semantics*). In Corollary 1 given in Section 4.2 we show that the unclocked semantics can be obtained from the clocked semantics by setting the clock context to T.

Unclocked Semantics. We now present semantics for LTL. The semantics is defined with respect to an infinite, finite, or empty word. The notation $w \models \varphi$ means that formula φ holds along the word w. The semantics is defined as follows, where b denotes a Boolean expression, φ and ψ denote formulas, and m, j and k denote natural numbers (i.e., non-negative integers).

  - $w \models b \iff |w| = 0$ or $w^0 \Vdash b$
  - $w \models b! \iff |w| > 0$ and $w^0 \Vdash b$
  - $w \models \neg\varphi \iff w \not\models \varphi$
  - $w \models \varphi \wedge \psi \iff w \models \varphi$ and $w \models \psi$
  - $w \models \mathsf{X}!^m\varphi \iff |w| > m$ and $w^{m\cdots} \models \varphi$
  - $w \models \varphi \mathsf{U} \psi \iff \exists k < |w|$ such that $w^{k\cdots} \models \psi$, and $\forall j < k$, $w^{j\cdots} \models \varphi$

Clocked Semantics. We define the semantics of an LTL$^@$ formula with respect to an infinite, finite, or empty word w and a context c, where c is a Boolean expression over P. We say that a finite word w *is a clock tick of* clock c if c holds at the last letter of w and does not hold at any previous letter of w. Formally,

Definition 2 (clock ticks)

- *We say that finite word w is a* clock tick *of c iff $|w| > 0$ and $w^{|w|-1} \Vdash c$ and for every natural number $i < |w| - 1$, $w^i \nVdash c$.*
- *For $m > 0$, we say that finite word w is m* clock ticks *of c iff there exists m words $w_1, w_2, \ldots, w_m$ such that $w = w_1 w_2 \ldots w_m$ and for every $1 \le i \le m$ the word w_i is a clock tick of c.*

The notation $w \models^c \varphi$ means that formula φ holds along the word w in the context of clock c. The semantics is defined as follows, where b, c and c_1 denote Boolean expressions, φ and ψ denote formulas, and m, j and k denote natural numbers (i.e., non-negative integers).

- $w \models^c b \Longleftrightarrow$ if $\exists k < |w|$ such that $w^{0..k}$ is a clock tick of c then $w^k \Vdash b$
- $w \models^c b! \Longleftrightarrow \exists k < |w|$ such that $w^{0..k}$ is a clock tick of c and $w^k \Vdash b$
- $w \models^c \neg\varphi \Longleftrightarrow w \nvDash^c \varphi$
- $w \models^c \varphi \wedge \psi \Longleftrightarrow w \models^c \varphi$ and $w \models^c \psi$
- $w \models^c X!^m\varphi \Longleftrightarrow \exists j < |w|$ s.t. $w^{0..j}$ is $m+1$ clock ticks of c and $w^{j..} \models^c \varphi$
- $w \models^c \varphi U \psi \Longleftrightarrow \exists k < |w|$ such that $w^k \Vdash c$ and $w^{k..} \models^c \psi$ and
$$\forall j < k \text{ such that } w^j \Vdash c, \; w^{j..} \models^c \varphi$$

- $w \models^c \varphi @ c_1 \Longleftrightarrow w \models^{c_1} \varphi$

3   Observations on the Semantics of LTL@

The following section provides some simple observation regarding the weak/strong next operators and their exponents. First we provide the direct semantics of the weak next operator, which was given as a syntactic sugaring of the strong next operator in Section 2.1.

Claim 1 (Weak next operator). *Let w be a word over Σ. Let c be a Boolean expression in B, m a non-negative integer and φ an LTL@ formula. Then*

$$w \models^c X^m\varphi \Longleftrightarrow \text{ if } \exists j < |w| \text{ s.t. } w^{0..j} \text{ is } m+1 \text{ clock ticks of } c \text{ then } w^{j..} \models^c \varphi$$

The following claim states that the weak/strong Boolean expressions can be stated in terms of the weak/strong next operator by setting m to zero. Note that this does not mean that the X^0 and $X!^0$ are redundant in the presence of weak and strong Boolean expressions. They are needed to provide an easy way to get to the closest tick (when the current cycle is not a clock tick) for general formulas.

Claim 2 (Weak/strong Boolean expressions). *Let w be a word over Σ. Let c and b be Boolean expressions in B. Then*

1. $w \models^c b! \Longleftrightarrow w \models^c X!^0 b$
2. $w \models^c b \Longleftrightarrow w \models^c X^0 b$

The following claim shows that the standard strong and weak next operators, as defined in [6], are obtained by setting m to one in $X!^m$ and X^m, respectively.

Claim 3 (Weak/strong simple next operators). *Let w be a word over Σ. Let c be a Boolean expression in B and φ an LTL$^@$ formula. Then*

1. *$w \models^c X!\varphi \Longleftrightarrow \exists j < k < |w|$ such that $w^{0..j}$ is a clock tick of c and $w^{j+1..k}$ is a clock tick of c and $w^{k..} \models^c \varphi$*
2. *$w \models^c X\varphi \Longleftrightarrow$ if $\exists j < k < |w|$ such that $w^{0..j}$ is a clock tick of c and $w^{j+1..k}$ is a clock tick of c then $w^{k..} \models^c \varphi$*

The following claim states that $X!^m$ can be obtained by m iterations of $X!$ and similarly for the weak version.

Claim 4 (Power characterization). *Let w be a word over Σ. Let c be a Boolean expression in B, m a integer and φ an LTL$^@$ formula.*

1. *$w \models^c X!^m\varphi \Longleftrightarrow w \models^c \underbrace{X!X!\ldots X!}_{m \ times}\varphi$*
2. *$w \models^c X^m\varphi \Longleftrightarrow w \models^c \underbrace{XX\ldots X}_{m \ times}\varphi$*

The following claim states that the next operators are additive. That is, composition of $X!^m$ (resp., X^m) operators corresponds to addition in the exponents (even if one or both exponents is zero).

Claim 5. *Let m and n be non-negative integers and φ and LTL$^@$ formula. Then*

1. *$X!^m X!^n \varphi \equiv X!^{m+n}\varphi$*
2. *$X^m X^n \varphi \equiv X^{m+n}\varphi$*

The proofs of these claims are given in the full version of the paper.

4   Meeting the Goals

In this section, we show that the logic LTL$^@$ satisfies all the goals of [6], as well as preserving the least and greatest fixed point characterization of the strong and weak until operators, respectively. We make use of the following notations.

The *projection* of a word w onto clock c, denoted $w|_c$, is the word obtained from w after leaving only the letters which satisfy c. For example, if $w = \ell_0\ell_1\ell_2\ldots\ell_{10}$ and $\ell_0 \not\Vdash c$, $\ell_1 \not\Vdash c$, $\ell_2 \not\Vdash c$, $\ell_3 \Vdash c$, $\ell_4 \not\Vdash c$, $\ell_5 \not\Vdash c$, $\ell_6 \Vdash c$, $\ell_7 \Vdash c$, $\ell_8 \not\Vdash c$, $\ell_9 \not\Vdash c$ and $\ell_{10} \not\Vdash c$ then $w|_c = \ell_3\ell_6\ell_7$.

Let φ be an LTL formula. We use $[\![\varphi]\!]$ to denote the set of all words satisfying φ. That is $[\![\varphi]\!] = \{w \mid w \models \varphi\}$. Let φ be an LTL$^@$ formula. We use $[\![\varphi]\!]_c$ to denote the set of all words satisfying φ under clock context c. That is, $[\![\varphi]\!]_c = \{w \mid w \models^c \varphi\}$. We say that two LTL formulas φ and ψ are *unclocked equivalent* ($\varphi \equiv \psi$) if $[\![\varphi]\!] = [\![\psi]\!]$. We say that two LTL$^@$ formulas φ and ψ are *clocked equivalent* ($\varphi \overset{@}{\equiv} \psi$) if $[\![\varphi]\!]_c = [\![\psi]\!]_c$ for every clock contexts c.

4.1 The Until Fixed Point Characterization

In standard LTL, interpreted over infinite words, $[\![\varphi \; \mathsf{U} \; \psi]\!]$ and $[\![\varphi \; \mathsf{W} \; \psi]\!]$ are the least and greatest (resp.) fixed points of the functional E defined as follows [15,3]:[3]

$$E(S) = [\![\psi \vee (\varphi \wedge \underline{\mathsf{X}}S)]\!] \tag{4}$$

where $\underline{\mathsf{X}}$ is the strengthless version of the $\mathsf{X}!$ and X operators that it used when LTL is interpreted solely on infinite words. When LTL is interpreted over finite words as well then $[\![\varphi \; \mathsf{U} \; \psi]\!]$ and $[\![\varphi \; \mathsf{W} \; \psi]\!]$ are the least and greatest fixed point of the functionals E^+ and E^- obtained from E by replacing $\underline{\mathsf{X}}$ with $\mathsf{X}!$ and X, respectively.

$$E^+(S) = [\![\psi \vee (\varphi \wedge \mathsf{X}!S)]\!] \tag{5}$$

$$E^-(S) = [\![\psi \vee (\varphi \wedge \mathsf{X}S)]\!] \tag{6}$$

This characterization does not hold for LTL$^{@}$. Consider the strong until operator. We have that $\psi \vee (\varphi \wedge \mathsf{X}!S)$ may be satisfied weakly if ψ is a weak formula, e.g. if ψ equals $\mathsf{X}p$ for some proposition p and the clock never ticks. Whereas $\varphi \; \mathsf{U} \; (\mathsf{X}p)$ demands (among other things) that there would be at least one clock tick. For this reason, [6] proposed the functional F_c^+ defined as follows:

$$F_c^+(S) = [\![(\mathsf{T}! \wedge \psi) \vee (\varphi \wedge \mathsf{X}!S)]\!]_c \tag{7}$$

where $\mathsf{T}!$ is the strong Boolean expression T asserting that there is a current cycle (and T holds on it). This characterization holds for singly-clocked formulas but not for multiply-clocked formulas. The following counter examples shows that the characterization breaks when multiple clocks are involved. Let p, q and $clkq$ be atomic propositions, and let $\psi = q@clkq$. Consider a word w such that $w^0 \models clkq \wedge q$ and for all $i > 0$, $w^i \not\models clkq \wedge q$, and $w^0 \not\models c$. Then $w \models^c \psi$ hence $w \models^c (\mathsf{T}! \wedge \psi) \vee (p \wedge \mathsf{X}!(p \; \mathsf{U} \; \psi))$. However, since $w^0 \not\models c$, and there is no state other than w^0 where $clkq \wedge q$ holds, $w \not\models^c (p \; \mathsf{U} \; \psi)$.

The following claim states that under the semantics given here, the strong until operator can be defined as a least fixed point of the following functional

$$G_c^+(S) = [\![\mathsf{X}!^0(\psi \vee (\varphi \wedge \mathsf{X}!S))]\!]_c \tag{8}$$

(even in the presence of multiple clocks). Since by definition $w \models^{\mathsf{T}} \mathsf{X}!^0\varphi \Longleftrightarrow |w| > 0$ and $w \models^{\mathsf{T}} \varphi$ this can be seen as a generalization of the standard characterization: The standard characterization assumes paths are non-empty and works with no clock context, or equivalently with T as the clock context - thus the $\mathsf{X}!^0$ operator can be removed. The obtained functional $G_\mathsf{T}^+(S) = [\![\psi \vee (\varphi \wedge \mathsf{X}!S)]\!]_\mathsf{T}$ is then the standard characterization. If we restrict also to infinite paths, the strength of the $\mathsf{X}!$ operator can be taken away as well.

---

[3] Earlier works (e.g. [2]) provided fixed point representation of the logic CTL by showing that it can be encoded in the propositional μ-calculus [13]. See [7] for the fixed-point characterization of the logic CTL* (that subsumes both LTL and CTL).

Theorem 1. *Let φ and ψ be LTL$^{@}$ formulas. Then $[\![\varphi \ U \ \psi]\!]_c$ is a least fixed point of the functional $G_c^+(S) = [\![X!^0 \, (\psi \vee (\varphi \wedge X! \, S))]\!]_c$.*

Proof: It is easy to see that the functional G_c^+ is monotonic and thus by Tarski-Knaster theorem [18] it has a least fixed point. First we show that $[\![\varphi \ U \ \psi]\!]_c$ is a fixed point of G_c^+ then we show that it is the least fixed point.

– Let φ and ψ be LTL$^{@}$ formulas. Let w be a word over Σ, and c a Boolean expression. We show that $[\![\varphi \ U \ \psi]\!]_c$ is a fixed point of G_c^+ by proving

$$\varphi \ U \ \psi \overset{@}{\equiv} X!^0 \, (\psi \vee (\varphi \wedge X! \, (\varphi \ U \ \psi))).$$

$w \models^{\underline{c}} X!^0 \, (\psi \vee (\varphi \wedge X! \, (\varphi \ U \ \psi)))$

$\Longleftrightarrow \exists \, j_0 < |w|$ s.t. $w^{0..j_0}$ is a clock tick of c and $w^{j_0..} \models^{\underline{c}} (\psi \vee (\varphi \wedge X! \, (\varphi \ U \ \psi)))$

$\Longleftrightarrow \exists j_0 < |w|$ such that $w^{0..j_0}$ is a clock tick of c and either $w^{j_0..} \models^{\underline{c}} \psi$ or $w^{j_0..} \models^{\underline{c}} (\varphi \wedge X! \, (\varphi \ U \ \psi)))$

$\Longleftrightarrow \exists j_0 < |w|$ such that $w^{0..j_0}$ is a clock tick of c and either $w^{j_0..} \models^{\underline{c}} \psi$ or $(w^{j_0..} \models^{\underline{c}} \varphi$ and $\exists j_1 < |w|$ such that $j_1 > j_0$ and $w^{j_0+1..j_1}$ is a clock tick of c and $w^{j_1..} \models^{\underline{c}} (\varphi \ U \ \psi))$

$\Longleftrightarrow \exists j_0 < |w|$ such that $w^{0..j_0}$ is a clock tick of c and either $w^{j_0..} \models^{\underline{c}} \psi$ or $(w^{j_0..} \models^{\underline{c}} \varphi$ and $\exists j_1 < |w|$ such that $j_1 > j_0$ and $w^{j_0+1..j_1}$ is a clock tick of c and $\exists k < |w^{j_1..}|$ such that $w^{j_1+k} \Vdash c$ and $w^{j_1+k..} \models^{\underline{c}} \psi$ and for every $j < k$ such that $w^{j_1+j} \Vdash c$, $w^{j_1+j..} \models^{\underline{c}} \varphi)$

$\Longleftrightarrow \exists k < |w|$ s.t. $w^k \Vdash c$ and $w^{k..} \models^{\underline{c}} \psi$ and $\forall j < k$ s.t. $w^j \Vdash c$, $w^{j..} \models^{\underline{c}} \varphi$

$\Longleftrightarrow w \models^{\underline{c}} \varphi \ U \ \psi$

– We have shown that $[\![\varphi U \psi]\!]_c$ is a fixed point of G_c^+. We now show that $[\![\varphi U \psi]\!]_c$ is the least fixed point. That is, given S is an arbitrary fixed point of G_c^+ we show that $[\![\varphi U \psi]\!]_c \subseteq S$. Let S be a fixed point of G_c^+. That is, S is a set of empty, finite, or infinite words such that $w \in S$ iff $w \models^{\underline{c}} X!^0(\psi \vee (\varphi \wedge X! \, S))$ where $w \models^{\underline{c}} S$ means $w \in S$. We have to show that for any word w, we have that $w \models^{\underline{c}} \varphi U \psi$ implies $w \in S$.

Let w be such that $w \models^{\underline{c}} \varphi U \psi$. Then there exists $k < |w|$ s.t. $w^k \Vdash c$ and $w^{k..} \models^{\underline{c}} \psi$ and for every $j < k$ s.t. $w^j \Vdash c$ we have $w^{j..} \models^{\underline{c}} \varphi$. From the fact that $w^{k..} \models^{\underline{c}} \psi$ and $w^k \Vdash c$ we get that $w^{k..} \models^{\underline{c}} X!^0 \psi$ and thus $w^{k..} \in S$. Let $0 \le j_0 < j_1 < \ldots < j_k < k$ be the set of all j's in w such $w^j \Vdash c$. Consider first j_k. We have that $w^{j_k} \Vdash c$, $w^{j_k..} \models^{\underline{c}} \varphi$ and $w^{k..} \in S$. Thus $w^{j_k..} \models^{\underline{c}} X!^0(\varphi \wedge X! \, S)$ and so $w^{j_k..} \in S$. By induction we get that for each such j_i we have that $w^{j_i..} \in S$. In particular $w^{j_0..} \in S$. Thus $w^{j_0..} \models^{\underline{c}} X!^0(\psi \vee (\varphi \wedge X! \, S))$. And since j_0 is the closest tick of c starting at 0 we get that $w^{0..} \models^{\underline{c}} X!^0(\psi \vee (\varphi \wedge X! \, S))$ as well. Thus, we have shown that $w \in S$. $\qquad\square$

We now show that the **weak until** operator is the greatest fixed point of the functional G^- below obtained from G^+ by weakening the next operators.

Theorem 2. *Let φ and ψ be* LTL$^@$ *formulas. Then $[\![\varphi \, W \, \psi]\!]_c$ is a greatest fixed point of the functional $G_c^-(S) = [\![X^0 (\psi \vee (\varphi \wedge X S))]\!]_c$.*

Proof: It is easy to see that the functional G_c^- is monotonic and thus by Tarski-Knaster theorem [18] it has a greatest fixed point. First we show that $[\![\varphi \, W \, \psi]\!]_c$ is a fixed point of G_c^- then we show that it is the greatest fixed point. In the following we make use of the direct clocked semantics of W as given by [8, Lemma 4.9].

$$w \models^c \varphi \, W \, \psi \text{ iff for all } 0 \leq k < |w| \text{ such that } w^k \Vdash c \text{ and } w^{k\cdots} \not\Vdash \varphi,$$
$$\text{there exists } 0 \leq j \leq k \text{ such that } w^j \Vdash c \text{ and } w^{j\cdots} \models^c \psi.$$

– Let φ and ψ be LTL$^@$ formulas. Let w be a word over Σ, and c a Boolean expression. We show that $[\![\varphi \, W \, \psi]\!]_c$ is a fixed point of G_c^- by proving

$$\varphi \, W \, \psi \overset{@}{\equiv} X^0 (\psi \vee (\varphi \wedge X (\varphi \, W \, \psi))).$$

$ w \models^c X^0 (\psi \vee (\varphi \wedge X (\varphi \, W \, \psi)))$

$\Longleftrightarrow$ if there exists $j \geq 0$ such that $w^{0\cdots j_0}$ is a clock tick of c then $w^{j_0\cdots} \models^c (\psi \vee (\varphi \wedge X (\varphi \, W \, \psi)))$

$\Longleftrightarrow$ if there exists $j_0 < |w|$ such that $w^{0\cdots j_0}$ is a clock tick of c then either $w^{j_0\cdots} \models^c \psi$ or $w^{j_0\cdots} \models^c (\varphi \wedge X (\varphi \, W \, \psi)))$

$\Longleftrightarrow$ if there exists $j_0 < |w|$ such that $w^{0\cdots j_0}$ is a clock tick of c then either $w^{j_0\cdots} \models^c \psi$ or ($w^{j_0\cdots} \models^c \varphi$ and if there exists $j_1 < |w|$ such that $j_1 > j_0$ and $w^{j_0+1\cdots j_1}$ is a clock tick of c then $w^{j_1\cdots} \models^c (\varphi \, W \, \psi))$

$\Longleftrightarrow$ if there exists $j_0 < |w|$ such that $w^{0\cdots j_0}$ is a clock tick of c then either $w^{j_0\cdots} \models^c \psi$ or ($w^{j_0\cdots} \models^c \varphi$ and if there exists $j_1 < |w|$ such that $j_1 > j_0$ and $w^{j_0+1\cdots j_1}$ is a clock tick of c then for all $0 \leq k < |w^{j_1\cdots}|$ such that $w^{j_1+k} \Vdash c$ and $w^{j_1+k\cdots} \not\Vdash \varphi$, there exists $0 \leq j \leq k$ such that $w^{j_1+j} \Vdash c$ and $w^{j_1+j\cdots} \models^c \psi)$

$\Longleftrightarrow$ for all $0 \leq k < |w|$ such that $w^k \Vdash c$ and $w^{k\cdots} \not\Vdash \varphi$, there exists $0 \leq j \leq k$ such that $w^j \Vdash c$ and $w^{j\cdots} \models^c \psi$

$\Longleftrightarrow$ $w \models^c \varphi \, W \, \psi$

– We have shown that $[\![\varphi W \psi]\!]_c$ is a fixed point of G_c^-. We now show that $[\![\varphi W \psi]\!]_c$ is the greatest fixed point. That is, given S is an arbitrary fixed point of G_c^- we show that $[\![\varphi W \psi]\!]_c \supseteq S$. Let S be a fixed point of G_c^-. That is, S is a set of empty, finite, or infinite words such that $w \in S$ iff $w \models^c X^0 (\psi \vee (\varphi \wedge X S)$ where $w \models^c S$ means $w \in S$. We have to show that for any word w, we have that $w \in S$ implies $w \models^c \varphi W \psi$.

  Let w be such that $w \in S$. Then $w \models^c X^0(\psi \vee (\varphi \wedge X S))$. Assume towards contradiction that $w \not\models^c \varphi W \psi$. Let $J = \{j_0, j_1, \ldots\}$ be the set of all j's such that $w^j \Vdash c$ with $0 \leq j_0 < j_1 < \ldots < |w|$. Note that $|J|$ may be empty, finite or infinite. Then, $w \not\models^c \varphi W \psi$ implies there exists a tick point j_k such that $w^{k\cdots} \not\Vdash \varphi$ and for every tick point $j_i \leq j_k$ we have that $w^{j_i\cdots} \not\Vdash \psi$. Thus

$w^{j_k \cdots} \notin S$ (since $w^{j_k \cdots} \not\models^{\underline{c}} X^0 \psi$ and $w^{j_k \cdots} \not\models^{\underline{c}} X^0 \varphi$). Therefore, $w^{j_k - 1 \cdots} \notin S$ (since $w^{j_k - 1 \cdots} \not\models^{\underline{c}} X^0 \psi$ and $w^{j_k - 1 \cdots} \not\models^{\underline{c}} X^0 X S$). For the same reason $w^{j_k - 2 \cdots} \notin S$. By induction we can show that for any $j_i \leq j_k$ we have $w^{j_i \cdots} \notin S$. In particular $w^{j_0 \cdots} \notin S$ and so $w = w^{0 \cdots} \notin S$ as well, contradicting our assumption. □

4.2   The Other Goals

Below we state that the semantics given here preserve the goals met in [6]. The work in [6] provides detailed explanations and motivations of the goals, as well as relation to other works. Here we provide a succinct motivation to the less obvious goals. The proofs are a slight modification of those of [6] and are given in the full version of the paper.

1. When singly-clocked, the semantics should be that of the *projection view*.
   Motivation:
   When only a single clock is involved we would like that a clocked formula $\varphi @ clk$ hold on a word w if and only if the unclocked formula φ holds on a word $w|_c$ (i.e. on the word obtained from w by projecting onto those states where clk holds).⌟

Proposition 1. *For any* LTL *formula* φ, *a Boolean expression* c *and an infinite, finite, or empty word* w, *the following holds:*

$$w \models^{\underline{c}} \varphi \quad \text{if and only if} \quad w|_c \models \varphi$$

The following is an immediate consequence of this.

Corollary 1. *for an* LTL *formula* φ, *and a word* w.

$$w \models^{\underline{T}} \varphi \quad \text{if and only if} \quad w \models \varphi$$

2. Clocks should not accumulate.
   Motivation:
   In many hardware designs, large chunks of the design work on some main clock, while small pieces work on a secondary clock. Rather than require the user to specify a clock for each subformula, we would like to allow clocking of an entire formula on a main clock, and pieces of it on a secondary clock, in such a way that the outer clock (which is applied to the entire formula) does not affect the inner clock (which is applied to one or more sub-formulas). That is, we want a nested clock operator to have the effect of "changing the projection", rather than further projecting the projected word.⌟

Proposition 2. *For any* LTL$^{@}$ *formula* φ *and Boolean expressions* c_1 *and* c_2 *the following holds:*

$$\varphi @ c_1 @ c_2 \stackrel{@}{\equiv} \varphi @ c_1$$

3. The clock operator should be its own dual.
   Motivation:
   Previous definitions of clock operators [1,4] introduces two kids of clocks, a
   weak clock and a strong clock (one is the dual of the other). Each of the
   definitions had drawbacks as we elaborate on items 4 and 5 below.⌐

   Proposition 3. *For any* LTL$^@$ *formula φ and Boolean expression b the following holds:*

   $$(\neg\varphi)@b \overset{@}{\equiv} \neg(\varphi@b)$$

4. For any atomic propositions p and q, there should be a clocked version of
   $(Fp) \wedge (Gq)$ that is meaningful on paths with a finite number of clock ticks.
   Motivation:
   In Sugar2.0 [4], a strongly clocked formula requires the clock to "tick
   long enough to ensure that the formula holds", while a weakly clocked
   formula allows it to stop ticking before then. Thus, for instance, the formula
   $(Fp)@clk!$ (which is strongly clocked) requires there to be enough ticks of
   clk so that p eventually holds, whereas the formula $(Fp)@clk$ (which is
   weakly clocked) allows the case where p never occurs, if it "is the fault
   of the clock", i.e., if the clock ticks a finite number of times. For the dual
   formulas we get that $(Gq)@clk!$ holds if the clock ticks an infinite number
   of times and q holds at every tick, while $(Gq)@clk$ holds if q holds at every
   tick, no matter how many there are. A disadvantage of this semantics is
   that the formula $(Fp) \wedge (Gq)$ cannot be satisfactorily clocked for a finite
   word, because $((Fp) \wedge (Gq))@clk!$ does not hold on any finite word, while
   $((Fp) \wedge (Gq))@clk$ makes no requirement on p on such a word.⌐

   Under the semantics given here we get that $((Fp) \wedge (Gq))@c$, holds if p holds
   for some state and q holds for all states on the projected word, which is
   indeed the intuitive desired semantics.

5. For any atomic proposition p, if $(Fp)@clk$ holds on a word, it should hold
   on any extension of that word.
   Motivation:
   In ForSpec [1], a strongly clocked formula requires only that the clock
   tick *at least once*, after which the only role of the clock is to define the
   projection of the word onto those states where the clock ticks. A weakly
   clocked formula, on the other hand, holds if the clock never ticks; if it does
   tick, then the role of the clock is the same as for a strongly clocked formula.
   Thus, the only difference between strong and weak clocks in ForSpec is on
   paths whose projection is empty. This leads to the strange situation that
   a liveness formula may hold on some word w, but not on an extension of
   that word, ww'. For instance, if p is an atomic proposition, then $(Fp)@clk$
   holds if there are no ticks of clk, but does not hold if there is just one tick,
   at which p does not hold.⌐

Proposition 4. *For Boolean expressions b, clk and c, a finite word w, and an infinite or finite word w', the following holds:*

$$w \models^c (Fb)@clk \implies ww' \models^c (Fb)@clk$$

6. For any clock c, two equivalent LTL formulas should remain equivalent when clocked with c.

   Proposition 5. *For LTL formulas φ and ψ, and a Boolean expression c, the following holds:*

   $$\varphi \equiv \psi \implies \varphi@c \stackrel{@}{\equiv} \psi@c$$

7. Substituting subformula ψ for an equivalent subformula h should not change the truth value of the original formula.

   Proposition 6. *If ψ is a subformula of φ, and $\psi' \stackrel{@}{\equiv} \psi$, then the following holds:*

   $$\varphi \stackrel{@}{\equiv} \varphi[\psi \leftarrow \psi']$$

   where $\varphi[\psi \leftarrow \psi']$ denotes the formula obtained from φ by replacing subformula ψ with ψ'.

8. For every word, the truth value of LTL$^@$ Formula (2) given in the introduction should be the same as the truth value of LTL Formula (3) given in the introduction.

   Proposition 7. *For every word w,*
   $$w \models^T (G(p \to Xq))@clka \iff w \models G((clka \wedge p) \to X(\neg clka \ W \ (clka \wedge q)))$$

4.3   Rewrite Rules

In [6] it was shown that the clock operator does not add expressive power. In fact there are rewrite rules that given an LTL$^@$ formula φ return an equivalent LTL formula. The rewrite rules form a recursive procedure $\mathcal{T}^{clk}()$, whose application starting with $clk = T$ results in an LTL formula with the same truth value in context T. The rewrite rules are given below. Note that by Claim 4 it suffices to provide rewrite rules for X!^{0} and X! instead of X!^{m}.

- $\mathcal{T}^{clk}(b) = (\neg clk \ W \ (clk \wedge b))$
- $\mathcal{T}^{clk}(b!) = (\neg clk \ U \ (clk \wedge b))$
- $\mathcal{T}^{clk}(\neg f) = \neg \mathcal{T}^{clk}(\varphi)$
- $\mathcal{T}^{clk}(\varphi \wedge \psi) = \mathcal{T}^{clk}(\varphi) \wedge \mathcal{T}^{clk}(\psi)$
- $\mathcal{T}^{clk}(X!^0 f) = (\neg clk \ U \ (clk \wedge \mathcal{T}^{clk}(\varphi)))$
- $\mathcal{T}^{clk}(X!\varphi) = (\neg clk \ U \ (clk \wedge X!(\neg clk \ U \ (clk \wedge \mathcal{T}^{clk}(\varphi)))))$
- $\mathcal{T}^{clk}(\varphi \ U \ \psi) = (clk \to \mathcal{T}^{clk}(\varphi)) \ U \ (clk \wedge \mathcal{T}^{clk}(\psi))$
- $\mathcal{T}^{clk}(\varphi@clk_1) = \mathcal{T}^{clk_1}(\varphi)$

Proposition 8. *Let φ be any LTL$^@$ formula, c a Boolean expression, and w a word.*

$$w \models^c \varphi \quad \text{if and only if} \quad w \models \mathcal{T}^c(\varphi)$$

The proof of this proposition as well as some additional rewrite rules are given in the full version of the paper.

5   Conclusions

In [6] a relatively simple definition of LTL augmented with a clock operator was given. The augmented logic is suitable for specifying properties in multiply-clocks designs [5, Chapter 14] and was adopted by the IEEE standard PSL. In this definition, the only role of the clock operator is to define a projection of the word, and it is its own dual. This definition was shown to answer a list of design goals. However it does not preserve the least fixed point characterization of the until operator. The characterization of until as a least fixed point is not merely a theoretical issue — it has practical aspects as some tools depend on it.

In this work we fix this problem with a minor addition to the semantics of [6]. The addition introduces an *exponent* to the next operator. The key of this solution is that by taking the zero exponent we get the operators $X!^0$ and X^0 which can be thought of as alignment operators, such as the ones in ECBV [9], taking us to the closest clock tick, if the current cycle is not a clock tick.

The suggested semantics can be seen as a way to abstract the word when multiple clocks are involved. The clock operator @ defines the current clock context, so that the temporal operators move according to this context. For example, $(\varphi U \psi)$ demands that ψ hold on some future tick of the context clock, and φ holds on all ticks preceding the tick where ψ holds. The alignment operators $X!^0$ and X^0 allow you to move to the closest tick of a clock, which is needed in the event of a clock switch.

The resulting semantics meets all the design goals listed in [6] and preserves the least and greatest fixed point characterization of the strong and weak until operators, respectively.

Acknowledgements

I would like to thank Katoen Joost-Pieter for asking a question at HVC that prompted Theorem 2, which was not a part of the originally submitted version of this paper. I would like to thank Doron Bustan, Cindy Eisner, John Havlicek and an anonymous referee for their important comments on an early draft of this paper. I would like to thank Orna Kupferman for helping me in tracking some of the references.

References

1. Armoni, R., Fix, L., Flaisher, A., Gerth, R., Ginsburg, B., Kanza, T., Landver, A., Mador-Haim, S., Singerman, E., Tiemeyer, A., Vardi, M.Y., Zbar, Y.: The ForSpec temporal logic: A new temporal property-specification language. In: Katoen, J.-P., Stevens, P. (eds.) ETAPS 2002 and TACAS 2002. LNCS, vol. 2280, Springer, Heidelberg (2002)
2. Clarke, E., Emerson, E.: Characterizing correctness properties of parallel programs as fixpoints. In: de Bakker, J.W., van Leeuwen, J. (eds.) Automata, Languages and Programming. LNCS, vol. 85, Springer, Heidelberg (1980)

3. Dam, M.: Temporal logic, automata and classical theories - an introduction. Lecture Notes for the 6th European Summer School on Logic, Language and Information (1994)
4. Eisner, C., Fisman, D.: Sugar 2.0 proposal presented to the Accellera Formal Verification Technical Committee (March 2002), http://www.haifa.il.ibm.com/verification/sugar/Sugar_2.0_Accellera.ps.
5. Eisner, C., Fisman, D.: A practical introduction to PSL. Springer, Heidelberg (2006)
6. Eisner, C., Fisman, D., Havlicek, J., McIsaac, A., Van Campenhout, D.: The definition of a temporal clock operator. In: Baeten, J.C.M., Lenstra, J.K., Parrow, J., Woeginger, G.J. (eds.) ICALP 2003. LNCS, vol. 2719, Springer, Heidelberg (2003)
7. Emerson, E.A.: Model checking and the Mu-calculus. In: Descriptive Complexity and Finite Models. DIMACS Series in Discrete Mathematics, vol. 31, pp. 185–214. American Mathematical Society, Providence, RI (1997)
8. Havlicek, J., Fisman, D., Eisner, C.: Basic results on the semantics of Accellera PSL 1.1 foundation language. Technical Report 2004.02 Accellera, (May 2004)
9. Havlicek, J., Levi, N., Miller, H., Shultz, K.: Extended CBV statement semantics, partial proposal presented to the Accellera Formal Verification Technical Committee (April 2002), http://www.eda.org/vfv/hm/att-0772/01-ecbv_statement_semantics.ps.gz
10. Annex E of IEEE Standard for SystemVerilog Unified Hardware Design, Specification, and Verification Language. IEEE Std 1800^{TM} (2005)
11. IEEE Standard for Property Specification Language (PSL). IEEE Std 1850^{TM} (2005)
12. Kaivola, R.: A simple decision method for the linear-time mu-calculus (1995)
13. Kozen, D.: Results on the propositional mu-calculus. Theoretical Computer Science 27(3), 333–354 (1983)
14. Manna, Z., Pnueli, A.: Temporal Verification of Reactive Systems: Specification. Springer, New York (1992)
15. Manna, Z., Wolper, P.: Synthesis of communicating processes from temporal logic specifications. ACM Trans. Program. Lang. Syst. 6(1), 68–93 (1984)
16. Pnueli, A.: The temporal logic of programs. In: Proc. 18th Annual IEEE Symposium on Foundations of Computer Science, pp. 46–57 (1977)
17. Pnueli, A.: In transition from global to modular temporal reasoning about programs. In: Apt, K. (ed.) Logics and Models of Concurrent Systems. NATO Advanced Summer Institute, vol. F-13, pp. 123–144. Springer, Heidelberg (1985)
18. Tarski, A.: A lattice-theoretical fixpoint theorem and its applications. Pacific J. Math. 5, 285–309 (1955)
19. Vardi, M.Y.: An automata-theoretic approach to linear temporal logic. In: Banff Higher Order Workshop, pp. 238–266 (1995)

Reactivity in SystemC Transaction-Level Models

Frederic Doucet[1], R.K. Shyamasundar[2], Ingolf H. Krüger[1], Saurabh Joshi[3],
and Rajesh K. Gupta[1]

[1] University of California, San Diego
[2] IBM India Research Laboratory
[3] Indian Institute of Technology, Kanpur

Abstract. SystemC is a popular language used in modeling system-on-chip implementations. To support this task at a high level of abstraction, transaction-level modeling (TLM) libraries have been recently developped. While TLM libraries are useful, it is difficult to capture the reactive nature of certain transactions with the constructs currently available in the SystemC and TLM libraries. In this paper, we propose an approach to specify and verify reactive transactions in SystemC designs. Reactive transactions are different from TLM transactions in the sense that a transaction can be killed or reset. Our approach consists of: (1) a language to describe reactive transactions that can be translated to verification monitors, (2) an architectural pattern to implement reactive transactions, and (3) the verification support to verify that the design does not deadlock, allows only legal behaviors and is always responsive. We illustrate our approach through an example of a transactional memory system where a transaction can be killed or reset before its completion. We identify the architectural patterns for reactive transactions. Our results demonstrate the feasibility of our approach as well as support for a comprehensive verification using RuleBase/NuSMV tools.

1   Introduction

Transaction-level models are useful in SystemC [1] to understand a system by abstracting the low-level bus signaling details. In this paper, we build upon this work by extending the transactions to support reactive features that are commonly found in frameworks such as Esterel [2]. Reactivity can provide one with the capability to kill or reset a transaction before the transaction completes. This is analogous - but for transactions - to the reactive features for processes that were present in the earlier versions of SystemC through the "wait" and "watching" syntactic constructs [3]. The "watching" constructed was later dropped from SystemC due to lack of use. However, as the libraries evolve and as the role of TLM models is increasing, we believe that these constructs would find greater use and simplify the design migration to higher levels of abstraction.

This investigation of specification and verification of reactive transactions was motivated by an experiment to model and verify a transactional memory using interaction descriptions and SystemC. The fundamental difference between the transactional memory model and the typical TLM models built with SystemC is

K. Yorav (Ed.): HVC 2007, LNCS 4899, pp. 34–50, 2008.

the following: in the transactional memory, a process that initiates a transaction can be reset before the transaction completes. Then, the pending transaction could be reset or not, depending on what the desired outcome is. Unfortunately, it is not possible to capture this kind of behavior with the current SystemC TLM libraries. Therefore, we had to re-think what a transaction is and what are the syntactical and architectural features that are necessary to capture the reset and kill behavior, and how to use the formal verification to guarantee the implementation of the transaction specifications.

We found three challenges for specifying implementing and verifying the reactive transactions with SystemC. The first one is to specify the transactions using the property specification languages. Because many events can potentially happen at the same time, the properties can be very tedious to specify. From our experience, as a specification can take many simultaneous events at one time, and because the properties need to describe every possible scenario, the properties become very large as one basically has to compute and write down the product of all possible event combinations for the TLM events. The second challenge is that it is difficult to implement reactive features within SystemC TLM models. This is because there are no do/watching statement we can use to capture the reactive behaviors and the necessary transaction handlers. Also, since the transaction events are atomic rendezvous in the specification and handshakes in the implementation, the implementation of the reactive transactions can be challenging as mismanaging the handshakes with the resets could easily cause synchronization problems such as deadlocks. Finally, the third challenge is to have an efficient SystemC verification framework that support the reactive transactions as a first-order construct and also includes the capability of verifying liveness properties.

In this paper, we present an approach to specify and reason about the reactive transactions by defining a language that will capture the transactions, and a tool to translate these specifications into verification monitors. While one could argue that such transactions could be specified using PSL [4], we believe the task can be slightly tedious as the properties become long and complex. This is evidenced by the continuing evolution of PSL into more elaborate higher-level design languages [5] where the specification can be a bit more high-level, making the specification easier to write. In that spirit, we use a specification language that is inspired by the process algebraic framework of CRP [6]. Our framework enables the specification of rendezvous communications a la CSP, as well as the reactive features provided by the Esterel constructs. We extend those ideas to add the features that are necessary for transactions.

The contributions described in this paper are as follows. First, we define a high-level language inspired by CRP to describe reactive transactions and their compositions as a first-order construct. Second, using the standard syntax, we provide a TLM extension in the form of an architectural pattern to capture the reactive transactions, with the cascading of resets. Third, we believe are the first to formally check TLM models with respect to transaction specifications rather than generic properties.

The rest of the paper is organized as follows. In the next section, we present the related work in monitor-based verification and SystemC verification. In Section 3, we describe a subset of the Transactional Memory example that motivated this work, and the problems and challenges of specifying and verifying reactive transactions. In Section 4, we describe how to specify reactive transactions, with the definition of the syntax and semantics of the specification language. In Section 5, we describe how to implement the reactive transactions in SystemC, and then present our experiments and results in Section 6, followed by a discussion and the conclusion.

2   Related Work

We broadly categorize the related work as being the specification of protocols and the generation of verification monitors, as well as the verification of SystemC designs. In some sense, this work bridges transaction specification with SystemC verification by using the specification of transactions for TLM verification.

2.1   Protocol Monitors

In the context of system-level design, a transaction is a concept that is a slight bit above the components. We need to capture the transactions spanning accross multiple components in the system into properties that can be used for verification. Specification languages do not clearly provide the necessary constructs, since there is no notion of global transactions.

To address this gap, there have been several attempts at describing transactions as high-level entities, at the level above the components. Seawright et al. [7] proposed an approach to describe the transaction that can happen at an interface using regular expressions. Such a protocol description can be used to generate interface monitors from the regular expressions. Siegmund et al. [8] followed this approach and showed how one can synthesize bus interface circuits from the regular expressions. The approach has the advantage that, instead of describing the producer and the consumer, the description models the protocol as a monitor that observes a set of variables. To describe the monitor, their language has four operators: "serial", "parallel", "repeat" and "select". A synthesis algorithm is used to generate the state machines for both the producer and the consumer. Although it greatly simplified complex hardware design, one of the limitations is that it can be difficult to specify and synthesize the reactive features (kill/reset) with the available operators.

Several more interesting contributions followed. Oliveira et al. [9] extended monitor-based specification languages by introducing storage variables, a pipeline operator, and also improved the algorithms for generating the protocol monitor. However, one drawback of their approach is the lack of formal semantics. Shimizu [10] addressed part of the problem by using a framework of concurrent guarded transitions, and showed how to model check the descriptions for useful properties.

Interface descriptions and monitors are now widely used for both documentation and validation [4] [11]. Many engineers use the PSL language (and extensions [5]) to describe the interfaces, and several tools exist to generate protocol monitors for simulation. There exist commercial tools that generate protocol monitors from such descriptions for simulation or verification, notably FoCs [12]. In this context, we see two opportunities stemming from this body of work: (1) to easily and elegantly capture the reactive features in the transactions, and (2) to have a compositional analysis from transactions to interface specification, which challenging to achieve with the reactive features.

2.2   SystemC Verification

The goal of the Transaction-Level Modeling (TLM) with SystemC [13] is to define a model where the details of the RTL bus communications are abstracted away either (1) instead of going through signal transitions, have a component directly call the method of another component, or (2) having the components communicating through buffered FIFO communications. In both cases abstract data types can also be used to bundle low-level bus data types into one chunk of data. The benefit of using a TLM model is that the simulator does not need to spend cycles on simulating all the RTL bus synchronizations, thus the design will simulate much faster. Typically, a SystemC TLM model simulates 2-3 orders of magnitude faster than an "equivalent" RTL model. There exists a number of verification approaches for both RTL and TLM models written in SystemC. These approaches support TLM models in the sense that they support the syntactic constructs found in the models, which include function calls, access to FIFO buffers, and reading and writing signals. However, it is difficult to verify a TLM model because (1) the model can be non-deterministic due to the shared variable communications within the channels, and (2) the number of elements queued in a FIFO buffers can grow without a bound. Thus, all existing approaches impose restrictions on the input syntax to avoid these problems.

The approach defined by Habibi et al. [14] uses a specification format based on PSL sequences or basic Message Sequence Charts, augmented with clocking guards. The properties range over the signals and the buffers in the architecture. A property is translated into a monitor, which is an automaton with fail, in-progress and accept states. Similarly, a SystemC design is translated into automaton and then the design and the property automata are composed together. During the composition, the ASML composition tool will expand the state machine and check that the monitor is always asserted. Similarly, the Lussy tool suite developed by Moy et al. [15] translates SystemC modules into an intermediate automaton based on the Lustre formalism. This approach also uses synchronous observers for verification. In this work, the notion of a transaction matches the SystemC TLM definitions, where the bus transactions which are abstracted into simple function calls. These function calls are then mapped to architectural blocks that capture the TLM communication through simple minimal handshakes. The approach by Kroening [16] provides efficient SystemC verification by using by translating a SystemC model to a SMV description, using predicate abstraction and other techniques. However, here again there is no explicit notion of a transaction.

3   Motivating Example: Transactional Memory

Figure 1 shows an example of how modules, channels and buffers are connected in the transactional memory system. There are three components with their own threads: the program segment, the controller and the cache. There are also two channels, which convert a SystemC TLM method call into a request/response handshake through buffers.

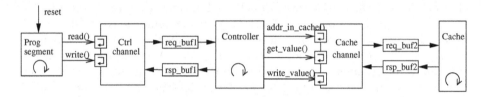

Fig. 1. Simplified example architecture for the Transactional Memory model

The program segment starts a **read()** or a **write()** transaction with a method call to the channel. Figure 2 depicts a scenario for the interactions for a read transaction. The channel converts the call to a request which it places on th **req_buf1 buffer**. The controller will pick up the request, and if it is a read request it is going to check if the address is in the cache by calling the **addr_in_cache** method of the cache channel. If it, then it will get the value by calling the **get_value** method. If it is a write request, it will just call the write value method. The methods of the cache channel will generate a request to the **req_buf2** buffer. The cache will then process the request and place the response on the response buffer **rsp_buf2**, and the response will eventually make its way to the program segment that will eventually pick it up through the value returned by the original method call. Note that for a read or write transaction, there is at least one sub-transaction that will be called the controller and the cache.

The **reset** signal is used to reset the program segment when there is a conflict on the cache. The program segment can be reset at anytime while a transaction is in progress. The main challenge in this example is the following: when the program segment is reset, what happens with the pending transactions? Should they complete or be killed? It is the responsibility of the designer (or the synthesis tool) to decide what the desirable outcomes in such situations are. However, in the current SystemC TLM standard, there is no support to handle these situations. Therefore, defining the required control signals and communication protocols to support these situations, both for specification and verification, is the central problem we are addressing in this paper.

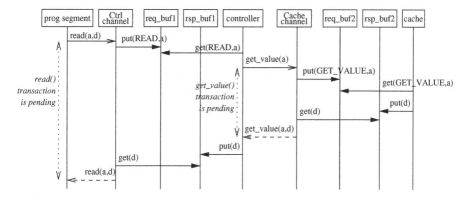

Fig. 2. Message exchange and scope for a read transaction

4   Specification of Reactive Transactions

We capture a transaction as a first-order entity, in the sense that it can be specified, it has a context, control signals and that it can describe behavior which can be distributed over many components in an architecture. Figure 3(a) depicts the "abstract" interface of a transaction: there is a **start** and a **done** signal, both being used as the normal and entry and exit event of the transaction. As its name indicates, the **kill** signal is used to terminate a transaction. The **status** is used by other components to observe the status of the transaction. The possible statuses are "ready", "done", "in progress" and "killed". Figure 3(b) and Figure 3(c) shows the abstract interface behavior for a terminating and a reactive transaction. The start and done signals are abstract in the sense that they can be mapped to given events in the system, such as specific reading a value for a buffer. In between and start and the completion of a transaction can be events, operations, and sub-transactions.

The specification language we use to capture transactions is rooted in CRP, but we augment it to capture the transactions as first-order constructs. The

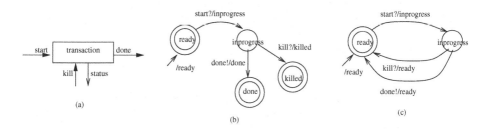

Fig. 3. Interface for Reactive Transaction: (a) control and status signals (b) normal transaction (c) reactive transaction

formal foundation of CRP [6] is composed of CSP [17], where we borrow the rendezvous communication, with the synchronous foundation in Esterel with its reactive features [2]. In the same fashion, we will define the semantics of our specification language with a semantics domain composed of an environment, which is a set of events, rendezvous actions, pending labels and status flag, and a set of state variables. The semantics of a specification description is defined through a transition system which is induced by operational semantics rule of the form:

$$(\langle stmt\rangle, \sigma) \xrightarrow[\langle E,A,L\rangle]{\langle E',A',L',b\rangle} (\langle stmt'\rangle, \sigma')$$

where:

- *stmt* is a specification statement, meaning the location of the program counter for the specification, and *stmt'* is the program text with the location of the program counter after the transition,
- σ and σ' are the states before and after the reaction respectively,
- E is the set of events in the environment before taking the transition
- L is the set of pending labels in the environment before taking the transition,
- E' is the set of events emitted by this transition,
- A' is the set of rendezvous labels agreed for this transition,
- L' is a set of pending labels, containing the pending labels after taking the transactions,
- b is a boolean flag indicating if the taken transition terminates (blocks) the instantaneous reaction or not.

Figure 4 shows the main statements in the language, and Table 1 and 2 show the functions defining the semantics for the transaction and reactive statements respectively. The statements to specify the behaviors of transactions are exec_start and exec_done, where exec_start t will denotes the beginning of a transaction t, synchronizing on rendezvous start(t), and posting a label pending(t) in the environment (to remember that transaction t is pending). Similarly, statement exec_done t denotes the completion of t, and synchronizes on rendezvous done(t), also removing the pending label t from the environment. The exec_start t and exec_done t statements are meant to be paired with rv_rcv t and rv_snd t rendezvous statements. The exec statements are to be used by the master process (the one initiating the transaction), and rendezvous statements are used by the slave process (the one receiving the transaction). The only difference between the exec and the rendezvous statement is the exec statements post and remove a transaction labels in the environment.

The rendezvous statements work like CSP rendezvous, with a slight variation to accommodate the synchrony hypothesis. The synchrony hypothesis, a concept defined in Esterel [2], is that at a given instant, all processes synchronously execute a sequence of statements instantaneously (up until the next pause). The rv_snd a and rv_rcv a statements synchronize on the shared action a only if that action is not in the preceding environment, and is present only in the output environment. This is to avoid the possibility of a rendezvous being taken twice during a synchronous reaction (synchronous as in synchrony hypothesis).

The watching statement is used to monitor events which will interrupt statement stmt when bexpr evaluate to true. When the condition evaluates to false, the watch computation will keep proceeding along stmt and its derivative (stmt can be a complex statement) until the termination of stmt. If the condition is true, then the computation of stmt will terminate immediately, and all the pending transactions will be killed, and L' will be empty. In other words, during a watch condition, if there is a pending transaction label, the transaction will be killed - including all transactions started by stmt. This ability to keep track of what transactions has been started, and be able to kill them in the event to a watch statement is the main feature of the reactive transaction specification language. This is the same as the hidden signals that are found in the composition operators (such as prefix) in process algebras, and used to simplify specifications. Note that it is possible to define scopes for the set L of pending labels to follow the hierarchical structure of the specification. But this leads to much more complicated semantic rules, which we will omit for the sake of space and simplicity.

The rest of the language borrows heavily from CRP, with the wait, emit, rendezvous, sequencing, choice, guarded actions and pause statements. The emit statement posts an event e into the set E', while a wait expression is evaluated in the incoming environment E. The pause statement terminate an instantaneous reaction. The language also has constructs for parallel compositions, arithmetic and Boolean expressions, and usual control flow statement etc. The syntax semantics of these and other statements in the language follow from the definitions Esterel and CSP with the addition of the transformation for the synchrony hypothesis, but are out of the scope of this paper.

```
stmt ::=
    exec_start t        /* start transaction t                */
  | exec_done t         /* wait for transaction t to be done  */
  | rv_snd a            /* rendezvous at a (can send data)    */
  | rv_rcv a            /* rendezvous at a (can receive data) */

  | do { stmt } watching bexpr         /* do/watching stmt    */
  | G(bexpr) {stmt} [] G(bexpr) {stmt} /* guarded selection   */
  | stmt |C| stmt       /* choice                             */
  | stmt ; stmt         /* sequence                           */

  | emit e              /* emit event e                       */
  | wait bexpr          /* wait for given boolean expression  */
  | pause               /* wait for a moment                  */
```

Fig. 4. Syntax of the specification language

Table 1. Semantics for the Transaction Statements

(rv-snd-1)	**(rv-snd-2)**
$$(\texttt{rv\_snd a},\sigma) \xrightarrow[\langle E,A,L\rangle]{\langle\emptyset,a,L,1\rangle} (\_,\sigma)$$ with $a \notin A$	$$(\texttt{rv\_snd a},\sigma) \xrightarrow[\langle E,A,L\rangle]{\langle\emptyset,\emptyset,L,0\rangle} (\texttt{rv\_snd a},\sigma)$$

$$\textbf{(rv-snd-1)} \qquad \dfrac{a \notin A}{(\texttt{rv\_snd a},\sigma) \xrightarrow[\langle E,A,L\rangle]{\langle\emptyset,a,L,1\rangle} (\_,\sigma)}$$

$$\textbf{(rv-snd-2)} \qquad (\texttt{rv\_snd a},\sigma) \xrightarrow[\langle E,A,L\rangle]{\langle\emptyset,\emptyset,L,0\rangle} (\texttt{rv\_snd a},\sigma)$$

$$\textbf{(rv-rcv-1)} \qquad \dfrac{a \notin A}{(\texttt{rv\_rcv a},\sigma) \xrightarrow[\langle E,A,L\rangle]{\langle\emptyset,a,L,1\rangle} (\_,\sigma)}$$

$$\textbf{(rv-rcv-2)} \qquad (\texttt{rv\_rcv a},\sigma) \xrightarrow[\langle E,A,L\rangle]{\langle\emptyset,\emptyset,L,0\rangle} (\texttt{rv\_rcv a},\sigma)$$

$$\textbf{(exec-start-1)} \qquad \dfrac{start(t) \notin A}{(\texttt{exec\_start t},\sigma) \xrightarrow[\langle E,A,L\rangle]{\langle\emptyset,start(t),\{L\cup pending(t)\},1\rangle} (\_,\sigma)}$$

$$\textbf{(exec-done-1)} \qquad \dfrac{done(t) \notin A}{(\texttt{exec\_done t},\sigma) \xrightarrow[\langle E,A,L\rangle]{\langle\emptyset,done(t),\{L\setminus pending(t)\},1\rangle} (\_,\sigma)}$$

$$\textbf{(exec-start-2)} \qquad (\texttt{exec\_start t},\sigma) \xrightarrow[\langle E,A,L\rangle]{\langle\emptyset,\emptyset,L,0\rangle} (\texttt{exec\_start t},\sigma)$$

$$\textbf{(exec-done-2)} \qquad (\texttt{exec\_done t},\sigma) \xrightarrow[\langle E,A,L\rangle]{\langle\emptyset,\emptyset,L,0\rangle} (\texttt{exec\_done t},\sigma)$$

5 Verifiable Implementation in SystemC

In this section we discuss the following challenges in the verifiable implementation of reactive transactions:

1. How to have an implementation of reactivity through a simple architectural pattern that is generalizable for reactive transactions, and
2. How to correlate the atomic events in a transaction specification to the non-atomic handshakes in the SystemC code.

5.1 Reactivity Through Exceptions and Architectural Patterns

To implement reactivity within TLM models, we need to use the reactive features that were removed from SystemC a short time ago. These watching-and-waiting statements have been using exceptions to throw special conditions designating reset conditions [3]. For this purpose, we follow a similar pattern and we introduce a new wait macro, which we call MYWAIT :

```
#define MYWAIT(event_expr, reset_cond) \
    wait(event_expr); \
    if (reset_cond) \
      throw 1;
```

Table 2. Semantics for the Reactive Statements

(do-watching-1)

$$\frac{\sigma \not\models bexpr \qquad (\texttt{stmt}, \sigma) \xrightarrow[\langle E,A,L\rangle]{\langle E',A',L',b\rangle} (\texttt{stmt'}, \sigma')}{(\texttt{do \{stmt\} watching (bexpr)}, \sigma) \xrightarrow[\langle E,A,L\rangle]{\langle E',A',L',b\rangle} (\texttt{do \{stmt'\} watching (bexpr)}, \sigma')}$$

(do-watching-2)

$$\frac{\sigma \not\models bexpr \qquad (\texttt{stmt}, \sigma) \xrightarrow[\langle E,A,L\rangle]{\langle E',A',L',b\rangle} (\_, \sigma')}{(\texttt{do \{stmt\} watching (bexpr)}, \sigma) \xrightarrow[\langle E,A,L\rangle]{\langle E',A',L',b\rangle} (\_, \sigma')}$$

(do-watching-3)

$$\frac{\sigma \models bexpr}{(\texttt{do \{stmt\} watching (bexpr)}, \sigma) \xrightarrow[\langle E,A,L\rangle]{\langle \forall t \in L: kill(t), \emptyset, \emptyset, \rangle} (\_, \sigma)}$$

The macro defines a wait statement, which will wait on a given list of events. This will be a regular transaction event, or a reset event. The second parameter is the reset condition, and it identifies which event condition means the transaction has been reset, and if this condition holds the macro will throw an exception (here just an integer). An example of how to use this macro is as follows:

```
MYWAIT( (clk.posedge_event() | reset.posedge_event()),
        (reset.event() && reset==1) );
```

where the event expression is either a clock up-tick or a reset up-tick, and the reset expression a reset event and the reset signal to one. The MYWAIT macro is meant to be used inside a try/catch statement. Here is an example of a process which invokes a **write** transaction on a **ctrl** channel:

```
try {
  ctrl->write(1,1)
} catch (int reset_code) {
  ctrl->kill__write();
}
```

When a reset event occurs, the exception will be thrown from inside the **write()** method implementing the transaction inside the ctrl channel. The exception will be caught by the outer handler– not in the channel but in the component. In this case, the process can choose to kill the transaction in the server by calling the **kill_write()** method on the channel to send the kill signal to the server.

In this case, the handling of the reactivity can be done inside the component, but in general an architectural pattern with a transaction controller and a separate controller helper to handle the reactivity can be used. Figure 5 shows the architectural pattern to use to separate the reset conditions from the regular TLM processing. A controller processes transactions and dispatches sub-transactions.

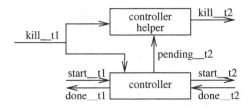

Fig. 5. Architectural pattern to propagate the transaction kills

With the architecture on the figure, assume a situation where a transaction t1 is started, followed transaction t2 being started by the controller, t2 being necessary to complete t1. When t2 is started, signal pending__t2 is sent to the controller to tell that t2 is pending. If t1 is killed while t2 is pending, then from pending__t2 the controller helper will go ahead and kill t2.

This pattern is useful when a controller helper can process and keep track of all the simultaneous transactions. Then, the controller it does not have to be concerned about keeping track of which sub-transactions to kill, matching the idea the designer has when using the transaction description algebra. An underlying question is how to implement this controller helper.

5.2   Non-atomicity of Rendezvous and Kill Handlers

In the specification, a rendezvous is atomic. However, in the SystemC TLM implementation, a rendezvous is not atomic but a handshake. The master component synchronizes with the slave (also called the transaction server - or just server) through a method call that leads to an exchange using a TLM FIFO buffer. Until the slave has picked up the data from the buffer, the exchange cannot be considered done, but only in progress. In that sense, the challenge here is implementing the transactions with the reactive features is to manage the kills that occur during the handshakes that are in progress. When a kill occurs during that time, there has to be special conditions to correlate the non-atomic exchange to the atomic exchange in the specification.

Figure 6 shows the scenarios that can occur when kill happens during a handshake. Each of these scenarios requires a specific handling strategy which will make sure the buffers are emptied and the transaction in the slave is cleanly killed. The first case, illustrated Figure 6(a), is when t2 gets killed before it started; this assumes that the server of t2 will be able to eventually unblock and pick up the request from the buffer, see the kill__t2 signal to be asserted, and then thus discard the request:

```
if ( pending__t2 and ready__t2 and full(t2_req_buf) ) {
  kill__t2 = 1;
  wait_until empty(t2_req_buf);
  kill__t2 = 0;
}
```

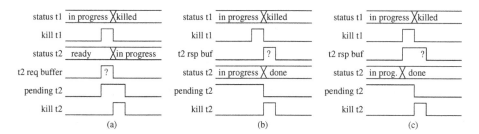

Fig. 6. Scenarios for handshakes with kill: (a) request posted but slave has not picked up yet, (b) slave is processing transaction, (c) slave is done but master has not picked up response yet

The second scenario is when t2 terminates at the same time it gets killed. In that case, the handler might need to pick up and discard the response:

```
if (pending__t2 and in_progress__t2_) {
  kill__t2 = 1;
  wait_until ready(t2) or kill(t2) or done(t2);
  kill__t2 = 0;
  if (full(t2_rsp_buf))
    get(rsp_buf)
}
```

The third scenario is when t2 is done serving the transaction, but the master has not yet picked up the response from the buffer. Then, the handler just picks up and discards the response from the buffer:

```
if (pending__t2 and ready__t2 and not full(t2_rep_buf)) {
  assert( full(t2_rsp_buf) );
  get(t2_rsp_buf);
}
```

We believe that, the transaction interfaces defined in our reactive transaction framework gives the tools to implement the handling strategies for reactive transactions. However, it is the *responsibility of the designer* to make sure there are no deadlocks and de-synchronization situations in the design. While we provide the signals and the patterns, correctly implementating the transaction controllers can be a challenging task. In that context, it is very valuable to have the verification support to be able to formally prove the correctness of the implementation.

6   Experiments and Results

Our verification setup is to use monitor-based model checking, where a monitor will check a SystemC component for any unallowed behaviors. Furthermore, we also use temporal logic formulas to ensure no deadlocks or stalls are reached. To convert a specification description into a verification monitor, we designed and implemented a Spec Analyzer tool. The conversion from specification to monitor directly follows the operational semantics rules, with the addition of the conversion for the synchrony hypothesis. The pass about the synchrony hypothesis is used to reduce a sequence of micro-transitions into one synchronous macro-transition, by following the termination flag (the b in the semantic rules). The Spec Analyzer generates a verification monitor which has a an error state which denotes a problem in the design, as well as a special state to handle the environment assumptions (whether we are "in-transaction" or not). Furthermore, using the Module Analyzer tool we previously presented [18], we convert the SystemC to a transition system described in an SMV file.

For the example, we implemented a simplified version of the transactional memory in SystemC with the reactive transactions library. Figure 7 shows the structure of the system we implemented and verified. The structure is the same as the one in Figure 1 with the addition of the reactive features. The program segment implements reactivity with a try/catch and takes care of the pending transactions in its catch handler. For the controller, we use the pattern with the controller helper as described in the previous section.

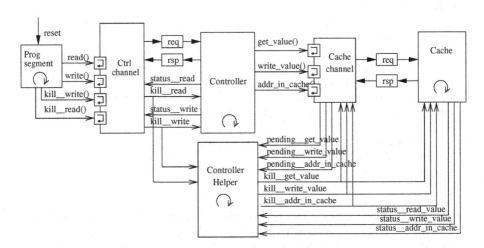

Fig. 7. Reactive architecture for the simplified Transactional Memory model

We have verified the design both at the system-level and at the component level. At the system-level, the global specification is an infinite sequence of read or write transactions that can be reset and restarted. We derived local component specifications from the global transactions for component-level verification.

Figure 8 lists the specification for the controller, which reads as follows: the controller will first wait for a rendezvous on either a read_start or write_start transaction. These transactions are to be initiated by the program segment using exec statements. Then, if controller picks up a read or a

```
while (true) {
        rv_rcv read__start |C| rv_rcv write__start ;
        G( read__start && !read__kill ) {
                do {
                        exec_start addr_in_cache;
                        exec_done  addr_in_cache;
                        exec_start get_value;
                        exec_done  get_value;
                        rv_snd read__done
                } watching read__kill__posedge_event
        } [] G( write__start && !write__kill ) {
                do {
                        exec_start write_value;
                        exec_done  write_value;
                        rv_snd write__done
                } watching write__kill__posedge_event
        } [] G( (!(read__start && !read__kill )) &&
                (!(write__start && !write__kill)) ) {
                // other guards are false
        };
}
```

Fig. 8. Specification for the Controller

write transaction and it was not killed at the same instant, it will proceed on it; if the transaction was killed it will discard the request go back to the rendezvous. When the controller processes the read transaction, it will execute two sub-transactions and complete with a done rendezvous - all this while watching the kill read condition. If a kill read occurs, the controller shall return to the initial rendezvous, and the pending transactions will get killed by the combination of exec and watching statements. A write transaction works similarly. Note that the controller can wait for an arbitrary amount of time between the rendezvous.

Table 3 lists the verification results for the example using NuSMV 2.4.3. For each run, the property we verify are the following:

1. *Monitor assertions:* AG !(monitor.state==ERROR)
   This guarantees all the behaviors of the implementations are permitted by the transaction specification;
2. *C++ assertions:* AG !(component.ERR)
   When an assertion inside a C++/SystemC module fails, it will set the ERR flag. This is often used to monitor the conditions inside the modules.
3. *Liveness assertions:* AG AF trans_starts or AG EF trans_starts
   The liveness property specifies that we can always eventually start a new transaction, or there always is a path leading to the start of a new transaction, depending on how strong the property has to be. This will prove absence of stalls or deadlocks with respect to those events and the branching conditions.

The verification times for all the properties are compounded in the entries of Table 3. The transaction channels are inlined inside the SystemC components. To keep track of transactions implemented through method calls, start and done events are added at the boundary of methods calls. We also currently limit the sizes of the TLM buffers to one unit only. The verifiation times are reasonable, and in line with the verification times for other SystemC verification frameworks. However, we cannot fairly compare our numbers with the numbers from other verification frameworks because the other frameworks do not capture the reactive transactions as we do, thus the specification is different. As for the numbers in the table, one can notice that the verification of the Controller + Controller Helper takes significantly more time and space than for the other components. This is because the controller interacts with all components - thus all buffers are there - and its environment model has many constraints.

Table 3. Verification results (with NuSMV)

Configuration	Time (sec)	Memory (KB)
full system	671	102864
prog segment	41	19168
controller (+ controller helper)	483	97368
cache	131	40300

Note that we did not prove the compositionality of the specification, and this is outside the scope of this paper. The system-level verification is important to prove that the reset of nonatomic rendezvous avoids all integration problems. In our case, we found several integration bugs and this lead us of to formulate those conditions. One of the next steps is to generalize those conditions and elaborate a proof structure to avoid having to do the system-level verification.

7   Summary and Future Work

In this paper, we have presented an approach to specify, implement and verify reactive transactions in SystemC. To specify the transactions, We defined a language that implicitly keeps track of pending transaction and a watching statement is used to abstract away the bookeeping details of propagating the reactivity to sub-transactions (propagating the reset and kill events).

Many of the implementation efforts are spent on explicitly instantiating these signals in an verifiable implementation pattern. Indeed, we provide the sketch of an architectural pattern to implement the reactive transactions in SystemC, as well as an outline of the conditions to correlate the non-atomic SystemC implementation of atomic transaction events. Our third contribution is the verification path, currently supported by SMV-based model checkers.

One of the broader goal of this work is to exploit the compositionality in the transaction specifications, as well as, when possible, its reflection in the architecture and proof structure. We believe that the style of specification we have developed will be amenable to the decomposition and consistency checks that are necessary for to support this example. In that context we are also investigating using equivalence checking techniques to address the verification problem more directly.

Acknowledgments

The authors would like to acknowledge the anonymous reviewers for their excellent suggestions.

References

1. Groetker, T., Liao, S., Martin, G., Swan, S.: System Design with SystemC. Kluwer Academic Publishers, Dordrecht (2002)
2. Berry, G.: The Foundations of Esterel. MIT Press, Cambridge (2000)
3. Liao, S., Tjiang, S., Gupta, R.: An Efficient Implementation of Reactivity for Modeling Hardware in the Scenic Design Environment. In: Proc. of the Design Automation Conf. (1997)
4. Marschner, E., Deadman, B., Martin, G.: IP Reuse Hardening via Embedded Sugar Assertions. In: Proc. of the Int. Workshop on IP SOC Design (2002)
5. Balarin, F., Passerone, R.: Functional Verification Methodology Based on Formal Interface Specification and Transactor Generation. In: Proc. Design Automation and Test in Europe Conf. (2006)
6. Berry, G., Ramesh, S., Shyamasundar, R.K.: Communicating Reactive Processes. In: Proc. of the Symposium on Principles of Programming Languages (1993)
7. Seawright, A., Brewer, F.: Clairvoyant: A Synthesis System for Production-based Specifications. IEEE Trans. on Very Large Scale Integration (VLSI) Systems 2, 172–185 (1994)
8. Siegmund, R., Muller, D.: Automatic Synthesis of Communication Controller Hardware from Protocol Specification. IEEE Design and Test of Computer 19, 84–95 (2002)
9. Oliveira, M., Hu, A.: High-level Specification and Automatic Generation of IP Interface Monitors. In: Proc. of the Design Automation Conf. (2002)
10. Shimizu, K.: Writing, Verifying, and Exploiting Formal Specifications for Hardware Designs. PhD thesis, Stanford University (2002)
11. Zhu, Q., Oishi, R., Hasegawa, T., Nakata, T.: System-on-Chip Validation using UML and CWL. In: Proc. of the Int. Conf. on Hardware-Software Codesign and System Synthesis (2004)
12. Abarbanel, Y., Beer, I., Glushovsky, L., Keidar, S., Wolfsthal, Y.: FoCs: Automatic Generation of Simulation Checkers from Formal Specifications. In: Proc. of the Int. Conf. on Computer Aided Verification. pp. 538–542 (2000)
13. Cai, L., Gajski, D.: Transaction-level Modeling: an Overview. In: Proc. of the Int. Conf. on Hardware/Software Codesign and System Synthesis, pp. 19–24. ACM Press, New York (2003)

14. Habibi, A., Tahar, S.: Design and Verification of SystemC Transaction-level Models. IEEE Transactions on Very Large Scale Integration Systems 14, 57–68 (2006)
15. Moy, M., Maraninchi, F., Maillet-Contoz, L.: LusSy: A Toolbox for the Analysis of System-on-a-Chip at the Transactional Level. In: Proc. of the Int. Conf. on Application of Concurrency to System Design (2005)
16. Kroening, D., Sharygina, N.: Formal Verification of SystemC by Automatic Hardware/Software Partitioning. In: Proc. of the Int. Conf. on Formal Methods and Models for Codesign (2007)
17. Hoare, C.A.R.: Communicating Sequential Processes. Series in Computer Science. Prentice-Hall International, Englewood Cliffs (1985)
18. Shyamasundar, R., Doucet, F., Gupta, R., Krüger, I.H.: Compositional Reactive Semantics of SystemC and Verification in RuleBase. In: Proc. of the Workshop on Next Generation Design and Verification Methodologies for Distributed Embedded Control Systems (2007)

Verifying Parametrised Hardware Designs Via Counter Automata*

A. Smrčka and T. Vojnar

FIT, Brno University of Technology,
Božetěchova 2, CZ-61266, Brno, Czech Republic
{smrcka,vojnar}@fit.vutbr.cz

Abstract. The paper presents a new approach to formal verification of generic (i.e. parametrised) hardware designs specified in VHDL. The proposed approach is based on a translation of such designs to counter automata and on exploiting the recent advances achieved in the area of their automated formal verification. We have implemented the proposed translation. Using one of the state-of-the-art tools for verification of counter automata, we were then able to verify several non-trivial properties of parametrised VHDL components, including a real-life one.

1   Introduction

Modern hardware description languages (HDL) such as VHDL or Verilog allow digital hardware to be designed in a way quite close to software programming. These languages offer many features whose use constitutes a challenge for the current formal verification technologies. One of such challenges is the possibility of *parametrisation* of the designed hardware components by values from a domain that is not bounded in advance. Parametrisation is widely used, e.g., when creating libraries of re-usable hardware components.

In this paper, we propose a novel way of verifying parametrised hardware components. Namely, inspired by the recent advances in the technology for verification of *counter automata*, we propose a translation from (a subset of) VHDL [11] to counter automata on which formal verification is subsequently performed. The subset of VHDL that we consider is restricted in just a limited way, mostly by excluding constructions that are anyway usually considered as erroneous, undesirable, and/or not implementable (synthesisable) in hardware.

In the generated counter automata, bit variables are kept track in the control locations whereas bit-vector (i.e. integer) variables—including parameters—are mapped to (unbounded) counters. When generating counter automata from VHDL, we first pre-process the input VHDL specification in order to simplify it (i.e. to reduce the number of the different constructions that can appear in

---

* This work was supported by the project CEZ MSM 0021630528 *Security-Oriented Research in Information Technology* of the Czech Ministry of Education, by the project 102/07/0322 of the Czech Grant Agency, and by the CESNET activity "Programmable hardware".

it), then we transform it to an intermediate form of certain behavioural rules describing the behaviour of particular variables that appear in the given design, and finally we put the behaviour of all the variables together to form a single counter automaton.

We concentrate on verifying that certain bad configurations specified by a boolean VHDL expression (which we call an error condition) over bit as well bit-vector variables is not reachable. We have built a simple prototype tool implementing the proposed translation. Despite there is a lot of space for optimising the generated counter automata and despite the fact that reachability analysis of counter automata is in general undecidable [10], we have already been able to verify several non-trivial properties of parametrised VHDL components, including a real-life component implementing an asynchronous queue designed within the Liberouter project (which aims at designing new network routing and monitoring systems based on the FPGA technology) [13,9].

Related work. Recently, there have appeared many works on automatic formal verification of counter automata or programs over integers that can also be considered as a form of counter automata (see, e.g., [6,18,1,15,8,4]). In the area of software model checking, there have also appeared works that try to exploit the advances in the technology of verifying counter automata for a verification of programs over more complex structures, notably recursive structures based on pointers [3,7,2]. In this work, we get inspired by the spirit of these works and try to apply it in the area of verifying generic (parametrised) hardware designs. We obtain a novel, quite general, and highly automated way of verification of such components, which can exploit the current and future advances in the technology of verifying counter automata.

Plan of the paper. In Section 2, we introduce some basics of VHDL, we comment on the VHDL constructions that we do not support, and explain the way we pre-process VHDL for the further transformations. We also introduce the notion of counter automata. In Section 3, we provide a translation from (simplified) VHDL to a certain form of intermediate behavioural rules. In Section 4, we present a translation from the intermediate format to counter automata. Section 5 comments on the reachability properties that we verify and on the way we facilitate their checking. In Section 6, we discuss our experimental results. Finally, in Section 7, we conclude and briefly discuss possible future improvements of our approach.

2   Hardware Design and Counter Automata Basics

2.1   Hardware Design

Nowadays, most of the digital hardware development is not done on the level of particular gates or transistors, but rather on the more abstract *register transfer level* (RTL). There are several languages for RTL hardware design, also known as *hardware description languages* (HDL), out of which the most widely used are VHDL and Verilog. A design specified in such a language is an input for hardware synthesis tools, and also for hardware simulation or verification tools. A process called *synthesis* transforms a generic RTL description of a system to the gate/transistor level of a concrete electronic circuit description. Such a description serves as an input for the further production of an integrated circuit (through the so-called place&route process) or as a configuration program for field programmable gate arrays (FPGA) if they are used to implement the system.

We build our counter automata-based models from the RTL level description via an *intermediate behavioural model*. This model cannot be created from the gate level as on that level the parametrisation of the system is lost—all the parameters are already instantiated. Moreover, in our model, we are only interested in the logical behaviour of the system, not in details such as propagation delays of the gates or the set of concrete hardware elements used to physically implement the given system.

Although VHDL and Verilog are different languages, their main expressive means are quite similar from our point of view of building a counter automaton model from an RTL hardware description (and running a verification on the counter automaton). That is why, in this paper, we will discuss only the VHDL language, which, moreover, has a better support for parametrised designs.

Hardware Design in VHDL. In VHDL [11], a more complex hardware system is described in a modular way using *components*. A component is described by a definition of its *interface* and its *body*. The interface defines the inputs and outputs of a component as well as its parameters which can make the component generic. The body of a component, also known as an *architecture*, consists of a declaration of internal variables and a collection of the so-called *parallel statements* describing the behaviour of the component.

VHDL offers two types of specifying the design of an architecture—structural and behavioural. Within a structural description, we view a digital circuit as a composition of objects that may be composed of other smaller objects. In terms of the parallel statements, this approach is based on using statements of *instantiations of subcomponents* and *parallel assignment statements* (e.g., `even <= not(a1 xor a2 xor a3)`;[1]). On the other hand, the behavioural approach directly describes the desired functionality of a component using the parallel statement `process` that is specified as a *sequence of statements* like *sequential assignments* or *conditionals*. We have to, however, note that sequential statements in VHDL have a different meaning than in typical programming languages—the sequence they are based on is not the execution sequence, but rather a sequence of preferences of how to proceed under different circumstances (we will get to this issue closer later on).

Since there is no way how to efficiently synthesise a hardware design from complex behavioural requirements, the behavioural description is widely used for a low-level description of parts of a system (e.g., logic functions, simple

---

[1] From a logical point of view, a variable such as **even** represents a symbolic name for the expression assigned to it only.

registers, counters), while the structural description is used for building more complex components or the entire system.

Transparent and Synchronous Mode. The so-called *transparent* and *synchronous* modes of hardware gates substantially influence the output of the gate. For example, let us have two gates connected in a cascade. If both gates work in the transparent mode (such gates are known as *latches*) and the input changes its value, the first gate instantly propagates the input to its output (the input of the second gate), and the same value propagation happens at the second gate. The result of the transparent mode is that the change of the input of the first gate instantly changes the value of the output of the second gate. Conversely, if both gates work in the synchronous mode (such gates are known as *flip-flops*), they propagate their inputs to the output one step at a time—the change of the input values of the first gate changes its output after one clock period, but this still does not immediately influence the output of the second gate (its output is changed only after another clock period). Let us add that some gates may be operated both as latches as well as flip-flops depending on some of their control inputs.

Not Considered VHDL Constructions and Behaviour. VHDL is a very rich specification language, and we do not cover it fully. However, most of the restrictions that we describe below correspond to constructions which are in theory possible, but are usually not used, represent undesirable design practices, are often not even synthesisable, or modern synthesis tools [12,14] at least issue warnings when they are used.

First, we do not support VHDL functions, procedures, delay information, and asserts which serve for a test-bench specification of the designed hardware and do not have an influence on the behaviour of the hardware.

Next, we disallow cyclic assignments in the transparent mode in a sequential description of a behaviour (e.g., q <= not(reset and not(set and q)), or if (reset = '1') then a <= b; b <= a; elsif).[2] Such assignments would complicate our constructions significantly, and in practice, they are anyway undesirable as they lead to a possible oscillation of the signals.

We concentrate on analysing reachable stable states of hardware components only. A *stable state* is a state which does not change until one or more input variables change their values. Unstable states arise due to transition and propagation delays of real gates changing their stable states (cf. Fig. 1). In general, even when we are interested only in stable states, if we do not consider unstable states at all, there is a risk that we will not capture flaws caused by reading and registering unstable values. Such a flaw can be caused either (i) by a signal path that is too long wrt. the clock frequency used, or (ii) by an asynchronous exchange of signals between two clock domains. However, the need to deal with the former issue is eliminated simply by taking into account the capabilities of standard synthesis tools. These tools automatically check that the delay arising

---

[2] A sequential gate works in the transparent mode when its output is controlled only by the level of the input signals.

in the longest signal path of a given circuit is safe wrt. the clock frequency used. The latter issue is a little more complicated but it is still usually solvable by using simple static analysis to check whether the given circuit uses proper synchronisation approaches (like Gray coding) for all clock domain crossing signals [17]. Hence, below, we do not consider unstable states any further.

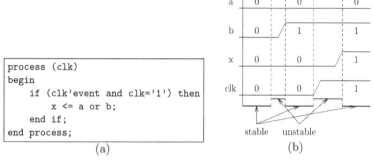

```
process (clk)
begin
    if (clk'event and clk='1') then
        x <= a or b;
    end if;
end process;
```

(a)   (b)

Fig. 1. (a) The source code of a simple component and (b) an example of a timed diagram of its behaviour illustrating the notion of stable and unstable states

Finally, we restrict the use of parameters a bit. Namely, we do not allow a bit-wise access to variables with a parametric range and we do not allow `for` loops over parametrised variables. Both of these restrictions could be lifted, but they would further complicate our translation to counter automata and also their analysis (as we would have to introduce a relatively complicated arithmetic to mask out the particular bits of the values of particular counters). We let experiments with these feature for our future research.

2.2 Simplifying VHDL Code

To avoid a very complex direct transformation from the rich VHDL language to the intermediate behavioural model introduced in Section 3 (which is then translated to counter automata in Section 4), we first simplify a VHDL source code to a form which is much simpler for all the subsequent steps.

As we mentioned before, VHDL components contain input/output ports, parameters, and internal variables—here, we consider all of them simply as *variables*. VHDL provides two basic types of variables: *1-bit (boolean) variables* and *arrays (vectors) of bits*. Further, there is also a possibility of user-defined structured types, but they are used as a form of syntactic sugar only. Therefore, before any further steps, we decompose structured variables to their elements. Similarly, if a bit vector variable is accessed bit-wise (i.e. there is at least one statement in the considered code that accesses single bits of the vector at a time), we replace the vector variable with its boolean components (if we had not disallowed the bit-wise access to parametrised-size vectors, we would have had to use a complex arithmetics to mask out the particular bits—e.g., to get a bit value at position p in the bit vector represented by an integer value n, we could use the expression $(n \text{ div } 2^p) \text{ mod } 2)$. The remaining vectors may then easily be mapped to counters of counter automata (whereas all 1-bit variables will be a part of their control states).

Further, we also remove all structural descriptions of circuits and replace them by the corresponding behavioural description (in a way similar to macro expansion in the C programming language). This can easily be achieved by unfolding (or flattening) of the structural description taking into account that a structural description simply describes from which subcomponents a given component is build of, what are the values of parameters of the subcomponents, and how the input/output ports of these subcomponents are connected to the input/output ports of the component and/or to each other (which is done via the internal variables of the component). We substitute references to the subcomponents by their behavioural description, connect their input/output ports to the internal variables of the component (and/or its input/output ports), and substitute parameters of the subcomponents by the appropriate arguments (which may be parameters of the component being processed).

Next, we transform the code such that the only statements that will remain (and that we will have to consider in the further steps) are the following:

1. *Assignment statements* of the form `signal <= expression;` appearing in an architecture definition as parallel statements or in a process section as sequential statements.
2. *Conditional* (`if`) *statements* appearing in process sections as sequential statements with the following syntax (and the obvious semantics): `if cond1 then stmt1; elsif cond2 then stmt2; ... ; else stmtN; end if;`

To this end, we rewrite any other statements to one or more assignment and/or conditional statements of the above form. In particular, this is the case of the VHDL *selected assignments* and `case` statements (cf. Fig. 2). Moreover, it is also the case of the VHDL `for` loops as we assume that they cannot be performed over parametric bit vectors—otherwise, we would have to model their effect by special purpose loops in our counter automata.

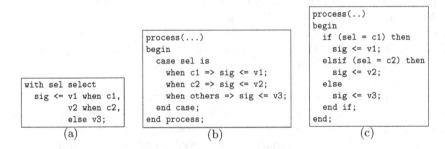

Fig. 2. A conversion of (a) *selected signal assignments* and (b) `case` statements to (c) `if` statements

Normalization of `if` Statements. After the pre-processing done above, the architecture of the component being examined is described by a set of parallel assignments and a set of **processes**, every such a process consists of a sequence of sequential assignments and (possibly nested) `if` statements. As we have already said, these sequential statements inside the processes are *not* executed sequentially—instead, for each variable, the last applicable assignment is searched and used, and all the statements preceding it are ignored. For example, for a sequence v <= e1; if c then v <= e2; endif;, if c holds, one performs the v <= e2; assignment, otherwise one performs the assignment v <= e1; (we may assume that the processes consist solely of assignments and—possibly nested—`if` statements).

In order to make dealing with the described semantics easier when generating the intermediate behavioural model, we perform one more pre-processing step. In particular, we transform each process into a single nested `if` statement in which it is clear under which conditions which assignment is to be applied (e.g., the example we mentioned above will be transformed to the statement if c then v <= e2; else v <= e1; endif;—more examples will come below). More precisely, for each sequential process and each variable v assigned by that process, we do the following steps (we ignore all assignments to other variables when handling v):

1. We add an empty `else` branch to each `if` statement of the given process that does not have such a branch.
2. Till there is some assignment or `if` statement s_1 in the given process that is just before an `if` statement s_2 (i.e. s_1 and s_2 are on the same level of nesting of `if` statements), we move s_1 to the beginning of the `else` branch of s_2, i.e. we nest s_1 into the `else` branch of s_2 and put it just before the statements that are already in this branch (cf. Fig. 3(a)).
3. If there are branches of `if` statements of the given process that do not contain any statement, we add the implicit assignment v <= v; to each of them.
4. We reduce every sequence of statements $s_1; s_2; ...; s_n; v <= e;$ within the given process to just v <= e;. Here, s_i for $1 \le i \le n$, $n \ge 1$, is a sequence of assignments or `if` statements. The fact that at the end of the sequence there is an assignment statement (and not an `if` statement) is guaranteed by the transformation done in the previous step.

2.3   Counter Automata

For an integer arithmetic formula φ, let $FV(\varphi)$ denote the set of free variables of φ.[3] For a set of variables X, let $\Phi(X)$ denote the set of integer arithmetic formulae with free variables from $X \cup X'$ where $X' = \{x' \mid x \in X\}$. If $\nu : X \to \mathbb{Z}$ is

---

[3] We do not further restrict the kind of integer arithmetics used. It naturally follows from the integer operations used in the hardware design being handled, to which our translation adds just an implementation of the implicit modulo arithmetics used in VHDL—we will get back to this issue in the next subsection.

```
                                          if c2 then
                                            v <= e2;
if c1 then          if c2 then            else                    if c2 then
  v <= e1;            v <= e2;              if c1 then              v <= e2;
end if;             else                     v <= e1;      -->    else
if c2 then    -->     if c1 then           else                     v <= e3;
  v <= e2;              v <= e1;             v <= v;              end if;
else                  end if;              end if;
  v <= e3;            v <= e3;             v <= e3;
end if;             end if;              end if;
        (a)                                        (b)
```

Fig. 3. Transformations of sequential statements: (a) moving all statements preceding an `if` statement to its `else` branch, (b) removing statements preceding an assignment (and thus being useless)

an assignment of $FV(\varphi) \subseteq X$, we denote by $\nu \models \varphi$ the fact that ν is a satisfying assignment of φ. A *counter automaton* (CA) is a tuple $A = \langle X, Q, q_0, \varphi_0, \rightarrow \rangle$ where X is a finite set of counters, Q is a finite set of control locations, $q_0 \in Q$ is a designated initial location, φ_0 is an arithmetic formula such that $FV(\varphi_0) \subseteq X$, describing an initial assignments of the counters, and $\rightarrow \in Q \times \Phi(X) \times Q$ is a finite set of transition rules.

A configuration of a CA is a pair $\langle q, \nu \rangle \in Q \times (X \rightarrow \mathbb{Z})$. The set of all configurations is denoted by $\mathfrak{C}$. The transition relation $\xrightarrow[A]{\varphi} \subseteq \mathfrak{C} \times \mathfrak{C}$ is defined by $(q, \nu) \xrightarrow[A]{\varphi} (q', \nu')$ iff there exists a transition $q \xrightarrow{\varphi} q'$ such that if σ is an assignment of $FV(\varphi)$, where $\sigma(x) = \nu(x)$ and $\sigma(x') = \nu'(x)$, we have that $\sigma \models \varphi$ and $\nu(x) = \nu'(x)$ for all variables x with $x' \notin FV(\varphi)$. We denote by $\xrightarrow[A]{}$ the union $\bigcup_{\varphi \in \Phi} \xrightarrow[A]{\varphi}$, and by $\xrightarrow[A]{*}$ the reflexive and transitive closure of $\xrightarrow[A]{}$. A *run* of A is a sequence of configurations $(q_0, \nu_0), (q_1, \nu_1), (q_2, \nu_2) \ldots$ such that $(q_i, \nu_i) \xrightarrow[A]{} (q_{i+1}, \nu_{i+1})$ for each $i \geq 0$ and $\nu_0 \models \varphi_0$.

2.4 Handling VHDL Integer Variables in Counter Automata

When translating operations on integer variables used in VHDL to operations on counters, we have to take care of the fact that in VHDL, arithmetical operations over integers are always implicitly evaluated *modulo the range of the appropriate integer variables*. In counter automata, we have to make the modulo computation explicit (e.g., an assignment `v1 <= v2+v3;` over integer variables represented on n bits has to be translated to an assignment of the form $v_1 := (v_2 + v_3) \bmod 2^n$).

For analysing the generated counter automata, we then, of course, need a tool that can cope with counter manipulations corresponding both to arithmetical, logical, and relational operators directly used in the considered VHDL design as well as to the additional operations stemming from implementing the implicit modulo computations (and if we add them in the future, then also the bit-wise manipulations on integer variables). Given a concrete counter automata analyser, the translation may need to be adjusted to respect the operations that the tool supports. If the tool does not offer all the needed operations (nor allows their implementation based on other supported operations), one has to restrict to the case when the appropriate integer variables have a fixed range (i.e. are not parameters) and can also be recorded as a part of the control states of counter automata.

3 An Intermediate Behavioural Model

In the previous section, we discussed the syntax and semantics of VHDL constructions that we will consider in the following, together with the notion of counter automata that we want to use to model (and analyse) these constructions. In order to make the translation from the simplified VHDL to counter automata smoother, we make it via an intermediate behavioural model that we will now present.

3.1 A Definition of the Intermediate Behavioural Model

The *intermediate behavioural model* of a hardware component is defined as a triple $M = (V, T, B)$, where V is a set of variables that are typed by a function $T : V \rightarrow \{\texttt{bool}, \texttt{int}\}$, and B is a set of *behavioural rules* that describe the behaviour of a given hardware component and that have a form which we introduce below.

Let $V_i \subseteq V$ be a set of input ports and $V_p \subseteq V$ a set of parameters. We define $\overline{V} = V \times \{\texttt{last}, \texttt{next}, \texttt{posedge}, \texttt{negedge}\}$ to be the set of possible references to the values of variables from V with the following meaning:

- $(v, \texttt{last}) \in \overline{V}$ refers to the value of v in the *last reached* (i.e. current) *state*— in expressions, we usually abbreviate it simply to v,
- $(v, \texttt{next}) \in \overline{V}$, abbreviated to v', denotes the value of v in the *next state*,
- $(v, \texttt{posedge}) \in \overline{V}$, abbreviated to $\uparrow v$, has the boolean meaning $\uparrow v = \neg v \wedge v'$ and denotes the *positive edge* of a 1-bit variable v (for which $T(v) = \texttt{bool}$),
- $(v, \texttt{negedge}) \in \overline{V}$, abbreviated to $\downarrow v$, has the boolean meaning $\downarrow v = v \wedge \neg v'$ and denotes the *negative edge* of a 1-bit variable v (for which $T(v) = \texttt{bool}$).

Further, let E be the set of all (well-typed) expressions that one can form over $\overline{V}$ using arithmetical $(+, -, *, ...)$, relational $(=, \neq, <, >, \leq, \geq)$, and logical $(\neg, \wedge, \vee, ...)$ operators, and let C be the subset of E containing all boolean valued expressions. Let $\bot \in E$ denotes an *empty* expression (see below).

We can now introduce the special conditional assignments that are the behavioural rules constituting the set B of an intermediate behavioural model. In particular, $B \subseteq C^* \times V \times E$. We write a behavioural rule $b \in B$ as

$$c \rightarrow v := e$$

for $c \in C^*$ being a list of enabling conditions, $v \in V$ the variable set by the rule, and $e \in E$ being an expression defining the new value of v. In other words, b

with $c = c_1c_2...c_n$ says that if $c_1 \wedge c_2 \wedge ... \wedge c_n$ holds for the evaluation of the variables, v will get a new value obtained by an evaluation of e. If $c = \varepsilon$, we consider it to be always true, and the assignment $v := e$ is always enabled.

For a behavioural rule $b : c \rightarrow v := e \in B$, let $cond(b) = c$ denote the enabling condition of b, $var(b) = v$ denote the variable to be set, and let $value(b) = e$ be the expression defining the new value of v. For $e \in E \cup C^*$, let $F(e)$ be the set of references to variables occurring in e. Finally, let $B(v) = \{b \mid b \in B, var(b) = v\}$ be the set of behavioural rules over a variable v.

3.2   Extracting Behavioural Rules from the Source Code

The architecture of a VHDL component consists of a set of parallel assignments and a set of sequential processes. With respect to the simple VHDL transformations described in Section 2.2, we may assume that the sequential processes consists of a single `if` statement for every variable set within it. In order to obtain the set of behavioural rules B from such a description, we extract the rules from VHDL statements as follows:

1. For each parallel assignment `v <= e;`, we add a rule $\varepsilon \rightarrow v := e$ into B.
2. For each sequential process that sets a variable v by a single, possibly nested, `if` statement (after the pre-processing, there is no other possibility), we proceed as follows. For each assignment statement `v <= e;` that appears on the leaf level of such a (nested) `if` statement, we add a rule $c'_1, c'_2, ..., c'_n \rightarrow v := e$ into B ($n \geq 1$). Here, $c_1, c_2, ..., c_n$ are all the branching conditions that one tests before reaching `v <= e`, and $c'_i = c_i$ if the condition is supposed to hold (i.e. we are nesting into an `if` c_i or `elsif` c_i branch) whereas $c'_i = \neg c_i$ if the condition is supposed not to hold. An example of such a transformation is shown in Fig. 4.

3.3   Adjustments of Behavioural Rules

The Environment of a Component. To be able to model check a component, we need a model of its environment too. Currently, we model the environment to behave in a completely random way. To do that, we extend the intermediate behavioural model by adding behavioural rules for all component inputs. For every such an input $v \in V_i$, we add the following behavioural rule $\varepsilon \rightarrow v := random$. Here, $random$ represents a random integer or boolean value. Note that we have to adjust the form of $random$ such that the CA analyser that want to use understands it.

Non-state Variables. We are only interested in stable states that are defined by the so-called *state variables*. In the hardware developers' jargon, such variables are also known as registers or signals which save their value. The remaining variables are *non-state variables* whose values are not registered and that, from our point of view, represent just a symbolic name for some expression. From a set of behavioural rules, a non-state variable can be identified by the fact

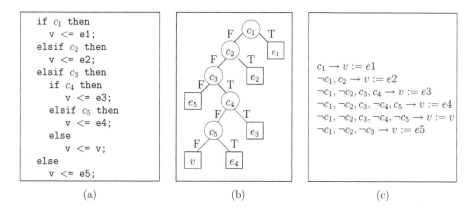

(a)   (b)   (c)

Fig. 4. Synthesis of behavioural rules wrt. the conditions passed till a certain assignment can be fired: (a) a normalized VHDL `if` statement, (b) the tree representing branching conditions, (c) the set of behavioural rules for variable v

that its value is set by a rule with the empty enabling condition (i.e. by an unconditional assignment[4]). The remaining variables are then state variables. The only exception are input variables whose values are defined and held by the environment of the modelled component. Formally, $v \in V \setminus V_i$ is a non-state variable iff $cond(b) = \varepsilon$ for the rule $b \in B$ such that $B(v) = \{b\}$. Let further $V_s = V_i \cup \{v \mid v \in V, cond(b) \neq \varepsilon\}$ be the set of state variables. Before generating counter automata, we change the intermediate behavioural model to use the state variables only. We remove the non-state variables v defined by rules $\varepsilon \rightarrow v := e$ present in B by iteratively searching for references to such variables in enabling conditions and value expressions of the rules in B and by replacing these references by e.

Behavioural Rules Over 1-bit Variables. Next, for technical reasons allowing us to ease the subsequent construction of CA from intermediate behavioural rules, we prefer to have all the manipulation of 1-bit state variables in guards of the rules. That is why, we transform every behavioural rule $b : c \rightarrow v := e$ over a 1-bit state variable $v \in V_s$, $T(v) = bool$, to the rule $b_{new} : c, v' = e \rightarrow v := e$.

Triggers of Behavioural Rules. Let $V_{\uparrow\downarrow} = \overline{V} \cap (V \times \{\texttt{posedge}, \texttt{negedge}\})$ be the set of edges of the values of variables from V. We define a mapping $R : B \rightarrow \{\tau\} \cup V_{\uparrow\downarrow}$ that assigns each rule either τ in case the rule models an assignment in the transparent mode or a signal edge (i.e. a *trigger*) that activates the rule if it models an assignment in the synchronous mode. Formally, for $b \in B$, let $R(b) = \tau$ iff $F(cond(c)) \cap V_{\uparrow\downarrow} = \emptyset$, and let $R(b) = t$ iff $F(cond(b)) \cap V_{\uparrow\downarrow} = \{t\}$ for some $t \in V_{\uparrow\downarrow}$. Note that this definition is correct as due to the hardware

---

[4] Note that as we require the rules not to be in a conflict, this is the only rule that is setting the value of such a variable.

description principles, there can be at most one positive or negative edge variable reference in a behavioural rule condition. Designs violating this requirement are exposed during the synthesis process.

For each rule $b \in B$ that works in the transparent mode, i.e. $R(b) = \tau$, we adjust the condition and assignment part of b such that each variable reference that appears there refers to the future. This is, we change every variable reference v that appears in $value(b)$ or $cond(b)$ to v'. The reference to the future assures that the rule is evaluated using values of variables that are computed at the same time step as the one at which we perform the evaluation (and not a step before as in the case of the synchronous mode). This is because gates working in the transparent mode immediately propagate their input values to the output. We can afford to use this transformation as we excluded the possibility of cyclic dependencies of the values of variables in the transparent mode. That is why, the variables changing in the transparent mode can be ordered according to their dependencies and evaluated in the given order starting with variables that are assigned a constant value (which happens, e.g., when the circuit is being reset) or from variables which are not changing at the given time step. For an illustration of this behaviour, see Fig. 5.

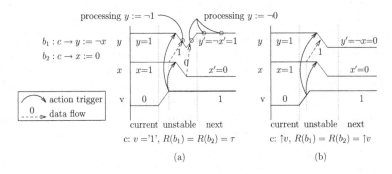

Fig. 5. A timing diagram illustrating the differences between the transparent and synchronous mode. For the transparent mode (a), both x and y are controlled by the *level* of the variable v, which causes a continuous change of their values (y is set to the negation of x via b_1, y is set to 0 via b_2). Due to the propagation delays of hardware which implements such a behaviour, there are several changes of the values until they are all stabilised, which we are, however, not interested in. The important thing to notice is that the resulting value of x is $\neg y'$ and not $\neg y$. On the other hand, in the synchronous mode (b), an *edge* triggers a change of the value of v, which holds until the next triggering event. In this case, the resulting value of x is $\neg y$ (and not $\neg y'$).

We have to do a similar adjustment as above also for the rules modelling the synchronous mode. For simplicity, we consider here the case of positive edges only. The case of negative edges is analogical. Within each rule $b \in B$ for which $R(b) = \uparrow v$ for some $v \in V$, $cond(b) = c_1 c_2 \ldots c_n \uparrow v c_{n+1} \ldots c_m$ for some $n, m \in \mathbb{N}$. Note that $F(c_1 c_2 \ldots c_n) \cap V_{\uparrow\downarrow} = \emptyset$. In this case, the way our algorithm for generating behavioural rules works implies that the set of generated behavioural rules B must also include behavioural rules $b_\tau \in B$ whose condition is built solely of the conditions $c_1, c_2, \ldots, c_n$ (possibly negated), hence $R(b_\tau) = \tau$. Due to the evaluation order of the conditions, the b_τ rules have a priority over b. At the same time, they model the transparent mode, hence they will work with the future values of variables. That is why, in order to exclude a possible conflict of the rules b_τ with b, we have to replace every variable reference v to v' in $c_1, c_2, \ldots, c_n$ in b. Then, if some of the b_τ rules is enabled, b is disabled as its enabling condition contains a negation of some of the enabling conditions of b_τ evaluated on the same values of variables. On the other hand, if this is not the case, the rest of b will work with the current values of the variables.

4   Generating Counter Automata

4.1   Counters, Control Locations, and Initialisation

Let us fix a hardware design with a set of variables V of types T and with a set of behavioural rules B generated from the design. We start building the counter automaton A representing the design by defining its *set of counters* as all integer-type state variables from V—formally, wrt. the definition of counter automata (Def. 2.3), $X = \{v \mid v \in V_s, \ T(v) = int\}$.

Further, we build control locations of A based on all possible evaluations of all *control state variables* in V, i.e. 1-bit state variables from the set $V_q = \{v \in V_s \mid T(v) = bool\}$. Formally, we define the set of control locations of A as $Q = \{q \mid q : V_q \to \{0, 1\}\}$.

The design of a component in VHDL does not include any specification of its initial state. In most cases, however, the specification of the component includes a combination of signals which *resets* the component to some initial state and assigns some constants to all its internal variables. For the generation of A, to obtain these constants and thus define the *initial location* and the *initial constraint on counters*, the user must explicitly specify the resetting signals by providing the appropriate evaluation of input variables that encodes them. By evaluating enabling conditions of all the rules in B under the given resetting valuation of the input variables, we get a subset of rules that are initially enabled. Each of such behavioural rules defines an initial value for one variable—by evaluating the assignment parts of these rules, we can initialise the variables. The obtained values of control state variables make up the definition of the initial location q_0, the evaluation of integer variables allows us to construct the initial constraint φ_0 on counters[5]. If the modelled component has no resetting signals or the desired initial state is not the reset state, the initialisation must be defined explicitly by the user.

---

[5] In fact, this applies only to the counters other than the ones representing parameters—if the possible values of parameters are also to be constrained somehow, it is up to the user to add the appropriate constraint into φ_0.

4.2 Transition Relation

For an expression $e \in E$ and two locations $q_1, q_2 \in Q$ of A, we denote by e^{q_1,q_2} the evaluation of e where for each $v \in V_q$, $(v, last)$ is evaluated as $q_1(v)$ and $(v, next)$ is evaluated as $q_2(v)$. We allow the evaluation to be partial—if e contains integer variables, they remain untouched. We construct the transition relation of A by checking for every pair of control locations $q_1, q_2 \in Q$, $q_1 \neq q_2$, whether the intermediate behavioural model allows us to connect them:[6]

1. For each $b \in B$ with $cond(b) = c_1c_2 \ldots c_n$ for some $n \in \mathbb{N}$, we (as far as possible) evaluate the enabling condition of b, i.e. we compute $guard^{q_1,q_2}(b) = \bigwedge_{1 \leq i \leq n} c_i^{q_1,q_2}$. Let $B_e = \{b \mid b \in B, var(b) \in V_s, guard^{q_1,q_2}(b) \neq false\}$ be the set of all (conditionally) enabled behavioural rules setting the value of state variables.

2. We further one-by-one consider all subsets $B_t \subseteq B_e$ such that B_t contains exactly one rule b such that $var(b) = v$ for each state variable $v \in V_s$. For each B_t, we perform the following steps:

   (a) In each rule $b \in B_t$, we iteratively substitute all references to the future values of counter variables by the expressions assigned to them within B_t. This is, we substitute each v' for $v \in V_s \setminus V_q$ by the expression $value(b_v)$ where $b_v \in B_t$ and $var(b_v) = v$.[7] We repeat this step till all references to future values of counters disappear.

   (b) Based on the set of rules B_t, we create a transition $q_1 \xrightarrow{\varphi} q_2$ of A where

   $$\varphi = \left(\bigwedge_{b \in B_t} guard^{q_1,q_2}(b)\right) \wedge \left(\bigwedge_{b \in B_t, var(b) \notin V_q} \alpha(value^{q_1,q_2}(b))\right) \text{ and } \alpha \text{ is a}$$

   function that transforms an assignment $v := e$ to a formula $v' = e$.

Let us add a few comments to the algorithm. For a given choice of states q_1 and q_2, the first step may lead to three situations: (i) If $guard^{q_1,q_2}(b) = false$, we know that b does not change the value of $var(b)$. (ii) If $guard^{q_1,q_2}(b) = true$, b is allowed to change the value of $var(b)$. (iii) Finally, if $guard^{q_1,q_2}(b)$ does not reduce to neither $false$ nor $true$ (i.e. if $guard(b)$ refers to some values of counters in a way that must be taken into account), we only know that b may be able to change $var(b)$, but subject to the values of the counters. If there is no (at least conditionally) enabled behavioural rule for some state variable, i.e. if $\exists v \in V_s, \forall b \in B(v).guard^{q_1,q_2}(b) = false$, no transition from q_1 to q_2 will be possible as we are unable to compute the next value of v in q_2—even for preserving the current value of v there is a behavioural rule which is forbidden by its guard. Otherwise, we have to explore all combinations of (at least potentially) enabled rules adjusting the value of the particular variables, which is done in the second step of the algorithm.

Suppose now that, for instance, $V_s = \{v_1, v_2, v_3, v_4\}$ where only v_4 is a 1-bit variable, and the first step of the algorithm yields a set of rules $B_e = \{g_1 \rightarrow v_1 :=$

---

[6] Note that we cannot have self-loops in A as the control states are stable, and some signal must change in order a change of the states happens.

[7] At this point, only the variables representing counters are considered as the references to future values of control state variable are taken care through the partial evaluation of the expressions.

$f_1(v_2'), g_{2,1} \rightarrow v_2 := f_{2,1}(v_3', v_1), g_{2,2} \rightarrow v_2 := f_{2,2}(v_3), g_3 \rightarrow v_3 := f_3(v_2), v_4' = \neg v_4 \rightarrow v_4 := \neg v_4\}$ (the rule for v_4 is transformed as we described in Section 3). We can find two subsets B_t that are to be handled by the second step of the algorithm—namely, $B_{t,1} = \{g_1 \rightarrow v_1 := f_1(v_2'), g_{2,1} \rightarrow v_2 := f_{2,1}(v_3', v_1), g_3 \rightarrow v_3 := f_3(v_2), v_4' = \neg v_4 \rightarrow v_4 := \neg v_4\}$ and $B_{t,2} = \{g_1 \rightarrow v_1 := f_1(v_2'), g_{2,2} \rightarrow v_2 := f_{2,2}(v_3), g_3 \rightarrow v_3 := f_3(v_2), v_4' = \neg v_4 \rightarrow v_4 := \neg v_4\}$. If we apply the steps described above for $B_{t,1}$, we obtain two CA transitions with a formula $g_1 \wedge g_{2,1} \wedge g_3 \wedge v_1' = f_1(f_{2,1}(f_3(v_2), v_1)) \wedge v_2' = f_{2,1}(f_3(v_2), v_1) \wedge v_3' = f_3(v_2)$ going between control states q_1 and q_2 such that $q_1(v_4) = \neg q_2(v_4)$. Note that the condition $v_4' = \neg v_4$ does not appear in the formula of the transition as its evaluation wrt. q_1, q_2 yields *true*.

5 Handling the Reachability Properties to Be Verified

In our work, we concentrate on verifying that certain *bad configurations* are not reachable. We assume the bad configurations to be given by a boolean VHDL expression—an *error condition*. The error condition may refer to 1-bit VHDL variables appearing in the design of the component being checked (which are represented as a part of the control location of the generated counter automata) as well to VHDL bit-vector variables (represented by the values of counters in the counter automata).

In order to facilitate verification of reachability of the bad configurations, we extend a generated counter automaton by a special *error state* whose reachability implies that a bad configuration is reachable in the component being checked. The error state is connected to the control states of the generated counter automaton that represent a valuation of the VHDL 1-bit variables which is not contradictory with the error condition. Moreover, the transitions to the error state are guarded by conditions on counters derived from the error condition by substituting the 1-bit variables by values that appear in the source control location of these transitions (after which, just a constraint on bit-vector variables remains).

6 Experiments

For our experiments, we implemented a Python-based prototype [16] of the proposed translation (up to some of the issues of the VHDL pre-processing mentioned in Section 2). In particular, we implemented a translation to counter automata in the input language of the ARMC tool [15] and also to integer programs in the C programming language in order to be able to use the Blast model checker [8] as well. Both of the tools provide us with the possibility of verifying reachability properties of counter automata (or, alternatively, integer programs) using techniques based on predicate abstraction and the counterexample-guided abstraction refinement (CEGAR) loop.

To test the proposed counter-automata-based model extraction method, we have first applied it to two small non-parametric components (having integer

Table 1. Experiments with counter automata extraction from VHDL and with their subsequent reachability analysis using ARMC and Blast

Component	Locations	Transitions	Counters	Extraction time	ARMC	Blast
Counter	5	13	2	< 1s	< 1s	1.5s
Register	9	43	2	1s	< 1s	< 1s
Synchronous LIFO	65	985	3	24s	40s	5m31
Asyn. FIFO (FE)	65	5060	12	1m12s	6m56s	N/A
Asyn. FIFO (Status)	129	6628	12	4m	4m16	N/A

variables, but of a fixed width). Then we applied the method to two more complex parametric components, including a real-life, highly specialised, parametric component developed within the Liberouter project [13].

The first two components (a counter and a register) represent basic elements from which hardware is built on the RTL level. For the *counter*, we verified that there is no overflow possible. For the *register*, we verified that the data transfer from its input to the output and the reset of the register work correctly. A more complex case study that we considered is a *synchronous LIFO* component which implements a stack with two operations—push and pop. The generic nature of this component is given by a parametrisation of the number of items the LIFO can save. This component implements—among other—signals that say whether it is empty or full. We verified whether these signals are always correctly set for any possible size of the LIFO.

The last verified component is an *asynchronous queue* (FIFO). This specialised parametric component was built to be used in network monitoring adaptors developed within the Liberouter project (with a stress on being as efficient as possible). Apart from signals about whether the component is empty or full, it also implements additional signals saying whether it is almost full or almost empty (less than some amount of items are free/occupied). For the component, we successfully verified two properties: (i) that the queue does not inform that it is empty and full at the same time, and (ii) that the status information about the queue being almost full is set correctly. For a more detailed description of the verified properties see [16].

The results of our experiments are summarised in Table 1. The first column gives the verified component—for the last component, there are two lines corresponding to the two different properties that we checked for it. The next column provides the number of control locations in the generated counter automata—note that the number corresponds to $2^n + 1$, which is the number of control locations over n 1-bit state variables, plus one location representing the bad state. The next two columns provide the number of transitions between control locations of the generated counter automata and the number of used counters (integer variables). The next columns gives the times used by our prototype tool to generate the counter automata. Finally, the last two columns provide the time used by ARMC and Blast, respectively, to verify the generated counter automata. The experiments were performed on an Intel Xeon X5355 processor with 16GB of memory. ("N/A" means that the verification did not finish.)

7 Conclusion and Future Work

We have presented a new, quite general and automated, approach to formal verification of parametrised VHDL components. The approach is based on an automated translation of the components to counter automata and on exploiting the constantly improving technology for verifying counter automata (or integer programs). We have built a prototype tool implementing our translation schema and successfully used it together with the ARMC tool [15] for verification of several interesting properties of parametrised VHDL components, including a real-life component developed within the Liberouter project [13].

In the future, we want to experiment with lifting some of the restrictions of our initial approach (e.g., allowing a bit-wise approach to parametrised components). Another interesting research direction is to investigate possibilities of reducing the size of the automata that we generate. Further, we would like to do more experiments with real-life components and also with using more different tools for handling counter automata (or integer programs).

Acknowledgement. We would like to thank Andrey Rybalchenko for his help with the use of the ARMC tool.

References

1. Bardin, S., Finkel, A., Leroux, J., Petrucci, L.: FAST: Fast Acceleration of Symbolic Transition systems. In: Hunt Jr., W.A., Somenzi, F. (eds.) CAV 2003. LNCS, vol. 2725, Springer, Heidelberg (2003)
2. Bardin, S., Finkel, A., Lozes, E.: From Pointer Systems to Counter Systems Using Shape Analysis. In: Proc. of AVIS 2006 (2006)
3. Bouajjani, A., Bozga, M., Habermehl, P., Iosif, R., Moro, P., Vojnar, T.: Programs with Lists are Counter Automata. In: Ball, T., Jones, R.B. (eds.) CAV 2006. LNCS, vol. 4144, Springer, Heidelberg (2006)
4. Chaki, S., Clarke, E., Groce, A., Ouaknine, J., Strichman, O., Yorav, K.: Efficient Verification of Sequential and Concurrent C Programs. Formal Methods in System Design 25(2–3), 129–166 (2004)
5. Chu, P.P.: RTL Hardware Design Using VHDL: Coding for Efficiency, Portability, and Scalability. John Wiley and Sons, Inc, Hoboken, New Jersey (2006)
6. Comon, H., Jurski, Y.: Multiple Counters Automata, Safety Analysis and Presburger Arithmetic. In: Vardi, M.Y. (ed.) CAV 1998. LNCS, vol. 1427, Springer, Heidelberg (1998)
7. Habermehl, P., Iosif, R., Rogalewicz, A., Vojnar, T.: Proving Termination of Tree Manipulating Programs. Verimag, TR-2007-1 (2007), www-verimag.imag.fr/index.php?page=techrep-list
8. Henzinger, T.A., Jhala, R., Majumdar, R., Sutre, G.: Software Verification with Blast. In: Ball, T., Rajamani, S.K. (eds.) Model Checking Software. LNCS, vol. 2648, Springer, Heidelberg (2003)

9. Kořenek, J., Pečenka, T., Žádník, M.: NetFlow Probe Intended for High-Speed Networks. In: Proc. of FPL 2005, IEEE Computer Society, Los Alamitos (2005)
10. Minsky, M.L.: Computation: Finite and Infinite Machines. Prentice-Hall International, Englewood Cliffs (1967)
11. IEEE Computer Society. IEEE Std 1076-2000. IEEE Standard VHDL Language Reference Manual. IEEE Std 1076-2000. Pages. 290. (2000) ISBN: 0-7381-1948-2
12. Leonardo Spectrum, Mentor Graphics (2007), www.mentor.com/products/fpga_pld/synthesis/leonardo_spectrum
13. Liberouter Project Homepage. www.liberouter.org
14. ModelSim, Mentor Graphics (2007), www.model.com
15. Podelski, A., Rybalchenko, A.: ARMC: The Logical Choice for Software Model Checking with Abstraction Refinement. In: Hanus, M. (ed.) PADL 2007. LNCS, vol. 4354, Springer, Heidelberg (2006)
16. Smrčka, A.: VHD2CA. In: A Prototype of a Translator from VHDL to Counter Automata, www.fit.vutbr.cz/~smrcka/projects/vhd2ca/
17. Šafránek, D., Smrčka, A., Vojnar, T., Řehák, V., Řehák, Z., Matoušek, P.: Verifying VHDL Design with Multiple Clocks in SMV. In: Brim, L., Haverkort, B., Leucker, M., van de Pol, J. (eds.) FMICS 2006 and PDMC 2006. LNCS, vol. 4346, Springer, Heidelberg (2007)
18. Yavuz-Kahveci, T., Bartzis, C., Bultan, T.: Action Language Verifier, Extended. In: Etessami, K., Rajamani, S.K. (eds.) CAV 2005. LNCS, vol. 3576, Springer, Heidelberg (2005)

How Fast and Fat Is
Your Probabilistic Model Checker?
An Experimental Performance Comparison[*]

David N. Jansen[1,3], Joost-Pieter Katoen[1,2], Marcel Oldenkamp[2],
Mariëlle Stoelinga[2], and Ivan Zapreev[1,2]

[1] MOVES Group, RWTH, Aachen, Germany
{David.Jansen@, katoen@cs., zapreevis@cs.}rwth-aachen.de
[2] FMT Group, University of Twente, Enschede, The Netherlands
h.a.oldenkamp@student.utwente.nl, marielle@cs.utwente.nl
[3] ICIS, Radboud University, Nijmegen, The Netherlands

Abstract. This paper studies the efficiency of several probabilistic model checkers by comparing verification times and peak memory usage
for a set of standard case studies. The study considers the model checkers ETMCC, MRMC, PRISM (sparse and hybrid mode), YMER and
VESTA, and focuses on fully probabilistic systems. Several of our experiments show significantly different run times and memory consumptions
between the tools—up to various orders of magnitude—without, however, indicating a clearly dominating tool. For statistical model checking YMER clearly prevails whereas for the numerical tools MRMC and
PRISM (sparse) are rather close.

1 Introduction

Model checkers such as PRISM [34] (with about 4,000 downloads), MRMC [23],
E⊢MC² [16], VESTA [35,36], YMER [39], and APMC [27] support the verification of discrete- and continuous-time Markov chains. Their engines are based
on combinations of numerical or simulation techniques for Markov chains and
traditional CTL model-checking algorithms. Tools such as PRISM are relatively
easy to use, have a graphical user interface and advanced built-in plot facilities.
This allows researchers from various areas to apply probabilistic model checking. Applications range from areas such as randomized distributed algorithms to
planning and AI, security [30], and even biological process modeling [28]. Probabilistic model checking engines have been integrated in existing tool chains
for widely used formalisms such as stochastic Petri nets [9], Statemate [6], the
stochastic process algebra PEPA [18], and a probabilistic variant of Promela [4].

---

[*] This research has been partially funded by the Netherlands Organisation for Scientific Research (NWO) under FOCUS/BRICKS grant numbers 642.000.505 (MOQS)
and 612.000.311 (MC=MC); the EU under grant number IST-004527 (ARTIST2);
the DFG/NWO bilateral cooperation programme under project number DN 62-600
(VOSS2); and by the DFG Research Training Group 1298 (AlgoSyn).

This paper provides a comparative experimental study of a substantial set of probabilistic model checkers. The aim of this study is to get more insight into the strengths and weaknesses of the various tools, and to compare different model-checking techniques. We focus on fully probabilistic models, that is, finite-state discrete- and continuous-time Markov chains (DTMCs and CTMCs). We consider the temporal logics: probabilistic CTL (PCTL) [13] and its continuous-time variant CSL [3,5]. These logics allow one to express constrained reachability probabilities, e. g., the probability to reach a goal state while visiting only legal states is at least 0.4567, and bounded versions thereof. In the discrete setting the bound is a number of steps while in the continuous case a time bound may be imposed on reaching the goal state. Finally, CSL allows for expressing steady-state properties such as: in the long run the probability to be in a goal state meets a certain bound. All these properties have been used in the experiments, as well as nested versions thereof and qualitative properties.

The experiments are focused on the verification time, i. e., the required time to verify a formula on a Markov chain, as well as peak memory usage, i. e., the maximal amount of memory needed during the verification. This was done for a set of five publicly available case studies, mostly examples that act as benchmarks for probabilistic model checking and that allow for varying state space sizes. Tools that were considered are E⊦MC^2, MRMC, PRISM, VESTA and YMER. All experiments were carried out on a standard PC, and care was taken that equivalent input models are used. Since models, properties, testing environment, and tool settings are all publicly available, all reported experiments are repeatable and verifiable. The number of experiments carried out is substantial, and each experiment is repeated several times. In total, about 15,000 verification runs have been considered. This paper presents a selection of the experiments from [31] and attempts to observe and explain relevant phenomena.

We found considerable differences in time and memory usage between the tools, due to variations in model checking techniques (statistical versus numerical), state space representation (MTBDDs versus sparse matrices or a combination) and implementation language (C/C++ versus Java). The tables in Sect. 6 show an overview of the results. In addition, we compared the user friendliness of the tools. Here PRISM is the clear winner.

Organisation of the Paper. Section 2 briefly presents the tools and Sect. 3 the case studies we analyzed. In Sect. 4 we discuss the set up of our measurements. Then, we compare and analyze the results of our experiments in Sect. 5. Finally, Sect. 6 summarizes the conclusions and provides tool recommendations.

2   Tools

ETMCC. E⊦MC^2 [16] (version 1.4.2, 2001), also written ETMCC, is a prototype model checker for CTMCs. The tool is written in Java and uses sparse matrices to represent the state space.

MRMC. MRMC [23] (version 1.1.1b, March 2006) is a model checker for discrete-time and continuous-time Markov reward models. MRMC is a command-line tool, implemented in C, and represents the state space by sparse matrices.

PRISM. PRISM [25] (version 2.1, September 2004[1]) stands for Probabilistic Symbolic Model Checker. The user interface and parsers are written in Java; the core algorithms are mostly implemented in C++. For state space representation, PRISM uses a modified version of the CUDD package [38].

PRISM offers a choice between two engines that use different data structures: a "sparse" and a "hybrid" engine, henceforth denoted as $PRISM^S$ and $PRISM^H$. It is expected that $PRISM^S$ is faster, whereas $PRISM^H$ consumes less memory. Regardless of the engine, PRISM always generates an MTBDD to represent the transition matrix, and $PRISM^S$ converts it to a sparse matrix, if necessary.

VESTA. VESTA [35] (version 2.0, 2005) is a Java-based tool for statistical analysis of probabilistic systems. It implements the statistical methods from [41,36], based on Monte-Carlo simulation and statistical hypothesis testing [19].

YMER. YMER [39] (version 3.0, February 2005) is a command-line tool, written in C and C++, for verifying transient properties of CTMCs and generalizations. YMER implements statistical CSL model checking techniques [41], based on discrete event simulation [37] and acceptance sampling. It also supports numerical techniques, where the numerical engine for model checking CTMCs is adopted from PRIMS's hybrid engine.

Other tools. We have also considered other tools for our comparison, for example APMC [27], FHP-Murphi [32], Probverus [14]. We restricted ourselves to the above five because other tools did not support our models or logics or were not available in a stable version.

2.1 Languages

Input Models. Most tools support both discrete- and continuous-time Markov chains. Support for discrete time is limited in E⊢MC²; YMER only supports (a superset of) CTMCs. Some tools also recognize other input models (MDPs, reward models) not considered here. PRISM has its own modelling language: A system is described as the parallel composition of a set of *modules.* A module state is determined by a set of finite-range variables and its behaviour is given using a guarded-command notation. E⊢MC² and MRMC do not use a specific modeling language; instead, they accepts models in (a subset of) the *.tra*-format as e. g. generated by the stochastic process algebra tool TIPPtool [15] and Petri net tool DaNAMiCS [?]. The state labelling with atomic propositions has to be

---

[1] This was the most recent version when we started our research. In the meantime, a newer version of PRISM has appeared.

Table 1. Minimal and maximal model sizes per case study

timing	study	min/max, param.	# states	# transitions
discrete	SLE	min, $n = 4, k = 2$	55	70
		max, $n = 8, k = 4$	458,847	524,382
	RDF	min, $n = 3$	770	2,845
		max, $n = 7$	5,454,562	44,070,594
	BDP	min, $m = 100$	101	202
		max, $m = 100,000$	100,001	200,002
continuous	TQN	min, $n = 2$	15	23
		max, $n = 1023$	2,096,128	7,328,771
	CPS	min, $n = 3$	36	84
		max, $n = 18$	7,077,888	69,599,232

provided in a separate *.lab* file. We used a recently added feature of PRISM to generate these files directly from PRISM models. The language used by YMER is a subset of the PRISM language with a few slight syntactic differences. VESTA uses a Java-based language to specify models. A model description consists of sequential statements in combination with Java code. Each statement consists of a guard, rate and action. The language offers no explicit parallel composition.

Requirements. All tools support the logics PCTL for DTMCs, or CSL for CTMCs. The tools that support other models, of course, also know additional property languages. In addition, E⊢MC^2 supports aCSL, an action-based variant of CSL; and VESTA accepts requirements specified using QuaTEx [1].

3   Case Studies

We selected five representative case studies, taken from the literature on performance evaluation and probabilistic model checking. The selected studies represent a spectrum of applications, both distributed algorithms and performance models, and are of diverse natures. There are three discrete-time and two continuous-time cases. For each case, we let the tools calculate the probability of some bounded and unbounded until properties, i.e. constrained reachability properties. They are the most important property type in the logic PCTL (and the only one that cannot be checked trivially). We also included a nested property (with multiple until operators) in a discrete-time case study. In the continuous-time case studies, we also checked for steady-state properties. The model types and the sizes of the smallest and largest models investigated are recorded in Table 1.[2]

Synchronous Leader Election (SLE). The Synchronous Leader Election protocol [21] solves the following problem: in a ring of n processors with

---

[2] Unfortunately we were not able to generate larger state spaces for the SLE case study due to an error obtained from the CUDD package.

synchronous unidirectional communication, the processors have to elect a unique leader by sending messages around the ring. The protocol proceeds in rounds. In a round, each processor (independently) chooses a random number from the set $\{1, \ldots, k\}$ as its id. Then, they pass their ids around the ring. If there is a unique id, then the processor with the largest unique id is elected leader; otherwise they begin a new round. We checked the SLE protocol for $n = 2$ with $k \in \{2, 4, 6, 8, 10, 12, 14, 16\}$ and $n = 4$ with $k \in \{2, 4\}$.

The protocol is used in several studies, e. g. [27,12,11]. We checked the properties: (1) eventually a leader is elected, i. e., $\mathcal{P}_{\geq 1}(\Diamond\ elected)$, (2) the probability to elect a leader within 5 steps is ≥ 0.85, i. e., $\mathcal{P}_{\geq 0.85}(\Diamond^{\leq 5}\ elected)$, and (3) the probability to elect a leader within 40 steps is ≥ 0.99, i. e., $\mathcal{P}_{\geq 0.99}(\Diamond^{\leq 40}\ elected)$.

Randomized Dining Philosophers (RDP). In the Dining Philosophers problem [10], one assumes a round table with n philosophers who spend their lives just thinking and eating. There is a large plate of spaghetti in the center of the table, which is constantly refilled. Between each pair of philosophers lies a chopstick. Whenever a philosopher feels hungry, he can eat using the two chopsticks on his sides. [33] describes a distributed randomized algorithm to avoid deadlocks: A philosopher picks the two chopsticks in random order. If he can only get one chopstick, he gives up eating (but may become hungry again later).

For $n \in \{3, 4, 6, 7\}$ we checked the properties: (1) eventually some philosopher will eat, i. e., $\mathcal{P}_{\geq 1}(\Diamond\ eat)$, and (2) the probability that some philosopher will eat within 20 steps is at least 0.9, i. e., $\mathcal{P}_{\geq 0.9}(\Diamond^{\leq 20}\ eat)$.

Birth–Death Process (BDP). Birth–death processes [29,22] are used in numerous fields, e. g. to model the growth of a population or queue size. States in a birth–death process are numbered by integers that denote the current population size n. An increase in size is denoted as "birth" whereas a decrease is denoted as "death." To get a finite Markov chain, we limited the maximum population size to a predetermined size m. The probability of birth decreases with the population size, until it is 0 when the maximum population is reached.

For $m \in \{100, 1000, 10000, 100000\}$ we checked the properties: (1) the probability to reach a quarter of the maximum population within $\frac{m}{2}$ steps is ≥ 0.9, i. e., $\mathcal{P}_{\geq 0.9}(\Diamond^{\leq \frac{m}{2}}(n = \frac{m}{4}))$, (2) eventually a population of 50 will be reached while the probability to reach a population of 70 within 100 steps never drops below 0.9, i. e., $\mathcal{P}_{\geq 0.8}(\mathcal{P}_{\geq 0.9}(\Diamond^{\leq 100}(n = 70))\mathcal{U}(n = 50))$, and (3) eventually the maximum population will be reached, i. e., $\mathcal{P}_{\geq 1}(\Diamond(n = m))$.

Tandem Queuing Network (TQN). The Tandem Queuing Network [17,34] (see also [16,40,35]) consists of two queues of capacity n in sequence. Messages arrive at the first queue; when they get served, they are routed to the second queue, from where they leave the system. The message arrivals are exponentially distributed with rate $\lambda = 4n$. The server handles messages from the first queue according to a two-phase Coxian [8] distribution. The time between departures from the second queue is exponentially distributed with rate $\kappa = 4$.

For $n \in \{2, 10, 50, 100, 255, 511, 1023\}$ we checked: (1) in equilibrium, the TQN is full with probability < 0.01, i.e., $\mathcal{S}_{<0.01}(\mathit{full})$, (2) the TQN is full within 0.5 to 2 time units with probability < 0.1, i.e., $\mathcal{P}_{<0.1}(\Diamond^{[0.5,2]} \mathit{full})$, and (3) if the second queue is full, eventually a departure will happen, i.e., $\mathcal{P}_{\geq 1}(\mathit{snd}\,\mathcal{U}\,\mathit{sndn})$.

Cyclic Server Polling System (CPS). A cyclic polling system [20] consists of n stations and a server. Each station has a buffer with capacity 1 and the stations are attended by a single server in cyclic order. The server starts by polling the first station. If this station has a message in its buffer, the server serves it. Once the station has been served, or if its buffer was empty, the server moves to the next station cyclically. The polling and service times are exponentially distributed with rates $\gamma = 200$ and $\mu = 1$, respectively. The arrival rate of messages at each station is exponentially distributed with rate $\lambda = \mu/n$. Applications of this case study can be found in e.g. [39,16,35,40].

For $n \in \{3, 6, 9, 12, 15, 16, 17, 18\}$ we checked properties like: (1) in the steady state, the first station is waiting for the server with probability < 0.2, i.e., $\mathcal{S}_{<0.2}(\mathit{busy}_1 \wedge \neg\mathit{serve}_1)$, (2) the probability that the first station will be served within time interval $[40, 80]$ is ≤ 0.99, i.e., $\mathcal{P}_{\leq 0.99}(\Diamond^{[40,80]} \mathit{serve}_1)$, (3) if the first station is busy, the probability that it will be served within time t is ≥ 0.5 (for $t \in \{5, 10, 20, 40, 80\}$), i.e., $\mathit{busy}_1 \implies \mathcal{P}_{\geq 0.5}(\Diamond^{\leq t} \mathit{poll}_1)$, and (4) if the first station is busy, it will be served eventually, i.e., $\mathit{busy}_1 \implies \mathcal{P}_{\geq 1.0}(\Diamond\,\mathit{poll}_1)$.

4   Experimental Setup

This section describes the details of our experiments measuring the verification time and peak memory usage of the various tools. To give our conclusions a solid scientific basis, the experiment design was guided by the following principles:

- *Repeatability and Verifiability:* Every one should be able to repeat and verify our experiments; this is achieved by the fact that our models, properties, scripts and tool settings are publicly available.
- *Statistical Significance:* This has been achieved by repeating experiments several times and computing the standard deviation.
- *Encapsulation:* Our experiments should measure what we claim to measure (i.e. model check times and memory usage), no other influences. This has been achieved by carefully measuring the time and memory usage of the processes (see below) and by using a dedicated machine, thus the effect of disturbing factors such as network traffic, background processes is avoided.

Moreover, we have considered the tools as black boxes. That is, we have executed the tools, but not changed their source code[3]. Also, we chose the verification parameters (e.g. the algorithm for solving matrix equations) to be the same across all tools. For details on the models and measurements, we refer to [31].

---

[3] A minor exception is E⊢MC², where we added command line support to facilitate scripting.

Software and Hardware Settings. All experiments were performed on a standard PC with an Intel® Pentium® 4 CPU 3.00 GHz processor and 2 GB of RAM. The operating system is SuSE Linux 9.1, because this is supported by all tools. Furthermore we ensured that the verification parameters and numerical solution methods of the tools match. For the numerical tools, e. g., the Jacobi method is used for solving systems of linear equations and the convergence accuracy ϵ is set to the default value 10^{-6}. For the statistical tools, we bound the probability of error (i. e. the chance of false negatives or positives) by $\alpha = \beta = 0.01$, which is the default setting for these tools, and half the width of the indifference region $\delta = 0.01$. The former agrees with possible choices of $\alpha = \beta$ from [40]. The choice of δ is somewhat arbitrary, and also taken from the literature.

Timing. In (probabilistic) model checking, two time factors are of interest: the *model construction time*, i. e. the time to build the internal representation from the input model, and the *model checking time*, i. e. the time to verify the property on the internal representation. We mainly focused on the bare model check time. One would often construct the model only once and then use it to verify multiple properties. In our comparison, we use the time as reported by the tools.

Memory Usage. We measured the peak memory usage of the model checker, i. e. the amount of memory that is allocated for the verification problem at hand. More precisely, we recorded the virtual memory size (RAM + swap) of the entire process (which includes model construction). It also includes memory that the process has allocated but does not actually use. We did so by running a script in parallel to the model checker that took a sample every 100 msec. Although this sampling method is not perfect, it gives us the means to conduct uniform measurements on all tools, and it provides a reasonable indication of the memory consumption of each tool. A disadvantage is that this method does not work for very small experiments that are too quick. Other methods, such as profiling tools, are less suitable as they e. g., require tool modifications.

Data Collection. All experiments and measurement procedures were automated using shell scripts. This enabled us to easily repeat experiments many times and collect data in a uniform way. An experiment consists of verifying one property on one particular model using one of the model checkers. The tools are restarted before each experiment; this prevents the interference of e. g., caching on the measurements. Each experiment was repeated 20 times, except that experiments for which a single run took more than 30 minutes were repeated only three times. From the collected data, we calculated mean and standard deviation. The latter is determined using Student's t distribution, which takes the number of experiments into account. The maximal completion time for a single experiment was set to 24 hours, i. e., experiments that took longer were aborted. The verification time of these experiments is indicated in the results as ∞.

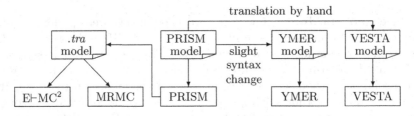

Fig. 1. The PRISM model is the central model, from which the other models are derived

Model Construction. The selected case studies were modeled using the model description language of each of the tools. For MRMC, E⊢MC² and PRISM the models were readily available, viz., from the PRISM webpage or from the example models included in the tool distribution. Although the tools use different modeling languages, we require the models to be equivalent across all tools. Thanks to the export facility of PRISM version 3.0 beta1, models in the PRISM language can be exported to the input format of E⊢MC² and MRMC. The YMER modeling language is almost identical to that of PRISM and only a few minor changes had to be made. The models for these four tools can thus safely be assumed to be equivalent on the state and transition level, so there is no bias for or against one of the tools. The TQN and CPS case studies are provided in the standard distribution of the VESTA tool. Only for the BDP case study, a re-modeling effort was needed. We were not able to generate the models for the RDP and SLE case studies due to parsing problems of VESTA (see also Fig. 1).

We attempted to generate models as large as possible by varying the model parameters. In addition to the RAM size, two factors restrict the model size: the size of the *.tra* files used by MRMC and E⊢MC² is limited to a maximum of 2 GB In a few cases, we could not generate (and verify) our model as PRISM crashed due to a (known) problem of the CUDD package used for MTBDDs.

As MRMC and E⊢MC² do not support a built-in modeling language, their overhead to generate a sparse matrix representation is low compared to the sparse matrix generation by PRISM. This aspect should be considered when interpreting the following experimental results.

5 Data and Analysis

5.1 Performance

The experimental results are discussed per type of formula, allowing us to compare phenomena across the various case studies. The results are presented by histograms where the x-axis indicates the model parameters that determine the state space size, and the y-axis indicates the verification time (in seconds) or the memory consumption (in KB). Note that the y-axis is log-scale. The legend of the plots is given by Fig. 2.

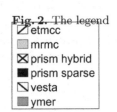

Fig. 2. The legend

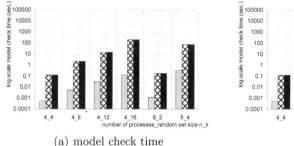
(a) model check time

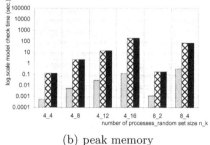
(b) peak memory

Fig. 3. Synchronous leader election: $\mathcal{P}_{\geq 1}(\lozenge \ elected)$

Almost Sure Reachability Properties. We first consider unbounded until formulas with probability bound ≥ 1. Figure 3 shows the verification time and memory usage for the SLE case study for various (n, k) pairs. (Recall that n is the number of nodes, and k the identity range.) As PRISM checks qualitative properties in a symbolic manner regardless whether it uses the sparse or hybrid engine, there is no difference in runtime nor in memory consumption between PRISM^S and PRISM^H. On increasing model parameters, the memory consumption of MRMC grows gradually (as expected) whereas for PRISM^S and PRISM^H only a slight increase is observed. This is due to the fact that PRISM requires a large base memory for the JVM, the CUDD package (around 40 MB) and the MTBDD it generates. The MTBDD for this case study is not very compact, as indicated by the following table:

(n, k)	$(4, 4)$	$(4, 8)$	$(4, 12)$	$(4, 16)$	$(8, 2)$	$(8, 4)$
MTBDD vertices	10K	165K	9M	2.8M	7.9K	1.1M
# states	0.8K	12K	62K	0.2M	2K	0.5M

As a result, PRISM needs substantially more memory than MRMC and the verification times differ up to several orders of magnitude. (For the smallest two problem instantiations, the memory consumption for MRMC is unavailable as its verification times are negligible.)

The SLE case study suggests that memory consumption for PRISM^S and PRISM^H is highly influenced by the MTBDD size. This observation is also substantiated by the CPS case study, for which the MTBDD sizes just increase slightly on a growth of the state space size:

n	3	6	9	12	15	18
MTBDD vertices	112	367	765	1282	1942	2745
# states	36	0.6K	7K	74K	0.7M	7M

Observe that the MTBDD is very compact, e.g., the model of 7 million states only requires 2745 MTBDD vertices, much less than in the SLE case study.

Some experimental results for a reachability property of the CPS case study are summarized in Fig. 4. In contrast to the previous study, PRISM needs less memory than MRMC for large models due to the small MTBDD size. As before, there is no difference between PRISM^S and PRISM^H. For small models,

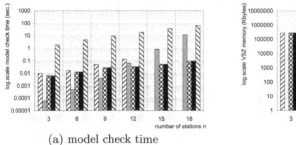
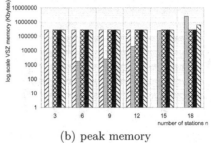

(a) model check time   (b) peak memory

Fig. 4. Cyclic polling server: $busy_1 \implies \mathcal{P}_{\geq 1}(\lozenge\, poll_1)$

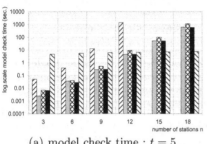
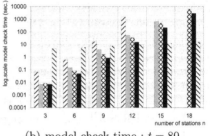

(a) model check time : $t = 5$ (b) model check time : $t = 80$

Fig. 5. Cyclic polling server: $busy_1 \implies \mathcal{P}_{\geq 0.5}(\lozenge^{\leq t}\, poll_1)$

MRMC is faster and less memory intensive, but for $n \geq 15$, it is outperformed by PRISM^S. This effect is to be expected to be more drastic for larger values of n as PRISM^S is able to check the CPS for $n > 18$ (roughly 26 M states) rather efficiently. As the file size of the *.tra* file for $n > 18$ exceeds 2 GB, we were unable to execute MRMC on it. For $n \geq 15$, E⊢MC^2 runs out of memory. The performance of E⊢MC^2 is worse than that of MRMC due to a less space-efficient sparse matrix representation, and the effect of the JVM. VESTA is about two orders of magnitude slower although – due to the use of Java – its memory usage is comparable to PRISM^S. The inefficiency of VESTA stems from the fact that it needs an excessive amount of sample paths to decide properties with bounds of the form ≥ 1, as shown in the following table:

n	3	6	9	12	15	18
# samples	34K	150K	395K	840K	1.6M	2.9M

Generally, statistical tools have difficulties to decide whether the probability of some property meets a bound if the actual probability and the bound are close. VESTA always gave the correct answer for these properties. For the BDP case study we experienced that for the property that almost surely eventually the population is maximal, VESTA reports an incorrect answer if the stopping probability – the likelihood that a sample path is stopped [36] – is not chosen appropriately. More precisely, if at some point during the simulation the stopping probability (in our case 0.05) is larger than that of reaching the state $n=m$ (in fact, a rare event), the sample path ends and it is concluded that $n=m$ is not reached. Re-simulation using a smaller stopping probability (e. g. 0.01) yields the correct answer. (VESTA always gives results for the initial state only; see the remarks with the next case study for details.) Note that YMER is not used here as it does not support unbounded reachability properties.

Bounded Reachability Properties. To show the effect of bounds, we consider a time-bounded variant of the property discussed before and observe what happens upon changing time bound t. Figure 5 depicts the verification times for the extreme bounds that we investigated in the CPS: $t=5$ and $t=80$, whereas Fig. 6 depicts the memory consumption for arbitrary t – the memory consumption does not depend on t. The verification time re-

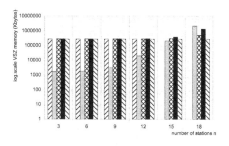

Fig. 6. Cyclic polling server, peak memory: $busy_1 \implies \mathcal{P}_{\geq 0.5}(\Diamond^{\leq t} poll_1)$

quired by MRMC is heavily influenced by t, e. g., for $n=15$ the time for $t=20$ is about four times longer than $t=5$. This is not surprising, as the time complexity of the underlying algorithm is linear in t. From $t=30$ on, the verification time is almost constant, due to a built-in steady-state detection [24]. Besides, for $t=80$ and $n=17$, MRMC requires about 1700 seconds (not depicted), and we obtained a timer overflow for larger instantiations. A similar behaviour is obtained for E⊢MC^2 but it runs out of memory rather quickly, as for simple reachability. PRISM^H is more efficient than PRISM^S due to the compact MTBDD (see previous case). As for MRMC, the verification time for PRISM^H and PRISM^S is linear in t, although this is less clear from the pictures due to the initial over-head of the MTBDD construction. A careful analysis of the logfiles reveals that the time *per iteration* is constant. Due to PRISM's steady-state detection, the verification time stops increasing around $t=30$. The verification time for VESTA for $t=5$ is rather constant as the number of samples (approx. 300,000) is more or less the same for each n. For $t=80$ the number of samples slightly increases (it raises from 0.2M for $n=3$ to about 1.1M for $n=18$). This explains the small increase in run time in Fig. 5(b). Unfortunately, VESTA gave wrong answers for low time bounds often: for $t = 5$, only 32.5 % of the answers were correct. Note that the property has also been checked by YMER, but as its run time is negligible – it immediately establishes that the initial state does not satisfy the premise of the implication – this is invisible in the figures. YMER thus has an "excellent" performance, but only checks the initial state whereas the other tools check *all* states. (VESTA also only provides answers for the initial state, but is unable to find the trivial satisfaction.)

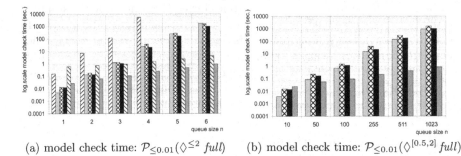

(a) model check time: $\mathcal{P}_{\leq 0.01}(\Diamond^{\leq 2} \ full)$ (b) model check time: $\mathcal{P}_{\leq 0.01}(\Diamond^{[0.5,2]} \ full)$

Fig. 7. Tandem queuing network: bounded reachability properties

Figures 7 and 8 show the results for checking a time-bounded property on the TQN case case study. YMER is for most cases much faster and smaller than all other tools. (For $n=2$ the verification time is too short to measure the memory consumption reliably.) As we have seen before, PRISM^H is more memory-efficient than PRISM^S, but the latter is faster. The memory usage of YMER is less than VESTA, and for both simulation tools independent of the model size (as expected). As in the other case studies we see that due to the base memory overhead (JVM+CUDD) usage, the PRISM memory consumption is less

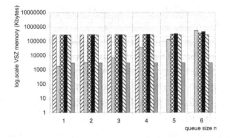

Fig. 8. Tandem queuing network, peak memory: $\mathcal{P}_{\leq 0.01}(\Diamond^{\leq 2} \ full)$

dependent on the model size than MRMC, and E⊢MC^2 is only able to handle relatively small models (up to few hundred thousands of states).

Figure 7(b) shows the timing for a bounded reachability property with both a positive lower and an upper bound. (E⊢MC^2 and VESTA do not support these bounds.) To check this formula, a model checker will calculate two reachability probabilities in different Markov chains. The results are similar to the above, as expected: YMER is, for most cases, the fastest tool; its runtime depends less on the model size than for the other tools. MRMC is slightly faster than PRISM^S, which is slightly faster than PRISM^H. The fact that YMER is fast is also confirmed by checking such bounded property on the CPS case study, e. g. on $n=16$, YMER just needs 1.2 sec whereas PRISM^S and MRMC require about 1500 sec, and PRISM^H about 3000 sec.

Steady State Properties. We only consider steady-state properties for CTMCs. The long-run operator for PCTL [2] is only supported by MRMC, and is therefore not used here. YMER and VESTA do not support steady-state properties, basically as it is unclear on when to stop the sample path generation. Figure 9 shows the runtime and peak memory for a steady-state property in the

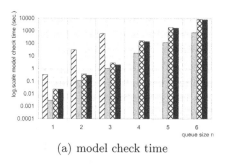
(a) model check time

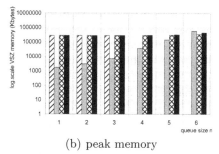
(b) peak memory

Fig. 9. Tandem queuing network : $\mathcal{S}_{>0.2}(\mathcal{P}_{>0.1}(\mathcal{X}\ snd))$

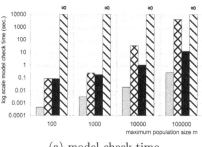
(a) model check time

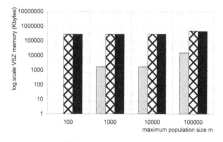
(b) peak memory

Fig. 10. Birth-death process : $\mathcal{P}_{\geq 0.8}(\mathcal{P}_{\geq 0.9}(\Diamond^{\leq 100}\ (n = 70))\ \mathcal{U}\ (n = 50))$

TQN case study. The experiments show similar results as before. E⊢MC^2 is the slowest tool and cannot handle large models (where $n > 100$). For the smaller models, the memory usage of PRISM is dominated by the overhead. For larger models, PRISM^S needs more memory than PRISM^H but is slightly faster. All experiments with steady-state formulas confirm our earlier observations: MRMC is faster and memory-wise more efficient than PRISM^S and PRISM^H, but for larger models, PRISM uses less memory than MRMC. The turn point, however, seems to occur at larger state spaces than experienced for reachability.

Nested Properties. We also checked the behaviour on nested quantitative reachability properties. Figure 10 shows the results of checking such property for the BDP case study. The tools check such nested formula in a bottom-up fashion, i.e., first the set of states satisfying the sub-formula is determined. The results are rather similar to the above findings. The MTBDD for the BDP case study is not very compact as the transition rates depend on the population size n, and as a result, most transition probabilities are distinct (resulting in many leaves in the MTBDD). As a result, MRMC outperforms PRISM^S and PRISM^H. Note however, that considered state spaces for this case study are relatively small which is favorable for MRMC. For all model instantiations, VESTA did not terminate simulation within 24 hours. We suggest as explanation that too many samples are required because the event $n=70$ is rather rare.

5.2 User Friendliness

Our experiments also gave insight in the user friendliness of the probabilistic model checkers. As recognised by many people in the field, we find PRISM the most user friendly tool, having a reasonably powerful modeling language, a GUI and many additional features, such as the ability to plot the probability for different model parameter values. VESTA was less powerful in this respect. It does have a nice GUI, but lacks a parallel composition operator. Hence one needs to combine the various parallel components into a single model by hand, which is a very cumbersome and error-prone task. Also, we find VESTA's syntax and error messages not so intuitive. PRISM is able to generate files that are readable for E⊢MC^2, MRMC and YMER. Whereas E⊢MC^2 and MRMC allow one to read these files directly, YMER uses a slightly different syntax, so PRISM models have to be slightly transformed before being used by YMER. Without a GUI, all three tools are less intuitive to use than PRISM. On the other hand, MRMC is more appropriate as back-end verification engine as it has a simple input format.

The following table summarizes the results ($++$ is best, $--$ is worst).

	E⊢MC^2	MRMC	PRISM	YMER	VESTA
ease of modeling	$++$ [a]	$++$ [a]	$++$	$+$	$--$
ease of use	$+$	$0/+$	$++$	0	$+$

[a] Exploiting the modeling facilities of PRISM (or TIPPtool).

6 Conclusion

We presented a performance comparison of five probabilistic model checkers. By ensuring that our experiments are repeatable, verifiable, statistically significant and free from external influences, our findings are based on a solid methodology.

From our experiments, we conclude that YMER is by far the fastest tool. Also, its memory usage is remarkably constant, hardly varying with the model size. Unfortunately, YMER only supports bounded and interval until formulas. Also, as statistical tool, YMER may report the wrong answer, and has done so during our experiments (in a few cases, as expected). In particular, YMER outperforms the other statistical model checker VESTA: VESTA's memory consumption is also rather constant, but more in the order PRISM's memory usage. However, its runtime varies a lot. For certain nested properties we checked, VESTA did not terminate within 24 h, even on a model with 100 states only.

E⊢MC^2 performs the worst in terms of memory, and frequently was unable to check models that were easy for the other tools.

For models up to a few million states, MRMC mostly performs better than PRISM^S both in time (although sparse matrix generation takes negligible time in MRMC compared to PRISM) and memory. This is mainly due to the overhead for MTBDD generation in PRISM. On larger models, PRISM^S and PRISM^H

perform better. This effect is more apparent whenever the MTBDD representation is compact. As expected, $PRISM^S$ is often faster than $PRISM^H$, but uses more memory. The results are summarized in the following tables.

We conclude that the differences between the numerical tools, which use the same algorithms [26], are based on differences in data structures used and more or less efficient implementations of the same algorithm. Statistical tools use different algorithms, so different behaviour – less dependent on model size than the numerical tools – meets the expectations.

speed	$E{\vdash}MC^2$	MRMC	$PRISM^S$	$PRISM^H$	YMER	VESTA
steady state	−	++	+	0/+ [a]	N/A	N/A
bounded until	−	+ [b]	+/++	0/+ [a]	++	+
unbounded until	−	+ [b]	+/++	+/++ [a]	N/A	−/0
nested	−	++	+	0/+ [a]	N/A [c]	−− [d]

[a] The time heavily depends on the MTBDD size.
[b] MRMC was faster in most cases, $PRISM^S$ on larger models.
[c] The property contained operators not supported by YMER.
[d] Based on one property, for which VESTA did not terminate.

memory	$E{\vdash}MC^2$	MRMC	$PRISM^S$	$PRISM^H$	YMER	VESTA
steady state	−	+ [a]	+	+/++ [a b]	N/A	N/A
bounded until	−	+ [a]	+	+/++ [a b]	++	+ [c]
unbounded until	−	+ [a]	+/++	+/++ [a b]	N/A	0/+ [c]
nested	−	+ [a]	+	+/++ [a b]	N/A	N/A [d]

[a] MRMC used least memory in most cases. For larger models $PRISM^S$ was between MRMC and $PRISM^H$, and $PRISM^H$ was the best.
[b] The MTBDD size varied much with the case study.
[c] Fairly constant; inefficient for small models, efficient for large ones.
[d] Based on one property, for which VESTA did not terminate.

Recommendations. Based on our experience, we have the following suggestions for improving the tools. For YMER, it would be very useful if it supported more CSL/PCTL operators, so that its "slim and fast" engine becomes applicable to a wider class of model checking problems. Also, it would be nice for YMER to use exactly the same syntax as PRISM, improving the tool interoperability. For VESTA, we suggest to improve its runtime efficiency. Also, its applicability would be enlarged by improving the modeling language, by either adding a parallel operator, or by supporting a modeling language similar to PRISM's. For PRISM, a tight connection with YMER could be of relevance – ideally, a user would call the YMER model checker by pressing a single button. For MRMC, we suggest to improve the performance for larger models.

Acknowledgement. We would like to thank Dave Parker and Gethin Norman for providing us with valuable feedback on a draft version of this paper.

References

1. Agha, G., Meseguer, J., Sen, K.: PMaude: Rewrite-based specification language for probabilistic object systems. ENTCS 153(2), 213–239 (2006)
2. Andova, S., Hermanns, H., Katoen, J.-P.: Discrete-time rewards model-checked. In: Larsen, K.G., Niebert, P. (eds.) FORMATS 2003. LNCS, vol. 2791, pp. 88–104. Springer, Berlin (2004)
3. Aziz, A., Sanwal, K., Singhal, V., Brayton, R.K.: Verifying continuous time Markov chains. In: Alur, R., Henzinger, T.A. (eds.) CAV 1996. LNCS, vol. 1102, pp. 269–276. Springer, Heidelberg (1996)
4. Baier, C., Ciesinski, F., Größer, M.: ProbMela and verification of Markov decision processes. SIGMETRICS Perform. Eval. Rev. 32(4), 22–27 (2005)
5. Baier, C., Haverkort, B., Hermanns, H., Katoen, J.-P.: Model-checking algorithms for continuous-time Markov chains. IEEE Trans. on Softw. Eng. 29(6), 524–541 (2003)
6. Bode, E., Herbstritt, M., Hermanns, H., Johr, S., Peikenkamp, T., Pulungan, R., Wimmer, R., Becker, B.: Compositional Performability Evaluation for STATEMATE. In: Quantitative Evaluation of Systems: QEST, pp. 167–178. IEEE CS, Los Alamitos (2006)
7. Changuion, B., Davies, I., Nelte, M.: DaNAMiCS: A Petri net editor (2007), http://www.cs.uct.ac.za/Research/DNA/microweb/danamics/DNAFrameH.html
8. Cox, D.R.: A use of complex probabilities in the theory of stochastic processes. In: Proc. Cambridge Philosophical Society, vol. 51, pp. 313–319 (1955)
9. D'Aprile, D., Donatelli, S., Sproston, J.: CSL model checking for the GreatSPN tool. In: Aykanat, C., Dayar, T., Körpeoğlu, İ. (eds.) ISCIS 2004. LNCS, vol. 3280, pp. 543–552. Springer, Heidelberg (2004)
10. Dijkstra, E.W.: Hierarchical ordering of sequential processes. Acta Informatica 1, 115–138 (1971)
11. Fokkink, W., Pang, J.: Simplifying Itai-Rodeh leader election for anonymous rings. ENTCS 128(6), 53–68 (2005)
12. Gupta, R., Smolka, S.A., Bhaskar, S.: On randomization in sequential and distributed algorithms. ACM Comput. Surv. 26(1), 7–86 (1994)
13. Hansson, H., Jonsson, B.: A logic for reasoning about time and reliability. Formal Aspects of Computing 6(5), 512–535 (1994)
14. Hartonas-Garmhausen, V., Campos, S., Clarke, E.M.: ProbVerus: probabilistic symbolic model checking. In: Katoen, J.-P. (ed.) AMAST-ARTS 1999, ARTS 1999, and AMAST-WS 1999. LNCS, vol. 1601, pp. 96–110. Springer, Heidelberg (1999)
15. Hermanns, H., Herzog, U., Klehmet, U., Mertsiotakis, V., Siegle, M.: Compositional performance modelling with the TIPPtool. Performance Evaluation 39(1–4), 5–35 (2000)
16. Hermanns, H., Katoen, J.-P., Meyer-Kayser, J., Siegle, M.: A Markov chain model checker. In: Schwartzbach, M.I., Graf, S. (eds.) ETAPS 2000 and TACAS 2000, LNCS, vol. 1785, pp. 347–362. Springer, Heidelberg (2000)
17. Hermanns, H., Meyer-Kayser, J., Siegle, M.: Multi-terminal binary decision diagrams to represent and analyse continuous-time Markov chains. In: Plateau, B., Stewart, W.J., Silva, M. (eds.) Num. Sol. of Markov Chains, Zaragoza, Prensas Universitarias, pp. 188–207 (1999)
18. Hillston, J.: A Compositional Approach to Performance Modelling. Cambridge University Press, New York (1996)
19. Hogg, R.V., Craig, A.T.: Introduction to Mathematical Statistics, 4th edn. Macmillan, New York (1978)

20. Ibe, O.C., Trivedi, K.S.: Stochastic Petri net models of polling systems. IEEE J. on Sel. Areas in Comm. 8(9), 1649–1657 (1990)
21. Itai, A., Rodeh, M.: Symmetry breaking in distributed networks. Inf. and Comp. 88(1), 60–87 (1990)
22. Karlin, S., McGregor, J.L.: The differential equations of birth-and-death processes, and the Stieltjes moment problem. Trans. of the AMS 85(2), 489–546 (1957)
23. Katoen, J.-P., Khattri, M., Zapreev, I.S.: A Markov reward model checker. In: Quantitative Evaluation of Systems, pp. 243–244. IEEE CS, Los Alamitos (2005)
24. Katoen, J.-P., Zapreev, I.S.: Safe on-the-fly steady-state detection for time-bounded reachability. In: Quantitative Evaluation of Systems: QEST, pp. 301–310. IEEE CS, Los Alamitos (2006)
25. Kwiatkowska, M., Norman, G., Parker, D.: PRISM: Probabilistic symbolic model checker. In: Field, T., et al. (eds.) TOOLS 2002. LNCS, vol. 2324, pp. 200–204. Springer, Heidelberg (2002)
26. Kwiatkowska, M., Norman, G., Parker, D.: Stochastic model checking. In: Bernardo, M., Hillston, J. (eds.) Formal methods for performance evaluation. LNCS, vol. 4486, pp. 220–270. Springer, Heidelberg (2007)
27. Lassaigne, R., Peyronnet, S.: Approximate verification of probabilistic systems. In: Hermanns, H., Segala, R. (eds.) PROBMIV 2002, PAPM-PROBMIV 2002, and PAPM 2002. LNCS, vol. 2399, pp. 213–214. Springer, Heidelberg (2002)
28. Lecca, P., Priami, C.: Cell cycle control in eukaryotes: A BioSpi model. Technical Report DIT-03-045, Informatica e Telecommunicazioni: University of Trento (2003)
29. Mohanty, S.G., Montazer-Haghighi, A., Trueblood, R.: On the transient behavior of a finite birth-death process with an application. Computers and Operations Research 20(3), 239–248 (1993)
30. Norman, G., Shmatikov, V.: Analysis of probabilistic contract signing. J. of Computer Security 14(6), 561–589 (2006)
31. Oldenkamp, M.: Probabilistic model checking: A comparison of tools. MSc thesis, Univ. of Twente, Netherlands (2007), http://www.cs.utwente.nl/~oldenkampha/
32. Penna, G.D., Intrigila, B., Melatti, I., Tronci, E., Zilli, M.V.: Finite horizon analysis of Markov chains with the Murphi verifier. STTT 8(4-5), 397–409 (2006)
33. Pnueli, A., Zuck, L.D.: Verification of multiprocess probabilistic protocols. Distributed Comput. 1(1), 53–72 (1986)
34. PRISM: Probabilistic symbolic model checker (2006), http://www.cs.bham.ac.uk/~dxp/prism/
35. Sen, K., Viswanathan, M., Agha, G.: Statistical model checking of black-box probabilistic systems. In: Alur, R., Peled, D.A. (eds.) CAV 2004. LNCS, vol. 3114, pp. 202–215. Springer, Heidelberg (2004)
36. Sen, K., Viswanathan, M., Agha, G.: On statistical model checking of stochastic systems. In: Etessami, K., Rajamani, S.K. (eds.) CAV 2005. LNCS, vol. 3576, pp. 266–280. Springer, Heidelberg (2005)
37. Shedler, G.S.: Regenerative Stochastic Simulation. Academic Pr, London (1993)
38. Somenzi, F.: CUDD: CU decision diagram package. Public software (1997), http://vlsi.colorado.edu/~fabio/CUDD/
39. Younes, H.L.S.: Ymer: A statistical model checker. In: Etessami, K., Rajamani, S.K. (eds.) CAV 2005. LNCS, vol. 3576, pp. 429–433. Springer, Heidelberg (2005)
40. Younes, H.L.S., Kwiatkowska, M., Norman, G., Parker, D.: Numerical vs. statistical probabilistic model checking. STTT 8(3), 216–228 (2006)
41. Younes, H.L.S., Simmons, R.G.: Probabilistic verification of discrete event systems using acceptance sampling. In: Brinksma, E., Larsen, K.G. (eds.) CAV 2002. LNCS, vol. 2404, pp. 223–235. Springer, Heidelberg (2002)

Constraint Patterns and Search Procedures for CP-Based Random Test Generation

Anna Moss

Intel Corporation, Haifa, Israel
anna.moss@intel.com

Abstract. Constraint Programming (CP) technology has been extensively used in Random Functional Test Generation during the recent years. However, while the existing CP methodologies are well tuned for traditional combinatorial applications e.g. logistics or scheduling, the problem domain of functional test generation remains largely unexplored by the CP community and many of its domain specific features and challenges are still unaddressed. In this paper we focus on the distinctive features of CP for the random functional test generation domain and show how these features can be addressed using a classical CP engine with custom extensions. We present some modeling and solving problems arising in this context and propose solutions. In particular, we address the way of model building in the problem domain of test generation which we refer to as *multi-layer modeling*. In this context we introduce constraint patterns of *composite variable*, *implied condition* and *implied composite variable condition*, define their semantics and propose schemes for their CSP modeling. The paper also addresses specific problems arising at the solving stage in the problem domain of random test generation. We propose solutions to these problems by means of custom random search algorithms. This approach is illustrated on the examples of the disjunction constraint and conditional variable instantiation. The latter algorithm addresses the feature of dynamic modeling required in the test generation task. To demonstrate the effectiveness of our approach we present experimental results based on the implementation using ILOG Solver as a CP engine.

1 Introduction

Design verification on the register transfer level (RTL) is a major task in processor design cycle. One of the commonly used methodologies for performing this task is simulation-based validation. This methodology involves developing a large amount of functional tests in an attempt to exercise various execution scenarios which could lead to bug detection. Unfortunately, it is not feasible to cover all possible test scenarios deterministically due to size and complexity of modern architectures. Hence, the common approach is to generate so called directed random tests, which are driven by constraints to express test intention yet employ randomness to extend the reach of the test. Automated test generation tools are being designed in order to facilitate the work of validation engineers. In recent years functional test generation has emerged as a new application area of CP technology. Constraint modeling is used to enable a

K. Yorav (Ed.): HVC 2007, LNCS 4899, pp. 86–103, 2008.
© Springer-Verlag Berlin Heidelberg 2008

declarative description of design under test as well as express test intention. Moreover, advanced CP algorithms are used by automated test generation tools to produce tests answering architectural and test intention requirements. However, while the existing CP methodologies are well tuned for traditional combinatorial applications e.g. logistics or scheduling, the problem domain of functional test generation remains largely unexplored by the CP community. Therefore, applying CP technology to test generation requires filling the gap between capabilities of classic CP engines and challenges presented by this specific problem domain. One of the possible approaches is to develop custom modeling and search tools for problems arising in test generation [1]. Another approach is to represent a test generation problem or sub problems as a classical CSP (Constraint Satisfaction Problem) and to use a standard CP engine with custom extensions for its modeling and solving [2]. While the former approach provides more flexibility in addressing domain specific features, the latter one achieves greater efficiency by making use of cutting edge CP algorithms. In this paper, we address the challenge presented by the second approach and show how some distinctive features of the functional test generation problem domain can be addressed within a classical CP framework. We demonstrate our ideas using ILOG Solver [3] as a CP engine. As observed in [2], our choice of the solver results from its high controllability and extensibility capabilities, including user-defined extensions to search heuristics, modeling and constraint propagation mechanism.

The first distinctive feature of CP for functional test generation considered in this paper arises from the way a CSP model is built. In traditional CP applications, a model is created by a single agent that possesses full knowledge of the problem and can exercise this knowledge to produce an efficient formulation of the problem as a CSP. On the other hand, in the domain of functional test generation, formulating a model is typically performed by several agents. For example, one of the agents contributing to a CSP model is an architectural description of the design under test. The corresponding part of the model reflects information that is not test specific. Another part of the model comes from a validation engineer who wishes to express the specific test intention by implying additional constraints on architectural variables. The validation engineer possesses the limited knowledge of the CSP model representing the architectural description. We refer to this modeling scheme in which parts of the model are built without full knowledge of other parts as *multi-layer modeling*. In this paper we present some of the challenges associated with multi-layer modeling and propose solution methods. Specifically, we introduce constraint patterns which we refer to as *composite variable* pattern, *implied condition* pattern and *implied composite variable condition* pattern, define their semantics and propose schemes for their CSP modeling. All of the presented patterns are related to the paradigm of conditional CSP. As a part of our modeling scheme, we propose the representation of conditional variables in terms of traditional CSP concepts.

Another distinctive feature which is characteristic of random functional test generation domain is the requirement that a solution to a CSP must be randomly distributed over the solution space according to a desired distribution. This requirement suggests the use of randomized search algorithms. The area of design and analysis of complete random search algorithms has received much attention in recent years (see [4] for a survey of research results in this area). However the focus of this research has been on analyzing and improving the performance of complete search methods by introducing randomization rather than addressing the randomness requirement. In this paper we design random search algorithms with a different purpose. Specifically, we wish to address problems arising in random test generation domain by taking advantage of the randomness requirement. While specific features of this problem domain render some of the classical search and constraint propagation techniques ineffective, the randomness requirement can be used to design random custom search algorithms that can effectively replace standard solving techniques. We illustrate this approach on the examples of the disjunction constraint and dynamic variable instantiation. The latter algorithm provides search level support for our conditional variable modeling.

The rest of the paper is organized as follows. Section 2 provides background definitions. In Section 3 we introduce some problems arising in multi-layer modeling and propose solutions based on the standard CP modeling concepts. Section 4 describes some problems in CP for random test generation arising at the search stage and presents random search algorithms that solve these problems. The description of algorithms is followed by experimental results to demonstrate the effectiveness of our approach. We conclude in Section 5 with the summary of results and future work directions.

2 Definitions

In this section we provide the CP background required for the presentation of our results. Also, the section contains description of selected ILOG Solver features that are referred to in the sequel of the paper. We begin by introducing the main concepts of Constraint Programming. An in-depth survey of this subject can be found in [5].

The CP paradigm comprises problem modeling as a CSP, constraint propagation, search algorithms, and heuristics. A CSP is defined by:

- a set of constrained variables. Each variable is associated with a (finite) domain which is a collection of values that the variable can potentially assume;
- a set of constraints. A constraint is a relation defined on a subset of variables which restricts the combinations of values that the variables can take simultaneously.

A *solution* to a CSP is an assignment of values to variables so that each variable is assigned a value from its domain and all the constraints are satisfied.

A *meta-constraint* is a constraint that is composed of other constraints by using operations on constraints, e.g. conjunction, disjunction, negation or implication.

A CSP formulation of a problem is processed by a constraint solver which attempts to find a solution using a search algorithm combined with reductions of variable domains based on constraint information. The latter mechanism is known as *constraint propagation.* During constraint propagation, domains of the variables involved in the constraint are reduced until some type of consistency is achieved. For example, one of the possible types of consistency is the *generalized arc consistency.*

This consistency type implies that for each value in the domain of a variable involved in the constraint, there exists a support in the domains of all other constraint variables. In other words, if any constraint variable is assigned any value from its domain, a way must exist for assigning other constraint variables so that the constraint is satisfied. To ensure the required type of consistency, a solver associates a specific propagation algorithm with each constraint type.

The *search space* is the Cartesian product of the variable domains. A complete search algorithm explores the search space systematically and is guaranteed to find a solution if such exists even though the time consumed by the search can sometimes be impractically large. At the first stage the search algorithm invokes initial constraint propagation to reduce variable domains defined in the CSP model. The algorithm then explores the search space by implicitly building a search tree. The nodes in such a tree correspond to so called *choice points* where search decisions can be made. The arcs descending from a choice point represent possible decisions. These decisions are taken according to some search strategy. For example, the possible search strategy is to pick a variable which has not been *fixed* yet (i.e. whose domain has not yet been reduced to a single value) and to try assigning each value in the domain in turn to the variable. In this case the search tree contains a choice point so that the arcs descending from this choice point correspond to possible value assignments to the variable. Each time a decision is taken at a choice point, domains of some variables get modified. These changes trigger the constraint propagation mechanism that ensures that each of the relevant constraints is propagated in respect to the new domains. A branch of the search tree *fails* if the domain of some variable becomes empty. In this case the search algorithm backtracks to one of the earlier choice points and tries to explore another branch. A solution is reached when all the variables get fixed. The search algorithm can apply various search heuristics regarding, for example, the order of variables to be chosen at choice points or the order of branch exploration.

To implement and test our methods we have used the ILOG constraint solver. This solver supports user extensions to the modeling capabilities, search engine and constraint propagation mechanism. In particular, a user can extend the search capabilities by implementing new search algorithms and heuristics. The search in the ILOG solver is implemented by means of so called *goal programming*. The algorithm maintains a stack of goals. Each goal is composed of the execution part and an (optional) sub goal that defines how the execution should be continued. While the stack is not empty, the search algorithm pops a goal from the top of the stack and executes it. At the end of its execution the goal pushes its sub goal (if any) on the stack. In this way, search goals can be pushed on the stack dynamically, depending on the state of the search. This mechanism allows implementing an algorithm where the sequence of events is not known in advance. An example of a predefined goal in the ILOG Solver is a *variable instantiation* goal which attempts to bind the variable to a value from its domain. Its algorithm creates a choice point where each branch corresponds to the assignment of a distinct domain value to the variable. A user is allowed to implement custom goals and to use them as building blocks of the search algorithm along with the predefined goals.

3   Constraint Patterns for Multi-layer Modeling

The need for identification of common constraint patterns arising in CSP models has been argued by Walsh in [6]. Following his argument, constraint patterns identification can help sharing modeling experience as well as exploiting these patterns by CSP solvers.

In this section we describe specific features of CSP model building for the task of functional test generation and identify constraint patterns applicable to this type of modeling. We define the semantics and propose implementation schemes for these constraint patterns. We start by describing the modeling paradigm characteristic of the test generation problem domain which we refer to as *multi-layer modeling*.

3.1 Multi-layer Modeling

In classical CP applications, a CSP model of a problem is built by a single agent that possesses full knowledge of the problem. However, this is not the case for the test generation task. In this task, the model is typically composed of a number of layers contributed by different agents. For example, one layer of the model is contributed by the architectural description of design under test. This layer defines architectural variables and constraints required to produce an architecturally valid test. This part of the model is constructed by an agent who possesses the knowledge of the architecture but is not aware of any specific test requirements. Another layer of the model comes from a validation engineer who augments the architectural layer of the model with constraints and new variables to express a specific test intention. The validation engineer has knowledge of the architectural concepts and must be provided access to the architectural variables introduced in the former layer of the model in order to formulate his constraints. However, his knowledge of the architecture need not be full and moreover, he does not possess the full knowledge of the CSP modeling of the architectural layer.

Formally, we consider a model building scheme where a CSP model is built in phases by layers contributed by different agents. Each of the agents has a limited knowledge of layers contributed by other agents in the preceding phases. These layers can share common variables. We refer to this scheme as multi-layer modeling. Fig. 1 illustrates the multi-layer modeling paradigm.

The main challenge posed by the multi-layer modeling scheme is providing a mechanism to allow variable sharing subject to limited knowledge of agents about the CSP modeling of their predecessors. In a typical variable sharing scenario, the current agent wishes to impose a constraint on a concept that has been modeled in one of the preceding layers. This concept is viewed by the current agent as a single variable. In the simple cases of variable sharing, the shared concept is modeled by a single CSP variable in one of the preceding layers. In these cases some naming convention can be agreed upon and used to pass the corresponding variable to the current agent. However, there are cases when a shared concept has a more complex representation in one of the preceding layers than a single variable.

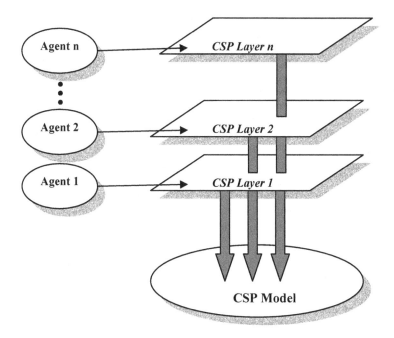

Fig. 1. Multi-Layer Modeling

In the remainder of this section we present constraint patterns arising in the context of multi-layer modeling and propose the ways for their implementation. The patterns described below are related to so called *conditional* variables, therefore we start with defining this concept and provide some background on conditional CSP.

3.2 Conditional Variables

As observed in [1], CP for functional test generation involves dynamic modeling. In dynamic modeling, the existence, or relevance, of some variables may depend on the values some other variables assume in the search process. Consider an example from IA-32 processor architecture [7]. This architecture implements a segmentation mechanism and supports several segment types, e.g. code segment and data segment. While data segment has an attribute indicating whether the segment is writable, the latter attribute is not applicable to a code segment. Clearly, a model part, e.g. a variable, representing this attribute should participate in the solution only if variables representing segment type are assigned values corresponding to a data segment type. The variables, whose relevance depends on values taken by other variables, are known as conditional variables, and problems involving conditional, or dynamic, parts are known as Conditional CSP (CCSP).

Since the formalism of CCSP was first introduced by Mittal and Falkenhainer [8], research has been done in this area and several algorithms have been developed for CCSP solving [9, 10, 11].

For the sake of completeness, below we present the definition of CCSP. CCSP is comprised of the following parts:

- Unconditional variables; these variables participate in all the solutions to the problem.
- Conditional variables; a conditional variable is associated with a condition referred to as *activity constraint*. The variable participates in a solution if and only if the condition is satisfied. In this case, a conditional variable is called *active*. An activity constraint can involve both conditional and unconditional variables. A group of conditional variables with the same activity constraint is known as *activity cluster*.
- *Compatibility constraints*; these constraints imply restrictions on combinations of values that the variables can simultaneously assume. Compatibility constraints can involve both conditional and unconditional variables. A compatibility constraint applies to a solution if and only if all of its conditional variables are active.

Next we describe our representation of CCSP in terms of the classical CSP. Unconditional variables are represented in our framework as standard CSP variables. Conditional variables are represented by a CSP variable and a CSP constraint. The latter constraint represents the activity constraint associated with the variable. Finally, compatibility constraints are represented as implication meta-constraints. Specifically, compatibility constraint C is represented by implication CSP constraint, implying that if the conditions associated with each of the conditional variables in C are satisfied, then C must also hold. We make the following assumptions about the activity constraints in our representation. First, we assume that the model does not contain activity circles. Namely, consider a graph where the nodes correspond to model variables and there is a directed edge from node a to node b if the variable b is conditional and the variable a participates in the activity constraint of b. The graph described above is known as a *dependency graph* [9]. Our assumption implies that the dependency graph is acyclic. While the general case of CCSP allows for activity cycles and [9,10] suggest methods to handle them, in our experience typical problems arising in the test generation tasks can be modeled without activity cycles. In general, we conjecture that activity cycles can be eliminated in most cases through more careful modeling. Next we describe our second assumption. Given that the dependency graph is acyclic, it can be assumed without loss of generality that if an activity constraint involves conditional variables then their conditions are also implied by the activity constraint. For example, consider a model which contains an unconditional variable $A[0..5]$, and conditional variables $B[0..5]$ and $C[0..5]$ where B is active if and only if $A > 5$, and C is active if and only if $B < 3$. Then we assume that activity constraint for C is formulated as $(A > 5)$ AND $(B < 3)$. Observe that if the second assumption does not hold, the activity constraints can be modified to make it hold while retaining an equivalent CCSP model. Specifically, following the assumption that the dependency graph is acyclic, one can compute a topological ordering of the dependency graph and append activity constraints of predecessors to an activity constraint of each variable.

In Section 4 we show how our representation of conditional variables in terms of CSP can be handled at the solving stage using a classic CP engine. In the rest of this section we present constraint patterns involving conditional variables that arise in the context of multi-layer modeling, and propose implementations for these patterns.

3.3 Composite Variable Constraint Pattern

Consider the case when an agent A wants to impose constraints on a concept C that has been modeled in some preceding layer L. Suppose the concept C may have different configurations depending on the values of other variables. More precisely, the concept C could be modeled in the layer L by a group G of conditional activity clusters with disjoint, i.e. mutually exclusive, activity constraints. The agent A does not possess the knowledge about the modeling of C in the layer L. Moreover, the modeling of C should remain transparent to A, and A would like to treat C as a single variable. Semantically, a constraint applied to C by the agent A must apply to each representation in the group G. We refer to this constraint pattern as a *composite variable* pattern.

For example, consider the paging mechanism in IA-32 processor architecture [7]. In certain modes, this mechanism allows pages of different sizes, namely, 4K and 4M. Linear to physical address translation passes through an architectural table called page directory. If the address being translated falls in a 4M page, then the base address of this page can be calculated from the *base* field of a page directory entry using a shift operation. Otherwise, address translation proceeds to another architectural table called page table, pointed by the page directory entry. In this case, the page base can be calculated from the *base* field of page table entry using a different shift operation. The resulting physical address is defined in terms of architectural table fields for each of the translation paths. Fig. 2 illustrates linear to physical address translation for 4M and for 4K pages. According to the mechanism described above, page base can be represented in the architectural layer of the CSP model by two different expressions. Each expression involves one distinct conditional variable and activity constraints of

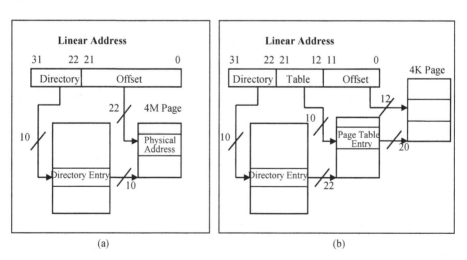

Fig. 2. Linear to physical address translation: (a) 4M pages; (b) 4K pages

these two variables are disjoint, implying that the page size is 4K or 4M, respectively. On the other hand, a validation engineer might wish to imply constraints on the page base, regardless of the page size. The modeling details of the page base should remain transparent to the validation engineer.

We propose to implement the composite variable pattern by adding a new variable and implication constraints to the layer L where the concept C is defined. Specifically, let $G=\{E_1,...,E_n\}$ be the group of variables or expressions representing different configurations of the concept C in the composite variable pattern. Then a new variable V should be added to the layer L. The domain of V equals the union of domains of $E_1,...,E_n$. Let C_i be an activity constraint of E_i, for $i=1,...,n$. Then for each i, an implication constraint must be added to the layer L, implying that if C_i holds then V equals E_i. Observe that these augmentations to the model of layer L are done not for the needs of this layer but for the purpose of sharing the composite concept with the following layers. In such an implementation, the following layers that wish to impose constraints on the concept C can apply the constraints directly to the variable V without the need to know about the expressions E_i.

In the page base example described above, one should add a new variable P representing the page base to the architectural layer. As the page base width is 32 bits the domain of the new variable is $[0..2^{32}-1]$. Moreover, one should add a constraint implying that if the page size is S then P equals the expression corresponding to the S-sized page translation path, for each S in $\{4K, 4M\}$.

3.4 Implied Condition Constraint Pattern

Like the composite variable constraint pattern defined in the previous subsection, the implied condition constraint pattern is related to conditional variables. This pattern arises when an agent imposes a constraint on a conditional variable defined in another layer. As the agent does not possess the knowledge of the CSP modeling of other layers, it may not be aware of the activity constraint of the variable or even of the fact that the variable is conditional. First, we define the semantics of such a constraint imposed on a conditional variable. We refer to a constraint which is not a meta-constraint as a *basic* constraint. Let L be the current layer and let V be a conditional variable defined in one of the layers preceding L. We suggest that any basic constraint λ on V in the current layer L should be interpreted as the conjunction of λ with the activity constraint of V. In other words, in order to satisfy λ, the variable V must be active. We observe that λ can be a part of a meta-constraint μ. In this case V should not necessarily be active since it might be possible to satisfy μ without satisfying λ. An alternative definition to that proposed above would be to require that the constraint λ should be taken into account only if the activity constraint of V is satisfied. Yet we think that the definition we propose better suits the framework of multi-layer modeling.

Consider the example of the writability attribute of a segment discussed in Section 3.2. Suppose this attribute is implemented by a conditional variable with an activity constraint, implying that the segment type must be that of a data segment. When a validation engineer imposes a constraint requiring a segment to be writable, the meaning of this constraint according to our definition is that the segment must be a data segment and must be writable.

To implement the proposed semantics within the standard CSP modeling framework, we use the representation of conditional variables described in Section 3.2. For each layer L, and for each basic constraint λ in L, conditional variables defined in layers preceding L are identified and their activity constraints are appended to λ using the conjunction operation.

3.5 Implied Composite Variable Condition Constraint Pattern

This pattern is a combination of the composite variable pattern and the implied condition pattern defined in the previous subsections. This pattern occurs when a concept C defined in layer L can have multiple configurations associated with disjoint activity constraints, like in the composite variable pattern, and in addition C itself is conditional. According to our semantics definition, a basic constraint on C imposed in a layer succeeding L implies that C must be active and the constraint must hold for all possible configurations of C.

For example, recall the page base example described in Section 3.3. When considered as a part of the address translation process, the paging mechanism itself is conditional. It is active if and only if paging is enabled. In this case, when a validation engineer imposes a basic constraint on the page base, in order to satisfy this constraint the paging mechanism must be active and the constraint on the page base must hold for any page size.

The proposed implementation of the implied composite variable condition pattern combines the ideas of the composite variable pattern and the implied condition pattern. In the layer L where the conditional concept C is defined, a new conditional variable S must be added with an activity constraint corresponding to the activity condition of C. The domain of S is defined as a union of domains corresponding to different configurations of C. Moreover, implication constraints are added to L, implying that if both the activity constraint of S and the activity constraint of a specific configuration hold then S must equal the expression corresponding to the specific configuration. When one of the following model layers imposes a constraint λ on S, the activity constraint of S is appended to λ using the conjunction operation.

4   Random Search Algorithms

In Section 0 we discussed distinctive modeling aspects of CP for functional test generation. In this section we present some challenges arising at the solving stage for this problem domain. We propose solutions to address these challenges. These solutions are based on the randomness requirement inherent to the random test generation task.

4.1   Random Search Algorithm for the Disjunction Constraint

Consider the following typical constraint arising in the random test generation task. Given an integer variable V with a very large domain, one wants to restrict the possible values for this variable to a finite set of ranges within the variable domain. The relative sizes of ranges with respect to the domain size can be small. Within the traditional CP framework, the described situation is modeled using a disjunction meta-constraint, where the disjunction is performed between the range constraints for each individual range.

The standard constraint propagation algorithm for the disjunction constraint is as follows. Let $C_1 \lor C_2 \ldots \lor C_n$ be a disjunction constraint. If C_i becomes false for each $i=1,\ldots,n$ except $i=j$ then add the constraint C_j to the solver. In particular, this propagation rule is implemented in ILOG Solver. Domain pruning achieved by this propagation rule is very weak as no pruning takes place until all but one constraint in the disjunction becomes violated. For example, for the range disjunction constraint described above, a solver would try to bind the variable V to arbitrary values in its large domain and since the percentage of valid values in the domain could be very small, this would cause the solver to backtrack numerous times until a valid value was found.

An improved method for disjunction constraint propagation is *constructive disjunction* [12]. Following this approach, each constraint in the disjunction is propagated independently, and the domain of each variable is computed as the union over its domains obtained in all of the branches. Returning to the example of range disjunction, the constructive disjunction rule implies that each of the range constraints must be propagated independently. This means that in each propagation branch, the domain of V will be reduced to the corresponding single range, and the domain of V after applying the constructive disjunction rule will be the union of valid ranges. While the constructive disjunction rule is very efficient in the example described above, in general cases it can be more time consuming compared to the standard propagation rule. For this reason, the constructive disjunction is not widely used by existing CP engines. Lhomme [13] proposed a further improvement to disjunction constraint propagation that achieves the same pruning as constructive disjunction but is more efficient in general cases. However, his algorithm involves iterating over domains of variables shared by constraints in the disjunction and has the complexity of $O(kd)$ where k stands for the number of shared variables and d is their maximum domain size. Therefore, this propagation rule is not efficient in cases of large domains as in the range disjunction example.

A completely different approach to handling disjunction constraints is to represent them by choice points at the solving stage rather than by CSP constraints. Such a choice point selects one constraint from the disjunction and adds it to a solver. This approach has been mentioned by Würtz and Müller [14]. They compare different approaches to disjunction constraints handling and argue that constructive disjunction is not efficient for all applications, and that real world applications might need the standard propagation method or choice points to handle disjunctions efficiently.

In this paper we propose to use the choice point approach in combination with randomization to handle disjunction constraints in the random test generation application. Specifically, we represent each disjunction constraint as a choice point in the search. The algorithm, which is performed at such a choice point, selects one of the constraints in the disjunction at random, with respect to uniform or any other desired distribution over individual constraints within the disjunction. The selected constraint is then added to the solver. In such an approach, only one constraint from the disjunction participates in the search at each given time. This algorithm is integrated into the standard search algorithm. If a failure occurs following a "bad" choice of a constraint from the disjunction, the algorithm backtracks to the choice point and tries another constraint.

We argue that the approach to disjunction constraints described above is the most suitable one for the random functional test generation problem domain. First of all, we observe that this approach answers in a natural way the requirement for random sampling of the solution space. Indeed, a typical use for disjunction constraints in the random test generation task is to enumerate over possible choices described by individual constraints. Since the validation task aims to cover all possible situations where bugs can reside, it is important that each possible architectural choice be represented with non zero probability in the resulting test. Therefore, such a disjunction can be viewed as a search decision regarding which choice will be represented in the test, and the desired probability can be assigned to each choice. Though this approach does not guarantee uniform or any other desired distribution over the solution space, it can serve as a good approximation to answer the validation needs. Second, as noted above, the existing constraint propagation methods for the disjunction constraint are generally not suited to the task of random test generation, because large variable domains typical to this task render these propagation methods ineffective. Finally, we use a standard CP engine to model and solve the tasks in test generation. However, as noted above, standard CP engines usually do not implement advanced propagation methods due to their high general case complexity. Extending an existing CP engine to include these advanced propagation algorithms would incur a substantial development effort, whereas the proposed algorithm can be more easily implemented by extending the search mechanism.

We have implemented the proposed method on top of ILOG Solver. As described in Section 2, the search algorithm in ILOG Solver is implemented using goal programming, where a goal serves as a building block of the search. We have implemented a custom goal *DisjunctionGoal* taking a list of constraints as a parameter. The outline of the algorithm is shown in Fig. 3.

```
goal DisjunctionGoal(Constraints[n])
    if n=1
            return goal(Constraint[0])
    else
            i ← rand(1,n)
            NewConstraints ← Constraints \
            Constraints[i]
            return ChoicePoint(goal(Constraint[i]),
                    DisjunctionGoal(NewConstraints[n-1])
```

Fig. 3. A random search algorithm for the disjunction constraint

The algorithm performed by *DisjunctionGoal* is as follows. The goal selects a constraint uniformly at random from the list of its parameters and discards this constraint from the list. If the reduced list is empty, then the goal adds the selected constraint to the solver and terminates. Otherwise, *DisjunctionGoal* creates a choice point. The first branch of the choice point adds the selected constraint to the solver. The second branch recursively activates another *DisjunctionGoal* that gets the reduced list of constraints as a parameter.

We observe that the algorithm described above can be easily generalized to handle arbitrary distribution over the constraint list, which can be passed to the algorithm as an additional parameter.

4.2 Random Search Algorithm for Conditional Variable Instantiation

In this section we apply the idea similar to that of the random search algorithm for the disjunction constraint to the problem of conditional variable instantiation.

The existing research results in the area of CCSP solving follow two main approaches. The first approach is to reformulate CCSP as a CSP and solve it with traditional CP methods. One way to obtain such reformulation is to represent the inactivity of a conditional variable by a special *null* value which is assigned to a variable when it is inactive [8,10]. Then activity constraints can be formulated as standard CSP constraints. Another way is to represent a CCSP by a collection of CSP problems that are solved separately [9]. The second approach is to design specialized algorithms for CCSP solving that aim to adopt the CSP techniques to the CCSP domain while eliminating the need for reformulation [10,11]. Experimental results presented in [10] show that the performance achieved by the second approach is much better than that of the first one.

None of the approaches described above fits the needs of our application. The reformulation methods are not acceptable due to performance consideration. Moreover, the choice of the null value in the case of null reformulation is problematic for integer variables in the test generation task. Such variables typically represent architectural fields with a domain of $[0..2^n-1]$ where n stands for the width of the field in bits. The representation used for these variables does not easily extend to include an additional dummy domain value. The approach of specialized CCSP modeling and solving techniques does not fit our purpose either since we aim to use the strengths of an existing CP engine for our task. In this paper we propose an approach to CCSP which employs traditional CP methods, addresses the specific features of the test generation problem domain, and does not require problem reformulation as a CSP. This is achieved by the following two steps. First, we represent conditional variables using concepts of traditional CSP as described in Section 3.2, without reformulating the problem as a CSP. Such modeling is implemented as a layer above the existing CP modeling tool. Second, we provide support for conditional variables in the solving engine. This is done by a custom extension to a CP solver within a standard CSP solving framework.

Next we describe our extension to the solving engine that allows instantiating conditional variables based on their activity status. As in the case of the disjunction constraint, we propose to view the activity status of a conditional variable as a search decision. The principle of random sampling of the solution space dictates that it might be desirable to represent both active and inactive statuses of each conditional variable with non zero probability in the resulting solution. Following this argument, we implement instantiation of conditional variables using the randomized decision procedure. The purpose of this procedure is to randomly decide on the activity status of the variable and to take actions according to the selected decision. Specifically, if the randomly taken decision is to make the variable active, its activity constraint must be added to the solver and the variable must be instantiated. Otherwise, the constraint opposite to the activity constraint of the variable must be added to the solver. Since the random decision can prove wrong and lead to no solution, the decision procedure creates a choice point where the randomly taken decision is checked first and its alternative is checked second in case the first branch leads to a search failure.

We observe that the requirement that an opposite constraint must exist for an activity constraint of the conditional variable is a limitation of our approach. However, the opposite constraint is defined for most of the common CSP constraints.

Like the disjunction constraint algorithm, the conditional instantiation algorithm described above was implemented using ILOG Solver. The outline of the algorithm is shown in Fig. 4. The algorithm *ConditionalGoal* takes a conditional variable represented as a CSP variable *var* and a CSP constraint *c* (activity constraint). To improve the performance of the algorithm we avoid backtracking in cases where the activity status of a conditional variable can already be determined at the current stage of the search. This is achieved by propagating the activity constraint of the variable prior to taking the random decision. If it is determined that the activity constraint is satisfied or violated, then the variable activity status is set deterministically and the corresponding actions are taken.

Observe that the algorithm described above can be used to instantiate a cluster of variables sharing the same activity constraint rather than a single variable. This provides a significant advantage over the null reformulation method where each variable needs to be instantiated regardless of its activity status. On the other hand, the proposed algorithm allows deactivating the whole cluster with a single condition check.

Recall that in our modeling, if an activity constraint involves a conditional variable it must also include the activity constraint of this variable. Therefore, when the algorithm adds the constraint *c* to the solver it can also imply the activity of additional variables required for the activity of *var*. Such implementation makes it possible to instantiate variables in an arbitrary order and not necessarily according to the topological ordering of the dependency graph defined in Section 3.2. Also, this achieves propagation of the activity status of conditional variables. Another observation is that in our algorithm, compatibility constraints propagate as soon as all of its variables become active. Indeed, recall that we represent a compatibility constraint C as an implication CSP constraint, where the left part is composed of activity constraints of all conditional variables in C, and the right part is C itself, formulated over CSP variables that correspond to both conditional and unconditional CCSP variables. Therefore, C begins to propagate when activity constraints of all the conditional variables it involves are satisfied.

```
goal ConditionalInstantiationGoal(var,c)
    Propagate(solver,c)
    if c is satisfied
         activity_status ← active
    else if c is violated
         activity_status ← inactive
    else
         activity_status ← rand(active,inactive)
    if activity_status = active
         return
         ChoicePoint(AndGoal(goal(c),InstantiateGoal(var)),
              goal(!c))
    else
         return ChoicePoint(goal(!c),
              AndGoal(goal(c),InstantiateGoal(var)))
```

Fig. 4. A randomized algorithm for conditional variable instantiation

Finally, we observe that like the algorithm for the disjunction constraint described in Section 4.1, the algorithm described above can be modified to take a probability parameter if some biasing for the activity status of a conditional variable is required.

4.3 Experimental Results

In this subsection we present experimental results to demonstrate the effectiveness of the random search algorithms described in the preceding subsections. Our results are obtained based on the implementation using ILOG Solver 6.3 as a CP engine. We performed the evaluation on Pentium M 1.7 GHz processor with 1GB of RAM.

First, we compare the performance of our random search algorithm for the disjunction constraint with the standard disjunction constraint propagation method implemented in ILOG Solver. Our test case includes one disjunction constraint on a single integer variable. The disjunction constraint is composed of four range constraints corresponding to sub ranges of the domain of the variable. The total number of valid values in all the ranges is 2^{10}. The test involves random instantiation of the variable subject to the disjunction constraint. We examined the performance for three cases, namely for variable domain size of 2^{16}, 2^{24} and 2^{31} respectively. For each case, we measured the run time of the solver, the number of search failures until the solution is found, and the memory usage of the solver. The results are summarized in Table 1. The figures shown in the table have been obtained as the average over 1000 random runs.

Table 1. Performance comparison results for disjunction constraint implementations by standard constraint propagation method implemented in ILOG Solver and custom random search algorithm *DisjunctionGoal*

Implementation	Domain Size	Run Time	Number of Fails	Memory Usage
ILOG Standard	2^{16}	1.2 ms	63	129 K
Constraint	2^{24}	100.8 ms	15970	836 K
Propagation	2^{31}	8850 ms	1407570	384697 K
	2^{16}	0.84 ms	0	105K
DisjunctionGoal	2^{24}	0.86 ms	0	105K
	2^{31}	0.88 ms	0	105K

The results below demonstrate clearly that while the standard disjunction constraint propagation method explodes in time and space, as the percentage of valid solutions in the variable domain decreases, the proposed random search algorithm achieves good performance regardless of the percentage of valid values.

Next we examine the performance of the proposed random search algorithm for conditional variable instantiation, *ConditionalGoal*. We compare the performance of *ConditionalGoal* with that of the CCSP implementation based on null reformulation as a CSP which has also been implemented using the ILOG Solver. As mentioned in Section 4.2, there exist methods for CCSP solving that achieve better performance than null reformulation. However, these methods require development of custom CP tools. Thus, the purpose of our experiments was to estimate the improvement that could be achieved within the framework of a traditional CP engine using our algorithm. Our test case includes two clusters of conditional variables of equal sizes, so that variables in the same cluster share the same activity constraint. In addition, the model involves unconditional variables and compatibility constraints involving both conditional and unconditional variables. We performed tests for three models of the structure described above but with different numbers of conditional variables, namely 10, 100, and 1000. For each test, we measured the run time and memory usage of each of the two algorithms averaged over 1000 random runs. Table 2 shows the results of the tests.

The results above show that the proposed method for conditional instantiation is more effective than null reformulation. Moreover, the advantage of the proposed algorithm becomes more evident with the increase of the clustering effect of conditonal variables in the model.

Table 2. Performance comparison results for conditional variable instantiation implementations by null reformulation and by custom random search algorithm *ConditionalGoal*

Implementation	Number of Conditional Variables	Run Time	Memory Usage
	10	0.8 ms	121 K
Null Reformulation	100	2.5 ms	271 K
	1000	33.4 ms	1789 K
	10	0.9 ms	121 K
ConditionalGoal	100	2.0 ms	213 K
	1000	18.1 ms	1219 K

5 Conclusion

In this paper we addressed some challenges arising in CP for the problem domain of functional test generation. Our focus has been on providing modeling and search solutions based on an existing CP engine. We argue that the use of a traditional CP engine for the test generation task both makes use of cutting edge CP technologies and saves a substantial implementation effort for test generator developers.

We considered both modeling and solving aspects of CP for test generation and provided solutions to specific problems arising in this domain. In particular, we addressed such a feature of CP for test generation as dynamic modeling, and proposed a method for modeling and instantiating conditional variables within the traditional CP framework with custom extensions. Also, we have identified specific modeling problems related to conditional variables in the modeling scheme characteristic of test generation domain. We defined constraint patterns associated with these modeling problems and proposed their implementation. Finally, we showed that replacing a standard disjunction constraint propagation method with a custom random search algorithm can boost the performance and thus overcome specific problems caused by large variable domains which otherwise could not be solved within reasonable time.

We intend to continue the research on the subjects discussed in this paper. In particular, we would like to generalize the constraint patterns presented in this paper by removing the current assumptions and restrictions. It would also be helpful to identify and implement additional constraint patterns arising in the context of multi-layer modeling. Moreover, regarding the random search algorithms presented in this paper, we believe that the performance of the proposed algorithm for conditional instantiation can be improved while remaining within the CP framework and we intend to perform further study in this direction.

Acknowledgements

The author would like to thank Asa Ben-Tzur and Boris Gutkovich for their valuable comments.

References

1. Bin, E., Emek, R., Shurek, G., Ziv, A.: Using a constraint satisfaction formulation and solution techniques for random test program generation. IBM Systems Journal 41(3), 386–402 (2002)
2. Gutkovich, B., Moss, A.: CP with Architectural State Lookup for Functional Test Generation. In: 11-th Annual IEEE International Workshop on High Level Design Validation and Test, 111–118 (2006)
3. ILOG Solver 6.3 Reference Manual (2006)
4. Gomes, C.: Randomized Backtrack Search. In: Milano, M. (ed.) Constraint and Integer Programming: Toward a Unified Methodology, pp. 233–283. Kluwer, Dordrecht (2003)
5. Smith, B.M.: Modeling for Constraint Programming. The 1-st Constraint Programming Summer School (2005)

6. Walsh, T.: Constraint Patterns. In: Rossi, F. (ed.) CP 2003. LNCS, vol. 2833, pp. 53–64. Springer, Heidelberg (2003)
7. IA-32 Intel Architecture Software Developer's Manual (2005)
8. Mittal, S., Falkenhainer, B.: Dynamic constraint satisfaction problems. In: Proceedings of 8-th National Conference on Artificial Intelligence, pp. 25–32 (1990)
9. Gelle, E., Faltings, B.: Solving Mixed and Conditional Constraint Satisfaction Problems. Constraints 8, 107–141 (2003)
10. Sabin, M., Freuder, E.C., Wallace, R.J.: Greater Efficiency for Conditional Constraint Satisfaction. In: Rossi, F. (ed.) CP 2003. LNCS, vol. 2833, pp. 649–663. Springer, Heidelberg (2003)
11. Geller, F., Veksler, M.: Assumption-Based Pruning in Conditional CSP. In: van Beek, P. (ed.) CP 2005. LNCS, vol. 3709, pp. 241–255. Springer, Heidelberg (2005)
12. Van Hentenryck, P., Saraswat, V., Deville, Y.: Design, Implementation, and Evaluation of the Constraint Language cc(FD). In: Podelski, A. (ed.) Constraint Programming: Basics and Trends. LNCS, vol. 910, pp. 293–316. Springer, Heidelberg (1995)
13. Lhomme, O.: An Efficient Filtering Algorithm for Disjunction of Constraints. In: Rossi, F. (ed.) CP 2003. LNCS, vol. 2833, pp. 904–908. Springer, Heidelberg (2003)
14. Würtz, J., Müller, T.: Constructive Disjunction Revisited. In: Görz, G., Hölldobler, S. (eds.) KI-96: Advances in Artificial Intelligence. LNCS, vol. 1137, pp. 377–386. Springer, Heidelberg (1996)

Using Virtual Coverage to Hit Hard-To-Reach Events

Laurent Fournier and Avi Ziv

IBM Research Laboratory in Haifa, Israel
{laurent, aziv}@il.ibm.com

Abstract. Reaching hard-to-reach coverage events is a difficult task that requires both time and expertise. Data-driven Coverage Directed Generation (CDG) can assist in the task when the coverage events are part of a structured coverage model, but is a-priori less useful when the target events are singular and not part of a model. We present virtual coverage models as a mean for enabling data-driven CDG to reach singular events. A virtual coverage model is a structured coverage model (e.g., cross-product coverage) defined around the target event, such that the target event is a point in the structured model. With the structured coverage model around the target event, the CDG system can exploit the structure to learn how to reach the target event from covered points in the structured model. A case study of using CDG and virtual coverage to reach a hard-to-reach event in a multi-processor system demonstrates the usefulness of the proposed method.

1 Introduction

Functional verification is widely acknowledged as one of the main challenges of the hardware design cycle [1,2]. The increasing complexity of hardware designs raises the need for the development of new techniques and methodologies that can provide the verification team with the means to achieve its goals quickly and with limited resources.

The current practice for functional verification of complex designs starts with the definition of a verification plan, comprised of a large set of events that the verification team would like to observe during the verification process. The verification plan is usually implemented using random test generators that produce a large number of test-cases and coverage tools that detect the occurrence of events in the verification plan. Analysis of the coverage reports allows the verification team to modify the directives for the test generators to better reach areas or specific events in the design that are not covered well [3].

The analysis of coverage reports and their translation to a set of test generator directives to guide and enhance the implementation of the test plan, results in major manual bottlenecks in the otherwise highly automated verification process. *Coverage directed test generation* (CDG) [4] is a technique to automate the feedback from coverage analysis to test generation. The main goals of CDG are to improve the coverage progress rate, to help reach non-covered events, and to

K. Yorav (Ed.): HVC 2007, LNCS 4899, pp. 104–119, 2008.
© Springer-Verlag Berlin Heidelberg 2008

provide many different ways to reach a given coverage event. Achieving these goals should increase the efficiency and quality of the verification process and reduce the time and effort needed to implement a test plan.

Data-driven CDG is a common approach to CDG. In data-driven CDG, the CDG system discovers relations between the directives that control the stimuli generation and coverage events based on observations of specific settings of the directives and the coverage events to which they lead. Reports on several CDG systems based on this approach have been published in recent years, including systems based on Bayesian networks [4], Markov chains [5,6], genetic algorithms [7], and inductive logic [8].

Data-driven CDG systems have been proven to work efficiently when there is some structure that connects the coverage events. The CDG system uses the structure to infer, from both the parameter settings that lead to covered events and the relation between these events and uncovered events, what are the best parameter settings for reaching the uncovered events. Cross-product coverage [9], which is the most commonly used form of structured coverage today, provides an easy-to-use structure for data-driven CDG. In cross-product coverage, the coverage model is defined as the cross-product of several attributes, each with a finite domain of possible values. Data-driven CDG systems can use this structure to break the problem of reaching a certain uncovered event into a set of smaller problems of reaching the values of each of the attributes of the event [8]. Simply stated, instead of trying to hit the event $< x_1, y_1 >$, the CDG system tries to reach the value x_1 in attribute X and the value y_1 in the attribute Y. Note that this approach works well even if the coverage attributes are not independent and are affected by the same parameters in the directive file.

While data-driven CDG works well for structured coverage models in general, and cross-product coverage models specifically, it is less capable of handling coverage models comprised of unrelated coverage events. This happens because the unstructured model does not provide the CDG system with an opportunity to learn how to reach uncovered events from covered events. To overcome this problem, we propose the use of *virtual coverage* to help data-driven CDG systems learn how to reach uncovered events in an unstructured coverage model or when only one coverage event exists.

The main idea is to define a structured coverage model, preferably a cross-product coverage model, around the target event, such that the target event is one of the coverage points in the structured events. With the structured coverage model around the target event, the CDG system can exploit the structure to learn how to reach the target event from covered points in the structured model. We named this idea virtual coverage because covering the structured coverage model is never a goal per-se of the verification process in general and the CDG system specifically. Instead, the CDG system tries to learn from this model and cover its coverage points only when this contributes to the goal of reaching the target event.

The idea of creating a virtual coverage model is reminiscent of a technique known as target enlargement [10] from the formal verification domain. There, the target space of the search is expanded into a set of nearby states. This expansion can be performed through an over-approximated BFS traversal from the target state or by adding additional states with small Hamming distance, to cite a few techniques. While the underlying concept of adding contributing states to the original coverage goal is similar in both target enlargement and virtual coverage, these techniques differ in one critical aspect: target enlargement uses these additional states as intermediate targets en route toward the real target, whereas in virtual coverage the important information is how these additional states are reached. This latter property makes it natural for exploitation in a learning environment in general and in a CDG framework in particular.

The virtual coverage model can be defined either manually or automatically. In manual definition, one can exploit domain knowledge to break the target event into smaller events and add related events or attributes around them. While manual definition can be difficult and time consuming, it has the potential to increase the chances of success when compared to any automated definition. This is due to the fact that the latter is naturally limited to more generic considerations. In effect, automatic definition can be realized by performing static and dynamic analysis on the design and the verification environment. For example, this can be done by breaking the target event expression into sub-expressions or finding the cone-of-influence of the target event.

To illustrate the benefits of using virtual coverage, we provide a case study where CDG and virtual coverage were used to reach a hard-to-reach event in a multi-processor system. The target event in this work was to fill a flow-through buffer in one of the nodes of the system. Direct attempts to reach this event yielded limited success. Defining a virtual coverage model around this event helped to identify relevant parameters that affect the utilization of the buffer. Designing and training a Bayesian network for the identified parameters and the virtual coverage model allowed our CDG system to generate directive files that reached the target event with a high probability.

The rest of the paper is organized as follows: Section 2 describes the concept of data-driven coverage directed generation and explains why it works well on structured coverage models. Section 3 presents virtual coverage as the solution for using data-driven CDG to reach singular coverage events. Section 4 describes the case study of filling the flow-through buffer. Conclusions and directions for future work are presented in Section 5.

2   Data-Driven Coverage Directed Generation

In the highly automatic verification environment used today, analysis of coverage information and usage of this information to direct the stimuli generator toward uncovered or lightly covered areas is one of the remaining human bottlenecks. Therefore, considerable effort is spent on finding ways to automate the covering procedure; that is, to close the loop of coverage analysis and stimuli generation. This automated feedback from coverage analysis to stimuli generation, known as *Coverage Directed stimuli Generation* (CDG), can reduce the manual work in the verification process and increase its efficiency. In general, the goal of CDG is to automatically provide the stimuli generator with directives that are based on coverage analysis [4]. Figure 1 presents a sketch of a verification environment with CDG. The CDG engine receives information from the coverage analysis tool about the state and progress of the coverage, and generates directives to the random test generator that are designed to achieve one or many of the CDG goals.

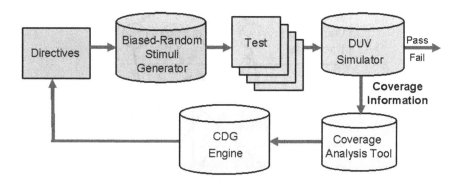

Fig. 1. Structure of a verification environment with CDG

There are two main approaches to CDG. In direct CDG, or model-based CDG, an external model of the design under verification is used to generate tests directives designed to accurately hit the coverage tasks [11]. In data-driven CDG, which is often called feedback-based CDG, the CDG system relies on inference of the required stimuli directives from observations of past behaviors [4]. This inference is usually done with machine learning techniques [4,7,8]. In this paper, we refer to CDG systems based on Bayesian networks [4], although the concept of virtual coverage described here can be used with other data-driven CDG approaches.

Bayesian networks are graphical models that represent distribution spaces [12]. A Bayesian network is a Directed Acyclic Graph (DAG) whose nodes are random variables and whose edges represent a direct influence between nodes. CDG based on Bayesian networks starts from the understanding that the space containing the directives to the stimuli generator on one side and the coverage model on the other side is a large distribution space. Moreover, it is assumed that this distribution space can be compactly represented using a Bayesian network.

The CDG process begins with construction of a Bayesian network model that describes the relations between the directives to the stimuli generator and the coverage space. Figure 2 illustrates a simple yet typical Bayesian network, which models an excerpt of the CDG setup used for covering dependencies in a pipeline of a microprocessor [4]. The network describes the relations between the directives that control the instructions generated by the stimuli generator and the coverage attributes of a cross-product coverage model. The network is comprised of input nodes that relate to stimuli generator directives (the top of the graph), coverage nodes (at the bottom), and hidden nodes, namely variables for which we don't have any physical evidence. The Bayesian network in Figure. 2 describes the causal relationships from the stimuli generation directives (causes) to the coverage model space (effects). For example, it encodes the expert knowledge that source and target registers together (nodes SR and TG in the figure) affect the ability to dispatch instructions into the pipelines.

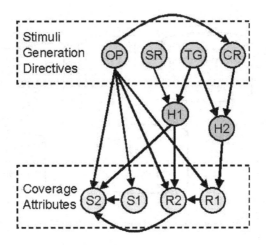

Fig. 2. Example of a Bayesian network for CDG

After being specified, Bayesian network structure is trained using a sample of directive files and the respective coverage events they cover. This is done by activating the simulation environment and constructing a training set out of the directives used and the resulted coverage tasks. The training process estimates the Bayesian network's parameters (i.e., set of conditional probability distributions).

To perform its job as the heart of a CDG system, the Bayesian network needs to infer the best directives to reach coverage events from coverage events it has seen during its training. To achieve this goal, the Bayesian network reduces the problem of reaching a specific goal into a set of simpler sub-goals.

Cross-product coverage models [9] provide a natural break of a specific coverage event into sub-goals of reaching the specific values of all the attributes in the coverage space. Simply stated, the CDG system can learn from positive and negative examples about the best settings of directives to reach a given value in each of the attributes and what settings should be avoided. Combing all the answers for the individual attributes together yields a good setting of the directives to the combined event. Figure 3 illustrates this. In the figure, covered events are marked by check marks and the target event is marked by a question mark (?). The CDG system can take advantage of events that reached the X coordinate of a target event but not the Y coordinate and events that reached the Y coordinate but not the X coordinate to infer how to reach the target event.

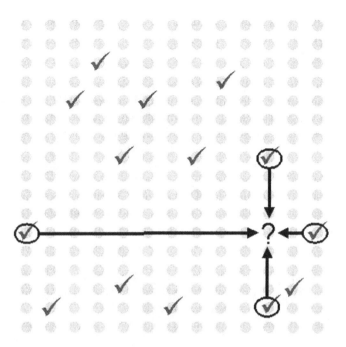

Fig. 3. Using the coverage model structure to learn how to reach an uncovered event in two-dimensional space

This simplified method works even when there are dependencies between the coverage attributes or when the coverage attributes depend on the same directive, as in the Bayesian network of Figure 2. In these cases, the structure of the Bayesian networks captures the dependencies between coverage attributes and their common dependencies. The learning algorithm can use the training data to catch the essence of the dependency encoded in the structure and save it in the conditional distributions stored in each node. When the network is queried about the most probable explanation for a coverage event, it can provide an answer that considers the dependencies in the network. For example, when the Bayesian network of Figure 2 is queried about the most probable explanation for instructions in stage 1 of the R and S pipes (nodes $R1$ and $S1$ in the figure), it looks for a setting in the opcode node (OP in the figure) that fits both the attributes *together*.

3   Virtual Coverage

While the common courtyard of the CDG technology includes a structured coverage model, there are many cases where the verification goals include generation of a very specific event, or a set of totally unrelated events (or at least events with unknown relationship). In the sequel, we will refer only to the case of a single event since it is simpler to describe; however, the results obtained can readily be adapted to the more general case of a set of uncorrelated events.

As an example of such a single event, Figure 4 depicts part of a typical modern superscalar microprocessor. It contains several (N) execution units implemented through pipelines including several stages. In regular operation, each instruction resides in a stage for a single cycle, after which it moves to the next stage and the stage becomes free for the next instruction. However, it may happen, for multiple different causes, that an instruction resides in a pipeline stage for several cycles. We then say that the instruction is held by the pipe stage, or that the pipe stage is on hold. Examples of causes for stages to be on hold are: long execution time of the instruction in the pipe, stalls caused by data hazards (i.e., the instruction is waiting for data), and stalls caused by control hazards (i.e., the instruction can not progress in the pipe because the following stage is on hold or other pipe ordering rules). When a pipe stage is on hold, the operations of previous stages in the pipeline are stalled. A particularly interesting event is one which occurs when all the initial stages of each pipeline are simultaneously on hold. In such a case, all the issue queues feeding the pipelines have to stall. This is undeniably an event of interest as it stresses the superscalar functionality, whereas the realization of this very specific scenario is, in general, extremely complicated.

It is obvious that when there is only a single event to generate such as the one above, there is no learning opportunity. The CDG learning engine cannot infer any knowledge on how to cover the desired event from the generation of other events. The trivial approach for coping with this problem is to invest extra-time in analyzing the event and to try to generate it by a process of trial and error.

To overcome this problem in a more efficient manner, we add a set of additional coverage goals, which we will call virtual coverage goals. On the one hand, they should be easier to cover than the original goal, and on the other hand their coverage should supply information to the CDG module on how to increase the probability of generating the original goal. More precisely, the solution adds structure around the targeted event to form a cross-product coverage model. Cross-product models have a structure defining a natural relationship, or distance, amongst the events and thus lend themselves well to learning. The CDG technology will then aim at covering the cross-product model as a means to reach the targeted event. In effect, the virtual coverage tasks yield a type of ladder to assist in reaching the targeted event. However, when driving the CDG technology, one should recall that the coverage of the virtual events is not a primary target. Hence, CDG should be operated in a special mode, in which it appropriately mixes exploration (with the hope of building the ladder) and exploitation (attempts to use the ladder to reach the desired event).

For example, the event described above can be generalized into a cross-product model in the following manner: select the state of each initial stage at the end of a cycle as an attribute, and have the virtual cross-product coverage model include all combinations of the possible states of the N initial stages. Note, there are many options for the possible state of a pipeline stage. However, the state of a stage can be a simple indicator whether the stage is on hold or not, in which

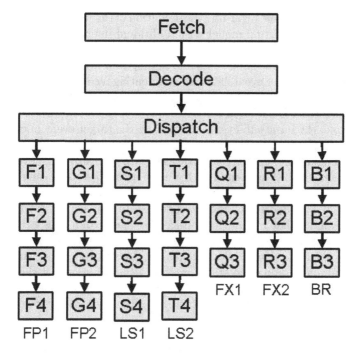

Fig. 4. Pipeline of a modern superscalar microprocessor

case the size of the cross-product space is 2^N events. A more detailed state can provide more information on the pipe stage and include values such as free (no instruction in the pipe stage), busy (instruction in the pipe stage but not on hold), on hold because of long execution time, on hold because of data hazard, etc. This more detailed state increases the size of the virtual space, but provides more opportunity for the CDG system to learn the relation between states of stages in the pipe.

An important issue regarding the use of virtual coverage models is how to define these cross-product models. The basic approach is to break the targeted corner case into sub-events, each with its own set of values, and define a coverage model represented by the Cartesian product of these values for each attribute. In our example, this basic approach can be easily applied because the target event is specified as a conjunction of sub-events. But there are many cases in which this basic approach cannot be easily used because breaking the event into sub-events is not intuitive. For example, consider the case of covering the event of forwarding data from stage $F2$ to stage $S3$ in the pipeline. For this event, the sub-events comprising it include: there is an instruction in stage $F2$, this instruction can forward data to $S3$, there is an instruction in $S2$, it can receive data from $S3$, certain timing constraints hold, etc. These sub-events are hidden in the definition of the microarchitecture of the processor. Therefore, expertise and domain knowledge are required to break the target event into necessary and sufficient sub-conditions.

Another intriguing issue regarding the definition of the virtual model is whether to augment the basic virtual model with additional information and how to do so. The basic virtual model can be augmented in two ways: adding values to the attributes representing the sub-events and adding new attributes that do not directly belong to the target event. The two augmenting techniques result in a larger virtual coverage space that contains more information, and thus more opportunities from which the CDG system can learn.

For example, the basic sub-events comprising the target event of our running example are whether a given stage in the pipeline is on hold or not. This definition of the sub-events results in a virtual coverage space with size of 2^N events. These basic sub-events can be augmented with a more detailed state of each pipe stage, as discussed above. This leads to a much larger coverage space with 5^N events. The additional information in the extended state can help the CDG system learn, for example, that free stages reduce the chance of stages being on hold in other pipes in future cycles. A second way to augment the virtual coverage model in our example is to add attributes for the states of other stages in the pipe. For example, adding the states of the execution stages of the pipes can help the CDG system learn how to bring instructions that are executed in these stages for long periods of time, thus increasing the probability of stalls caused by control hazards in the entry stages.

Note that increasing the size of the coverage space in a virtual model has less severe effects on the verification process because covering the virtual space is not a direct target of the verification process. Still, using a virtual space that is too large reduces the ability of the CDG system to learn it or requires more examples in the training set.

Our discussion so far dealt with the manual creation of a virtual coverage model. In such cases, the eventual success of the approach is dependent on the adequateness of the selected attributes and partition. If domain knowledge is low, it can be difficult to come up with an adequate set of attributes. To cope with this problem, cross-product models can be created in an automatic manner. In fact, even if domain knowledge is high, the automatic method might be preferred for efficiency and precision. There are several possible methods for automatic extraction of the virtual coverage model. For example, when the event is represented as a property in a property specification language, sub-properties can be used as the sub-events. When the target event is represented as a signal in the design, we can extract from the design the cone-of-influence of the event, and use each element in the cone-of-influence as an attribute in the cross-product model. This extraction can be done automatically through standard methods of static analysis on the design.

4   Case Study – Filling the Flow-Through Buffers

In this section we demonstrate the effectiveness of using virtual coverage and coverage directed generation to reach a very hard-to-reach event in an attempt to recreate a bug found in the lab.

4.1   The Target System

The bug occurred in the flow-through buffers in the multi-processor computing system depicted in Figure 5. The system is comprised of four nodes, with
each node containing several processing elements, caches, and memory and I/O
controllers (all of which are in the PE boxes in the middle of the nodes). The
nodes are connected using two one-way rings. The rings are used to transfer data
between nodes in the system, for example, to transfer data to and from remote
memories. To control the flow of transactions between the nodes, each node contains two flow-through buffers that store transactions in transition. Each ring
has one such buffer in each of the nodes. The flow-through buffer stores transactions only in intermediate nodes in the path from a source to a destination node.
Transactions arriving at a node from the previous node on the path are stored in
the flow-through buffer until the next node in the path is ready to accept them.
For example, a transaction from Node 0 to Node 2 traveling clockwise on the
inner ring is stored in the flow-through buffer of Node 1 until Node 2 is ready
to accept it. Transactions are always routed in the shortest path between the
source and destination nodes. For example, transactions from Node 2 to Node 1
are always sent on the outer ring counterclockwise. Transactions between nodes
on the opposite side of the ring are sent on the path with the least-loaded intermediate node. Note that because of the routing scheme and the number of
nodes in the system, the flow-through buffers store only transactions between
nodes on opposite sides of the ring.

The system can operate in two modes. In normal mode, all the nodes in the
system exist and both rings are fully operational. This mode is also called *closed
ring mode*. The system can also work in *open ring mode* when one (or more) of

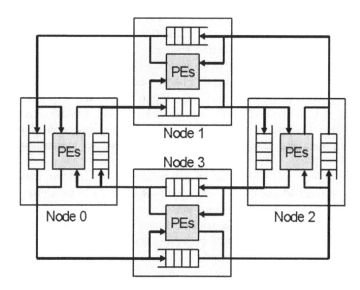

Fig. 5. Multi-processor system with flow-through buffer

the nodes are not available. In this case, only the parts of the rings that connect live nodes are available. For example, if Node 3 is missing, only the two links between Node 0 and Node 1 and the two links between Node 1 and Node 2 are working. In this case, the utilization of the flow-through buffers in Node 1 increases because there is only one path from Node 0 to Node 2 and back.

4.2   Description of the Bug

The bug found in the lab caused the flow-through buffers to overflow in some very rare conditions. Overflow in a flow-through buffer causes lost of transactions that are supposed to be stored in it. This, in turn, can cause the system to hang. Attempts to recreate the bug in simulation, and to understand the rare conditions that cause it, failed. However, analysis revealed that an important necessary condition for the bug is to fill the flow-through buffer and keep it full for long periods of time. Attempts to create this condition in simulation were not very successful. The verification team could reach this event only in a very small number of simulation runs and could not identify a proper setting of the verification environment that would increase the probability of this event.

By the time work with CDG and virtual coverage started, the bug was fixed, the fix was tested successfully at the lab, and the general belief was that overflow in the flow-through buffer was impossible in the fixed design. Still, to increase the confidence that the bug fix was correct, it was decided to put some effort into trying to reach the important necessary condition in simulation, or in other words, fill the flow-through buffer and keep it full for long periods of time. The exact goal was to fill the buffer and keep it full for more than 50 cycles.

4.3   Definition of the Virtual Coverage Model

The work to find directives that can reach the target event on a regular basis was done in three main steps. The first step was to define a virtual cross-product coverage space around the event to be used by the CDG engine as a foundation for learning how to reach the event. The second step was to design and train a Bayesian network as part of the CDG engine. The third step was to use the CDG engine with the trained Bayesian network to generate directives that could reach the event. To improve the chance of success, it was decided to simulate the system in open ring mode because this mode increases the utilization in the flow-through buffers.

The first step in the work was to create a mechanism that would help us measure if we reached the target event or how close to it we were. The mechanism that we used for this purpose was a cross-product coverage space that captured many properties of ring transactions. This virtual coverage space (we never intended to cover the entire coverage space or even portions of it) was designed in such a way that it would be able to provide the CDG engine with as much information as possible on how to reach the target event. In this sense, we were not satisfied with the two basic sub-events that built the target event, namely, the buffer is full and the time from arrival of the current transaction to the next departure from the buffer is more than 50 cycles. Instead, we used the two augmentation methods described in the previous section to increase the amount of information provided to the CDG system, thus increasing its ability to learn how to reach the target event. Overall, our coverage space was built of attributes of two types. First, we used attributes for the sub-events of the target event. In our case, these attributes were:

- The number of used entries in the buffer when a new transaction arrives. When this attribute was equal to the buffer capacity, the buffer was full. Note that for this attribute we used the number of used entries instead of an indicator whether the buffer is full or not to increase the information given to the CDG system.
- Time between arrival of the current transaction into the flow-through buffer and the next departure from the buffer. When the last free entry in the buffer was filled by a given transaction and the value of this attribute for this transaction was greater than 50, the target event was reached.

In addition to these two attributes, we used other attributes that were correlated to the target event. Adding these attributes to the Bayesian network helped it learn the relation between the parameters in directive files and behavior of transactions, so it could better reach the target event. Some of these attributes were:

- Number of cycles the transaction was in the flow-through buffer. This attribute was correlated to the service time required by the transaction, the utilization of the buffer when it arrived, and the ability of the flow-through buffer to send the transaction to the next node. All of these affected the ability to reach the target event.
- Time from arrival of the transaction to the arrival of the next transaction. This attribute was an indicator of the arrival rate to the buffer, and thus it was correlated to the buffer utilization.
- Transaction command (i.e., the opcode of the transaction). This attribute directly affected the service time of the transaction, thus contributing to the amount of time it was stored in the buffer.

4.4   The CDG System

The second step was designing and training a Bayesian network for the CDG engine. This step was done in several sub-steps that included identifying relevant parameters that affect the attributes in the coverage space, designing of the Bayesian network, and its subsequent training. More details on this CDG process can be found in [4].

To identify relevant parameters for creating transactions on the rings, we started with directive files designed by the verification team to reach the event. These directive files contained many parameters that were supposed to be relevant. To identify the parameters that had the greatest effect, we automatically generated a set of directive files that nicely span the parameter space using standard design-of-experiment techniques [13]. We then simulated the generated directive files and performed sensitivity analysis between the parameters and the coverage events created during the simulation. The sensitivity analysis was done using measures of mutual information [14] between parameters and coverage attributes and other statistical tests. This analysis helped reveal correlation between changing parameters and attributes in the coverage space. The parameters that we found to be most relevant included parameters that control instruction fetch and data loads and stores in the processing elements in each node, parameters that control i/o transactions in the nodes, and parameters that control addresses.

Next, we designed and trained the Bayesian network that relates the parameters and the coverage attributes. The network was designed based on information obtained from the sensitivity analysis and domain knowledge provided by the verification team. The network included nodes for the relevant parameters, the coverage attributes, and internal hidden nodes that captured specific aspects in the behavior of the system [4].

4.5   Results and Analysis

The trained network was used to generate directive files that increase the probability of the target event. This was done using the CDG engine by providing the trained Bayesian network with the target event as an evidence and querying for the most probable explanation to it in the parameters space [4]. In fact, we generated several sets of parameters using slightly different versions of the query and several versions of the Bayesian network. We simulated the generated directive files and simulation results indicated that most of these directive files hit the target event with a high probability and in many cases they were able to keep the buffer full for periods of time much longer than the required 50 cycles. See Table 1 for some details on the results.

Table 1. Results of flow-through buffer work

	Open Ring Mode	Closed Ring Mode
Probability of reaching the event	50%	30%
Maximal full time	200 cycles	140 cycles

After the success with the initial goal, we decided to improve our results by moving from the open ring mode to the normal closed ring mode. This was done by changing the configuration of the simulated system and adding parameters relevant to the forth node in the Bayesian network. After training the new Bayesian network, we generated a new set of directive files with the same goals (full utilization for long period of time). This new set of directive files was able to achieve its goals, although the results were not as good as in the open ring mode. The probability of reaching full utilization for more than 50 cycles was around 30% and the maximal full buffer utilization period was 130 cycles.

Analysis of the generated directive files revealed no surprises in how the CDG engine chose to set the various parameters. To reach the target event in the clockwise flow-through buffer in Node 1, the CDG engine generated parameters for Node 0 that pushed data to Node 2, parameters for Node 2 that pulled data from Node 0, and parameters for Node 1 that utilized the ring section from Node 1 to Node 2. Still, there are some differences between the directive files generated by the CDG engine and the manually created directive files. The main difference between the directive files was the control of the node with the flow-through buffer (Node 1 in the example above). The original understanding of the verification team was that activity of a node has very little influence on the utilization of its flow-through buffers. The sensitivity analysis revealed that the activity of the node has major effect on the utilization since the node can block the ring from the flow-through buffer because of its activity and need to communicate with the neighboring node. Another difference between the manual directive files and the ones generated by the CDG engine was in the split of distributions between the various processor and i/o commands that generate transactions on the ring. It seems that the CDG engine was able to find better distributions than the manual directive files. The effect of this difference on the ability of reaching the targeted event is less severe than the first difference, but it is not negligible.

The work described in this section took about four months and required about three person months and several workstations working almost non-stop either simulating directive files or training Bayesian networks. Although this work did not result in finding a bug in the flow-through buffers, it is a success because it helped achieve the goal of improving the confidence that no such bug exists. The high effort invested in the work indicates that using virtual coverage with manual definition of the coverage model and manual design of the Bayesian network is a solution only if the target event is extremely important and difficult to cover, or if the effort can be used for covering many events.

5   Conclusions

Data-driven coverage directed generation is shown to be an efficient means for closing the loop from coverage analysis to directives to the stimuli generation. These CDG systems rely on observations of directives to the stimuli generator and coverage events they reached, to infer how to reach uncovered events. This makes the systems inefficient when the target events are singular. To overcome this problem, we proposed the use of virtual coverage models. Virtual coverage models are structured coverage models defined around the singular target event. Virtual coverage models are used as a type of ladder to assist in reaching the targeted event without being the actual target of the verification process.

A case study of using CDG and virtual coverage to fill a flow-through buffer in a multi-processor system illustrates the usefulness of the proposed method in reaching hard-to-reach cases. This case study also demonstrates one of the main weaknesses of the proposed method, namely the effort required to achieve the goal. The high effort required means that this method is practical only if the target event is extremely important and difficult to cover. To overcome this problem and make virtual coverage useful in more cases, more automation in the process is required. This automation can come in two steps in the covering process. The first opportunity for increasing the automation is in the definition of the virtual coverage model. Another potential place for increasing the automation is in the design and implementation of the CDG system for covering the virtual coverage model. We are currently investigating both these opportunities.

Acknowledgments

We would like to thank Shai Fine for his help in developing the virtual coverage concept and his contribution to the flow-through buffer work. We also would like to thank Vesselina Zaharinova-Papazova, Steve Mittermaier, Jim Schafer, Jayen Ashar, and Ari Freund for their advice and work in the flow-through buffer work.

References

1. Bergeron, J.: Writing Testbenches: Functional Verification of HDL Models. Kluwer Academic Publishers, Dordrecht (2000)
2. Wile, B., Goss, J.C., Roesner, W.: Comprehensive Functional Verification - The Complete Industry Cycle. Elsevier, Amsterdam (2005)
3. Fournier, L., Arbetman, Y., Levinger, M.: Functional verification methodology for microprocessors using the Genesys test-program generator. In: Proceedings of the 1999 Design, Automation and Test in Europe Conference, pp. 434–441 (1999)
4. Fine, S., Ziv, A.: Coverage directed test generation for functional verification using Bayesian networks. In: Proceedings of the 40th Design Automation Conference, pp. 286–291 (2003)
5. Tasiran, S., Fallah, F., Chinnery, D.G., Weber, S.J., Keutzer, K.: A functional validation technique: biased-random simulation guided by observability-based coverage. In: Proceedings of the 2001 International Conference on Computer Design, pp. 82–88 (2001)
6. Wagner, I., Bertacco, V., Austin, T.: Microprocessor verification via feedback-adjusted Markov models. IEEE Transactions on Computer-Aided Design of Integrated Circuits and Systems 26(6), 1126–1138 (2007)
7. Bose, M., Shin, J., Rudnick, E.M., Dukes, T., Abadir, M.: A genetic approach to automatic bias generation for biased random instruction generation. In: Proceedings of the 2001 Congress on Evolutionary Computation CEC2001, pp. 442–448 (2001)
8. Hsiou-Wen, H., Eder, K.: Test directive generation for functional coverage closure using inductive logic programming. In: Proceedings of the High-Level Design Validation and Test Workshop, pp. 11–18 (2006)
9. Piziali, A.: Functional Verification Coverage Measurement and Analysis. Springer, Heidelberg (2004)

10. Yang, C.H., Dill, D.L.: Validation with guided search of the state space. In: Proceedings of the 35th Design Automation Conference, pp. 599–604 (1998)
11. Ur, S., Yadin, Y.: Micro-architecture coverage directed generation of test programs. In: Proceedings of the 36th Design Automation Conference, pp. 175–180 (1999)
12. Pearl, J.: Probabilistic Reasoning in Intelligent Systems: Netwrok of Plausible Inference. Morgan Kaufmann, San Francisco (1988)
13. Barker, T.: Quality by Experimental Design. CRC, Boca Raton, (1994)
14. Cover, T.M., Thomas, J.A.: Elements of Information Theory. John Wiley, New York, (1991)

Test Case Generation for Ultimately Periodic Paths

Saddek Bensalem[1], Doron Peled[2], Hongyang Qu[3], Stavros Tripakis[4],
and Lenore Zuck[5]

[1] Laboratoire Verimag, 2 Avenue de Vignate, 38610 Gieres, France
[2] Dept. of Computer Science, Bar Ilan University, Ramat Gan 52900, Israel
[3] Dept. of Computing, Imperial college London, London, SW7 2RH, UK
[4] Cadence Berkeley Labs, 2150 Shattuck Ave, 10th floor, Berkeley, CA 94704, USA
[5] Dept. of Computer Science, University of Illinois at Chicago, IL 60607, USA

Abstract. Software verification is a hard yet important challenge. In
general, the problem is undecidable. Nevertheless, it is still beneficial
to look at solutions that either restrict the generality or are heuristic in
nature (and do not guarantee to terminate). In this paper, we concentrate
on a related problem, that of verifying that a cycle in the flow chart
of a program does not terminate. We show some exact and sufficient
conditions for cycle nontermination, and provide application for program
verification. This allows us to check sequential and concurrent programs
against temporal properties, using a truly symbolic approach, and to use
temporal logic to guide the selection of test cases in such programs.

1 Introduction

Software verification was suggested four decades ago [6,10] as a method for validating that programs satisfy their specification. Although exhibiting beautiful
theoretical approach and introducing important influential concepts for software
development (such as the notion of an invariant), the goal of verifying software
in-the-large was not achieved. In particular, program verification is in general
undecidable, and requires considerable time and expertise. *Model Checking* [3,17]
restricts the verification problem to the finite state case. Different algorithmic
approaches are used to combat the inherently high complexity of the problem.
Completing the landscape of formal methods, *testing* is an approach for sampling and checking the code based on the intuition and experience of the testers.
Testing is often somewhat informal, prescribing various alternative strategies for
the generation of test cases.

The main formal methods provide a large spectrum of approaches for improving the quality of software. They offer a tradeoff between the amount of
effort required and the assurance provided. Combining these methods can help
alleviating some of their limitations. In particular, the method presented here is
related to [9], and is based on searching the flow chart paths, guiding the search
using the calculated path conditions, in the style of SPIN [11] . A specification
property, supplied by an experienced tester, corresponds to executions suspicious

K. Yorav (Ed.): HVC 2007, LNCS 4899, pp. 120–135, 2008.
© Springer-Verlag Berlin Heidelberg 2008

of being erroneous. The path condition for each generated path that potentially matches the given specification is checked for satisfiability. The checked path is extended by appending another flow chart node that also matches the checked property. When the path condition is found to be unsatisfiable, the search backtracks and a different successor node (if one exists) can be appended to the path. Upon success in finding a path that satisfies the specification, the path condition is instantiated with satisfying values before its execution. This forces testing the execution through the selected path while satisfying the given specification.

This, truly symbolic approach, is not a complete decision procedure for validating properties of software. Yet, it provides a useful human assisted tool, as was implemented in the PET system [9] for generating test cases based on a given temporal specification. A constraint that is lifted in this paper is that, formerly in [9], the specification provided refers to finite execution sequences. This is appropriate for sequential code, but sometimes not enough for concurrent algorithms or protocols that do not have a scheduled termination time. Moreover, since the given specification may refer to faulty executions, nonterminating executions may be exactly the goal of the search for errors in sequential code that *is* supposed to terminate.

In this paper we address the problem of calculating a path condition for infinite executions. This allows extending the application of the above symbolic approach for dealing with temporal properties, e.g., using the popular linear temporal logic (LTL) [14]. In particular, we apply a model-checking-like search for ultimately periodic (also called "lasso shaped") sequences. Such sequences consist of a finite prefix, followed by a cycle, of the flow chart graph. We provide some criteria for deducing that such an infinite sequence executes forever. Our approach, which calculates conditions for nontermination of code, complements the approach of proving termination (see e.g., [1,5,15,16]).

2   Overall Architecture

The system takes as input a program, which consists of either a single process or multiple processes. It translates it into flow charts, one per process. The system also takes as input an LTL specification, which is translated into a Büchi automaton. As an outcome of this latter transformation, the automaton nodes contain two kinds of assertions, referring to the program variables and the program labels (program locations), respectively. Inspired by model checking, we conduct a search for a path of the flow chart that satisfies the temporal specification. The search commences on the product of the flow chart(s) and Büchi automaton, for finding a path that satisfies the temporal property. Each node in the search is a tuple, containing a component from each process flow chart, and a component from the Büchi automaton. The two kinds of assertions in the Büchi automaton nodes are treated separately.

Program location assertions. The search algorithm progresses to extend the current path with a new tuple. Exactly one flow chart component progresses from its current location to a successor to form the next tuple (for modeling synchronous communication we would have to allow for two processes to progress simultaneously). While one flow chart progresses, the Büchi automaton also progresses from the current node to a successor. These simultaneous moves are done such that the flow chart nodes locations correspond to the location assertions (of the form $at\,l$) in the Büchi automaton nodes (and regardless of the Büchi automaton assertions on program variables, which will be taken into account when calculating the path conditions). That is, when assertion $at\,l$ is present in the Büchi component, where l is a label in process P, then the current node of the flow chart of P must be at location l (and similarly, when the assertion is $\neg at\,l$, it must *not* be at location l).

Program variables assertions. We calculated a path condition to execute the finite path searched so far, while satisfying the assertions on the program variables appearing in the Büchi components. We apply a SAT solver to the path condition. If the path condition is found to be unsatisfiable, the search is forced to backtrack.

A tuple of nodes reached during the search may correspond to multiple states, due to different values of the program variables. Therefore, when a tuple that is already in the search stack occurs again, we are not allowed to backtrack immediately as done in DFS (depth first search). Accordingly, we are also not allowed to conclude that a cycle that corresponds to an infinite execution is being closed when such a tuple is reached while already existing on the search stack. Thus, we may have such a tuple coexisting multiple times on the search stack. When such a tuple occurs in the search while being also in the search stack, it generates a path with a lasso shape. In case the periodic part includes an accepting Büchi component, we want to check whether this provides an infinite execution. We use the conditions in Section 4 to check whether the ultimately periodic path provides nonterminating execution sequence(s). Recall that since a tuple may occur on the stack several times, there are several potential lasso shapes that may need to be checked.

3 Preliminaries

3.1 Flow Charts

A flow chart of a program or a procedure is a graph, with nodes corresponding to assignments and conditions, and edges reflecting the flow of control between the nodes. A flow chart can be obtained by automatic compilation of sequential code. There are several kinds of nodes, where the most common are

- a *diamond* containing a *condition c*, which is a first order formula over the program variables, and
- a *box* containing an *assignment* of the form $x := e$, where x is a program variable and e is an expression,
- an *oval* denoting the *beginning* or *end* of the program (procedure).

Edges exiting from a diamond node are marked with either 'yes' or 'no' to denote the success or failure of the condition, respectively. A *transition* is either (1) an assignment node or (2) a condition together with the corresponding exit edge.

We assume that each node has a unique program counter value. This value can be a label that is provided with the code, or automatically generated by a translation tool. Passing an edge out of one node and into another entails a corresponding change of the program counter value. A *path* of a program is a sequence of consecutive nodes in the flow chart.

A *state* is a mapping providing values to the program variables from their predefined domain(s). An *augmented state* is a state that also provides a value to the program counter.

An *execution* is a (finite or infinite) sequence of states $g_0 \, g_1 \, \ldots \, g_n \, \ldots$, where each state g_i is obtained from its predecessor g_{i-1} by executing a flow chart node, as described below.

Let $\tau = t_1, t_2, \ldots t_n, \ldots$ be a path in a flow chart. Let $\Gamma = g_0, g_1, \ldots, g_n, \ldots$ be a sequence of non augmented program states (i.e., not including the program counter values). The sequence Γ is an *execution* of τ if for each $i \geq 1$ we have that

1. t_i is a diamond node, with condition c and the edge from t_i to t_{i+1} is marked with "yes". Then we must have $g_{i-1} \models c$ and $g_i = g_{i-1}$.
2. t_i is a diamond node, with condition c and the edge from t_i to t_{i+1} is marked with "no". Then we must have $g_{i-1} \models \neg c$ and $g_i = g_{i-1}$.
3. t_i is an assignment node labeled $x := e$. Then $g_i = g_{i-1}[e[g_{i-1}]/x]$, which denotes that g_i is the same as g_{i-1}, except for the variable x, which has the value of e, interpreted according to the state g_{i-1}.

In each one of these cases, we say that the transition t_i is *enabled* in the state g_{i-1}. We denote the executions of a path τ by $exec(\tau)$. Note that in a finite path, if the last node t_n is a diamond, we must also include its outgoing edge in order to figure out the complete information about the transition. An *augmented execution* must satisfy in addition that the program counter value in each state g_{i-1} corresponds to the location of the node t_i. In general, a path may correspond to multiple (augmented) executions.

A *path condition* $\wp_\mu(\varphi)$ for a given path of length (i.e., number of transitions) n is a first order predicate that is satisfied exactly by states from which the path μ *can* be executed, and moreover *each* such execution ends with a state satisfying φ. (A path condition does not refer to the program counter values.) Formally, this means that $\wp_\mu(\varphi)$ characterizes (i.e., is satisfied by) the set of all states g_0 such that there exist states $g_1, \ldots, g_n$, such that: (1) $g_0, \ldots, g_n$ is an execution of μ, and (2) $g_n \models \varphi$. When $\varphi = true$, we also denote the path condition by $\wp_\mu$. We extend the definition of a path condition also to infinite paths. Then φ must be *true*. In this case, the path condition is a predicate that is satisfied by states from which the path *can* be executed.

In deterministic code, there is at most one way of extending a state into an execution sequence. Hence, in this case, *all* the executions that start with a state satisfying $\wp_\mu$ are executions of the path μ (or, if μ is finite, the collection of paths with prefix μ).

We extend the notion of a path to cope with concurrent (multithreaded) software. In this case, we have a finite collection of flow chart graphs. A *concurrent path* is a sequence of nodes from the collection of graphs, such that the projection of the nodes on each flow chart forms a path. In other words, we *interleave* several flow chart paths to form a single concurrent path. In concurrent code, a *global* state is a combination of (local) states from the different processes. This gives a mapping of values to the collection of variables from all the processes. An execution is defined as before, but between any successive states there is a progress in one process. This assumes a model of programs with shared variables. For other models, e.g., that of synchronous message passing, two, or even more process, involved in sending and receiving a message, may progress from one global states to an adjacent one.

Concurrent code is thus *nondeterministic* in the sense that there may be more than a single way to continue the execution from the current state. For a nondeterministic code, the states satisfying the a path condition $\wp_\mu$ do not guarantee following the path μ; this is only true if, in addition, the nondeterministic choices will also agree with it. On the other hand, any state *not* satisfying the path condition $\wp_\mu$ will *not allow* the path μ to be executed. We still assume that transitions are deterministic in the sense that a transition that is executed from a particular state will result in a unique state.

In this paper we are in particular interested in *infinite paths*. In order to deal with infinite paths in situations where the execution terminates or deadlock, we can artificially extend each finite *maximal* path (including in particular concurrent paths), i.e., a path that cannot be extended by an executable flow chart node, by adding some fixed no-op assignment node (for example, containing $x := x$). We will use the following properties of $\wp$:

Compositionality: $\wp_{\sigma\rho}(\varphi) = \wp_\sigma(\wp_\rho(\varphi))$.
Monotonicity: If $\varphi \to \psi$ then $\wp_\mu(\varphi) \to \wp_\mu(\psi)$.
Distribution over Conjunction: $\wp_\mu(\varphi \wedge \psi) = \wp_\mu(\varphi) \wedge \wp_\mu(\psi)$.

3.2   Calculating Finite Path Conditions

We calculate the path condition backwards. The *accumulated path condition* represents the condition to move from the current point in the calculation to the *end of the path*. The current point in the path moves at each step in the calculation of the path condition backwards, over one node to the previous point (edge). We start with the condition *true* at the end of the path, if we are computing $\wp_\mu$, or with the condition φ, in case we are computing $\wp_\mu(\varphi)$. That is, for an empty path ϵ, $\wp_\epsilon = true$ and $\wp_\epsilon(\varphi) = \varphi$. The calculation of the path condition for a path $t\sigma$, can thus be defined formally according to cases of the executed transition t as follows:

- t is a diamond with condition c and exit marked as "yes". Then $\wp_{t\sigma} = \wp_\sigma \wedge c$.
- t is a diamond with condition c and exit marked as "no". Then $\wp_{t\sigma} = \wp_\sigma \wedge \neg c$.

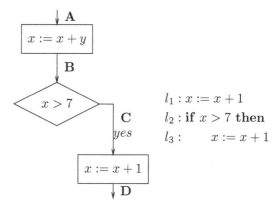

Fig. 1. An example path

- t is an assignment node, labeled $x := e$. Then $\wp_{t\sigma} = \wp_\sigma[e/x]$. (The notation $\phi[e/x]$ means replacing textually in the predicate ϕ every free occurrence of x by e.)

We can also calculate the *accumulated variable transformation* of a path μ. This is a transformation of the set of variables (a multiple assignment) of the path. Again, we perform the calculation backwards. We denote such a transformation as $\bar{x} := tr_\mu(\bar{x})$, i.e., a set of assignments to the variables $\bar{x}$. Denote by $tr(\bar{x})[e/x]$ the transformation where we substitute syntactically each occurrence of x in any right hand side of assignment in $tr(\bar{x})$ by e. Denote also by $tr_\mu(\bar{x})\triangle x := e$ the set of assignments obtained by adding to $tr_\mu(\bar{x})$ the assignment $x := e$ only if it does not contain already an assignment to x (otherwise, $tr_\mu(\bar{x})$ remains unchanged). We then have the following cases:

- t is a diamond, then $tr_{t\sigma}(\bar{x}) = tr_\sigma(\bar{x})$.
- t is an assignment, labeled $x := e$, then $tr_{t\sigma}(\bar{x}) = tr_\sigma(\bar{x})[e/x]\triangle x := e$.

Calculating the path condition for the example in Figure 1 backwards, we start at the end of the path, i.e., point **D**, with a path condition *true* and empty transformation. Going backwards to point **C**, we have still an accumulated condition *true*, and the transformation becomes $x := x+1$. At point B we obtain the accumulated path condition $x > 7$, while the transformation does not change. Then going back to point **A**, the path condition becomes $x + y > 7$, and the transformation becomes $x := x + 1 + y$.

We can henceforth represent any finite path μ using the pair $\wp_\mu \hookrightarrow tr_\mu$. The path in Figure 1 can then be represented by $x + y > 7 \hookrightarrow x := x + 1 + y$.

4   Conditions for Nontermination of Cycles

Consider the following problem: given a finite path σ followed by a cycle ρ; find conditions under which the ultimately periodic (lasso shaped) $\sigma\rho^\omega$ executes. Ultimately, we would like to compute $\wp_{\sigma\rho^\omega}$.

4.1 The Equality Method

We handle here the case where the execution of the path ρ starts each time with the same variable values, i.e., same state. Let $\bar{x}$ be the state before executing ρ, and $\bar{x}'$ be the state afterwards. Then we are interested in the case where $\bar{x} = \bar{x}'$, or equivalently, $\bar{x} = tr_\rho(\bar{x})$, since $\bar{x}' = tr_\rho(\bar{x})$. We can propagate this condition backwards to obtain the following condition on $\sigma\rho^\omega$:

$$\wp_{\sigma\rho} \wedge \wp_\sigma(\wp_\rho \wedge \bar{x} = tr_\rho(\bar{x}))$$

This is a *stronger* condition than $\wp_{\sigma\rho^\omega}$. This condition can be simplified (using the distribution of the $\wp$ predicate over conjunction) into

$$\wp_{\sigma\rho} \wedge \wp_\sigma(\bar{x} = tr_\rho(\bar{x})) \tag{1}$$

For nondeterministic programs, a similar result asserts that condition (1) is satisfied exactly by those states from which $\sigma\rho^\omega$ *can* be executed, given the right nondeterministic choices.

As an example, consider the following program.

```
0: z:=z-1;
1: while x>0 do begin
2:            y:=x;
3:            x:=(x*2+z+y)/3 end;
```

Let σ be the assignment z:=z+1 and ρ be one iteration of the loop. The transformation of the path ρ is then $(x, y) := ((x \times 2 + z + x)/3, x)$. We have $\wp_\rho = \wp_{\sigma\rho} = x > 0$. The condition for keeping the variable values the same over the loop ρ, i.e., $\bar{x} = tr_\rho(\bar{x})$ is $x = (x \times 2 + z + x)/3 \wedge y = x$, which is equivalent to $z = 0 \wedge y = x$. Pushed backwards over σ, which consists of the node $z := z - 1$, we obtain $\wp_\sigma(\bar{x} = tr_\rho(\bar{x})) = z - 1 = 0 \wedge y = x$, or equivalently $z = 1 \wedge y = x$. Thus, overall, the condition for executing the cycle with no change in value after each complete iteration, after initially decrementing z is $x > 0 \wedge z = 1 \wedge y = x$.

4.2 The Monotonicity Method

Consider the following trivial example.

```
0: x:=1;
1: while x>0 do
2:            begin x:=x+1 end;
```

Let σ be the assignment x:=1 and let ρ be one iteration of the loop. We have $\wp_{\sigma\rho} = true$. However, the condition $\bar{x} = tr_\rho(\bar{x})$ is in this case $x = x + 1$, which is equivalent to *false*. Thus, the equality predicate is also *false*. To be able to handle examples such as this one we introduce the monotonicity method described below.

For a loop ρ to execute infinitely many times, it is sufficient to find a loop invariant I such that $I \rightarrow \wp_\rho(I)$. Thus, the loop invariant guarantees that the loop executes once and after that the invariant continues to hold. The weakest such potential invariant is $I = \wp_\rho(true)$. To see this, notice that since $I \rightarrow true$, we have by monotonicity of $\wp_\rho$ that $\wp_\rho(I) \rightarrow \wp_\rho(true)$. Recall that we require $I \rightarrow \wp_\rho(I)$. Thus, if this holds, by transitivity, $I \rightarrow \wp_\rho(true)$. Now if we set $I = \wp_\rho(true)$, in the implication $I \rightarrow \wp_\rho(I)$, we obtain that $\wp_\rho \rightarrow \wp_{\rho\rho}$ is a sufficient condition for loop nontermination. Note that $\wp_{\rho\rho} = \wp_\rho(\wp_\rho) = \wp_\rho \wedge \wp_\rho[tr_\rho(\bar{x})/\bar{x}]$. The first conjunct is the condition to execute ρ once. The second conjunct expresses the condition to execute ρ after the first iteration; that is, $\wp_\rho$ holding *after* an iteration of ρ, then this condition is relativized to the values of the variables *before* the first iteration of ρ. Thus, the condition $\wp_\rho \rightarrow \wp_{\rho\rho}$ can be rewritten as

$$\wp_\rho \rightarrow \wp_\rho[tr_\rho(\bar{x})/\bar{x}] \tag{2}$$

Condition (2) states that if the loop can be executed once, then it can be executed indefinitely. To handle the case where σ precedes the infinite iteration of ρ, we have the following condition:

$$\wp_{\sigma\rho} \rightarrow \wp_\sigma(\wp_\rho[tr_\rho(\bar{x})/\bar{x}]) \tag{3}$$

We now proceed, for simplicity of the presentation, to elaborate on how to check Condition (2).

Consider first the simple case where the path condition $\wp_\rho$ is of the form $e \geq 0$ and let $e' = e[tr_\rho(\bar{x})/\bar{x}]$. Then Condition (2) is equivalent to $e \geq 0 \rightarrow e' \geq 0$. In this case, a sufficient condition is $e' \geq e$. That is, the value of the expression e is monotonically nondecreasing during the execution of the ρ loop. The same idea works when instead of $e \geq 0$, $\wp_\rho$ is of the form $e > 0$; in this case the condition is $e' > e$. When we have $e_1 \geq e_2$ or $e_1 > e_2$, we can use $e = e_1 - e_2$. or more general $\wp_\rho$ conditions, we can apply the following principles:

Conjunction principle. When $\wp_\rho$ is a conjunction $e_1 \geq 0 \wedge e_2 \geq 0$, it is sufficient to show that $e_1' - e_1 \geq 0$ and $e_2' - e_2 \geq 0$. To see this, observe that if $\wp_\rho$ is of the form $e_1 \geq 0 \wedge e_2 \geq 0$, then $\wp_\rho[tr_\rho(\bar{x})/\bar{x}]$ is of the form $e_1' \geq 0 \wedge e_2' \geq 0$, where $e_i' = e_i[tr_\rho(\bar{x})/\bar{x}]$, for $i = 1, 2$. Thus, Condition (2) is in this case equivalent to $(e_1 \geq 0 \wedge e_2 \geq 0) \rightarrow (e_1' \geq 0 \wedge e_2' \geq 0)$.

Disjunction principle. When $\wp_\rho$ is a disjunction $e_1 \geq 0 \vee e_2 \geq 0$, we strengthen the path condition to either $e_1 \geq 0$ or $e_2 \geq 0$. It is then sufficient to show either that $e_1' - e_1 \geq 0$ or that $e_2' - e_2 \geq 0$, respectively. This means requiring at least one of the disjuncts to grow monotonically. Of course, in this way we give up the ability to handle the case where expressions alternate in growth.

An equality $e_1 = e_2$ can be transformed into a conjunction $e_1 - e_2 \geq 0 \wedge e_2 - e_1 \geq 0$ and the conjunction principle can then be applied. An inequality $e_1 \neq e_2$ can be transformed into a disjunction $e_1 - e_2 > 0 \vee e_2 - e_1 > 0$ and the disjunction principle (which effectively strengthens the inequality by ignoring one of the disjuncts) may then be applied. Applying these rules repeatedly allows us to treat more complicated Boolean combinations.

The monotonicity method can easily handle the above example (where $\wp_\rho$ is $x > 0$ and $x + 1 = e' > e = x$ holds for all x). Still, monotonicity provides only a sufficient and not a necessary condition for nontermination. To see this, consider the loop $\mu: x \geq 0 \hookrightarrow (x, y) := (x - y, y/2)$, where variables x and y take rational values. Assume initially $y > 0$ and $x > 2 \times y$. In that case, the loop does not terminate. However, the value of x is reduced and converges towards the value of $x - 2 \times y$ (with the initial values of x and y) rather than diverges.

4.3   Mixed Ultimately Periodic Paths

In an infinite state space, nontermination of execution can be caused by a non-ultimately periodic path. Consider the following program, where the condition $PowerTwo(y)$ holds when y is a power of two of some natural number. Consider the following code:

```
α: while x>1 do
            begin β: if PowerTwo(x-1) then
                         γ: x:=4*(x-1)
            else        δ: x:=x-1        end
```

For example, we can have the following value of x, when the loop starts with $x = 4$:

$$4 \to 3 \to 8 \to 7 \to 6 \to 5 \to 16 \to 15 \to \ldots$$

We distinguish the condition β with the "yes" exit as β^+, and with the "no" exit as β^-. Then the nonterminating executions are not ultimately periodic. Instead, the number of $\beta^-\delta$ iterations roughly doubles (from k times to $(k \times 2) + 1$ times) between each successive iterations of $\beta^+\gamma$.

We provide a solution that works for deterministic code (that is, we do not allow any other processes to interleave with this loop). Our solution is also limited to identifying conditions for ultimately periodic executions when a temporal property is not given. We shrink each one of the paths i inside the loop into a path condition and transformation pair $c_i \hookrightarrow \bar{x}_i := \bar{e}_i$. As the code is deterministic, we obtain a transition t that includes a choice between all these pairs, depending on the (unique) condition that holds in the current state. Then path condition of $t\sigma$ (executing the transition t, followed by the sequence σ) can be formulated as follows:

$$\wp_{t\sigma}(\varphi) = \bigvee_i (c_i \wedge (\wp_\sigma(\varphi)[\bar{x}/\bar{e}_i])) \tag{4}$$

In the above example we shrink the path $\beta^+\gamma$ into $PowerTwo(x - 1) \hookrightarrow x := 4 * (x - 1)$, and the path $\beta^-\delta$ into $\neg PowerTwo(x - 1) \hookrightarrow x := x - 1$. We thus combine these two alternatives, which are mutually disjoint into a new kind of transition that selects (denoted using the operator $\square$) the transformation depending on the truth value of the condition:

$$t: PowerTwo(x - 1) \hookrightarrow x := 4 * (x - 1)\square\neg PowerTwo(x - 1) \hookrightarrow x := x - 1$$

The calculation of $\wp_{t\sigma}$ is defined in Equation (4). Let B be the obtained transition, representing the loop body, and α is the loop condition. Then it is easy to check that in this case $\wp_{\alpha B} \rightarrow \wp_{\alpha B \alpha B}$ holds.

5   Translating Temporal Specification

Our aim is to guide the search for a test case or an execution sequence matching the specification using a temporal property. The property may refer to labels that such paths pass, and to some relationship between the program variables. It can be given in various forms, e.g., an automaton or a temporal formula. The translation and search algorithm described in this section are an adaptation of the ones in [9]. The main changes from previous work are the use of specification on infinite sequences, and the use of partial order reduction. Due to limited space, the description here is terse, and the reader is referred to [9].

The specification includes the following two kinds of *basic formulas*. *Program counter predicates* are of the form $at\ l$, where l is a program counter label. If there are several processes, we may need to disambiguate this kind of predicate by mentioning also the process name, e.g., $P_3\ at\ l$. Such a predicate holds in a state if the program counter is at the location whose label is mentioned, i.e., on the edge *entering* a node with the mentioned label. *Program variables assertions* include the program variables (and do not include further Boolean operators). Such a predicate is interpreted over a state according to the usual first order semantics.

These formulas may be combined using Boolean and temporal operators. Our implementation uses the Linear Temporal Logic (LTL) syntax as follows:

$$\varphi ::= (\varphi)\ |\ \neg\varphi\ |\ \varphi \vee \varphi\ |\ \varphi \wedge \varphi\ |\ \bigcirc\varphi\ |\ \Box\varphi\ |\ \Diamond\varphi\ |\ \varphi\,\mathcal{U}\,\varphi\ |\ p$$

where $p \in \mathcal{P}$, with $\mathcal{P}$ a set of basic formulas. For a propositional sequence σ over $2^{\mathcal{P}}$, we denote the ith state (where the first state is numbered 0) by $\sigma(i)$, and the suffix starting from the ith state by $\sigma^{(i)}$. Let $|\sigma|$ be the length of the sequence σ, which is a natural number. The semantic interpretation of LTL as follows:

- $\sigma \models \bigcirc\varphi$ iff $\sigma^{(1)} \models \varphi$.
- $\sigma \models \varphi\,\mathcal{U}\,\psi$ iff $\sigma^{(j)} \models \psi$ for some $j \geq 0$ such that for each $0 \leq i < j$, $\sigma^{(i)} \models \varphi$.
- $\sigma \models \neg\varphi$ iff it is not the case that $\sigma \models \varphi$.
- $\sigma \models \varphi \vee \psi$ iff either $\sigma \models \varphi$ or $\sigma \models \psi$.
- $\sigma \models p$ iff $\sigma(0) \models p$.

The rest of the temporal operators can be defined using the above operators in a standard way.

The specification is translated into a Büchi automaton [7]. Let (S, Δ, I, F, L) be a finite state automaton with nodes (states) S, a transition relation $\Delta \subseteq S \times S$, initial nodes $I \subseteq S$, accepting nodes $F \subseteq S$ and a labeling function L from S to some set of labels. A *run* of the automaton is a maximal (finite or infinite) sequence of nodes $s_1 s_2 \ldots s_n$ (n can be ω for an infinite sequence) where $s_1 \in I$, and for each $1 \leq i < n$, $(s_i, s_{i+1}) \in \Delta$. An *accepting* run satisfies further that it passes infinitely many times through some state in F.

The *property automaton* is $A = (S^A, \Delta^A, I^A, F^A, L^A)$. Each property automaton node is labeled by a set of negated or non-negated basic formulas. The flow chart can also be denoted as an automaton $B = (S^B, \Delta^B, I^B, S^B, L^B)$ (where all the nodes are accepting, hence $F^B = S^B$). Each node in S^B is labeled by (1) a single program counter value, (2) a node shape, e.g., box or a diamond, respectively), and (3) an assignment or a condition, respectively. The transition relation Δ^B corresponds to the edges in the flow chart. The initial nodes are $I^B \subseteq S^B$.

We can extend the automaton B to represent a collection of n flow charts that execute concurrently. In this case, S^A will be the set of n-tuples of flow chart nodes, one per each flow chart. The relation Δ^B forces *exactly one* flow chart to progress according to its flow chart edge, while other flow chart nodes are not changed. I^B will be an n-tuple of initial nodes, where each component is an initial node in the corresponding flow chart.

The *intersection* between a property automaton A and a flow chart B is an automaton $A \times B = (S^{A \times B}, \Delta^{A \times B}, I^{A \times B}, F^{A \times B}, L^{A \times B})$ as follows:

- The nodes $S^{A \times B} \subseteq S^A \times S^B$ have matching labels: if $(a, b) \in S^{A \times B}$ then the program counter of the flow chart(s) node (tuple) b must satisfy the program counter predicate(s) labeling the property automaton node a.
- The transitions are $\{((a, b), (a', b')) | (a, a') \in \Delta^A \wedge (b, b') \in \Delta^B\} \cap (S^{A \times B} \times S^{A \times B})$.
- The initial states are $I^{A \times B} = (I^A \times I^B) \cap S^{A \times B}$.
- The accepting states are $F^{A \times B} = (F^A \times S^B) \cap S^{A \times B}$. Thus, membership in $F^{A \times B}$ depends only on the A automaton component being accepting.
- The label on a matched pair (a, b) in the intersection contains the union of labels from a and b.

Note that acceptance of runs by the intersection automaton as defined above ignores the program variable assertions on the nodes S^A and the assignments and conditions labeling the nodes S^B. The program variable assertions will affect the path condition, as will be shown later.

We assume that each node $s \in S^A$ of the property automaton is annotated by some set of program variables assertions whose conjunction is η_s and some set of program counter predicates whose conjunction is μ_s. This annotation is generated automatically when translating an LTL formula into an automaton.

Now consider an accepting sequence of the intersection of the property automaton A and the flow chart B of the form $\tau = t_1, t_2, \ldots, t_n \ldots$. Projecting τ over the components of the flow chart gives a path. Thus, we may observe τ as a path with some assertions added to it.

We are interested in the set of execution sequences of τ that also satisfy the corresponding temporal property expressed using the automaton A. When A is constructed as a translation of an LTL property ψ then $\rho \models \psi$. We denote the condition for such executions by $\wp_{\tau, \psi}$.

Consider first the simpler case of a temporal specification on program counters only. For example, executions of paths that pass through label l_2 twice may be suspected of leading to some incorrect use of resources. The tester may express such paths in LTL as

$$(\neg at\, l_2)\mathcal{U}(at\, l_2 \wedge \bigcirc((\neg at\, l_2) \wedge ((\neg at\, l_2)\mathcal{U}\,at\, l_2))). \tag{5}$$

Note that since the above temporal specification ψ involves only the program counters but not the program variables, for each path ρ there can be only two cases:

- All the executions of $exec(\rho)$ satisfy ψ, or
- None of the executions of $exec(\rho)$ satisfy ψ.

In the former case, $\wp_{\tau,\psi} = \wp_\tau$ and in the latter case $\wp_{\tau,\psi} = false$. In this case, by taking the intersection of the property automaton A for ψ and the flow chart B, the paths that are the runs of the intersection are exactly those that have all of their executions satisfying ψ .

In symbolic execution, we are often incapable of comparing states. Consequently, we cannot check whether we reach the same state again. We may not assume that two nodes in the flow chart with the same program counter labels are the same, as they may differ because of the values of the program variables. We also may not assume that they are different, since the values of the program variables may be the same.

We now show how to take into account also the program variables assertions. The specification formula (5) was based only on the program counters. Suppose that we also want to express that when we are at the label l_2 for the first time, the value of x is greater or equal to the value of y, and that when we are at the label l_2 the second time, x is at least twice as big as y. We can write this specification as follows:

$$\psi = (\neg at\, l_2)\mathcal{U}(at\, l_2 \wedge x \geq y \wedge \bigcirc((\neg at\, l_2) \wedge ((\neg at\, l_2)\mathcal{U}(at\, l_2 \wedge x \geq 2 \times y)))) \tag{6}$$

The translation from a temporal formula to an automaton results in the program variables assertions $x \geq y$ and $x \geq 2 \times y$ labeling two of the nodes of the resulted automaton. They do not participate in the automata intersection, but we need to incorporate them when calculating the path condition $\wp_{\tau,\psi}$. According to the (rather technical) definition of the automata intersection, the conjunction of the program variables assertions labeling the property automaton nodes is assumed to hold in the path condition *before* the effect of the matching flow chart node. Accordingly, if we add a condition η from some property automaton node to an assignment node in the flow chart, the assignment will take effect right after η has to hold.

In general, when calculating a path condition for a path τ obtained from the intersection of the property automaton for a property ψ and a flow chart, we need to take into account the program variables assertions that appear on it (coming from the property automaton components). We can do that by transforming the path as follows. Observe that each node in the intersection is a pair (a, b), where a is a property automaton node, and b is a flow chart node in the current path. The label of b agrees with the program counter predicates in a. Otherwise, the path is automatically rejected to be in the intersection during the search (and $\wp_{\tau,\psi} = false$). We transform each such pair into two sequential nodes. First, b remains as it appears in the flow chart. We insert a new diamond node to the current path, just before b. The inserted node contains as its condition the conjunction of the program variables assertions labeling the node a (and *true* if there are no program variables assertions labeling a). The edge between the new diamond and b is labeled with 'true' corresponding to the case where the condition in a holds. The edge that was formerly entering b now enters the new diamond. Then the path condition $\wp_{\tau'}$ for the path τ' obtained by the transformation is exactly $\wp_{\tau,\psi}$. We use the methods introduced in Section 4 on the resulted (and ultimately periodic) path τ' rather than on τ.

It is important too observe vethat the LTL to automata translation generates nodes that are labeled by a set of basic formulas, either negated or non-negated. Our separation of the search depends on the fact that we do not allow any basic formula that includes both program variables and program counters, as in $(at\ l_3) \times v$. Such formulas can usually be translated (unfortunately with some increase to the size of the formula) into formulas that make the required separation.

Independence among program actions is useful for reducing the effective state space needed in searching through a finite state system. Model checking for reducing the search space using independence or commutativity are generically called *partial order reduction methods* see, e.g., [4]. Two nodes t_1 and t_2 in different processes will be called *independent* if their sets of referred variables (variables tested or set by the nodes) are disjoint. Let T be the set of all the nodes of a tested program. We denote by $I \subseteq T \times T$ the independence relation between the nodes. Let v and w be two sequences of nodes, then the following holds (as can be proved on the possible nodes t_1 and t_2):

$$\wp_{vt_1t_2w}(\varphi) = \wp_{vt_2t_1w}(\varphi) \tag{7}$$

Note that if a temporal specification is involved, it must not distinguish between the executions vt_1t_2w and vt_2t_1w.

This observation can be generalized as follows (and proved by induction): when w is obtained from v be repeatedly permuting adjacent independent nodes, then

$$\wp_v(\varphi) = \wp_w(\varphi) \tag{8}$$

Two such sequences v and w are called *trace equivalent* [13]. This observation may reduce considerably the number of paths through which we search. In particular, there is no need to search through equivalent paths.

We use a reduction method that is suggested in [2]. For finite state spaces, the reduction is shown to coincide with sleep sets [8]. Like sleep sets, for finite systems, it is not guaranteed that a DFS will visit all of the program states. However, in our case, the state space is essentially infinite, and effectively cycle free; as we do not identify two identical tuples of control points reached during the search as the same. The result is that we do not lose coverage (the reduction technique in [2] also does not lose coverage when using BFS instead of DFS).

Since we search through an infinite state space, we apply iterative deepening, starting with some depth of search and increasing it gradually, as long as we did not find the desired path. Now consider the case where a tuple that exists in the search stack, at the end of a path σ, appears again, with a path ρ between these occurrences If an accepting Büchi component appears on ρ, we check whether $\sigma\rho^\omega$ is executable, using the techniques of Section 4. As discussed before, due to limited knowledge on values of program variables, such a tuple can exist more than once on the search stuck, and such a comparison and check then is required per each occurrence.

6   Implementation and Discussion

The equality and monotonicity methods have been implemented in Java. We use Mathematica [18] to compute the satisfiability of boolean formulas. We tested our methodology with the following example. A system is composed of two concurrent programs, as follows:

```
l1: while x<=y and z>0 do begin        l5: while x>=y do begin
l2:      y := y / 2;                    l6:      x := x - 1;
l3:      x := x * 2;                    l7:      y := y + 1
l4:      z := z - 1 end;                l8:      z := z * 2 end;
```

We assume that the variables x, y and z are integers. An interesting point in the example is that it contains infinitely many infinite loops if x, y and z can never overflow. In fact, if they are rationals, we can obtain preconditions like $y = 4 \wedge x = 2 \wedge z = \frac{4}{3}$ (repeating the execution of the program on the left once, and then the one on the right twice). We search for infinite-loops using the property $\square\lozenge(at\ l_1)$.

Figure 2 and 3 gives the result reported by our implementation. The maximum depth was set to 12. When it found an infinite loop, it did not stop, but continued looking for other loops until it checked all paths bounded by the maximum depth. The time in each row tells us when it found the corresponding lasso. The memory usage is not high, and thus we do not show it in the figure. Generally speaking, we are not guaranteed to obtain the shortest path for a loop, due to the order of matching a transition with a Büchi automaton node if there are multiple nodes available.

The approach presented in this paper provides a useful method for generating test cases. There are several constraints that we study here. One of the problems is undecidability of satisfiability. Finding satisfying values of unquantified first order formulas is in general undecidable. This follows from the undecidability of Hilbert's 10th problem [12]. In fact, there are simple cases where nontermination is still an open problem. For example, consider the following classical

Time (second)	Precondition	σ	ρ
11.634	$x = 1 \wedge y = 4 \wedge z = 3$	l_1, l_2, l_3, l_4	$l_1, l_5, l_2, l_6, l_3, l_4, l_7, l_8$
11.752	$x = 1 \wedge y = 4 \wedge z = 2$	l_1, l_2, l_3, l_4	$l_1, l_5, l_2, l_6, l_3, l_7, l_8, l_4$
80.658	$x = 1 \wedge y = 2 \wedge z = 2$	ϵ	$l_1, l_2, l_3, l_4, l_5, l_6, l_7, l_8$
83.322	$x = 1 \wedge y = 2 \wedge z = 1$	ϵ	$l_1, l_2, l_3, l_5, l_6, l_7, l_8, l_4$
155.521	$x = 2 \wedge y = 2 \wedge z = 2$	ϵ	$l_1, l_2, l_5, l_6, l_3, l_4, l_7, l_8$
159.314	$x = 2 \wedge y = 2 \wedge z = 1$	ϵ	$l_1, l_2, l_5, l_6, l_3, l_7, l_8, l_4$
1540.97	$x = 3 \wedge y = 2 \wedge z = 1$	l_5, l_6	$l_1, l_2, l_7, l_8, l_5, l_6, l_3, l_4$
1542.839	$x = 2 \wedge y = 1 \wedge z = 2$	l_5, l_6, l_1	$l_7, l_2, l_3, l_4, l_1, l_8, l_5, l_6$
1551.269	$x = 2 \wedge y = 1 \wedge z = 1$	l_5, l_6, l_1	$l_7, l_2, l_3, l_8, l_4, l_1, l_5, l_6$
1737.07	$x = 3 \wedge y = 1 \wedge z = 1$	l_5, l_6, l_7	$l_1, l_2, l_8, l_5, l_6, l_3, l_4, l_7$

Fig. 2. Results of the equality method

example (Collatz Problem): `while x>1 do begin if even(x) then x:=x/2 else x:=3×x+1 end;`

Another problem is the existence of nonperiodic infinite executions. For example, when there is a loop with two alternatives, α and β, one may have an infinite execution such as $\alpha\beta\alpha^2\beta^2\alpha^3\beta^3\ldots$. We provided a method for addressing such cases, which lumps together different loop transitions (in this case α and β). However, due to shrinking and lumping together different paths inside loops, the step by step synchronization of the program paths with the Büchi automaton is lost. Hence, this method can be used only with a restricted class of specifications (e.g., when each complete iteration of the loop happens to satisfy some state predicate φ that needs to be satisfied infinitely often).

Time (second)	Precondition	σ	ρ
12.128	$x = 1 \wedge y = 4 \wedge z \geq 3$	l_1, l_2, l_3, l_4	$l_1, l_5, l_2, l_6, l_3, l_4, l_7, l_8$
12.252	$x = 1 \wedge y = 4 \wedge z \geq 2$	l_1, l_2, l_3, l_4	$l_1, l_5, l_2, l_6, l_3, l_7, l_8, l_4$
83.031	$x = 1 \wedge y = 2 \wedge z \geq 2$	ϵ	$l_1, l_2, l_3, l_4, l_5, l_6, l_7, l_8$
85.715	$x = 2 \wedge y = 4 \wedge z \geq 2$	ϵ	$l_1, l_2, l_3, l_4, l_5, l_6, l_7, l_8, l_5, l_6, l_7, l_8$
85.96	$x = 1 \wedge y = 2 \wedge z \geq 1$	ϵ	$l_1, l_2, l_3, l_5, l_6, l_7, l_8, l_4$
88.723	$x = 2 \wedge y = 4 \wedge z \geq 1$	ϵ	$l_1, l_2, l_3, l_5, l_6, l_7, l_8, l_4, l_5, l_6, l_7, l_8$
163.198	$x = 2 \wedge y = 2 \wedge z \geq 2$	ϵ	$l_1, l_2, l_5, l_6, l_3, l_4, l_7, l_8$
167.107	$x = 3 \wedge y = 4 \wedge z \geq 2$	ϵ	$l_1, l_2, l_5, l_6, l_3, l_4, l_7, l_8, l_5, l_6, l_7, l_8$
167.358	$x = 2 \wedge y = 2 \wedge z \geq 1$	ϵ	$l_1, l_2, l_5, l_6, l_3, l_7, l_8, l_4$
171.36	$x = 3 \wedge y = 4 \wedge z \geq 1$	ϵ	$l_1, l_2, l_5, l_6, l_3, l_7, l_8, l_4, l_5, l_6, l_7, l_8$
173.994	$x = 4 \wedge y = 4 \wedge z \geq 1$	ϵ	$l_1, l_2, l_5, l_6, l_7, l_8, l_5, l_6, l_3, l_4, l_7, l_8$
236.517	$x = 3 \wedge y = 3 \wedge z \geq 2$	ϵ	$l_1, l_5, l_6, l_7, l_2, l_3, l_4, l_8, l_5, l_6, l_7, l_8$
239.229	$x = 3 \wedge y = 3 \wedge z \geq 1$	ϵ	$l_1, l_5, l_6, l_7, l_2, l_3, l_8, l_4, l_5, l_6, l_7, l_8$
1543.048	$x = 3 \wedge y = 2 \wedge z \geq 1$	l_5, l_6	$l_1, l_2, l_7, l_8, l_5, l_6, l_3, l_4$
1553.643	$x = 2 \wedge y = 1 \wedge z \geq 2$	l_5, l_6	$l_1, l_7, l_2, l_3, l_4, l_8, l_5, l_6$
1558.596	$x = 2 \wedge y = 1 \wedge z \geq 1$	l_5, l_6	$l_1, l_7, l_2, l_3, l_8, l_4, l_5, l_6$
1745.278	$x = 3 \wedge y = 1 \wedge z \geq 1$	l_5, l_6, l_7	$l_1, l_2, l_8, l_5, l_6, l_3, l_4, l_7$
1749.518	$x = 4 \wedge y = 2 \wedge z \geq 1$	ϵ	$l_5, l_6, l_7, l_1, l_8, l_5, l_6, l_7, l_2, l_3, l_4, l_8$

Fig. 3. Results of the monotonicity method

References

1. Biere, A., Artho, C., Schuppan, V.: Liveness Checking as Safety Checking. FMICS 2002, Malaga, Spain, ENTCS 66(2) (2002)
2. Bosnacki, D., et al.: On Commutativity Based Edge Lean Search. In: Arge, L., et al. (eds.) ICALP 2007. LNCS, vol. 4596, pp. 158–170. Springer, Heidelberg (2007)
3. Clarke, E.M., Emerson, E.A.: Design and Synthesis of Synchronization Skeletons Using Branching-Time Temporal Logic. In: Kozen, D. (ed.) Logics of Programs. LNCS, vol. 131, pp. 52–71. Springer, Heidelberg (1982)
4. Clarke, E.M., Grumberg, O., Peled, D.: Model Checking. MIT Press, Cambridge (1999)
5. Cook, B., Podelski, A., Rybalchenko, A.: Termination proofs for systems code. In: PLDI 2006, Ottawa, Ontario, Canada, pp. 415–426 (2006)
6. Floyd, R.: Assigning meanings to programs. In: Proceedings of Symposia in Applied Mathematics, vol. 19, pp. 19–32 (1967)
7. Gerth, R., Peled, D., Vardi, M., Wolper, P.: Simpler on-the-fly automatic Cverification of linear temporal logic. In: PSTV 1995, Warsaw, Poland, pp. 3–18 (1995)
8. Godefroid, P., Wolper, P.: Using Partial Orders for the Efficient Verification of Deadlock Freedom and Safety Properties. In: Larsen, K.G., Skou, A. (eds.) CAV 1991. LNCS, vol. 575, pp. 176–185. Springer, Heidelberg (1992)
9. Gunter, E.L., Peled, D.: Unit Checking: Symbolic Model Checking for a Unit of Code. In: Dershowitz, N. (ed.) Verification: Theory and Practice. LNCS, vol. 2772, pp. 548–567. Springer, Heidelberg (2004)
10. Hoare, C.A.R.: An Axiomatic Basis for Computer Programming. Communication ACM 12(10), 576–580 (1969)
11. Holzmann, G.J.: Design and Validation of Computer Protocols. Prentice Hall, Englewood Cliffs (1990)
12. Matiyasevich, Y.V.: Hilbert's 10th Problem. MIT Press, Cambridge (1993)
13. Mazurkiewicz, A.W.: Basic Notions of Trace Theory. In: de Bakker, J.W., de Roever, W.-P., Rozenberg, G. (eds.) Linear Time, Branching Time and Partial Order in Logics and Models for Concurrency. LNCS, vol. 354, pp. 285–363. Springer, Heidelberg (1989)
14. Pnueli, A.: The Temporal Logic of Programs. In: FOCS 1977, Rhode Island, pp. 46–57 (1977)
15. Podelski, A., Rybalchenko, A.: A Complete Method for the Synthesis of Linear Ranking Functions. In: Steffen, B., Levi, G. (eds.) VMCAI 2004. LNCS, vol. 2937, Springer, Heidelberg (2004)
16. Podelski, A., Rybalchenko, A.: Transition Invariants. LICS 2004, 32–41, Turku, Finland (2004)
17. Queille, J.-P., Sifakis, J.: Iterative Methods for the Analysis of Petri Nets. In: Selected Papers from the First and the Second European Workshop on Application and Theory of Petri Nets Bad Honnef, Informatik-Fachberichte 52, pp. 161–167 (1981)
18. Wolfram, S.: The Mathematica Book, 5th edn, Wolfram Media (2003)

Dynamic Testing Via Automata Learning[*]

Harald Raffelt[1], Bernhard Steffen[2], and Tiziana Margaria[3]

[1] University of Dortmund, Chair of Programming Systems,
Otto-Hahn-Str. 14, 44227 Dortmund, Germany
`harald.raffelt@uni-dortmund.de`
Tel.: ++49-231-755-7759, Fax. ++49-231-755-5802
[2] University of Dortmund, Chair of Programming Systems,
Otto-Hahn-Str. 14, 44227 Dortmund, Germany
`steffen@cs.uni-dortmund.de`
[3] Chair of Services and Software Engineering, Universität Potsdam,
August-Bebel-Str. 89, 14482 Potsdam, Germany
`margaria@cs.uni-potsdam.de`

Abstract. This paper presents *dynamic testing*, a method that exploits automata learning to systematically test (black box) systems almost without prerequisites. Based on interface descriptions, our method successively explores the system under test (SUT), while it at the same time extrapolates a behavioral model. This is in turn used to steer the further exploration process. Due to the applied learning technique, our method is optimal in the sense that the extrapolated models are most concise in consistently representing all the information gathered during the exploration. Using the LearnLib, our framework for automata learning, our method can elegantly be combined with numerous optimizations of the learning procedure, various choices of model structures, and last but not least, with the option to dynamically/interactively enlarge the alphabet underlying the learning process. All these features will be illustrated using as a case study the web application Mantis, a bug tracking system widely used in practice. We will show how the dynamic testing procedure proceeds and how the behavioral models arise that concisely summarize the current testing effort. It has turned out that these models, besides steering the automatic exploration process, are ideal for user guidance and to support analyzes to improve the system understanding.

1 Motivation

Testing was, is and will be an inevitable part of system development. No formal verification methodology can change that, because it fails to fully integrate the actual platform. However, formal methods are very valuable also for testing. E.g. model-based testing led to a qualitative change of the testing technology,

---

[*] This work has been partially supported by the European Union Specific Targeted Research Project SHADOWS (IST-2006-35157), exploring a Self-Healing Approach to Designing cOmplex softWare Systems.
The projects web page is at `https://sysrun.haifa.ibm.com/shadows`

K. Yorav (Ed.): HVC 2007, LNCS 4899, pp. 136–152, 2008.

by providing means to measure quality of testing and to generate test suites according to some given notion of coverage or some specifically defined goal. One particularly interesting technique here is conformance testing, which generate test suites that guarantee a notion of equivalence between a model and an implementation under certain additional assumptions. In fact, there is a wealth of powerful techniques dealing with the case when systems come with a formal model. However, what can be done if there is no or only a partial formal model?

In this paper, we present *dynamic testing*, a method that exploits automata learning to systematically test (black box) systems, e.g. component-based systems with third party components, and legacy systems, almost without prerequisites: Based on interface descriptions, our method successively explores the system under test (SUT), while it at the same time extrapolates a behavioral model. This is in turn used to steer the further exploration process. In essence, our method can be regarded as an on-the-fly conformance model generation and testing process [1], which we enhance here with interactive steering mechanisms, which are necessary to scale to system sizes interesting in practice. In addition the models generated on the fly are ideal means for generating test suites for regression testing, where one wants to check if well-known and loved features still function as expected.

Due to the applied learning technique, our method is optimal in the sense that the extrapolated models are most concise in consistently representing all the information gathered during the exploration. Using the LearnLib, our framework for automata learning, our method can elegantly be combined with numerous optimizations of the learning procedure, various choices of model structures, and last but not least, with the option to dynamically/interactively enlarge the alphabet underlying the learning process. The latter is very important in particular for testing Web applications, where the net-based exploration process inevitably leads to the dynamic "discovery" of new actions (in terms of links, forms, Web pages), which must be dynamically integrated in the learning process as extensions of the underlying alphabet.

All these features will be illustrated using as a case study the Web application Mantis, a Web-based bug tracking system widely used in practice. We will show how the dynamic testing procedure works and how the behavioral models arise that concisely summarize the current testing effort. It has turned out that these models, besides steering the automatic exploration process, are ideal for user guidance and to support analyzes to improve the system understanding. Moreover, using our dynamic testing technology behavioral models of Web applications are automatically kept up to date.

Our learning-based dynamic testing technology bases on longer term experiences with our *Integrated Test Environment* (ITE) [2], a platform for system-level testing of complex, distributed systems. The ITE is used here for executing the test cases proposed during the learning process. The core of the ITE, the *test coordinator*, is an independent system that drives the generation, execution, evaluation and management of the system-level tests. In general, it has access to all the involved subsystems and can manage the test execution through a

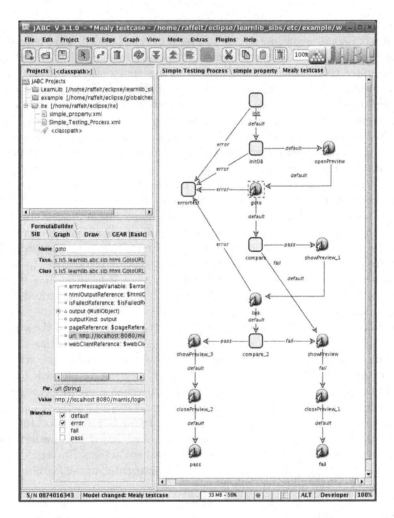

Fig. 1. Test case generated by the LearnLib for the case study: jABC executable model

coordination of different, heterogeneous test tools. These test tools, which locally monitor and steer the behavior of the software on the different clients/servers, are technically treated just as additional units under test. The ITE has been successfully applied to real-life examples of IP-based and telecommunication-based solutions: the test of a Web-based application (the Online Conference Service, used e.g. for the support of the program committee operations of over 60 LNCS conferences and the test of IP-based telephony scenarios, e.g. Siemens' testing of the Deutsche Telekom's Personal Call Manager application [3,4], which supports among other features the role based, Web-based reconfiguration of virtual switches. In those settings, we used ITE to execute tests and regression tests. Now we use the ITE as execution engine for the LearnLib's elementary queries.

In the remainder of the paper, we first present the LearnLib, our framework for automata learning, together with the basic principles of automata learning in Section 2.2. Afterwards we discuss the specifics of our technology for testing Web applications, namely the necessity to dynamically increase the alphabet underlying the learning process (Section 3). We then consider a concrete application example, the Mantis bug tracking systems, in Section 4, where we focus on the extrapolation of models, the kernel of the dynamic testing technology. The paper closes with some conclusions and perspectives in Section 5.

2   The LearnLib

LearnLib [5] is a library of tools for automata learning. It is implemented in C++ and tested under Linux and Solaris, and it currently consists of 150 classes and almost 50.000 lines of code. Originally, LearnLib has been designed to systematically build finite state machine models of unknown real world systems. In the meantime, it also became a platform for experimentation with different learning algorithms and to statistically analyze their characteristics in terms of learning effort, run time and memory consumption. The LearnLib consists of three libraries:

- The *automata learning* library contains the basic learning algorithms,
- the *filter* library provides several strategies to suppress redundant tests during the dynamic testing process, and
- a library based on ideas from conformance testing. It is essential for steering the model-based selection of individual test cases during the dynamic testing process.

Before discussing our learning technology in more detail at the end of this section, which is necessary to provide a better feeling of the essence of the proposed dynamic testing approach, we briefly sketch the LearnLib's integration as a plugin into our general modelling, development, and execution framework, the jABC.

2.1   Integration into the jABC

The jABC is a framework [6,7] for modelling, development, and execution of applications and services. Predecessors of jABC have been used since 1995 to design, among others, industrial telecommunication services [7], Web-based distributed decision support systems [8], and test automation environments for Computer-Telephony integrated systems [9].

jABC allows users to easily develop services and applications by composing reusable building-blocks to (flow-) graph structures. This development process is supported by an extensible set of plugins that provide additional functionality in order to adequately support all the activities needed along the development lifecycle like animation, rapid prototyping, formal verification, debugging, code generation, testing, and evolution. It does not replace but rather enhance other modelling practices like the UML-based Rational Unified Process [28,10].

Modelling the dynamic testing process in the jABC directly provides us with:

- **Customizability.** Processes can easily be customized, not only in their process structure, which can be modified conveniently using a graphical interface, but also in their look and feel and their organization in terms of taxonomies. Thus it is easily possible to adopt the notational and symbolic standards of the application domain.
- **Executability.** jABC's execution environment allows one to execute both the overall dynamic testing process and the individual test runs generated during the extrapolation process in order to realize the membership queries mentioned below.

  As an example, Fig. 1 shows one of the executable test cases produced in the course of the case study by the learning algorithm. The jABC graphs can be interpreted as control flow graphs. Nodes represent atomic actions that are executed successively, and the edges control the execution by determining the next step. The example contains the initialization, the call of a Web page (goto) followed by the comparison with the expected result, and the following of a hyperlink with successive comparison of the reached page.
- **Verification.** jABC provides model checking and checks for local consistency. These can be applied to the overall dynamic testing process to guarantee predefined rules, which may be required to avoid that the testing process gets stuck. As a typical example, test runs should leave the system under test in a state, where further test runs can continue.

  As an example, Fig. 2 shows how to ensure that jABC models (in this case the test case of Fig. 1) respect certain properties of interest. In this case, the property is that an *openPreview* is always followed by a *closePreview*. The red (resp. dark gray) dotted frames mark the violating paths: after *openPreview* no *closePreview* is reachable. Parts that do not violate the property are framed in green (resp. light grey).

  Model checking can also be applied to enforce behavioural properties of the models extrapolated during the dynamic testing process. This may be e.g. advantageous to steer the testing/learning process in certain directions.

In the dynamic testing described here, we use the ITE plugin for the jABC to model, verify, and enact the single test cases, as shown in the two previous pictures, and the LearnLib plugin to steer the learning process that underlies the dynamic testing.

The *learning process modelling mode* [11] of the LearnLib enables the user to control the entire learning process, comprising the context-specific choice of optimizations, strategies of search, as well as the setting of interaction points for a truly interactive learning process. Fig. 3 shows our process model for dynamic testing.

2.2   Supported Learning Technology

Machine learning deals in general with the problem of how to automatically generate system descriptions. Besides the synthesis of static soft- and hardware

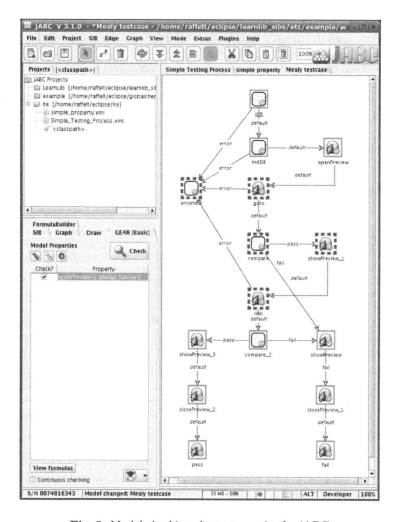

Fig. 2. Model checking the test case in the jABC

properties, in particular invariants [12], [13], [14], the field of *automata learning*, also called regular extrapolation [15] or regular inference [16], is of particular interest for soft- and hardware engineering [17], [19], [20], [21]. [18] for example aims at the derivation of automata from runtime observations, in combination with invariants from [12]. In this sense, it is a passive learning method.

We have used automata learning techniques in a number of contexts, e.g. to automatically construct models of common midrange telephony switch [22] and to enhance incomplete specifications of biological systems [23].

In this paper we apply automata learning for flexibly testing systems which are (in part) under-specified, i.e. systems containing third party components, black box systems, or simply systems which have become legacy systems over time. The following two subsections sketch 1) the basic technology, which provides the means for the organization of the dynamic testing process and the choice of individual tests, and 2) optimizations, which are essential for achieving practicality.

Classical Learning. Automata learning tries to construct a deterministic finite automaton that matches the behavior of a given target automaton on the basis of observations of the target automaton and perhaps some further information on its internal structure. In [15,24,22] we have discussed the method in detail. Here we only summarize the basic aspects of our realization, which is based on Angluin's learning algorithm L^* from [25]. A slight elaboration of Angluin's algorithm is depicted graphically in Fig. 3.

Definition 1

A deterministic finite automaton (DFA) is a tuple $M = (S, s_0, \Sigma, \delta, F)$ *where*

- S *is a finite nonempty set of* states,
- $s_0 \in S$ *is the* initial state,
- Σ *is a finite* alphabet,
- $\delta : S \times \Sigma \to S$ *is the* transition function, *and*
- $F \subseteq S$ *is the set of accepting states.*

Intuitively, a DFA evolves through states $s \in S$, *and whenever one applies an input symbol (or action)* $a \in \Sigma$, *the machine moves to a new state according to* $\delta(s, a)$. *A word* $q \in \Sigma^*$ *is accepted by the DFA if and only if the DFA reaches an accepting state* $s_i \in F$ *after processing the word starting from its initial state. We write* $s \xrightarrow{a} s'$ *to denote that on input symbol* a *the DFA moves from state* s *to state* s'. *The transition function* $\delta : S \times \Sigma \to S$ *can be extended to* $\delta' : S \times \Sigma^* \to S$ *such that forall states* $s, s' \in \Sigma$, *letters* $a \in \Sigma$, *and words* $w \in \Sigma^*$ *the following holds:* $\delta'(s, \varepsilon) = s$, *and* $\delta'(s, aw) = \delta'(\delta(s, a), w))$.

L^*, also referred to as an *active* learning algorithm, learns deterministic finite automata by *actively* posing *membership* queries and *equivalence* queries to the target automaton in order to extract behavioral information, and by refining successively an own hypothesis automaton based on the answers. A membership query tests whether a string (a potential run) is contained in the target automaton's language (its set of runs), and an equivalence query compares the hypothesis automaton with the target automaton for language equivalence, in order to determine whether the learning procedure was (already) successfully completed. In this case the experimentation can stop.

In its basic form, L^* starts with the one state hypothesis automaton that treats all words over the considered alphabet (of elementary observations) alike and refines this automaton on the basis of query results iterating two steps. Here, the dual way of how L* characterizes (and distinguishes) states is central:

- from *below*, by words reaching them. This characterization is too fine, as different words may well lead to the same state.
- from *above*, by their future behavior wrt. a dynamically increasing set of words. These future behaviors are essentially bit vectors, where a '1' means

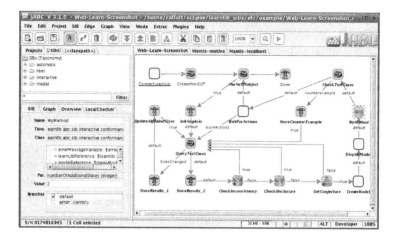

Fig. 3. Learning Process Modelling Mode: Design of a Web learning algorithm

that the corresponding word of the set is guaranteed to lead to an accepting state and a '0' captures the complement. This characterization is typically too coarse, as the considered sets of words are typically rather small.

The second characterization directly defines the hypothesis automata: each occurring bit vector corresponds to one state in the hypothesis automaton. The initial hypothesis automaton is characterized by the outcome of the membership query for the empty observation. Thus it accepts any word in case the empty word is in the language, and no word otherwise.

The learning procedure (1) iteratively establishes local consistency, after which it (2) checks for global consistency.

Local Consistency. This first step (also referred to as automatic *model completion*) again iterates two phases: one for checking wether the constructed automaton is *closed* under the one-step transitions, i.e., each transition from each state of the hypothesis automaton ends in a well defined state of this very automaton. And one for checking *consistency* according to the bit vectors characterizing the future behavior as explained above, i.e., whether all reaching words with an identical characterization from above possess the same one step transitions. If this is not the case, a distinguishing transition is taken as an additional distinguishing future guaranteeing that the two reaching words with different transition potential are no longer considered to represent the same state.

Global Equivalence. After local consistency has been established, an equivalence query checks whether the language of the hypothesis automaton coincides with the language of the target automaton. If this is true, the learning procedure successfully terminates. Otherwise the equivalence query returns a counterexample, i.e., a word which distinguishes the hypothesis and the target automaton. This counterexample gives rise to a new cycle of modifying the hypothesis automaton and starting the next iteration.

In any practical attempt of learning truly unknown systems, the equivalence tests can only be approximated, but membership queries can be answered by testing the target systems [15,24]. In particular it is in general impossible to decide, whether the hypothesis automaton is equivalent to the target system. We therefore use ideas from conformance testing in order to reduce equivalence queries to sets membership queries.

Web applications are typically reactive systems. They do not distinguish between accepting states and non accepting states but produce output when stimulated. We therefore use our adaptation of Angluin's algorithm for Mealy machines [22], which is suitable for this class of applications.

Definition 2. *A Mealy machine is defined as a tuple* $\mathsf{M} = (S, s_0, \Sigma, \Gamma, \delta, \gamma)$ *where*

- *S is a finite nonempty set of states,*
- *$s_0 \in S$ is the initial state,*
- *Σ is a finite input alphabet,*
- *Γ is a finite output alphabet,*
- *$\delta : S \times \Sigma \rightarrow S$ is the transition function, and*
- *$\gamma : S \times \Sigma \rightarrow \Gamma$ is the output function.*

A Mealy machine behaves very similarly to a DFA. It evolves through states $s \in S$, and whenever one applies an input symbol (or action) $a \in \Sigma$, the machine moves to a new state according to $\delta(s, a)$. However, in contrast to a DFA, it also produces an output symbol $x \in \Gamma$ according to $\gamma(s, a)$.

Optimizations. Central bottleneck in practice of automata learning, and consequently of our dynamic testing approach, is the overwhelming amount of arising membership queries. We employ application-specific and structure-specific optimizations in order to suppress redundant test cases [9,26]. We exploit e.g. prefix closure, a property valid for all testable systems, structural symmetry, typically given for systems consisting of a number of similar devices, and independence of observations. This already accelerated the learning process by several orders of magnitude. For our dynamic testing process, methods for steering the test selection process, e.g. using temporal properties for defining test goals, are additionally applied in order for our technique to scale further.

3   Dynamic Testing of Web Applications

Automata learning techniques have been proposed to deal with underspecified systems [15]. Web applications are a very specific kind of this class of systems, characterized by very small and well defined interfaces: using and testing a Web application boils down to invoking sequences of http- put and get methods on a Web-server, which simplifies the interaction with the system required during the learning process.

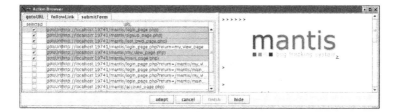

Fig. 4. Action Browser with opened gotoURL-Tab

Our algorithm traverses the Web application like a real user or agent. Not only does it retrieve and analyze the pages generated by the application like a Web robot, but it also uses the applications functionality. Thus executing a test typically has tangible effects, like a changed password after a change password operation or a update file after some change operation. These effects are visible in the next test run, which now has to deal with the new situation. In contrast to common Web crawlers, which recursively operate on all the retrieved URL's, our learning-based approach does not only consider the URL's, but also the dynamical behavior of the underlying application.

We use the jABC to graphically model the entire learning process, which comprises the modelling of conditional and interactive behavior. The nodes in this model represent arbitrary executable statements, in particular including all atomic functionalities of the LearnLib, and the edges specify in which order and under which condition they are processed, in a control flow fashion.

Fig. 3 depicts the control flow graph of the dynamic testing process for Web applications. The process starts with connecting the graphical user interface to the LearnLib *ConnectLearnLib*, before an interface to the Web application is created *CreateHtmlSUT*. The specific features of the Web application interface are presented in Sec.3.1. After these first initialization steps the learning process is started by initializing Angluin's algorithm L^* [25]. The learning algorithm now generates a test suite, which must be executed via the SUT interface in the next step. The *QueryTestCase* component executes the traces contained in the test suite (by means of repeated use of the ITE) and records the response of the SUT. At this point the SUT interface may discover that the implementation offers more possibilities to be stimulated than currently specified. When learning Web applications this is very common, since every discovered Web page may lead to new actions and can offer new hyperlinks and forms. This special feature is handled by the two components connected to the *sizesChanged* branch. First the results of querying the SUT are stored in the learning algorithm, then the alphabet is updated. If the alphabet is unchanged the results are stored as well and the observations are checked for the two well-formedness checks *CheckClosure* and *CheckConsistency*. If the observations are both closed and consistent, L^* constructs a conjecture model (*GetConjecture*), otherwise the learning algorithm provides a new test suite and the main loop continues.

After the main loop, the conjecture can be visualised (*CreateModel* and *DisplayModel*), before one enters the check for global equivalence. In this example

Fig. 5. Action Browser with opened followLink-Tab

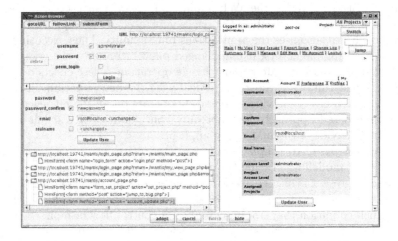

Fig. 6. Action Browser with opened SubmitForm-Tab

this is done by checking (*CheckTestCases*) the test suite generated using *Wp-Method* [27]. If the conjecture does not conform to the SUT, a counterexample is returned, and the learning algorithm continues. Otherwise the user can decide to introduce further actions (*WaitForActions*), or continue with the next SUT (*HasNextSubject*).

The execution of this control flow graph can be interactively steered using the *Tracer*, a plugin of the jABC for executing jABC models. The Tracer additionally provides useful debugging functionalities, which allow users to investigate the data exchanged between the nodes resp. atomic functionalities. This way the user can visualize at any time the sets of membership queries (realized via ITE test cases) and intermediate finite state models generated during the dynamic testing process.

3.1   Web Application Interface

Web applications can be regarded as Mealy machines. HTTP requests like "open a certain URL", "submit a form with some field set to predefined strings", or "follow a specified link" can be mapped to the input symbols (or actions) of a

Mealy machine, and the HTML pages generated by the Web application can be regarded as the corresponding output symbols.

Considering all possible input and output actions for a Web application is practically impossible, in particular in a learning context, which is an order of magnitude more expensive than exhaustive testing by means of conformance testing [1]. Thus abstraction must be applied in order to control the complexity. Typical is the grouping of the inputs and outputs according to their type or their role: It may be sufficient to check the application just using single data or one prototypical user. If this is insufficient, one can refine e.g. to distinguishing internal and external users, males or females, customers of administrators etc.. Our approach supports manual abstraction of input and output. This allows application experts to focus the learning process on different aspects of the application interactively on demand. The right choice of abstraction is vital for the success of the learning process.

A major challenge for inferring models of real life systems is the mapping between the abstract world of models and the concrete system scenario. From the (abstract) learning perspective, membership queries are just sequences of abstract (input) symbols that have to be answered by sequences of abstract (output) symbols. These queries need to be mapped to concrete test cases for the system, which requires concrete stimuli. Conversely, the generated concrete outputs must be abstracted to fit into the world of the models. The management of these mappings, which is beyond the scope of this paper, is part of the design of our integrated test environment (ITE) discussed in the introduction.

3.2   Interactive Specification of Input Actions

Learning Web applications does not only expose new behavioral structure but also new basic facts: the HTML-analysis of Web pages revealed during the learning process typically exposes new links and forms. Making them accessible to the learning procedure requires to dynamically extend the alphabet during the learning procedure. We offer the following three interaction for this purpose: 1) store a bookmark to a page for later reuse, 2) select a hyperlink, and 3) fill and submit a form.

Fig. 4 shows the corresponding *Action-Browser*. Note that choosing input actions using the *Action-Browser* can be done in parallel to executing test cases on the system under test. This allows one to introduce new input actions at any time, and prevents the LearnLib and the user from blocking each other.

The Action-Browser provides three tabs, corresponding to the three kinds of Web application input. On the left hand side of the ActionBrowser's *gotoURL*-Tab all available bookmarks are listed. By marking a check-box in the left column the user can instruct the learning algorithm to add a certain bookmark action to the learning alphabet. Added actions are highlighted in grey in the table. The right hand side is used to present a preview of visited pages. It can be selected by clicking on a bookmark in the left hand side panel.

The second kind of interactions a Web applications provides are hyperlinks, see Figure 5. In order not to treat each hyperlink individually, hyperlinks can be identified by their destination addresses or their ID-Tag. ID-Tags are optional HTML-attributes of almost every HTML-element, meant to uniquely identify an element on a Web page. Analogously, the right hand side previewer shows the links available on the page under test.

The third kind of interactions concerns submitting forms. The corresponding dialog is depicted in Figure 6. As before, the the right side is used to show a preview of a selected Web page. The left-hand side is split into three areas. The lowest area is used to list and select all forms revealed by the LearnLib process so far. The top area lists all form input actions that are considered to be used as input to the Web application. After selecting a form from the lower area, the user can specify in the middle area which concrete values should be used when submitting the form. For example, to learn the login process of a Web application one should try the login form with data of an authorized user and a bad user/password combination.

The Action-Browser dialog is used to realize abstraction on the input. Abstraction of the outputs is realized by xpath expressions. A corresponding GUI is currently under development.

4   Mantis: A Case Study

Mantis [29] is a popular Web-based bugtracking system. It is written in the PHP scripting language and requires a MySQL or PostgreSQL database and a Web-server. Mantis is platform-independent and has been installed on Windows, Mac OS, OS/2, and a variety of Unix operating systems. Almost any Web browser is able to function as a client. It is released under the terms of the GNU General Public License (GPL).

Reactive systems and in particular Web applications are designed to run forever. Thus that they do not need and therefore do not support an efficient reset operation. This also applies to Mantis. On the other hand, most automatic testing approaches as well as automata learning algorithms require a reliable and fast reset. Fortunately, Mantis can use a PostgreSQL database backend and PostgreSQL in order to clone databases. This enables us to realize the required reset operations via snapshots.

Fig. 7 shows the model extrapolated when restricting the input alphabet so that 1) all discovered bookmarks and follow-link actions in the public part of the application are enabled and 2) filling the autentification form with valid and an invalid username/password combinations are enabled. The part on the right-hand side is the portion visible to unauthorized users, and the smaller left-hand side portion can only be visited after a successful login. The strict separation of the left and the right part visually "verifies" that the confidential part on the left can only be visited after successful autentification.

We then additionally allowed the Mantis user to change his password by enabling two more actions: goto the user management page, and submit the new

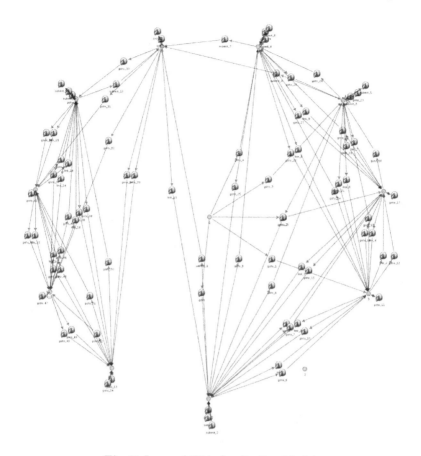

Fig. 7. Learned Web Application Model

password form. The new model adds the new aspect to the previous one, resulting in a diagram that is much more connected: for example, one can see that the
management feature and its subgraph are reachable from every state where login
was successful. We see here confirmed our feeling that complete models of such
systems are large and hardly analyzable in a visual manner, but that they can
be constructed by successive, aspect oriented exploration, adding further details
only at need. Views (for example, extracting only the user management after a
successful login) are here very useful, and they can be e.g. computed by model
checking.

5   Conclusion

We have presented *dynamic testing*, a method exploiting automata learning to
systematically test (black box) systems almost without prerequisites. Based on
interface descriptions, our method successively explores the system under test,

while at the same time extrapolating a behavioral model. This model is in turn used to steer the further exploration process. In addition, it is an ideal means for generating test suites for regression testing. Using the LearnLib, our framework for automata learning, our method can elegantly be combined with numerous optimizations of the learning procedure, various choices of model structures, and last but not least, with the option to dynamically/interactively enlarge the alphabet underlying the learning process. In particular the last feature is of vital importance for dynamically testing Web applications, where determining the alphabet is a major part of the extrapolation process. This has been illustrated in the case of the Web application Mantis, a bug tracking system widely used in practice.

Our current research focuses on scalability, the central bottleneck of dynamic testing (and learning). First experiments showed ways how to gain another couple of orders of magnitude by exploiting further domain-specific features and optimizing the internals of the LearnLib. Another interesting research direction we follow is the combination of dynamic testing and regression testing. Here we build on early experience in the area of Computer Telephony testing, where extrapolated models led to enormous performance gains [26]. Finally, we intend to use the gained models as basis for self-healing of Web applications, as investigated in the SHADOWS EU project.

References

1. Berg, T., Grinchtein, O., Jonsson, B., Leucker, M., Raffelt, H., Steffen, B.: On the correspondence between conformance testing and regular inference. In: Cerioli, M. (ed.) FASE 2005. LNCS, vol. 3442, pp. 175–189. Springer, Heidelberg (2005)
2. Niese, O., Margaria, T., Hagerer, A., Steffen, B., Brune, G., Goerigk, W., Ide, H.D.: Automated regression testing of cti-systems. In: ETW'01. Proc. of the IEEE European Test Workshop, Washington, DC, USA, p. 51. IEEE Computer Society, Los Alamitos (2001)
3. Margaria, T., Niese, O., Steffen, B., Erochok, A.: System level testing of virtual switch (re-)configuration over ip. In: ETW 2002. Proc. of the IEEE European Test Workshop, pp. 67–74. IEEE Computer Society Press, Los Alamitos (2002)
4. Hagerer, A., Margaria, T., Niese, O., Steffen, B., Brune, G., Ide, H.D.: Efficient regression testing of cti-systems: Testing a complex call-center solution. Annual Review of Communication, Int. Engineering Consortium (IEC), Chicago (USA) vol. 55, pp. 1033–1040 (2001)
5. Raffelt, H., Steffen, B., Berg, T.: Learnlib: A library for automata learning and experimentation. In: FMICS 2005. Proc.of the 10th International Workshop on Formal Methods for Industrial Critical Systems, Lisbon, Portugal, pp. 62–71. ACM Press, New York (2005)
6. Jörges, S., Kubczak, C., Nagel, R., Margaria, T., Steffen, B.: Model-driven development with the jabc. In: Bin, E., Ziv, A., Ur, S. (eds.) HVC 2006. LNCS, vol. 4383, Springer, Heidelberg (2007)
7. Margaria, T., Steffen, B., Reitenspieß, M.: Service-oriented design: The jabc approach. In: SOC 2005. Proc. of Service Oriented Computing, Internationales Begegnungs- und Forschungszentrum für Informatik (IBFI), Schloss Dagstuhl, Germany (2005)

8. Karusseit, M., Margaria, T.: Feature-based modelling of a complex, online-reconfigurable decision support service. Electr. Notes Theor. Comput. Sci. 157(2), 101–118 (2006)

9. Hungar, H., Margaria, T., Steffen, B.: Test-based model generation for legacy systems. In: ITC 2003. Proc. of 2003 International Test Conference, Charlotte, NC, pp. 971–980. IEEE Computer Society, Los Alamitos (September 2003)

10. Hörmann, M., Margaria, T., Mender, T., Nagel, R., Schuster, M., Steffen, B., Trinh, H.: The jabc approach to collaborative development of embedded applications. In: CCE 2006. Int. Workshop on Challenges in Collaborative Engineering - State of the Art and Future Challenges on Collaborative Design, April 2006 (Industry Day), Prag (CZ) (2006)

11. Raffelt, H., Steffen, B., Berg, T., Margaria, T.: LearnLib: A library for automata learning and experimentation. International Journal on Software Tools Technology Transfer (Submitted, 2005)

12. Ernst, M.D., Czeisler, A., Griswold, W.G., Notkin, D.: Quickly detecting relevant program invariants. In: ICSE 2000. Proc. of 22nd Int. Conf. on Software Engineering, pp. 449–458 (June 2000)

13. Nimmer, J.W., Ernst, M.D.: Automatic generation of program specifications. In: ISSTA 2002. Proc. of the 2002 Int. Symposium on Software Testing and Analysis, Rome, Italy, pp. 229–239 (July 22–24, 2002)

14. Brun, Y., Ernst, M.D.: Finding latent code errors via machine learning over program executions. In: ICSE 2004. Proc. of the 26th Int. Conf. on Software Engineering, pp. 480–490 (May 2004)

15. Hagerer, A., Hungar, H., Niese, O., Steffen, B.: Model generation by moderated regular extrapolation. In: Kutsche, R.-D., Weber, H. (eds.) ETAPS 2002 and FASE 2002. LNCS, vol. 2306, pp. 80–95. Springer, Heidelberg (2002)

16. de la Higuera, C.: A bibliographical study of grammatical inference. Pattern Recognition 38, 1332–1348 (2005)

17. Cook, J.E., Wolf, A.L.: Discovering models of software processes from event-based data (TOSEM) ACM Transactions on Software Engineering and Methodology 7(3), 215–249 (1998)

18. Mariani, L., Pezzè, M.: A technique for verifying component-based software. In: TACoS 2004. Proc. of Int. Workshop on Test and Analysis of Component Based Systems, pp. 17–30 (March 2004)

19. Xie, T., Notkin, D.: Mutually enhancing test generation and specification inference. In: Petrenko, A., Ulrich, A. (eds.) FATES 2003. LNCS, vol. 2931, pp. 60–69. Springer, Heidelberg (2004)

20. Peled, D., Vardi, M.Y., Yannakakis, M.: Black box checking. In: Wu, J., Chanson, S.T., Gao, Q. (eds.) FORTE/PSTV 1999. Proc. of the Joint Int. Conference on Formal Description Techniques for Distributed System and Communication/Protocols and Protocol Specification, Testing and Verification, pp. 225–240. Kluwer Academic Publishers, Boston, MA (1999)

21. Cook, J.E., Du, Z., Liu, C., Wolf, A.L.: Discovering models of behavior for concurrent systems. Technical report, New Mexico State University, Deppartment of Computer Science, NMSU-CS-2002-010. (August 2002)

22. Steffen, B., Margaria, T., Raffelt, H., Niese, O.: Efficient test-based model generation of legacy systems. In: HLDVT 2004. Proc. of the 9th IEEE Int. Workshop on High Level Design Validation and Test (HLDVT'04), Sonoma (CA), USA, pp. 95–100. IEEE Computer Society Press, Los Alamitos (2004)

23. Margaria, T., Hinchey, M.G., Raffelt, H., Rash, J., Rouff, C.A., Steffen, B.: Completing and adapting models of biological processes. In: BiCC 2006. Proc. of IFIP Conf. on Biologically Inspired Cooperative Computing, Santiago (Chile) (2006)
24. Steffen, B., Hungar, H.: Behavior-based model construction. In: Zuck, L.D., Attie, P.C., Cortesi, A., Mukhopadhyay, S. (eds.) VMCAI 2003. LNCS, vol. 2575, pp. 5–19. Springer, Heidelberg (2002)
25. Angluin, D.: Learning regular sets from queries and counterexamples. Information and Computation 2(75), 87–106 (1987)
26. Margaria, T., Raffelt, H., Steffen, B.: Knowledge-based relevance filtering for efficient system-level test-based model generation. Innovations in Systems and Software Engineering 1(2), 147–156 (2005)
27. Fujiwara, S., von Bochmann, G., Khendek, F., Amalou, M., Ghedamsi, A.: Test selection based on finite state models. IEEE Transactions on Software Engineering 17(6), 591–603 (1991)
28. Rational unified process (seen June 2007), http://www-306.ibm.com/software/awdtools/rup/
29. Mantis bug tracker. (seen June 2007), http://www.mantisbt.org

On the Architecture of
System Verification Environments

Mark A. Hillebrand[1,*] and Wolfgang J. Paul[2]

[1] German Research Center for Artificial Intelligence (DFKI),
P.O. Box 15 11 50, 66041 Saarbrücken, Germany
mah@dfki.de
[2] Saarland University, P.O. Box 15 11 50, 66041 Saarbrücken, Germany
wjp@cs.uni-sb.de

Abstract. Implementations of computer systems comprise many layers and employ a variety of programming languages. Building such systems requires support of an often complex, accompanying tool chain.

The Verisoft project deals with the formal pervasive verification of computer systems. Making use of appropriate formal specification and proof tools, this task requires (i) specifying the layers and languages used in the implementation, (ii) specifying and verifying the algorithms employed by the tool chain (or, alternatively, validating their actual output), and (iii) proving simulation statements between layers, arguing about the programs residing at the different layers. Combining the simulation statements for all layers should allow to transfer correctness results for top-layer programs to their bottom-layer representation; in this manner, a verified stack can be built.

Maintaining all formal artifacts, the actual system implementation, and the (verification) tool chain is a challenging task. We call sets of tools that help addressing this task *system verification environments*. In this paper, we describe the structure, contents, and architecture of the system verification environment used in the Verisoft project.

1 Introduction

We begin with a simple question: do we know how to formally verify software? At first, the answer would be 'yes', because (i) software consists of programs, (ii) ways to formally specify program behavior can be looked up in any textbook on programming language semantics, e.g., [1, 2], (iii) it has been known since decades how to produce paper and pencil proofs for programs based on formal semantics [3, 4, 5], and (iv) these proofs could be mechanically checked by a modern computer-aided verification (CAV) system. Thus, at least in principle the problem should be solved.

However, this is an oversimplification. Software engineering does not just deal with 'programs written in a programming language' but with complex software

---

* Work funded by the German Federal Ministry of Education and Research (BMBF) under grant 01 IS C38.

K. Yorav (Ed.): HVC 2007, LNCS 4899, pp. 153–168, 2008.

systems. These consist of many programs, which are written in different programming languages and interact with each other (and their environment) in nontrivial ways.

Thus, even the most benevolent software engineer would doubt the usefulness of software verification if programs requiring standard operating system services—e.g., file and terminal I/O, inter-process and network communication—cannot be handled. Even if such facilities could be handled, the verification results would be relative to the correctness of the underlying system and therefore questionable unless the hardware and the operating system (in particular its kernel and the device drivers) could also be verified.

In some software systems, errors have potentially disastrous consequences for body or purse and software correctness is particularly desirable. For example, security-critical systems implement cryptographic protocols to guarantee secrecy or authenticity of message exchange over untrusted networks. The systems controlling our cars, trains, or air planes are distributed and must meet hard real-time requirements.

The mission of the German Verisoft project [6] is to develop methods and an integrated set of tools permitting to handle all issues listed above and to demonstrate these by verifying entire systems of industrial interest. We call integrated sets of tools supporting the collaborative formal verification of computer systems (hardware plus software or software alone) *system verification environments*. Verification environments are themselves software systems, and like any substantial software system they should better have an architecture. This paper is about the architecture of such verification environments.

Present computer systems have a common structure: from the hardware to the applications they are organized in layers of abstraction with well-defined interfaces. For every pair of adjacent layers the lower system layer simulates the upper system layer and implements its interface. Any reasonable theory of correctness of concrete computer systems will reflect this structure. We will argue that this determines the architecture of system verification environments to a very large extent. As an example we will describe in this article the environment that was developed and is currently being used in the Verisoft project. We also announce a web site, where we expose those portions of this environment (including constructions and formal proofs) that appear sufficiently stable and do not contain confidential data of industry partners.

Overview. The remainder of this paper is structured as follows. In Sect. 2 we describe three concrete systems, which cannot be verified unless all the issues raised in the introduction are dealt with. These systems (and their requirements) were chosen together with Verisoft industry partners as concrete examples, whose complete formal verification should be made feasible by our system verification environment. Of course they will also serve as concrete examples in this paper.

Section 3 deals with computational models for describing the systems under consideration and their components. The range of these models is necessarily large, ranging from processors and devices at the low end via abstract C machines and operating systems to communicating distributed applications at the high end. Some of these models serve as building blocks, which are referenced by concurrent and distributed models. Any system verification environment must contain formal specifications of these models. There is no complete functional correctness proof of a C program without a formal C semantics. There is no complete functional correctness proof of a driver without a formal device model. There is no complete functional correctness proof of a program making a system call unless the semantics of that call is defined somewhere.

Section 4 deals with verified components. Clearly, in a technology capable of producing verified systems it is desirable to develop a library of verified standard components *together* with their correctness proofs. Indeed, such a library is indispensable if *pervasive* system verification [7, 8] is attempted, i.e., the verification of entire systems across several layers of abstraction. It turns out that that standard components often provide a simulation in terms of the models from Sect. 3. Processors for instance simulate assembler programs by registers, memories, and gates. Compilers translate source programs into target programs simulating the source programs.

In Sect. 5 we consider another hierarchy different from the hierarchy of system layers, namely the hierarchy of semantic models. In its basic form, this hierarchy and its associated soundness results are classical material from textbooks on programming language semantics [1]. We consider small step semantics, big step semantics, and Hoare logic. We use small step semantics in our system models where we need to argue about communicating systems, sometimes doing rely / guarantee style proofs [9]. Big step semantics and Hoare logic are equivalent and allow to prove pairs of pre and post conditions. Because the abstraction level is higher than in small step semantics, proofs can be generated with higher productivity than in small step semantics; for the Hoare logic we also make use of a verification condition generator.

In addition to program state and functions, we also allow abstract state and functions at the Hoare logic layer. This way, proofs in the Hoare logic may be conducted relative to low-level functions or libraries. Consider a driver writing some C variables to a disk. Although that driver has in line assembler code (otherwise it cannot access the ports of the hard disk controller) its effect can be specified in the Hoare logics by a pre and post condition pair operating on abstract state representing the disk configuration. Hoare logics of this kind we call *extended Hoare logics*; soundness results for such Hoare logics are relative to the postulated extended semantics.

Section 6 deals with proof tools. There must be a combination of interactive and automatic proof tools. Automatic tools increase productivity, thus they cannot be ignored in an engineering effort. Because the complete verification of entire systems is out of reach for present automatic tools, at least one 'general purpose' interactive prover must be present. We mainly use Isabelle/HOL [10] as general purpose prover. Isabelle/HOL also serves as an integration platform for most automatic proof tools.

Section 7 we shortly describe how the contents of the system verification environment are stored and related to each other in a version control system.

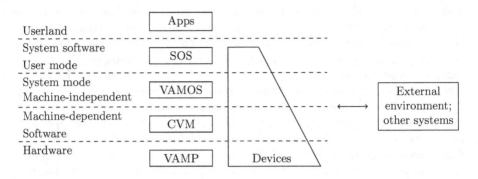

Fig. 1. Implementation layers of the academic system (Verisoft subproject 2)

Also, we describe the portions of the environment which are currently made public. We summarize in Sect. 8.

2   Overview of Systems

In this section, we describe three systems for which the formal pervasive verification is attempted in the Verisoft project: the 'academic system' (Verisoft subproject 2), the 'chipcard-based biometric identification (CBI) system' (Verisoft subproject 4), and the 'automotive system' (Verisoft subproject 6). All these systems use the same implementation languages and also share significant parts of the hardware and system software implementation. In particular, the employed hardware architecture and the architecture-specific parts of the microkernel implementation are reused for all described systems.

Academic system. The academic system is a computer system for writing, signing, and sending emails. It covers all implementation layers from the gate-level hardware to communicating concurrent programs and thus represents a vertical cross section of a general-purpose computer system.

Let us describe the components of the academic system in bottom-up fashion (see also Fig. 1). The lowest layer of the academic system consists of a *hardware architecture*, featuring the VAMP, a DLX-like processor with address translation, and abstractions of memory-mapped I/O devices (timer, network interface card, keyboard, terminal, and hard disk). The next layer of *communicating virtual machines (CVM)* establishes a hardware-independent programming interface for a microkernel and a virtual computation environment for concurrently running processes. Some parts of CVM must be implemented in assembler since C0, a subset of regular C, lacks low-level programming constructs. The *microkernel*, which is called VAMOS, is based on the CVM interface and contains no assembler parts. On the next-higher layer the *simple operating system* (SOS) is located, which runs as a (privileged) user process. It offers file I/O, inter-process communication, sockets, and remote procedure calls to user processes. Last but not least several user processes are needed to implement the desired functionality of the academic system; these include a signing software, an SMTP client (and, on the receiving side, an SMTP server), and a simple mail user agent.

Chipcard-based biometric identification system. The chipcard-based biometric identification (CBI) system is an access solution, which grants system access based on the similarity between fresh biometric data and reference biometric data. Fresh biometric data is sampled using a biometric sensor. The reference biometric data is read from a chipcard, which belongs to the user. Biometric data is considered personal data in Germany and has to be kept confidential in accordance with German privacy regulations. Additionally, communication between the host system and the user's chipcard must have certain cryptographic properties like authenticity and integrity of messages. This is established by running a cryptographic protocol between host and chipcard.

Automotive system. The automotive system is the prototype of an automatic emergency call system, which is meant to contact the public-safety answering point (PSAP) automatically in case of a (severe) car crash. The system is realized as a distributed system, namely a cluster of electronic control units (ECUs) connected to each other via a shared serial bus. Bus communication is time-triggered, i.e., access to this bus is granted to the individual ECUs according to a static, periodical schedule. The schedule period is called a *round*; rounds are evenly divided into *slots*, which represent the minimal bus allocation intervals. In each slot, the sending ECU may broadcast a *frame* to all other ECUs. Frames contain *messages* as a payload. Messages have types. On each ECU runs a small operating system, which is called OLOS. OLOS maintains a buffer for each message type. Incoming messages are stored into this buffer and outgoing messages are transmitted from that buffer (according to another, static schedule). Applications may access the message buffer using system calls. The user view of the whole cluster is as follows: applications are executed on all ECUs in lock-step while they seem to communicate over shared variables.

In order for this hardware / software stack to work as specified, the following two aspects concerned with timing are crucial. Already at the hardware level, a clock synchronization algorithm must be used to compensate for the different hardware clock frequencies of the ECUs (due to manufacturing tolerances or environmental conditions). Otherwise, ECUs will violate slot and round boundaries, in the long run causing bus contention and compromise of the communication mechanism. At the software level, for the system to operate in lock-step fashion, both the system software and the applications must run fast enough to observe slot and round boundaries. To show that these constraints are met, a worst-case execution time analysis for all the software is necessary.

3   Computational Models

The repository of computational models plays a very central role in the system verification environment. Typically, each model is referenced in three situations:

(i) in correctness proofs for programs in this model, (ii) in simulation theorems showing that the model is simulated by a model from an adjacent *lower* system layer, and (iii) in simulation theorems showing that the model simulates a model belonging to an adjacent *higher* system layer (which may also be a program correctness proof). In the remainder of this sections, we shortly sketch standard models (for languages and systems without devices), devices models (for systems with devices), and distributed models (for systems communicating over devices).

Standard models. We consider the following standard models for languages: (i) the model of the machine language / instruction set architecture (ISA) of the VAMP [11, 12], a variant of the DLX architecture [13], (ii) the model of VAMP assembler, (iii) the semantics of C0, which is the subset of C we use [14], and (iv) the semantics of C0A, which is C0 with in line assembler code. In the latter model, we have to consider both the computation of a (compiled) C0 program and of an assembler program. These computations influence each other in cases where in line assembler instructions update C0 variables, e.g., when a processor register is copied to a C0 variable. This requires knowledge about the memory layout employed by the C0 compiler, which allocates C0 variables to VAMP memory ranges.

Standard system models are obtained by combining one (or more) of the above models with specifications of special operations (e.g., system calls). In the academic system, we consider the following system models: (i) Communicating virtual machines (CVM), a generic model of operating system kernels permitting to abstract from the use of in line assembler in the lower-level kernel implementation [15]. This is a concurrent model of computation consisting of an abstract kernel modeled as a C0 program and user processes modeled as VAMP assembler programs. At any time either the kernel or one of the user processes are running. The kernel is non preemptive and may only be interrupted by reset. If interrupts occur during user process execution, the kernel is entered. No memory is shared between user processes or (C0 variables of) the abstract kernel. (ii) VAMOS, the abstraction of an instantiation of CVM with a specific kernel [16]. User processes may be assembler programs, or, in an extension of this model, also C0 programs. In the latter case, we also abstract from the concrete VAMOS scheduler. (iii) The model of the simple operating system (SOS), which specifies the system calls provided for C0 or assembler user applications.

Device models. With the standard models above we cannot yet handle the numerous situations where I/O is performed in the academic system (swap memory, terminal, file, and network access). This makes a generalization of the hierarchy above necessary. We have to define models for specific devices for use in the specific layers of the model stack. Depending on the layer and its level of abstraction, even variants of models for a device may be required. From one layer to the next, a more abstract variant of a device model is employed when the lower layer implements a (nontrivial) driver for that device.

We distinguish the following models. (i) Hardware with devices. Devices employed at this stage may be gate-level implementations of devices and, if this is the case, must be part of the hardware correctness proofs. (ii) Instruction set architecture with devices. For special cases (e.g., hard disk) this may be a nonconcurrent model [17]. In the general case, this model is nondeterministic, concurrent, and, when communication between computer systems is considered, also distributed, cf. [18, 19]. The obvious next two models are (iii) assembler with devices permitting to program device drivers in assembler (e.g., [20]) and (iv) C0A with devices permitting to use these drivers in C0A programs. (v) As a next step we turn the drivers into external functions. This permits to return to the syntax of ordinary C0. For nontrivial drivers (which are not only used to expose devices directly to user-level device drivers), more abstract variants of a device may be employed. For example, we abstract a hard disk used for swapping into a 'swap memory', which by the page fault handler via driver calls to swap in or swap out pages. This model we call C0 with devices.

In the system models devices can only be accessed by (or through) the kernel; device ports are never mapped to user memory and interrupts are relayed over the kernel. For each system model, we have an extended model with devices. From one system model to the next, certain devices may be hidden completely, e.g., the timer used by the microkernel's scheduler is not visible to the upper layers.

Extensions for distributed and communicating systems. In the automotive system several processors together with their bus interfaces form a cluster of electronic control units (ECUs), which communicate over a FlexRay like shared serial bus. A technically interesting complication arises from the fact that each ECU has a private oscillator with a clock period close but not equal to a reference clock period. As a consequence the bus interfaces contain serial interfaces and hardware implementing a clock synchronization algorithm [18, 19].

Thus, in the automotive system, the following distributed models are considered: (i) A distributed hardware model, which extends the usual digital hardware model in two ways. The hardware of the entire system is partitioned into portions with the same oscillator (the ECUs). Moreover, for the drivers and registers directly connected to the bus set up and hold times (and metastability of flip-flops) must be considered [19,21]. (ii) A distributed ISA model with FlexRay like devices modeling the communicating ECUs at the ISA level. (iii) A distributed assembler model with FlexRay like devices modeling the communicating ECUs at the assembler level. (iv) Employing the real-time kernel OLOS (OSEKtime like operating system) [22], which provides access to the FlexRay to C0 user applications, we obtain a distributed OLOS model. (v) The top level model used in the automotive system is a model of communicating automata called AutoFocus Task Model (AFTM) [23].

The model for academic systems communicating over the Internet is slightly simpler because only discrete systems are considered. From any computational model with network interface card as device, a distributed version of the model can be derived. This is simply the distributed system consisting of copies of the basic model and the model for their connection, i.e., the Internet, which includes a model of packet loss.

4 Verified Components

Based on models of computation of the previous section we may now proceed to present a library of verified components. A verified component has five parts: (i) a formal specification of the component, which defines user visible data structures and operations, (ii) a formal specification of the model in which the component is implemented, (iii) formal specifications of subcomponents used in the construction of the component (if any), (iv) an implementation of the component, and (v) a formal proof that the construction meets the specification. Formal specifications used in components may coincide with the specification of the computational models from Sect. 3, e.g., for components implementing system layers. Currently, a large number of verified components is under development or completed. For the components listed below at least the first four parts are completed and the formal proof is either completed or under construction.

Hardware. (i) VAMP processors built from ordinary hardware (i.e., gates, registers, and memories). Formal proofs against the VAMP ISA are completed in PVS [12,24] and under construction in Isabelle/HOL. (ii) processors with devices constructed from ordinary hardware devices specified at the hardware level. The specification of such processors is given by the computational model of VAMP ISA with devices. The correctness proof is a not completely obvious extension of 'ordinary' processor correctness theorems, because the ISA model of a processor with one or more devices is in general distributed and nondeterministic; the nondeterminism is resolved by the implementation's timing behavior. (iii) For the automotive system, interfaces for a FlexRay like bus have been constructed at the gate-level. The correctness proof for these devices is conducted in the distributed hardware model described above. Both the correctness of a serial interface and the implementation of a clock synchronization algorithm in hardware have to be shown. For paper and pencil proofs see [18,19]. The part of the formal correctness proof dealing with setup and hold times of registers is reported in [21].

Basic data structures and algorithms. For use by other C0 programs, we currently provide three libraries of basic data structures and algorithms: a library for doubly linked lists, a string library [25], and a big number library [26]. All libraries are programmed in C0. Specification and correctness proofs of the library functions are done in the Hoare logic for C0. The list library is used by the other two libraries.

Compiler. (i) The C0 compiler (backend) translates abstract syntax trees of C0 programs into VAMP assembler programs [14]. It is specified in C0 small steps semantics and uses the list library. The correctness is shown using C0 Hoare logic. Correctness with respect to small steps semantics is inferred using the soundness of the Hoare logic (cf. Sect. 5). (ii) A fairly straightforward extension, assuming 'acceptable' behavior of in line assembler portions, gives the correctness of the C0A compiler. (iii) A more involved extension of the compiler is a copying garbage collector [27], which is crucial for certain (application) code, such as the big number library. (iv) The simulation of the model C0A with devices by the model assembler with devices works only under certain software conditions: compiled C0 instructions, e.g., of the kernel, must not be interrupted and devices may only be accessed with in line assembler and not by compiled C0 statements. This guarantees that the execution of compiled C0 statements and device transitions do not interfere with each other. Note that user programs never directly access devices in our systems and can be interrupted, which has the effect of the non-interruptible kernel taking over control.

Device drivers. (i) Elementary device drivers are pieces of assembler program copying data between a region of memory in the processor and a device specific region of memory on the device, e.g., disk space. Elementary device drivers are specified and programmed in the model assembler with devices. For a paper and pencil correctness proofs of elementary device drivers for a disk and a UART see [17, 20]. (ii) Elementary device drivers may be embedded into functions of a C0A program. As these device drivers usually abstract from their assembler implementation, their specification can be done relative to the C0 model with devices. Typically, these drivers provide an abstracted view of the device they control. Note that for interfacing reasons, the correctness proofs of any C0A programs has to refer C0 calling convention and memory layout. (iii) User-level devices are implemented using system calls for device access provided, e.g., by the model VAMOS with devices. They may be verified relative to the specifications of these system calls in an extended Hoare logic (cf. Sect. 5). An example of such a driver is the hard disk driver used by the simple operating system to implement a simple file system. In contrast to the elementary device driver used for swapping, this disk driver is interrupt-driven.

System software. The specification of the generic operating system kernel CVM is directly given by the model CVM with devices. The so called concrete kernel, which is the CVM implementation for a given abstract kernel, is obtained by linking and compiling the abstract kernel with a C0A program. This program implements the CVM functionality. Its major data structures are the process control blocks and the page tables. Its major functions are swap memory management, page fault handling, context switching, and operations on the user assembler machines, such as user memory copy operations [15]. As the kernel is non-preemptive parts of its correctness (in particular the page fault handler's) can be shown in an extended Hoare logic (cf. Sect. 5).

VAMOS [16] is an instantiation of CVM, which was inspired by the L4 microkernel [28]. It calls CVM functions and is therefore implemented in the model CVM with devices. Proofs can make use of extended Hoare logics relative to a specification of this model. Thus, e.g., the correctness of inter-process communication (IPC) operations, which implement a rendezvous protocol, may be shown relative to the correctness of the user memory copy operations provided by CVM. In the VAMOS model allowing C0 user programs, two additional abstractions have to be justified. First, the scheduler is abstracted away. This requires to prove fairness of the scheduler. Second, some user processes are allowed to be C0 programs, which must be linked against a system call library implemented in C0A. Proving the library correct, requires another application of compiler correctness in the correctness proof.

The implementation of the simple operating system makes use of VAMOS, drivers for disk, terminal, and network interface and an implementation of TCP. On top of the disk driver, a simple file system is implemented. On top of the TCP implementation, socket management functions have been implemented.

To implement remote procedure calls (RPC) for SOS applications a port mapper, user-level primitives for the implementation of remote procedure call (RPC) on top of SOS, and an interface compiler have to be provided [29]. SOS and the applications running under it form a distributed system. Computations of user processes and of SOS are interleaved. Correctness proofs about applications interacting via RPC thus need to use rely / guarantee arguments (e.g., [30]).

Applications. Applications in the academic system are (i) an SMTP client and server for email transfer [30], (ii) a signature server used to sign electronic mails and (iii) an email client, which uses the previous applications and implements a user interface [31]. The applications run under SOS, make use of SOS RPC and the SOS file system. The signature server also makes use of formally verified cryptographic primitives (e.g., [32]). For the biometric identification system, security properties of the cryptographic protocol have been formally modeled and proven using VSE [33, 34]. Certain properties of the emergency call application in the automotive system were formally verified in the AutoFocus task model (AFTM) using the AutoFocus tool [23].

5   Semantics Hierarchy

Because we need to consider interleaved programs in several places of the Verisoft project (e.g., RPC clients and servers), the standard models listed in Sect. 3 are *all* small steps semantics. Although in the end we need many program correctness theorems with respect to small steps semantics, we produce the correctness proofs as much as possible using the verification condition generator (VCG) of a Hoare logic for C0 [35]. This needs to be justified by a hierarchy of C0 semantics, which is also part of the system verification environment: the small steps semantics of C0 (Sect. 3), a big steps semantics for C0 [35], and a Hoare logic with the VCG mentioned above as a proof tool.

In order to go back and forth between the three levels of C0 semantics we have proven formal versions of classical textbook theorems. First, the soundness of the big step semantics with respect to the small steps semantics. Second, the equivalence between Hoare logic and big step semantics. Because of the shallow embedding of the Hoare logic into Isabelle/HOL there can be no general (program-independent) equivalence proof in Isabelle because such a proof would require to quantify over all types of Isabelle [35, Chapter 8]. We expect, however, that the proofs obligations for individual C0 programs can be automatically proven.

We also use an extended version of this semantics stack with which (noninterrupted) C0 programs may be verified in the Hoare logic relative to an abstract specification, e.g., a system model providing system calls. This may be used in the verification of drivers (user or kernel level), abstract kernels, or user applications. The abstract specification is represented in the Hoare logic with ghost (i.e., non-program) variables and postulated pre and post condition pairs. All assumptions made in this manner need of course to be verified; the soundness results for this semantics are only relative to the assumed specifications. These assumptions must be discharged when transferring concrete properties from the Hoare logic to the small steps semantics.

6   Proof Tools

In our system verification environment we use interactive provers (mainly Isabelle/HOL [10]) as the central platform for formal modeling and verification tasks. All computational and semantic models are expressed as Isabelle/HOL theories. Components (hardware and software) to be verified are usually written relative to one of the semantic models in a deep embedding. There are two important exceptions to this rule. In the C0 Hoare logic, C0 expressions are shallow embedded to improve verification productivity [35]; special care must be taken about soundness here, as mentioned earlier. Also, hardware models are formulated in a synthesizable subset of Isabelle/HOL [36]. Since gate-level hardware constitutes the bottom of our model stack, we cannot show soundness here.

The benefit of having a general purpose interactive theorem prover as a central component is that there is always a verification tool of last resort when automatic verification fails. However, increasing automation is clearly the key to success in the verification of industrial computer systems. We have integrated a number of automatic proof tools into Isabelle/HOL via Isabelle's oracle interface. These tools either hook into one of the semantic model described above or Isabelle/HOL directly. We trust the tools to produce correct results; hence, currently, no proof objects are imported into Isabelle for automatically proven goals.

Proof tools that have been integrated into Isabelle include classical symbolic model checkers [36], software model checkers and shape analysis tools [37, 38, 39, 40], translation validation tools [41], and first-order logic theorem provers [42, 43]. As mentioned earlier, the C0 Hoare logic includes a verification condition generator [35]. For the automotive system, we use AbsInt's worst-case execution time analyzer aiT [44] based on abstract interpretation, which is, however, not directly integrated into Isabelle/HOL.

7   Repository Implementation and Public Releases

To form a viable platform for the development of system correctness proofs, we keep all afore-mentioned artifacts (computation models, proof objects, tools, etc.) in a central repository. We make use of the version control system Subversion [45], which provides revision tracking and concurrent operation in an easy-to-use fashion. In addition to the artifacts relevant for the formal verification, we also store system implementations, the development tool chain, and additional documentation in the repository. All of these items are organized

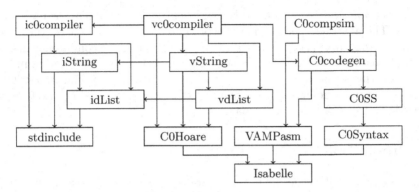

Fig. 2. Example of modules and their dependencies

in so-called *modules*, often on a more fine-grained level than described earlier (e.g., to share commonly used definitions or results across modules). Modules are related to each other via *dependencies*, which have to be acyclic.

Figure 2 shows a number of modules from our repository, which are related to the verification of our non-optimizing C0 compiler [14]. The four boxes on the left-hand side represent the implementation modules of the compiler: the compiler itself, the libraries that it needs, and standard headers. The latter need not to be verified. For the other three implementation modules, there is a corresponding code verification module. All proofs therein are conducted in the C0 Hoare logic [35], which is implemented in Isabelle/HOL [10]. In the top-level code verification module, vc0compiler, the output of the C0 compiler implementation is shown to be equivalent to the output of an (abstract) code generation algorithm [46]. This algorithm maps syntax trees of C0 programs to VAMP assembler programs, whose specifications are both modeled in Isabelle/HOL. In the module C0compsim, the correctness of the code generation, expressed as a simulation theorem over C0 and VAMP assembler computations, is shown.

We will make available self-contained portions of the repository, which appear to be appear sufficiently stable and do not contain confidential data of industry partners. Currently, four releases have been made public.[1] Two of the releases deal with the code-level verification of the C0 string library [25] and the C0 compiler [46], covering all the modules shown in Fig. 2 except C0compsim, which is planned to be released next. As mentioned above, the code verification is conducted in the C0 Hoare logic verification environment. For this purpose, the C0 implementations in concrete syntax have been translated into their Hoare logic representation. The translator is also included in the latest release. In the C0 Hoare logic, Hoare triples for partial and total correctness have been shown. In addition to the functional correctness and termination, the absence of certain runtime errors has been proven (e.g., integer overflows and out-of-bounds array access). These properties would be required at a later stage to translate total

---

[1] http://www.verisoft.de/VerisoftRepository.html

correctness results at the Hoare logic level down to our lower-level semantics, i.e., in the end to compiled program running on the target architecture.

The third release deals with the code-level verification of the C0 big integer library, implementing arbitrary-precision integer operations based on a linked-lists representation of integers. Supported operations include addition, subtraction, multiplication, division, remainder, and exponentiation modulo an integer.

The fourth release deals with the code-level verification of the email client of the academic system relative to the services provided the operating system and applications for signing and email transfer [31]. In addition to modules described earlier, it contains modules for the email client implementation and proofs.

8   Summary

We have presented an overview of the system verification environment used in the Verisoft project to carry out the formal pervasive verification of entire systems of industrial interest. The architecture of our verification environment is to a large extent determined by each system's architecture and its requirements. The system's layers, its implementation languages, its components, and its tool chain are all represented in the verification environment, thus enabling to formally reason on system requirements. The form of the representations is on the one hand shaped by the system requirements and on the other hand by verification productivity concerns: we are employing small-steps semantics to reason on concurrent, communicating programs, but we switch to more abstract semantics (for which we have verification condition generation and integration of automatic provers) wherever possible. Soundness and simulation theorems of the higher-level relative to lower-level semantics justify this approach. Thus, in addition to the stack of computational models, which inherit from the system implementation structure, a semantic stack is build. We have announced a web site, where we have started to publish portions of our verification environment.

References

1. Winskel, G.: The formal semantics of programming languages. MIT Press, Cambridge (1993)
2. Nielson, H.R., Nielson, F.: Semantics with Applications: A Formal Introduction. John Wiley & Sons, Chichester (1992)
3. Hoare, C.A.R.: An axiomatic basis for computer programming. Comm. ACM 12, 576–580 (1969)
4. Dijkstra, E.W.: Guarded commands, nondeterminacy and formal derivation of programs. Comm. ACM 18, 453–457 (1975)
5. Gries, D.: The Science of Programming. Springer, Heidelberg (1987)
6. The Verisoft Project. http://www.verisoft.de/
7. Bevier, W.R., Hunt, Jr., W.A., Moore, J.S., Young, W.D.: An approach to systems verification. Journal of Automated Reasoning 5, 411–428 (1989)

8. Moore, J S.: A grand challenge proposal for formal methods: A verified stack. In: Aichernig, B.K., Maibaum, T.S.E. (eds.) Formal Methods at the Crossroads. From Panacea to Foundational Support. LNCS, vol. 2757, pp. 161–172. Springer, Heidelberg (2003)
9. de Roever, W.P., de Boer, F., Hannemann, U., Hooman, J., Lakhnech, Y., Poel, M., Zwiers, J.: Concurrency Verification: Introduction to Compositional and Non-compositional Methods. Cambridge Univ. Press, Cambridge, UK (2001)
10. Nipkow, T., Paulson, L.C., Wenzel, M.: Isabelle/HOL. LNCS, vol. 2283. Springer, Heidelberg (2002)
11. Mueller, S.M., Paul, W.J.: Computer Architecture: Complexity and Correctness. Springer, Heidelberg (2000)
12. Beyer, S., Jacobi, C., Kröning, D., Leinenbach, D., Paul, W.: Instantiating uninterpreted functional units and memory system: Functional verification of the VAMP. In: Geist, D., Tronci, E. (eds.) CHARME 2003. LNCS, vol. 2860, Springer, Heidelberg (2003)
13. Hennessy, J.L., Patterson, D.A.: Computer Architecture: A Quantitative Approach. Morgan Kaufmann, San Francisco (1996)
14. Leinenbach, D., Paul, W., Petrova, E.: Towards the formal verification of a C0 compiler: Code generation and implementation correctness. In: Aichernig, B., Beckert, B. (eds.) SEFM 2005, pp. 2–11 (2005)
15. Gargano, M., Hillebrand, M., Leinenbach, D., Paul, W.: On the correctness of operating system kernels. In: Hurd, J., Melham, T.F. (eds.) TPHOLs 2005. LNCS, vol. 3603, pp. 1–16. Springer, Heidelberg (2005)
16. Dörrenbächer, J.: (VAMOS microkernel, formal models and verification) Talk given at the International Workshop on System Verification, SV 2006, Sydney, Australia (August 7–8, 2006), http://www.cse.unsw.edu.au/~formalmethods/events/svws-06/VAMOS_Microkernel.pdf
17. Hillebrand, M., In der Rieden, T., Paul, W.: Dealing with I/O devices in the context of pervasive system verification. In: ICCD 2005, pp. 309–316. IEEE Computer Society, Los Alamitos (2005)
18. Knapp, S., Paul, W.: Realistic Worst Case Execution Time Analysis in the Context of Pervasive System Verification. In: Reps, T., Sagiv, M., Bauer, J. (eds.) Wilhelm Festschrift. LNCS, vol. 4444, pp. 53–81. Springer, Heidelberg (2007)
19. Knapp, S., Paul, W.: Pervasive verification of distributed real-time systems. In: Broy, M., Grünbauer, J., Hoare, T. (eds.) Software System Reliability and Security, Trento, Italy. NATO Security Through Science Series. Sub-Series D: Information and Communication Security, vol. 9, pp. 239–297. IOS Press, Amsterdam, Trento, Italy (2007)
20. Alkassar, E., Hillebrand, M., Knapp, S., Rusev, R., Tverdyshev, S.: Formal device and programming model for a serial interface. In: Beckert, B. (ed.) Proceedings, 4th International Verification Workshop (VERIFY), Bremen, Germany, pp. 4–20 (2007)
21. Schmaltz, J.: A formal model of lower system layer. In: Gupta, A., Manolios, P. (eds.) FMCAD 2006, pp. 191–192. IEEE Computer Society, Los Alamitos (2006)
22. Knapp, S.: Towards the verification of functional and timely behavior of an eCall implementation. Master's thesis, Saarland Univ. (2005), http://www-wjp.cs.uni-sb.de/publikationen/Knapp05.pdf
23. Botaschanjan, J., Gruler, A., Harhurin, A., Kof, L., Spichkova, M., Trachtenherz, D.: Towards modularized verification of distributed time-triggered systems. In: Misra, J., Nipkow, T., Sekerinski, E. (eds.) FM 2006. LNCS, vol. 4085, pp. 163–178. Springer, Heidelberg (2006)

24. Dalinger, I., Hillebrand, M., Paul, W.: On the verification of memory management mechanisms. In: Borrione, D., Paul, W. (eds.) CHARME 2005. LNCS, vol. 3725, pp. 301–316. Springer, Heidelberg (2005)
25. Starostin, A.: Formal verification of a C-library for strings. Master's thesis, Saarland Univ. (2006), `http://www-wjp.cs.uni-sb.de/publikationen/St06.pdf`
26. Fischer, S.: Formal verification of a big integer library including division. Master's thesis, Saarland University (2007)
27. Appel, A.W., Ginsburg, M.: Modern Compiler Implementation in C. Cambridge Univ. Press, New York (1998)
28. Liedtke, J.: On micro-kernel construction. In: SOSP 1995. Proceedings of the 15th ACM Symposium on Operating systems principles, pp. 237–250. ACM Press, New York (1995)
29. Shadrin, A.: Design and implementation of the portmapper and RPC primitives in the context of the SOS. Master's thesis, Saarland Univ. (2006), http://www-wjp.cs.uni-sb.de/publikationen/Sh06.pdf
30. Langenstein, B., Nonnengart, A., Rock, G., Stephan, W.: A history-based verification of distributed applications. In: Beckert, B. (ed.) Proceedings, 4th International Verification Workshop (VERIFY), Bremen, Germany, pp. 70–84 (2007)
31. Beuster, G., Henrich, N., Wagner, M.: Real world verification – Experiences from the Verisoft email client. In: Sutcliffe, G., Schmidt, R., Schulz, S. (eds.) ESCoR 2006. CEUR Workshop Proceedings. CEUR-WS.org, vol. 192, pp. 112–125 (2006)
32. Lindenberg, C., Wirt, K., Buchmann, J.: (Formal proof for the correctness of RSA-PSS) Cryptology ePrint Archive, Report 2006/011, `http://eprint.iacr.org/2006/011`
33. Cheikhrouhou, L., Rock, G., Stephan, W., Schwan, M., Lassmann, G.: Verifying a chipcard-based biometric identification protocol in VSE. In: Górski, J. (ed.) SAFECOMP 2006. LNCS, vol. 4166, pp. 42–56. Springer, Heidelberg (2006)
34. Hutter, D., Langenstein, B., Sengler, C., Siekmann, J.H., Stephan, W., Wolpers, A.: Verification Support Environment. In: Hutter, D., Stephan, W. (eds.) Mechanizing Mathematical Reasoning. LNCS (LNAI), vol. 2605, pp. 476–493. Springer, Heidelberg (2005)
35. Schirmer, N.: Verification of Sequential Imperative Programs in Isabelle/HOL. PhD thesis, Technical University of Munich (2006)
36. Tverdyshev, S.: Combination of Isabelle/HOL with automatic tools. In: Gramlich, B. (ed.) FroCos 2005. LNCS (LNAI), vol. 3717, pp. 302–309. Springer, Heidelberg (2005)
37. ACSAR: Automatic Checker of Safety properties based on Abstraction Refinement. `http://www.mpi-inf.mpg.de/~seghir/ACSAR/ACSAR-web-page.html`
38. ARMC: Abstraction refinement-based model checker for safety and liveness properties. `http://www.mpi-inf.mpg.de/~rybal/armc/`
39. Jahob and Bohne: Verifying data structure consistency. `http://www.mit.edu/~vkuncak/projects/jahob/`
40. Daum, M., Maus, S., Schirmer, N., Seghir, M.N.: Integration of a software model checker into Isabelle. In: Sutcliffe, G., Voronkov, A. (eds.) LPAR 2005. LNCS (LNAI), vol. 3835, pp. 381–395. Springer, Heidelberg (2005)
41. Emeliyanenko, P.: Automatic verification of conditions for absence of interrupts. Bachelor's thesis, Saarland Univ. (2006) `http://react.cs.uni-sb.de/fileadmin/user_upload/react/theses/PEmeliyanenko.pdf`
42. SPASS: An Automated Theorem Prover for First-Order Logic with Equality. `http://spass.mpi-sb.mpg.de/`

43. e-SETHEO prover system. http://www4.in.tum.de/~stenzg/
44. Ferdinand, C., Heckmann, R.: Verifying timing behavior by abstract interpretation of executable code. In: Borrione, D., Paul, W. (eds.) CHARME 2005. LNCS, vol. 3725, pp. 336–339. Springer, Heidelberg (2005)
45. Subversion: An open-source revision control system. http://subversion.tigris.org/
46. Petrova, E.: Verification of the C0 Compiler Implementation on the Source Code Level. PhD thesis, Saarland University, Computer Science Department (2007)

Exploiting Shared Structure in
Software Verification Conditions

Domagoj Babić and Alan J. Hu

Computer Science Department
University of British Columbia

Abstract. Despite many advances, today's software model checkers and extended static checkers still do not scale well to large code bases, when verifying properties that depend on complex interprocedural flow of data. An obvious approach to improve performance is to exploit software structure. Although a tremendous amount of work has been done on exploiting structure at various levels of granularity, the fine-grained shared structure among multiple verification conditions has been largely ignored. In this paper, we formalize the notion of shared structure among verification conditions, propose a novel and efficient approach to exploit this sharing, and provide experimental results that this approach can significantly improve the performance of verification, even on path- and context-sensitive and dataflow-intensive properties.

1 Introduction

Verification conditions (VCs) are logical formulas, constructed from a system and desired correctness properties, such that the validity of verification conditions corresponds to the correctness of the system. Constructing and proving VCs are both essential steps in software verification, and both have been active areas of research. In this paper, we focus on proving the validity of VCs more efficiently.

The trend today is to use automated decision procedures to prove or disprove the computed VCs. Unfortunately, this process is computationally extremely expensive and is the main bottleneck to the wider application of formal and semi-formal software verification methods. Previous work has focused on the computation of VCs (e.g. [11,15]), abstraction to make the VCs simpler for the decision procedure (e.g. [4,5]), and the efficiency of the decision procedures themselves (e.g. [9,3,12,19,20]).

In our previous work [1], we showed how the structure of a single interprocedural verification condition can be exploited at a coarse function level. This paper explores a different direction for improving efficiency — namely, exploiting shared structure among multiple VCs at the level of individual expressions — and proposes a technique that exploits this structure. Since solving VCs is typically expensive, elimination of this redundancy has the potential to significantly improve performance of static checking. In this paper, we present our insights, formalize the notion of shared structure, propose an algorithm for exploiting this shared structure, and provide experimental evidence that our approach can cut runtime by almost one third and reduce the number of timeouts.

K. Yorav (Ed.): HVC 2007, LNCS 4899, pp. 169–184, 2008.

1.1 Background and Related Work

Static Checking The work in this paper fits in the context of static checking of software. The distinction between static checking and model checking is fuzzy, but historically, static checking has emphasized fast bug hunting and scalability to large software, at the expense of precision (and often soundness and/or completeness), whereas model checking has emphasized precision and soundness, with the primary research challenge being scalability. Our overall goal is to maintain the precision of a bit-accurate software model checker like CBMC [14], while matching or exceeding the scalability of static checkers like Boogie [17] or Saturn [27].

We use our static checker CALYSTO, but the contribution of this paper can be applied to any static checker that uses a decision procedure, assuming some reasonable properties of VCs (see Sec. 2). Boogie and Saturn are the closest relatives of CALYSTO. Boogie is a mature tool that performs *intraprocedural* analysis and requires user-provided function/class interface invariants. Boogie uses abstract interpretation to compute sound invariants of certain types of loops found in programs, while others are unrolled and terminated with an assumption that the loop test is false [16]. CALYSTO is less mature and handles loops either by unrolling them (unsound) as in ESC/Java [10] or by considering all loop-carried values unconstrained (sound). Standard, more precise loop invariant computation techniques can be used to replace loops with loop invariants, as a CALYSTO-preprocessing technique. The most significant difference is that CALYSTO requires no user-provided interface invariants. Instead, CALYSTO performs path- and context-sensitive *interprocedural* analysis. Such analysis is inherently more expensive than the intraprocedural analysis in Boogie, so we focus on exploiting structure at various levels of granularity to achieve scalability. For instance, in our previous work [1], we showed how structure can be exploited to avoid the exponential blowup of context-sensitive analysis in many cases. Saturn is path-sensitive, but performs only partially context-sensitive analysis by computing summaries as projections onto a set of predicates. CALYSTO, on the other hand, is fully context sensitive, which means that it can handle dataflow-related properties more precisely. Saturn demonstrated that SAT solvers can be used to prove VCs, but it uses off-the-shelf SAT solvers. In our experience, we have found that tight integration of the static checker with a custom-tailored decision procedure offers significant performance improvements, hence our research on exploiting structural properties of VCs by the decision procedures.

Verification Conditions Traditionally, VCs are computed by Dijkstra's weakest precondition transformer [8], as is done for example in ESC/Java [10] and Boogie. A naïve representation of VCs computed by the weakest precondition can be exponential in the size of the code fragment being checked, but this blow-up can be avoided by the introduction of fresh variables to represent intermediate expressions [26,11,15]. Equivalently, we can keep the formulas in the form of graphs that correspond to the abstract syntax trees of the parsed formulas, with common sub-expressions shared. Such graphs make structural reasoning easier, so we shall use the graph representation in this paper. This representational difference is otherwise insignificant.

Two things set our research apart from previous work on VCs. First, as mentioned above, we do not assume user-provided interface invariants, but rather perform context-sensitive interprocedural analysis. Second, we focus on exploiting common subexpressions shared among multiple VCs. Our goal is to explore how much we can learn from solving a set of VCs and how we can apply that knowledge to solve the remaining VCs more efficiently.

Learning. Our contribution can be viewed as an automatic learning technique. Given a set of VCs, the technique learns from the implicants that a decision procedure implied, and attempts to reuse that knowledge later if the remaining VCs share some subexpressions with the already solved ones.

Learning is an efficient technique for speeding up decision procedures, and has been especially effective in boolean satisfiability (SAT) solvers [28]. The new aspect of the problem that we are considering is *context-dependence* — facts learned about a shared subgraph while solving one VC might not hold in the context of others.

Stump and Dill [25] proposed context-dependent caching and proof compression for an Edinburgh LF decision procedure, but they considered caching only for subgraphs of a single formula and did not consider sharing between multiple formulas. While solving each individual VC, our static checker CALYSTO already eliminates common subexpressions, and our SAT-based decision procedure SPEAR features its own *intra-VC* learning (caching) mechanism. In contrast, the contribution of the present paper is *inter-VC* learning.

Structure Exploitation. Many researchers have looked into how to exploit structure for more efficient verification. Starting from the coarsest level of granularity, Rountev at al. [23] observed that large libraries change less frequently than the applications that use them, so the libraries can be pre-analyzed for speeding up verification of the applications. Conway et al. [6] observed that programs are usually modified in small incremental steps. So, after the application was verified once, only the modified functions and functions that transitively call them have to be re-verified. Our work explores a new dimension of the problem that has not (to the best of our knowledge) been explored before. Namely, we are interested in elimination of redundancy at a finer level of granularity — individual expressions. This redundancy is inherent to any software verification technique simply because a large majority of execution paths share some common sequence of statements. Our technique is orthogonal to the above mentioned approaches, and can be combined with them.

2   Preliminaries

In this section, we give definitions of some basic concepts required for understanding the rest of the paper and present the assumptions on which our method relies.

Decision Procedure. We are interested in bit-precise software verification in order to be able to catch frequent integer under/over-flow bugs[1]. So, all of our analysis will be

---

[1] For instance, the 2004 JPEG security exploit (see e.g. [2]).

assuming modular (machine bit-vector) arithmetic. Our decision procedure SPEAR[2] is based on a SAT solver and supports all standard modular arithmetic operators on finite bit-vectors, including expensive operators (like multiplication and division). Although we use modular arithmetic, the contribution is largely independent of the chosen logic.

When automated decision procedures are used for proving VCs, the validity of a verification condition VC is usually being proven by asking the decision procedure to prove unsatisfiability of the formula $VC = \text{false}$. Its satisfiability means that there is a possible bug in the program from which the VC was constructed.

Representation As mentioned, we represent VCs as acyclic graphs. This representation simplifies the reasoning about the structure of the formulas. In addition, using simple node hash tables, we eliminate all common subexpressions. Such graphs, in which all redundancies have been eliminated, are known as maximally-shared graphs:

Definition 1 (Maximally-Shared Graph)
Given an acyclic graph $G = (N, E)$, let $\mathcal{L}$ stand for a labeling function $\mathcal{L} : N \longrightarrow$ string. Define the arity of a node n, denoted as $|n|$, as the number of outgoing edges. The outgoing edges are ordered, and the i-th edge of a node n will be denoted as $child_i(n)$. Two operator nodes n_1 and n_2 are defined to be equivalent ($n_1 \triangleq n_2$) if and only if $|n_1| = |n_2|$, $\mathcal{L}(n_1) = \mathcal{L}(n_2)$, and $\forall i : 0 \leq i \leq |n_1| : child_i(n_1) \triangleq child_i(n_2)$. (This is standard bisimulation equivalence, but applied to a graph representing the static structure of a VC, rather than the more typical application to a transition system.) Graph G is maximally-shared if $\neg \exists n_1, n_2 \in N : n_1 \neq n_2 \wedge n_1 \triangleq n_2$.

CALYSTO computes verification conditions directly as maximally-shared graphs. The graph representation can be transformed into a conjunction of expressions by standard renaming. We shall identify nodes in the graph with the variables used for renaming. This is a one-to-one mapping. We shall represent equality (resp. inequality) in formulas and algorithms as $=$ (resp. $\neq$), while in the code snippets and graphs $=$ will stand for assignment, and $==$ (resp. $!=$) for equality (resp. inequality).

Graph Relations If there is an edge connecting two nodes, $n \longrightarrow m \in E$, then n is a *predecessor* of m, and m is a *successor* of n. The set of predecessors of a node n will be denoted as $Pred(n)$, and the set of its successors as $Succ(n)$. The nodes in the transitive closure of $Pred(n)$ are *ancestors* of n, and the nodes in the transitive closure of $Succ(n)$ are *descendants* of n, denoted $Desc(n)$.

To analyze the shared subgraphs, we rely upon the dominance relation [21]:

Definition 2 (Dominance Relation)
A node n dominates node m if and only if all the paths from the entry node to m go through n, written as $n \trianglerighteq m$. If $n \neq m$, n strictly dominates m, denoted $n \gg m$.

The dominance relation is a partial order (reflexive, antisymmetric, and transitive) and can be computed in $\mathcal{O}(N\alpha(E, N))$ [18] time, where α is the extremely slowly growing inverse of Ackermann's function. In practice, a simpler $\mathcal{O}(E \log N)$ algorithm [18] is

---

[2] http://www.domagoj.info/index_spear.htm

faster, even for very large graphs, and that is what we are using for the results in this paper.

The dominance relation, as defined above, requires a unique entry node. The technique presented in this paper always considers the root node that represents a single VC to be the entry node for the computation of the dominance relation.

Assumptions The work presented in the paper relies on several assumptions, which are either almost always satisfied in practice or can be satisfied with a trivial amount of post-processing.

First, as mentioned already, we assume that the VCs are representable by acyclic graphs corresponding to abstract syntax trees obtained by parsing the formula. Most software static checking tools (including Saturn, ESC/Java, Boogie, and CALYSTO) produce VCs that have such structure. An example of a graph representation of two VCs that share some subgraphs is shown in Fig. 1.

Second, the decision procedure must be able to identify facts of the form *variable = constant* that are implied by formulas being solved. For instance, if the decision procedure is based on a SAT solver, learned unit literals are such facts. Decision procedures based on the Nelson-Oppen [20] framework generate conjunctions of equalities (providing that the individual theories are convex), and it is easy to extract the equalities that satisfy our requirement.

Third, we assume complete propagation of equalities with constants, i.e. we require that the decision procedure generates facts of the form $a = 7, b = 7, c = 7$ instead of $a = 7, b = a, c = b$. This is trivial to accomplish by a linear time constant propagation post-processing even if the decision procedure does not make such guarantees. Assuming that the formula is satisfiable, both SAT solvers and E-graphs [7], on which the Nelson-Oppen framework is based, satisfy this requirement.

Fourth, we assume that the proper subexpressions of a VC are logically consistent. Every expression that can be translated into an acyclic circuit-like representation satisfies this requirements because circuits themselves are logically consistent — every input produces some output. Two small examples provide the intuition behind this assumption.

Example 1 Consider an obviously inconsistent formula $a < 0 \land a > 0$. By introduction of fresh variables $n_0, \cdots, n_2$ we get:

$$n_0 = a < 0$$
$$n_1 = a > 0$$
$$n_2 = n_0 \land n_1$$

This is a logically consistent set of constraints which corresponds to the circuit-like representation in Fig. 1. Note that the constraints force n_2 to be always false, but the constraints themselves are satisfiable. Variable n_2 corresponding to the root node in Fig. 1 can be seen as a *circuit output*.   □

As mentioned earlier, the goal is to prove validity of a VC, i.e., that the value of the output node is always true. We can check this by adding constraint *root_node = false*

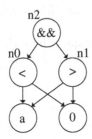

Fig. 1. Small maximally-shared graph representing $a < 0 \wedge a > 0$. Successors of non-commutative operators are ordered in the natural order (from left to right). Operator nodes are labelled with the operator (inscribed) and the name of corresponding variable used in renaming (adjacent to the node).

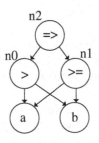

Fig. 2. Graph corresponding to the set of constraints in Example 2

and then check satisfiability. If the resulting formula is satisfiable, the original VC is not valid. Only by adding the additional constraint can the constraints become inconsistent, as in the next example.

Example 2 Given the formula: $VC = (a > b \Rightarrow a \geq b)$, we can construct the set of constraints:

$$n_0 = a > b$$
$$n_1 = a \geq b$$
$$n_2 = n_0 \Rightarrow n_1$$

which is consistent. Now, to check validity, we add constraint $n_2 = $ false to the set, forcing the output to false. The set of constraints becomes unsatisfiable, meaning that the original VC was valid. □

If the consistency assumption were violated, then the decision procedure could imply arbitrary implicants, because false can imply anything. The consistency assumption ensures that the implicants derived from a subexpression are meaningful.

3   Exploiting Shared Structure

In software, many paths share common statements, which means that computed VCs will share common subexpressions. However, it is less obvious how to exploit that structure.

A direct approach is to construct a disjunction of all (negated) verification conditions, give it to the theorem prover, and for each solution, report a bug, then add a blocking clause to eliminate that disjunct from further consideration. Everything that the theorem prover learns can be re-used, so this is a "perfect solution". Unfortunately, it suffers from the same problem as clause learning in a SAT solver: there is too much information that is learned, with very little of it being useful later. Instead, we seek to distill out implicants learned while solving one VC that are useful for solving another VC. However, not all implicants can be re-used, because they can depend on the context of the first VC, which might not be true of the other VC.

The crux of the problem is that decision procedures can propagate information in any direction. Consider the VC shown in Fig. 2 with the additional constraint $n_2 = $ false. Most decision procedures would start solving the VC by propagating constants. From $n_2 = $ false, it follows that $n_0 = $ true and $n_1 = $ false. From $n_1 = $ false it follows that $a < b$. The last implicant contradicts $a > b$, hence the set of constraints represented by the graph is unsatisfiable. This propagation of information from *above* introduces assumptions that might not hold in all other contexts. Any other VC that contains the subexpression represented by n_2 and does not enforce $n_2 = $ false cannot reuse the previously computed solution.

Intuitively, we want a way to figure out which implicants were implied from *below*. For instance, if a decision procedure can infer that node n_2 is always true just by considering its descendants, then the same decision procedure will be able to infer the same result if n_2 appears as a subexpression of any other VC. In other words, $n_2 = $ true becomes a *context-independent invariant*.

The concept of "context" can be defined in many ways. Since we study the fine-grained structure of expressions computed from software, it is helpful to define context on the maximally-shared graphs as follows: We say that an expression represented by a node in a maximally-shared graph is context-independent if its value is uniquely implied by its sub-expressions, otherwise the relation is context-dependent. For instance, in Example 2 (Fig. 2) the implicant $n_0 = $ true is context-dependent because the implication chain came from the predecessor n_2. On the other hand, $n_2 = $ true is a context-independent invariant as it follows from the nodes below n_2.

Decision procedures can generate a large number of implicants. For example, SAT solvers usually generate a single implicant per conflict. Keeping even only 10% of implicants from each VC requires excessive amounts of memory. In addition, not all implicants are context-independent invariants. So, we use a more restricted form of invariants to represent learned facts:

Definition 3. *Let n be some node in a maximally-shared graph and ψ an invariant derived by the decision procedure of the form $n = $ constant. We shall say that n is* fixed *by the decision procedure. Define predicate $fix_{DP}(n)$ to be* true *iff n is fixed by the decision procedure. If $fix_{DP}(n) = $ true, define operator $FixVal_{DP}(n)$ to be an operator that returns the constant to which the node n was fixed.*

The invariants derived by the decision procedure represent knowledge gained about the solved VC; these invariants can be either context-dependent or context-independent. We need to separate out the context-independent ones, as those can be used later when other VCs are solved. So, we define a subset of nodes that were fixed by the decision procedure in a context-independent manner as:

Definition 4. *Let n be a node fixed by the decision procedure to $FixVal_{DP}(n)$. If the invariant $n = FixVal_{DP}(n)$ was derived only by considering a subgraph rooted at n, we* *shall say that n was* fixed from below. *Define predicate fix$_\uparrow$ (n) to be* true *iff n is fixed from below.*

There are two basic approaches to establishing context independence. First, the decision procedure could record the implication graph for each inferred relation. Second, one could attempt to reconstruct the chain of reasoning from the relations produced by the decision procedure once it terminates. In our experience, the first approach is impractical for decision procedures based on SAT solvers, as it requires excessive resources, and slows down the core of the solver by several orders of magnitude. However, it might be a viable approach within the Nelson-Oppen framework if all the combined theories are convex [20][3]. We present a reconstruction-based approach: a simple algorithm that given a set of nodes fixed by the decision procedure, efficiently computes a safe approximation of the set of nodes fixed in a context-independent manner.

It is worth noting that simple incrementality [13] cannot be used for handling multiple contexts. When the contexts are changed, assumptions and their implicants unrelated to the new context have to be removed, so the implication graphs have to be recorded — exactly what we are trying to avoid. Some automated theorem provers, like Yices [9] and CVC [24], feature push/pop commands that allow undoing logical reasoning since the last checkpoint (push). Even with these commands, we would need to push a new context for each potentially shared node, which would be prohibitively expensive. Furthermore, if lazy construction of VCs is used, then it is not known *a priori* which nodes will end up being shared, so every single subexpression would need to be pushed as a new context.

3.1 Algorithm

Depending on the client, the queries to the decision procedures might be available all at once, or computed in a lazy manner. For example, a static checker that relies on some form of abstraction might compute incrementally more refined VCs, or process the call graph of the verified application in an incremental manner. Other clients, like invariant generators, might construct a number of queries at once, and ask for invariants common to all the queries. Because CALYSTO performs lazy structural abstraction [1], we focus on the case where queries are posed in an online manner: VCs are checked one-by-one and future queries are not known. Obviously, the same algorithm can also handle the the case where all VCs are available in advance.

Algorithm 1 computes a safe approximation of the set of nodes that are fixed from below. The values of nodes fixed from below are stored in an associative table *Fixed*, indexed by the nodes. Later, if another VC contains a node n that exists in the table, the value that is read from the table, *Fixed*[n], is used to create an additional constraint $n =$ *Fixed*[n]. Adding this additional constraint to the set of constraints representing the VC being solved saves computation effort because the decision procedure can immediately start propagating the *Fixed*[n] constant.

---

[3] Modular arithmetic, as well as the theory of integers, are not convex, so even decision procedures based on Nelson-Oppen framework would need some form of bookkeeping, similar to implication graphs, to be able to exactly identify a set of assumptions from which each implicant was implied.

Algorithm 1. Approximation of the set of nodes fixed from below. Predicate *isConstant*(n) returns true if the node n is a constant node, predicate *isRoot*(n) returns true if the node n represents a VC (root of the graph), while *isOperator*(n) is true iff n represents an operator. Results of the analysis are stored in the table *Fixed*, indexed by nodes. The set of descendants (resp. predecessors) of a node n is denoted as $Desc(n)$ (resp. $Pred(n)$).

```
 1: procedure FIX(n, Fixed)
 2:     for each s ∈ Succ(n) do
 3:         FIX(s, Fixed)
 4:     if ¬isRoot(n) ∧ isOperator(n) ∧ fix_DP(n) then
 5:         for each d ∈ Desc(n) do
 6:             if ¬isConstant(d) ∨ n ≫̸ d then
 7:                 return
 8:         for each p ∈ Pred(n) do
 9:             if fix_DP(p) then
10:                 return
11:         Fixed[n] ← FixVal_DP(n)
```

Line 4 performs some basic technical checks. The value of the root node is fixed from above (to false because we are checking for unsatisfiability), so the root node is eliminated from consideration. Note that there is no reason why the root node couldn't be fixed from below as well. However, in that case, our analysis is not capable to resolve whether the implication chain came from above or from below. In order to resolve this ambiguity, the theorem prover would need to track implication graphs — a technique which we consider too expensive.

Only three basic types of nodes can be present in the expression graph: constants, variables, and operators. Constants are always fixed from below, variables are always considered unconstrained, so it makes sense to attempt to fix the values of only the operator nodes.

Intuitively, the algorithm works as follows. Lines 5–7 check whether the node dominates all its descendants. If n does not dominate some descendant d, it follows that d is reachable from the root of the graph by at least one path that does not go through n. Consequently, d appears in at least two contexts (one represented by the path that passes through n and the other by path that avoids n). Without reconstructing the implication graph that led the decision procedure to imply $n = FixVal_{DP}(n)$, it is not possible to distinguish between these cases: (1) The invariant was implied from below, relying only on the descendants of n. (2) The invariant was implied from above, possibly all the way from the root node. (3) The constant propagation chain came from above, avoiding n, fixed the value of some descendant of n, which in turn implied the invariant. The dominance test eliminates the third case. The purpose of lines 8–10 is to eliminate the second case. Obviously, if no predecessor of n was fixed, the constant propagation chain must have come from below. Remember that we assume complete propagation of constants, so each constant propagation chain has to have its beginning and its end. The nodes that pass both tests can be safely considered fixed from below.

Implementations should mark visited nodes and avoid revisiting them. As each node has to be visited only once, and each node can have at most $|N|$ descendants and predecessors together (G is acyclic), the worst case complexity is $\mathcal{O}(|N|^2)$, but that is a very pessimistic bound. We found that in practice the algorithm runs almost in linear time if a depth-first-search is used to iterate over the descendants in lines 5–7. Intuitively, the deeper the node is, the larger the probability that it is shared (simpler expressions are more frequently shared than complex ones). Hence, the probability of running into a node not dominated by n is becoming larger as we get further away from n (downwards). The dominance relation can be computed in $\mathcal{O}(|N|\alpha(|N|,|E|))$, as noted before.

How good is the approximation? The algorithm is able to fix only the nodes that are at the end of a constant propagation chain. Intuitively, the last fixed node in the constant propagation chain is the node that required the largest amount of reasoning. For instance, let $n_1, \cdots, n_k$ be a sequence of nodes whose values were fixed from below, all lying on the same path. Assume that there are k VCs such that first contains n_1, second n_2 but not n_1, and so on. The last VC contains only n_k. Since all node values were fixed from below, it is likely that the decision procedure will repeat the same steps while solving each of those k VCs, so eventually, all nodes in the constant propagation chain might become fixed from below, and constraints $n_i = FixVal_{DP}(n_i)$ can be used later if any of the n_i nodes becomes a part of other VCs. Even though this approximation is crude, it is very fast even for large VCs. In Sec. 4, we will evaluate whether the algorithm is fast enough and can find enough context-independent invariants to improve overall performance.

To prove that Alg. 1 really computes a set of nodes fixed from below, we start with the following lemma.

Lemma 1. *Let n be the subgraph of graph G such that n is fixed by the decision procedure $fix_{DP}(n) = $ true. Assume that $\forall p \in Pred(n) : \neg fix_{DP}(p)$ and $\forall d \in Desc(n) : n \gg d$, then $fix_{\uparrow}(n) = $ true*

Proof. As n dominates all descendants, the decision procedure could have inferred that $n = FixVal_{DP}(n)$ by a chain of constant propagations either from the descendants in G of n or from its ancestors. Due to the definition of dominance, the constant propagation chain can enter the subgraph rooted at n only passing through n, or has to start in the subgraph and propagate upwards. According to our assumptions (Sec. 2), the decision procedure completely propagates constants. So, if the the chain starts in some ancestor of n, at least one predecessor has to be fixed. If that's not the case, we can deduce that $n = FixVal_{DP}(n)$ must have been implied from the descendants of n.

Theorem 1. *All of the expressions $n = FixVal_{DP}(n)$ computed by Alg. 1 are context-independent invariants.*

Proof. Follows from Lemma 1

Finally, we give the overall algorithm (Alg. 2) to verify multiple VCs with sharing, as implemented in CALYSTO. Given a graph representation of a VC, the main loop first translates the graph into the form suitable for the given decision procedure, producing a set of constraints C, and negates the VC. For each node n whose value was fixed from below, the algorithm adds the corresponding constraint $n = FixVal_{DP}(n)$ to the set of constraints. The decision procedure is called with the set of constraints as a parameter. If the decision procedure finds the negated VC satisfiable, it reports a possible bug and continues. In the last step, Alg. 1 visits the nodes in the graph, and computes an

Algorithm 2. Checking the Validity of VCs with Shared Structure. Function TRANS-
LATE translates the graph representation to a representation suitable for the decision
procedure. SOLVE is the call to the decision procedure with the set of constraints C.

1: clear table *Fixed*
2: **for each** VC_i **do**
3:    $C \leftarrow \text{TRANSLATE}(VC_i) \cup VC_i = \text{false}$
4:    **for each** $n \in Desc(VC_i)$ **do**
5:       **if** n is a valid index into table *Fixed* **then**
6:          $C \leftarrow C \cup n = Fixed[n]$
7:    $status \leftarrow \text{SOLVE}(C)$
8:    **if** $status = satisfiable$ **then**
9:       Report bug
10:   $\text{FIX}(VC_i, Fixed)$

---

approximation of the set of nodes whose values were fixed from below by the most
recent call to the decision procedure, for use in solving subsquent VCs.

3.2 Example

In this section, we go through an example that is similar to what we have found in
practice. The example illustrates expression sharing among VCs. Variables a, b, c are
machine integers, and s,t,u,v,y,x are boolean variables. All operators used in the example are standard C-like operators.[4]

```
1   int f(int a, int b, bool s, bool t) {
2       if (a % 2) { a++; }
3       if (b % 2) { b++; }
4
5       int c = a * b;
6       int d = c & 3;
7       bool u = (d != 0);
8       bool v = (s == t);
9       bool y = (u || s);
10      bool x = (y || v);
11
12      if (x) {
13          assert(t); // VC1
14          ...
15      } else {
16          assert((a + b) % 2 == 0); // VC2
17          ...
18      }
19      ...
20  }
```

There are two assertions in the example: the first assertion can be violated, while the
second can't. Lines 2–3 increment odd numbers, so at line 5 both a and b are even.

---

[4] Operator % is the modulo operator, & is bitwise-and, || is logical-or, and ++ is post-increment.

Table 1. The first column gives the name and version of the benchmark. KLOC is the number of source code lines, in thousands, before preprocessing. #VCs is the number of checked VCs. As is typical, almost all VCs are UNSAT, since satisfiable VCs correspond to bug reports. The next four columns give the total VC checking time in seconds (including timeouts) and the number of timeouts, for the base approach (i.e., the same system without the newly proposed method) vs. the newly proposed method. The timeout limit was 300 secs. Experiments were on a dual-processor AMD X2 4600+ machine with 2 GB RAM, running Linux 2.6.15. Memory consumption was not a bottleneck on any of the benchmarks.

Benchmark	KLOC	#VCs	Base Approach		New Approach	
			Time (sec)	Timeouts	Time (sec)	Timeouts
Bftpd v1.6	4	1130	725.8	0	582.5	0
HyperSAT v1.7	9	1363	5.3	0	5.1	0
Licq v1.3.4	20	2009	199.6	0	214.5	0
Dspam v3.6.5	37	8627	3478.6	8	3157.6	6
Xchat v2.6.8	76	8090	368.5	0	365.8	0
Wine v0.9.27	126	9000	1881.4	2	1266.7	0

Thus, their product is a multiple of four. Therefore, the last two bits of the product will be zero, even in the case of an overflow. Hence, d is always zero.

In our implementation, the VCs are computed directly as maximally-shared graphs, as shown in Fig. 3, from the SSA [22] provided by the compiler front-end. A large part of the graph is shared. This sharing is especially valuable when expensive operations are shared, like multiplication.

How would a SAT-based decision procedure handle these constraints? Each VC is solved independently of the others, and additional constraints are kept only for nodes fixed from below. We start solving VC1 by adding the constraint $VC_1 = \text{false}$. The decision procedure could deduce by constant propagation from the root: $x = \text{true}, t = \text{false}$, and those are all the invariants that can be found by trivial constant propagation. A typical SAT solver could continue with enumeration of possible solutions that would satisfy node c, which corresponds to the product of two conditionally defined variables. If a (resp. b) is odd, it will be incremented, so a (resp. b) is even at line 5. As mentioned previously, the least significant bit of even numbers is zero, so the two least significant bits of a product of even numbers are zero as well. Hence, the decision procedure eventually implies $d = 0$. By constant propagation it follows that $u = \text{false}$. At that point, the decision procedure has to make another case split, and by setting $s = \text{true}$, VC1 is satisfied, meaning that the assertion can be violated. When VC1 is being solved, node u dominates all leaves of its subgraph (each root node is solved independently, so VC2 still doesn't exist at this point). Node u was not fixed from above, but considering the subgraph rooted at u, the decision procedure was able to infer that $u = \text{false}$. Since both conditions required by the Alg. 1 are met, u can be marked as fixed from below. Later, when VC2 is constructed, the additional constraint $u = \text{false}$ can be added to the set of constraints. Adding the constraint quickly prunes away most of the left branch of VC2, focusing the effort on the right branch. Since the sum of two even numbers is divisible by two, the right branch is true, meaning that $VC_2 =$ false is unsatisfiable. Hence, the second assertion is valid.

4 Experimental Results

To test our approach, we used CALYSTO to generate VCs for six real-world, publicly-available C/C++ applications, ranging in size from 4 to 126 thousand lines of code (KLOC) before preprocessing. The benchmarks are the Bftpd ftp server, the Dspam spam filter, our boolean satisfiability solver HYPERSAT, the Licq ICQ chat client, the Wine Windows OS emulator, and the Xchat IRC client. For each program, for each pointer dereference, we generated a VC to check that the pointer is non-NULL (omitting VCs that were solved trivially by our expression simplifier). Although we demonstrate our approach on checking for NULL pointers, our method is independent of the property being verified, as long as the assumptions in Sec. 2 are met.

The experimental results are given in Table 1. The runtimes represent the time our SAT-based modular arithmetic decision procedure SPEAR needed for solving all the

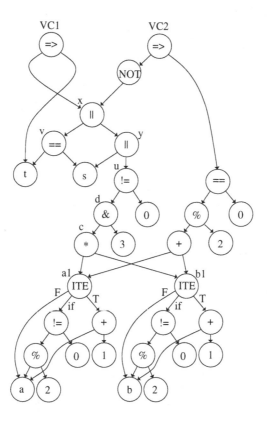

Fig. 3. Maximally-shared graph representing two negated VCs. To simplify the graph layout, some constants are not shared. Edges of if-then-else (ITE) nodes are labelled with if for the condition branch, and T (resp. F) for true (resp. false) branches.

VCs and include computation of the dominance relation. On only one of the smaller benchmarks, Licq, was the new approach somewhat slower. In all other cases, the new approach is faster. On Wine, the largest benchmark, the proposed approach speeds up the solving phase by 32%. There were also fewer timeouts with the new approach (meaning that the reported results are lower bounds on the speedup).

The key question is whether the derived context-independent invariants are able to accelerate the solver enough to overcome the cost of deriving them. The results show that the overhead of our approach is very low, yet in some cases, it provides a substantial speedup. SPEAR was already highly optimized, and features several techniques (like abstraction, lazy interpretation [1], gate-optimal VC encoding, and several others) that result in significant performance improvements over a standard, direct "bit-blasting" translation of the VCs into SAT. The results presented in Table 1 show that exploiting shared structure can push a state-of-the-art static checker even further.

5   Future Work

It would be useful to improve the quality of approximation of the set of nodes fixed from below, while maintaining the low computational cost. Since we observed more structure-sharing in practice than our technique is able to exploit, we believe that improvements in that direction could provide even more significant speedups.

Finding more expressive context-independent invariants could also boost the performance of static checking. Such context-independent learning would probably run into similar problems as learning in decision procedures — which implicants to keep and for how long. Considering that learning has proven itself in SAT solvers as an indispensable technique without which no solver today is competitive, we believe that this direction is particularly promising.

We have focused on the case where VCs are solved one-by-one. If multiple VCs are available all at once, solving the VCs in a different, heuristically-chosen order might allow deriving more context-independent invariants. Furthermore, it should be possible to analyze the maximally shared graph to quickly find the shared subgraphs between the multiple VCs. Only these nodes need to be considered as candidates to be context-independent invariants, reducing the overhead of our approach.

6   Conclusion

We have demonstrated a novel way to exploit shared, expression-level structure available in verification conditions. The approach relies on simple invariants inferred by automatic decision procedures. The proposed technique computes a subset of those invariants which can be used safely in a context-independent manner. Our experimental results demonstrate that the technique can substantially improve the performance of static checking. As scalability is the primary limitation of automatic software verification tools, these results are a step towards more widely applicable, practical formal verification of software.

References

1. Babić, D., Hu, A.J.: Structural abstraction of software verification conditions. In: Damm, W., Hermanns, H. (eds.) CAV 2007. LNCS, vol. 4590, pp. 371–383. Springer, Heidelberg (2007)
2. Babić, D., Musuvathi, M.: Modular Arithmetic Decision Procedure. Technical Report TR-2005-114, Microsoft Research Redmond (2005)
3. Ball, T., Lahiri, S.K., Musuvathi, M.: Zap: Automated theorem proving for software analysis. In: Sutcliffe, G., Voronkov, A. (eds.) LPAR 2005. LNCS (LNAI), vol. 3835, pp. 2–22. Springer, Heidelberg (2005)
4. Ball, T., Majumdar, R., Millstein, T., Rajamani, S.K.: Automatic predicate abstraction of C programs. In: PLDI, ACM SIGPLAN Notices, vol. 36, pp. 203–213 (2001)
5. Bryant, R.E., Kroening, D., Ouaknine, J., Seshia, S.A., Strichman, O., Brady, B.: Deciding bit-vector arithmetic with abstraction. In: Grumberg, O., Huth, M. (eds.) TACAS 2007. LNCS, vol. 4424, pp. 358–372. Springer, Heidelberg (2007)
6. Conway, C.L., Namjoshi, K.S., Dams, D., Edwards, S.A.: Incremental Algorithms for Interprocedural Analysis of Safety Properties. In: Etessami, K., Rajamani, S.K. (eds.) CAV 2005. LNCS, vol. 3576, pp. 449–461. Springer, Heidelberg (2005)
7. Detlefs, D., Nelson, G., Saxe, J.S.: Simplify: A Theorem Prover for Program Checking. Technical report, HP Laboratories Palo Alto, Technical Report HPL-2003-148 (2003)
8. Dijkstra, E.W., Scholten, C.S.: Predicate calculus and program semantics. Springer, New York (1990)
9. Dutertre, B., de Moura, L.M.: A Fast Linear-Arithmetic Solver for DPLL(T). In: Ball, T., Jones, R.B. (eds.) CAV 2006. LNCS, vol. 4144, pp. 81–94. Springer, Heidelberg (2006)
10. Flanagan, C., Leino, K.R.M., Lillibridge, M., Nelson, G., Saxe, J.B., Stata, R.: Extended static checking for Java. In: PLDI, ACM SIGPLAN Notices, pp. 234–245 (2002)
11. Flanagan, C., Saxe, J.B.: Avoiding exponential explosion: Generating compact verification conditions. In: POPL, pp. 193–205. ACM Press, New York (2001)
12. Ganzinger, H., Hagen, G., Nieuwenhuis, R., Oliveras, A., Tinelli, C.: DPLL(T): Fast Decision Procedures. In: Alur, R., Peled, D.A. (eds.) CAV 2004. LNCS, vol. 3114, pp. 175–188. Springer, Heidelberg (2004)
13. Hooker, J.N.: Solving the incremental satisfiability problem. J. Log. Program. 15(1-2), 177–186 (1993)
14. Kroening, D., Clarke, E., Yorav, K.: Behavioral Consistency of C and Verilog Programs Using Bounded Model Checking. In: DAC, pp. 368–371. ACM Press, New York (2003)
15. Leino, K.R.M.: Efficient weakest preconditions. Inf. Process. Lett. 93(6), 281–288 (2005)
16. Leino, K.R.M., Logozzo, F.: Loop invariants on demand. In: Yi, K. (ed.) APLAS 2005. LNCS, vol. 3780, pp. 119–134. Springer, Heidelberg (2005)
17. Leino, K.R.M., Müller, P.: A verification methodology for model fields. In: Sestoft, P. (ed.) ESOP 2006 and ETAPS 2006. LNCS, vol. 3924, pp. 115–130. Springer, Heidelberg (2006)
18. Lengauer, T., Tarjan, R.E.: A fast algorithm for finding dominators in a flowgraph. ACM Trans. Program. Lang. Syst. 1(1), 121–141 (1979)
19. Moskewicz, M.W., Madigan, C.F., Zhao, Y., Zhang, L., Malik, S.: Chaff: Engineering an efficient SAT solver. In: DAC, pp. 530–535. ACM Press, New York (2001)
20. Nelson, G.: Techniques for program verification. PhD thesis, Stanford University (1979)
21. Prosser, R.T.: Applications of boolean matrices to the analysis of flow diagrams. In: Proceedings of the Eastern Joint Computer Conference, pp. 133–138. Spartan Books (1959)
22. Rosen, B.K., Wegman, M.N., Zadeck, F.K.: Global value numbers and redundant computations. In: POPL, pp. 12–27. ACM Press, New York (1988)
23. Rountev, A., Kagan, S., Marlowe, T.J.: Interprocedural dataflow analysis in the presence of large libraries. In: Mycroft, A., Zeller, A. (eds.) CC 2006 and ETAPS 2006. LNCS, vol. 3923, pp. 2–16. Springer, Heidelberg (2006)

24. Stump, A., Barrett, C., Dill, D.: CVC: A Cooperating Validity Checker. In: Brinksma, E., Larsen, K.G. (eds.) CAV 2002. LNCS, vol. 2404, Springer, Heidelberg (2002)
25. Stump, A., Dill, D.L.: Faster Proof Checking in the Edinburgh Logical Framework. In: Voronkov, A. (ed.) CADE 2002. LNCS (LNAI), vol. 2392, pp. 392–407. Springer, Heidelberg (2002)
26. Tseitin, G.S.: On the complexity of derivation in propositional calculus. In: Siekmann, J., Wrightson, G. (eds.) Automation of Reasoning 2: Classical Papers on Computational Logic 1967-1970, pp. 466–483. Springer, Heidelberg (1983)
27. Xie, Y., Aiken, A.: Scalable error detection using boolean satisfiability. In: POPL, pp. 351–363. ACM Press, New York (2005)
28. Zhang, L., Madigan, C.F., Moskewicz, M.H., Malik, S.: Efficient conflict driven learning in a boolean satisfiability solver. In: ICCAD, pp. 279–285. IEEE Press, Los Alamitos (2001)

Delayed Nondeterminism in Model Checking Embedded Systems Assembly Code

Thomas Noll[1] and Bastian Schlich[2]

[1] Software Modeling and Verification Group
RWTH Aachen University
52074 Aachen, Germany
noll@cs.rwth-aachen.de
[2] Embedded Software Laboratory
RWTH Aachen University
52074 Aachen, Germany
schlich@cs.rwth-aachen.de

Abstract. This paper presents an approach to the efficient verification of embedded systems. Such systems usually operate in uncertain environments, giving rise to a high degree of nondeterminism in the corresponding formal models, which in turn aggravates the state explosion problem. Careful handling of nondeterminism is therefore crucial for obtaining efficient model checking tools. Here, we support this goal by developing a formal computation model and an abstraction method, called *delayed nondeterminism*, which instantiates nondeterministic values only if and when this is required by the application code. It is shown how this technique can be integrated into our CTL model checking tool *[mc]square* by introducing symbolic abstract states which represent several concrete states. We also give a simulation relation between the concrete and the abstract state space, thus establishing the soundness of delayed nondeterminism with respect to "path-universal" logics such as ACTL and LTL. Furthermore, a case study is presented in which three different programs are used to demonstrate the effectiveness of our technique.

1 Introduction

Embedded systems are frequently used in safety critical systems. Full testing of these systems is often not possible due to fast time to market or uncertain environments. To address these problems, industry recognized model checking as a promising future tool for the analysis of such systems.

The first model checking tools available worked on proprietary models (e.g., SMV [1], Spin [2] and Uppaal [3]). To use them, the user had to remodel the system under consideration in the input language of the corresponding tool. Then, there were model checking tools which worked on higher level programming languages (e.g., C, C++ or Java). Nowadays, model checking of assembly language (machine level language) gets into focus of research, cf. [4,5,6,7,8].

Model checking assembly language has several advantages. Writing microcontroller programs in higher level languages usually involves direct hardware access

K. Yorav (Ed.): HVC 2007, LNCS 4899, pp. 185–201, 2008.
© Springer-Verlag Berlin Heidelberg 2008

or embedded assembly instructions, which is not supported by most of the tools. Moreover, the assembly code is the code that is actually deployed to the hardware. Hence, it is not an intermediate representation as the C code. Thus, all errors introduced during the complete development process can be found in the assembly code, including, for instance, errors in the compiler and errors in handling the hardware. The model checker does not have to consider the behavior of the compiler as when model checking C code. In contrast to C code, assembly code usually has a clean, formal and well documented semantics.

On the other side, model checking assembly code has two disadvantages. First, the created state spaces tend to be bigger than when model checking higher level languages as more details are involved. Second, the analysis is hardware dependent, and hence, model checking tools have to be adapted to every processor that should be supported.

In order to tackle this problem, we have developed [mc]square[1], which is a discrete, (mostly) explicit state, on-the-fly, Computation Tree Logic (CTL) [1] model checker. It is capable of model checking assembly code written for certain microcontrollers (ATMEL ATmega and Infineon XC167). It was important for us not to restrict the set of supported constructs and to process arbitrary assembly code given by the user (including, e.g., direct and indirect memory access, recursions, and functions). Additionally, the user should not be forced to provide an environment. To address the disadvantage of being hardware-dependent, we developed an extensible architecture, which was described in [9]. To deal with the state explosion problem, we implemented different abstraction techniques in [mc]square. One of these, which is described in this paper, is called *delayed nondeterminism*.

Delayed nondeterminism is an abstraction technique featuring two aspects which help to reduce the state space size. First, it tries to limit the number of bits (bytes) that have to be split up when determining nondeterministic values (e.g., when input is read from the environment and not all bits are needed for evaluation). Second, it tries to delay the split up as long as possible, i.e., nondeterministic values only have to be instantiated when the corresponding values are needed for evaluation. Delayed nondeterminism is implemented by introducing abstract states into [mc]square. That is, a state in [mc]square no longer represents a single concrete state, but may represent many concrete states.

This paper is structured as follows. We start with the presentation of related work. Then, a basic introduction to [mc]square is given. In the following section, our formal approach to modeling microcontrollers is presented. As an example, the model of the ATMEL ATmega16 microcontroller is detailed. Then, the abstraction technique of delayed nondeterminism is introduced. It is shown that delayed nondeterminism induces a simulation relation between the concrete and the abstract state space. After that, a case study is presented which demonstrates the effect of delayed nondeterminism on the state space size of three different programs. In the end a conclusion is drawn and some potential directions for future improvements are shown.

---

[1] http://www-i11.informatik.rwth-aachen.de/mc_square.html

2   Related Work

Motivated by the observation that usually memory is the limiting factor in the application of model checking, many approaches have been developed to combat the state explosion problem (see [1] for an overview). The abstraction technique presented in this paper, *Delayed NonDeterminism* (DND), is dynamically applied at runtime. To the best of our knowledge, no comparable approach has been developed so far to control the effect of nondeterminism in modeling embedded systems.

There is, however, a verification method for concurrent systems called *narrowing* which is based on a similar idea, and which is described in [10]. Here, the states and transitions of the system are symbolically represented by terms and rewriting steps, respectively. Terms can contain variables to abstract from details of the system state which currently are not "interesting", but which can be later expanded by substitution steps if necessary. Thus, in some sense, variables correspond to the nondeterministic values in our approach.

Another direction of work which is worth mentioning is the consideration of nondeterminism in connection with functional programming languages. The paper [11] studies the implementation of nondeterministic choice in this setting and refers to the problem of copying nondeterministic values, which is also the reason for over-approximation in our model.

Symbolic or X-valued simulation is another technique that is similar to the technique applied in *[mc]square*. Here, symbolic values are used in place of explicit values. In our approach parts of the states used can be symbolic, but whenever the simulator or the model checker needs to access symbolic parts of a state, these parts are instantiated, and hence become explicit. All parts of a state that are not accessed remain symbolic. In [12], a symbolic simulator is used to verify hardware systems. Whenever an X (denoted by * in our approach) is accessed and a value is needed, new symbolic variables are added and simulation has to be repeated. In our approach a dynamic refinement is conducted. There are some approaches combining *explicit* and *symbolic executions* (cf. [13, 14]), but these approaches do explicit execution and symbolic execution in parallel.

Other model checkers that handle machine languages or languages that are similar to machine languages are *Java PathFinder* (*JPF*) [15], *StEAM* [16], and *Estes* [5], all being explicit model checkers as is *[mc]square*. JPF accepts Java bytecode and employs collapsing techniques for efficiently storing states. Our experiments have shown that such methods do not pay off in the case of *[mc]square* since its states have a less complex structure. Another difference is that *JPF* has to deal with parallel processes and therefore employs abstraction techniques such as partial order reduction, which cannot be done in *[mc]square*. Moreover the memory model used within *JPF* makes it possible to apply symmetry reduction techniques. Again, this is not possible in *[mc]square* because the order of data within memory is important. *StEAM* model checks bytecode for the Internet C Virtual Machine. In this approach an existing Virtual Machine (VM) is monitored and model checking is conducted on the states created by this VM. *Estes* model checks assembly code for a certain processor. Similar to *StEAM*, it uses

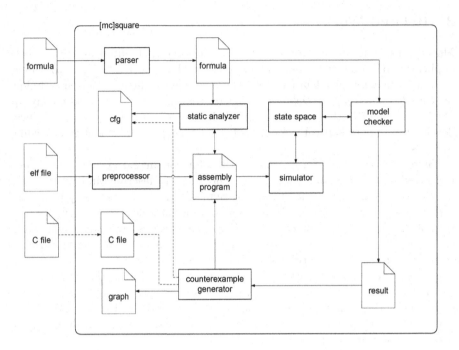

Fig. 1. Process used in *[mc]square*

an existing VM (the GNU debugger) to create the state space. In our approach, we concentrate on the creation of the state space, that is, we concentrate on the domain-specific abstractions implemented within the simulator. We do not want to use existing simulators as we think that significant savings can be achieved by a tailored implementation. In contrast to *Estes* we abstract from time because the state explosion observed when temporal aspects were taken into account was too big. Model checking considering time leads to real-time model checking (cf. [3]).

3   Introduction to *[mc]square*

This section gives an introduction to *[mc]square*, which is a discrete, (mostly) explicit state, on-the-fly, CTL model checker. It accepts assembly code written for certain microcontrollers (ATMEL ATmega and Infineon XC167). More information about *[mc]square* can be found in [6,9].

The process that is applied in *[mc]square* is shown in Fig. 1.

First, the user inputs the program as an Executable and Linking Format (ELF) file and the specification as a CTL formula. If the C code is available, the user can also provide the C code file. The formula is parsed and transformed into a formula object, which is utilized by the static analyzer and the model checker component. The ELF file is preprocessed and converted into an human readable assembly program.

Then, the static analyzer component starts inspecting the assembly program. During this analysis, it uses information from the formula object (registers, variables and memory locations used within the atomic propositions) to preserve validity of the results. In the first step of the static analysis, a Control Flow Graph (CFG) of the assembly program is created. This CFG is used later on by the counterexample generator to present counterexamples or witnesses. In the end, the static analyzer adds annotations to the assembly program which are used by the simulator to reduce the state space size.

After that, model checking starts. First, the model checker requests the initial state from the state space. It checks this state for certain parts of the formula, and depending on the result of this check, it requests successor states of this state from the state space. Then, it again checks these states for specific parts of the formula. This process continues until a goal state is reached (proving or disproving the validity of the formula) or the complete state space is built. The model checking algorithm used was taken from [17]. A first version of this algorithm was presented in [18]. As the simulator implemented in *[mc]square* creates a safe over-approximation of the real state space, validity of ACTL[2] formulae is preserved. If a CTL formula containing an existential path quantifier is found to be correct, the user has to check whether the witness is a valid one, i.e., whether it is feasible in the concrete state space and not caused by the over-approximation. In the latter case, the user can deactivate some of the options used in the simulator to build a more accurate state space. However, this generally increases the number of states.

Whenever successors of a state are requested that are not created yet, the state space component uses the simulator to on-the-fly create the needed states. To do so, it passes the state to the simulator and calls a `step()` method. The simulator creates all possible successors of this state including, e.g., occurrences of interrupts, different input values from the environment etc. If, e.g., an instruction IN R18 PINA reads input from the environment into register R18, and all eight bits of port A are nondeterministic (used for input), this state has 256 successors (all values between 0 and 255). If at another location an instruction IN R4 PINB reads input from port B and, this time, only two bits of this port are nondeterministic (all other bits are used for output and not for input) and one interrupt is active, five successor states are created. In one successor the interrupt handler is entered, and in the other four successors the IN instruction is executed and register R4 gets the four different possible values. During this step *[mc]square* uses some abstraction techniques to minimize the state space size. It is important to notice that all these abstractions lead to a safe over-approximation of the concrete state space (preserving ACTL). One of these techniques is delayed nondeterminism, which is detailed in this paper.

In the last step, the counterexample generator derives a counterexample or a witness depending on the formula checked and the result of the model checking

---

[2] The universal fragment of CTL; see [19]

process. This counterexample/witness is then presented in the assembly code, in the C code, as a state space graph, and in the CFG of the assembly code. Hence, the user can choose the representation that suits his requirements best to find the error. In this representation, he or she can also check whether a witness of an non-ACTL formula is a feasible one.

4   The Formal Model

This section introduces our formal modeling approach for microcontroller systems, consisting of hardware, software and environment. The motivation of this development is twofold:

- It allows us to formally establish the correctness of our *delayed nondeterminism* abstraction technique, showing that it yields an over-approximation: every possible behavior of the original system is also represented in the abstract system, i.e., the abstract system simulates the concrete system (see Section 4.4 for details).
- The model is very general, meaning that it allows to formalize virtually any microcontroller system. Thus, it could be used as a kind of intermediate specification, supporting the rapid development of model-checking tools for embedded systems. This aspect will be investigated in our future work.

4.1   Handlers and Guarded Assignments

In our approach, the state of a (microcontroller) system will be decomposed into a control state and a data state. More concretely, we assume that the data space is organized as a global memory with linear byte addresses. The latter are denoted by A and are assumed to have a length of m bytes (in our application, $m = 2$). Thus, $A := \mathbb{C}^m$ where $\mathbb{C} := \mathbb{B}^8$ and $\mathbb{B} := \{0, 1\}$. Here the bth bit of a byte $c \in \mathbb{C}$ is denoted by $c[b]$.

In order to incorporate nondeterminism, we extend this definition by introducing a *nondeterministic bit value* $*$, and let $\mathbb{B}_* := \mathbb{B} \cup \{*\}$ and $\mathbb{C}_* := \mathbb{B}_*^8$. Moreover we distinguish a set of *deterministic addresses* $D \subseteq A$ in which only deterministic values are allowed to be stored. These will later be used for certain I/O registers and for the (symbolic) addresses occurring in the formula to be verified. Thus, *memory states* can be represented as mappings in the set $V := \{v \mid v : A \to \mathbb{C}_*\}$ where $v(a) \in \mathbb{C}$ for every $a \in D$.

The behavior of a system is determined by its current *control location*, which is the program counter in our case. It is represented by a finite set Q. Thus, the set of *(system) states* is given by $S := Q \times V$. State changes are specified by three so-called *handlers*:

- a *nondeterminism handler* of the form $g_1; \ldots; g_k$ where $k \geq 0$, which introduces nondeterministic values where necessary,
- an *interrupt handler* of the shape $h_1 : q_1 > \ldots > h_l : q_l$ where $l \geq 0$ and $q_1, \ldots, q_l \in Q$, which specifies the system's reaction to extraordinary events such as interrupts, and

- for each control location $q \in Q$, an *instruction handler* of the form $q : h'_1 : q'_1 > \ldots > h'_m : q'_m$ where $m \geq 1$ and $q'_1, \ldots, q'_m \in Q$, which defines the normal execution of machine instructions.

Here each g_i, h_i, h'_i is a *guarded assignment* of the shape $e_0 \rightarrow x_1 := e_1, \ldots, x_n := e_n$ where $n \geq 0$, $e_0, \ldots, e_n$ are value expressions, and $x_1, \ldots, x_n$ are (disjoint) address expressions (see below). A guarded assignment is called *enabled* if its guard e_0 evaluates to 1 in the current memory state. Its execution yields a new memory state in which, for every $1 \leq i \leq n$, the value stored at x_i is determined by e_i. The guard e_0 can be omitted if it is the constant 1.

Given a current state $(q, v) \in S$, the next state is determined by

1. executing every enabled guarded assignment g_i in the nondeterminism handler in the given order, followed by
2. an application of the first enabled guarded assignment h_i in the interrupt handler, stopping at the corresponding control location q_i. If no such assignment exists, then
3. again the complete nondeterminism handler is executed and, finally,
4. the first enabled guarded assignment h'_j in the instruction handler for q is applied, stopping at q'_j.

Formally, given the handlers of the above form, the successor state $(q', v') \in S$ is defined as follows:

$$(q', v') := \begin{cases} (q_i, [\![h_i]\!](v_1)) & \text{if } I \neq \emptyset \text{ and } i = \min I \\ (q'_j, [\![h'_j]\!](v_2)) & \text{if } I = \emptyset, J \neq \emptyset, \text{ and } j = \min J \\ (q, v_2) & \text{if } I = J = \emptyset \end{cases}$$

where

$$v_1 := [\![g_k]\!](\ldots ([\![g_1]\!](v))\ldots),$$
$$v_2 := [\![g_k]\!](\ldots ([\![g_1]\!](v_1))\ldots),$$
$$I := \{i \in \{1, \ldots, l\} \mid h_i \text{ enabled in } v_1\}, \text{ and}$$
$$J := \{j \in \{1, \ldots, m\} \mid h'_j \text{ enabled in } v_2\}.$$

Here $[\![g]\!] : V \rightarrow V$ denotes the meaning of a guarded assignment g as a mapping on memory states; it will be defined in Section 4.3.

In our application, the nondeterminism handler is employed to deal with interrupts: it checks which interrupts can (potentially) occur, and nondeterministically sets the corresponding flags. The actual processing of the interrupt is done by the interrupt handler. It first tests (in the order of descending interrupt priority) whether an interrupt is raised, and jumps to the corresponding handling routine in this case. Only if no interrupt has to be handled (i.e., $I = \emptyset$), it again runs the nondeterminism handler and finally executes the actual machine instruction at the current control location by applying the corresponding instruction handler.

Here the repeated call of the nondeterminism handler is required since after the interrupt handler has ignored a cleared interrupt flag, the latter could be set by some external event before the machine instruction is executed. Moreover it is important to observe that the nondeterminism handler performs every enabled guarded assignment while the execution of the interrupt and the instruction handler stops after applying the first guarded assignment which is enabled.

As mentioned earlier, each guarded assignment is of the shape $e_0 \rightarrow x_1 := e_1, \ldots, x_n := e_n$ with value expressions e_i and address expressions x_j. *Address expressions* are of the form a or $a{\downarrow} + d$ or $a[b]$ where $a \in A$, $b \in \{0, \ldots, 7\}$, and $d \in \mathbb{Z}$. The first two cases are byte addresses, either given directly or indirectly by dereferencing the address stored at a and by adding displacement d. The expression $a[b]$ refers to the bth bit of the byte which is stored at a. *Value expressions* are of the form $op(y_1, \ldots, y_k)$ where op is an operation of the type $op : T_1 \times \ldots \times T_k \rightarrow T_0$ such that, for every $1 \leq j \leq k$, $T_j \in \{\mathbb{C}, \mathbb{C}_*, \mathbb{B}, \mathbb{B}_*\}$ and y_j is an address expression. Here, we always assume that operations respect memory sizes, i.e., that $T_j \in \{\mathbb{C}, \mathbb{C}_*\}$ ($T_j \in \{\mathbb{B}, \mathbb{B}_*\}$) whenever y_j denotes a byte (bit) address. A similar restriction applies to the result type T_0 and to the corresponding left-hand side address x_i. Moreover, we require the result type of the guard e_0 to be $\mathbb{B}$.

The *semantics of an address expression* α depends on the current memory state $v \in V$, and is denoted by $[\![\alpha]\!]_v$. For byte address expressions, we let $[\![a]\!]_v := a \in A$ and $[\![a{\downarrow} + d]\!]_v := a' + d \in A$ if $a' = v(a) \ldots v(a + m - 1) \in A$. Thus, in the second case, the result is the address a' which is stored at a, adding displacement d. The semantics is undefined if a' is not a valid address, i.e., contains a nondeterministic bit value $*$. For bit address expressions, we let $[\![a[b]]\!]_v := (a, b) \in A \times \{0, \ldots, 7\}$.

To determine the *semantics of a value expression*, we have to apply the corresponding operation to the argument values: if $op : T_1 \times \ldots \times T_k \rightarrow T_0$ and $[\![y_j]\!]_v \in T_j$ for every $1 \leq j \leq k$, then $[\![op(y_1, \ldots, y_n)]\!]_v := op([\![y_1]\!]_v, \ldots, [\![y_k]\!]_v)$. Otherwise the result is again undefined.

Note that the admissible types of operations in value expressions support non-deterministic bit values as both arguments and results. Thus it is possible, e.g., to describe a simple copy instruction by choosing the identity on $\mathbb{C}_*$ or $\mathbb{B}_*$ as the operation. On the other hand, nondeterministic values in argument addresses can be excluded by choosing the argument type $\mathbb{C}$ or $\mathbb{B}$. In such a case, the access to an address containing a nondeterministic values requires instantiation; see Section 4.3 for details. Moreover it is possible to mix deterministic and non-deterministic values: if, e.g., a * bit is multiplied by 0, the operation can still be evaluated by 0.

The next section shows how the microcontroller system under consideration can be represented by our formal model. Thereafter, we will continue with formally defining the meaning of guarded assignments.

4.2   Modeling the ATMEL ATmega16

In order to model the execution of machine code on the ATMEL ATmega16 microcontroller, the general framework developed in the previous section has to be instantiated as follows:

- Since the machine code is stored in flash memory, control locations in Q correspond to flash memory addresses.
- Each address comprises $m := 2$ bytes.
- The following distinguished addresses are denoted by symbolic names:
  - C variables used in the application program
  - status register SREG with flag bits C $(= 0)$, Z $(= 1)$, N $(= 2)$, ..., I $(= 7)$
  - general-purpose registers R0, ..., R31
  - indirect addressing registers X = R27:R26, Y = R29:R28, Z = R31:R30
  - I/O registers such as
    - * timer registers such as TIMSK, TIFR and TCCR0,
    - * interrupt registers such as GICR and GIFR,
    - * stack pointers (SPL, SPH),
    - * data direction registers (DDRA, ...) and
    - * port registers (PORTA, ...)
    and single bit positions within these (CS00, ...).
- The deterministic addresses in D comprise the addresses which are referenced in the formula to be verified and certain I/O registers such as the DDR and PORT registers.
- The nondeterminism handler, which is repeatedly executed before the interrupt and the instruction handler, sets the input registers and checks whether interrupts can potentially occur. Here we only consider a timer and an external interrupt; other interrupts can be handled similarly:

$$\text{TCCR0}[\text{CS02}] = 1 \lor \text{TCCR0}[\text{CS01}] = 1 \lor \text{TCCR0}[\text{CS00}] = 1$$
$$\rightarrow \text{TIFR}[\text{TOV0}] := nd(\text{TIFR}[\text{TOV0}]);$$
$$\text{DDRB}[\text{DDB2}] = 0 \rightarrow \text{GIFR}[\text{INTF2}] := nd(\text{GIFR}[\text{INTF2}]); \ldots$$

where $nd : \mathbb{B}_* \to \mathbb{B}_*$ is defined by $nd(*) := *$, $nd(0) := *$, and $nd(1) := 1$.
- The interrupt handler is specified as follows (again only considering timer and external interrupts):

$$\text{SREG}[\text{I}] = 1 \land \text{TIMSK}[\text{TOIE0}] = 1 \land \text{TIFR}[\text{TOV0}] = 1 \rightarrow: 18\downarrow >$$
$$\text{SREG}[\text{I}] = 1 \land \text{GICR}[\text{INT2}] = 1 \land \text{GIFR}[\text{INTF2}] = 1 \rightarrow: 36\downarrow > \ldots$$

- Every machine instruction which is stored at some location $q \in Q$ gives rise to an instruction handler. We give some exemplary instructions:
  - ADD Ri,Rj:
    $q : \text{R}i := \text{R}i + \text{R}j, \text{SREG}[\text{Z}] := (\text{R}i + \text{R}j = 0), \text{SREG}[\text{C}] := \ldots, \ldots : q + 2$
  - RJMP k: $q :: q + k + 1$
  - IJMP: $q :: \text{Z}\downarrow$
  - JMP k: $q :: k$
  - SBRC Ri,b: $q : \text{R}i[b] = 0 \rightarrow: q + 2 > \text{R}i[b] = 1 \rightarrow: q + 3$
  - BREQ k: $q : \text{SREG}[\text{Z}] = 1 \rightarrow: q + k + 1 > \text{SREG}[\text{Z}] = 0 \rightarrow: q + 2$
  - MOV Ri,Rj: $q : \text{R}i := \text{R}j : q + 2$
  - LD Ri,X+: $q : \text{R}i := \text{X}\downarrow, \text{X} := \text{X} + 1 : q + 2$
  - LD Ri,-X: $q : \text{R}i := \text{X}\downarrow - 1, \text{X} := \text{X} - 1 : q + 2$
  - LDD Ri,X+d: $q : \text{R}i := \text{X}\downarrow + d : q + 2$
  - IN Ri,A: $q : \text{R}i := pin(\text{DDRA}, \text{PORTA}) : q + 2$ where $pin : \mathbb{C} \times \mathbb{C} \to \mathbb{C}_*$ is, for every $b \in \{0, \ldots, 7\}$, defined by $pin(c,d)[b] := d[b]$ if $c[b] = 1$ and $*$ otherwise.

4.3   Coping with Nondeterminism

In our formal model, nondeterministic bit values can arise due to the application of an operation $op : T_1 \times \ldots \times T_k \to T_0$ with result type $T_0 \in \{\mathbb{C}_*, \mathbb{B}_*\}$. In the simplest case, op is just the identity, that is, the assignment is of the form $x := y$ with $[\![y]\!]_v = a \in A \setminus D$ and $v(a) \notin \mathbb{C} \cup \mathbb{B}$. A more involved example is the formalization of the IN machine instruction (see Sect. 1 and 4.2) where a zero bit in the DDRA register causes a nondeterministic bit value to be assigned.

In the standard implementation, this situation is handled by *immediate instantiation*, meaning that each assignment of nondeterministic bit values is resolved by considering all possible assignments of concrete values instead. It is clear that this involves an exponential blowup, e.g., the assignment of byte value $*^8$ gives rise to 256 different successor states.

Our goal is to avoid this overhead by *delaying nondeterminism*, i.e., by replacing nondeterministic by concrete values only if and when this is required by the following computation. Here "if" and "when" refer to two different aspects of this optimization, which both lead to a reduction of the number of states created. First, delayed nondeterminism only instantiates those bits (bytes) that are used by some instruction, and hence, all other bits (bytes) may remain nondeterministic. This lowers the number of successors which have to be created. Second, delayed nondeterminism defers the splitting of nondeterministic values until they are really needed. Hence, successors are created at a later point in time. Both aspects help to minimize the number of created states, while still preserving a safe over-approximation (as will be shown in Sect. 4.4).

In order to formally develop this abstraction technique, we introduce a partial order $\sqsubseteq \subseteq \mathbb{B}_* \times \mathbb{B}_*$, given by $0 \sqsubseteq *$ and $1 \sqsubseteq *$, and lift it to bytes and memory states by pointwise extension: $c[7] \ldots c[0] \sqsubseteq c'[7] \ldots c'[0]$ iff $c[b] \sqsubseteq c'[b]$ for every $b \in \{0, \ldots, 7\}$, and $v \sqsubseteq v'$ iff $v(a) \sqsubseteq v'(a)$ for every $a \in A$. Thus $v \sqsubseteq v'$ if v' is "more general" than v.

Immediate Instantiation   Immediate instantiation follows the principle that in the course of the computation only deterministic values may be stored. (Nevertheless, it is still possible, due to the initial choice of the memory state, that $v(a) \in \mathbb{C}_* \setminus \mathbb{C}$ for specific addresses $a \in A \setminus D$.)

We say that a guarded assignment of the form $e_0 \to x_1 := e_1, \ldots, x_n := e_n$ is *enabled* in memory state $v \in V$ if $[\![e_0]\!]_v = 1$. Its execution nondeterministically yields every $v' \in V$ which is obtained by first evaluating every right-hand side expression e_i, by taking every possible instantiation of nondeterministic bit values, and by updating v accordingly. Formally, $v' := v[[\![x_i]\!]_v \mapsto c_i; 1 \leq i \leq n]$ such that $c_i \in \mathbb{C} \cup \mathbb{B}$ with $c_i \sqsubseteq [\![e_i]\!]_v$ for every $1 \leq i \leq n$. Here $v[a \mapsto c]$ denotes the modification of v at address a by storing the new value c.

Composing the effects of the nondeterminism, the interrupt, and the instruction handler for the current control location $q \in Q$ as described in Section 4.1, we obtain a *concrete transition* $(q, v) \xrightarrow{h} (q', v')$ where h is the first enabled guarded assignment of the interrupt or the instruction handler, and q' is the corresponding successor location. Given an initial system state $s_0 \in S$, this yields a *concrete transition system* $T^c = (S, \bigcup_{h \in G} \xrightarrow{g}, s_0)$ where the set G collects all guarded assignments in the interrupt and the instruction handlers.

Delayed Nondeterminism As described earlier, our goal is to instantiate nondeterministic bit values as late as possible, i.e., not necessarily when they are computed but only if and when they are required by a subsequent computation step. More concretely, the instantiation of bit address $(a, b) \in A \times \{0, \ldots, 7\}$ with $v(a)[b] = *$ in state $(q, v) \in S$ is required for a guarded assignment g of the form $e_0 \to x_1 := e_1, \ldots, x_n := e_n$ if

- (a, b) is referred by the guard e_0 (*guard* case), or
- g is enabled and some e_i refers to (a, b) in an operation argument position which does not allow nondeterministic bit values (*argument*), or
- g is enabled and some x_i dereferences a (*indirection*), or
- g is enabled and for some $1 \leq i \leq n$, the evaluation of e_i yields a nondeterministic value which cannot be stored at address x_i since it is in D (*target*).

Here, we say that a bit address (a, b) is *referred* by a value expression $op(y_1, \ldots, y_k)$ if it is referred by some address expression y_j, which is the case if $y_j = a[b]$, $y_j = a$, $y_j = a{\downarrow} + d$, or $y_j = a'{\downarrow} + d$ for some $a' \in A$ such that $[\![a'{\downarrow} + d]\!]_v = a$.

We can now formalize the above distinction of cases by the following incremental instantiation procedure: a guarded assignment g of the form $e_0 \to x_1 := e_1, \ldots, x_n := e_n$ yields $v' \in V$ if there exist intermediate memory states $v_1, v_2, v_3, v_4 \in V$ such that

1. $v_1 \sqsubseteq v$ with $v_1(a, b) \neq v(a, b)$ iff $v(a, b) = *$ and (a, b) is referred by e_0 (*guard*), and
2. g is enabled in (q, v_1), i.e., $[\![e_0]\!]_{v_1} = 1$, and
3. $v_2 \sqsubseteq v_1$ with $v_2(a, b) \neq v_1(a, b)$ iff $v_1(a, b) = *$, some e_i is of the form $op(y_1, \ldots, y_n)$ with $op : T_1 \times \ldots \times T_n \to T_0$, and (a, b) is referred by some y_j where $T_j \in \{\mathbb{C}, \mathbb{B}\}$ (*argument*), and
4. $v_3 \sqsubseteq v_2$ with $v_3(a, b) \neq v_2(a, b)$ iff $v_2(a, b) = *$, some x_i is of the form $a{\downarrow} + d$, and $b \in \{0, \ldots, 7\}$ (*indirection*), and
5. $v_4 := v_3[[\![x_i]\!]_{v_3} \mapsto [\![e_i]\!]_{v_3}; 1 \leq i \leq n]$, and
6. $v' \leq v_4$ with $v'(a, b) \neq v_4(a, b)$ iff $v_4(a, b) = *$, $[\![x_i]\!]_{v_4} \in \{a, (a, b)\}$ for some $1 \leq i \leq n$, and $a \in D$ (*target*).

Similarly to the previous section, the composition of nondeterminism, interrupt, and instruction handlers yields *abstract transitions* of the form $(q, v) \xRightarrow{h} (q', v')$ where h and q' are again determined by the first enabled guard in the interrupt handler or the instruction handler for q. Together with an initial system state $s_0 \in S$, this induces an *abstract transition system* $T^a = (S, \bigcup_{h \in G} \xRightarrow{g}, s_0)$.

4.4 Establishing Correctness

Our goal is to verify the correctness of the program under consideration by model checking it with respect to a specification. The latter is given by a temporal formula over a set P of bit value expressions which act as the atomic propositions. These propositions yield an extension of both the concrete and the abstract transition system to a *labeled transition system (LTS)*. In the first case, it is of the form $L^c = (S, \bigcup_{h \in G} \xrightarrow{h}, s_0, \lambda)$ where $\lambda : S \to 2^P : (q, v) \mapsto \{p \in P \mid [\![p]\!]_v = 1\}$ labels each state by the set of all propositions which are valid in that state. Note that the choice of the deterministic addresses D, comprising all addresses in the formula, guarantees that $[\![p]\!]_v$ is always defined. Analogously, $L^a = (S, \bigcup_{h \in G} \overset{h}{\Longrightarrow}, s_0, \lambda)$ is obtained in the abstract case.

The idea is to model check the "small" abstract LTS rather than the "big" concrete one. Since, as we will now show, every computation in L^c corresponds to a computation in L^a, this excludes "false positives": whenever every abstract computation satisfies the given specification, this also applies to every concrete computation. The converse, however, is not true: copying nondeterministic bit values may have the effect that the "same" nondeterministic value is replaced by different concrete values. Thus, L^a is an over-approximation of L^c. This may lead to "false negatives", i.e., spurious computations in L^a which violate the specification.

Formally the connection between L^c and L^a is given by a *simulation*, which is a binary relation $\rho \subseteq S \times S$ such that $s_0 \rho s_0$ and, whenever $s_1 \rho s_2$,

- $\lambda(s_1) = \lambda(s_2)$ and
- for every transition $s_1 \xrightarrow{h} s_1'$, there exists $s_2' \in S$ such that $s_2 \overset{h}{\Longrightarrow} s_2'$ and $s_1' \rho s_2'$.

Indeed, it can be shown that L^a simulates L^c, i.e., that every sequence of guarded assignments with immediate instantiation can be reproduced using delayed instantiation. More concretely, the simulation relation is given by the partial order on bit values: $(q_1, v_1) \rho (q_2, v_2)$ iff $q_1 = q_2$ and $v_1 \sqsubseteq v_2$. In summary, this means that our delayed nondeterminism abstraction is sound with respect to "path-universal" logics such as ACTL and LTL.

5   Case Study

This section describes a case study demonstrating the effect of delayed nondeterminism on the state space size of different programs. The case study is conducted on a laptop equipped with a Intel Core Duo CPU at 2.33 GHz, 4 GB main memory, and a hard disk with a capacity of 100 GB. *[mc]square* is completely written in Java, and hence, every operating system can be used.

All programs used in this case study were developed by students during lab courses, exercises, diploma theses, or their working time. None of them was intentionally written to be model checked. All programs were run on the ATMEL ATmega16 microcontroller.

In this case study, we execute four runs for each program. We use the following four combinations of abstraction techniques: no abstraction technique, Dead Variable Reduction (DVR) and Path Reduction (PR), Delayed Nondeterminism

Table 1. Effect of delayed nondeterminism on the state space size

Program	Options used	# states stored	# states created	Size [MB]	Time [s]	Reduction
plant	none	801,616	854,203	240	23.19	-
	DVR & PR	54,788	1,297,080	16	17.98	93%
	DND	188,404	195,955	57	4.39	76%
	all	11,524	222,636	3.5	3.02	99%
traffic light	none	35,613	38,198	10	0.78	-
	DVR & PR	2,585	55,370	0.75	0.71	93%
	DND	10,004	10,520	2.73	0.24	72%
	all	523	13,069	0.21	0.17	99%
window lift	none	10,100,400	11,196,174	2,049	416.98	-
	DVR & PR	119,331	5,123,942	36	69.42	99%
	DND	323,450	444,191	96	9.09	97%
	all	10,699	463,129	3.26	7.43	100%

(DND), and finally, DVR, PR, and DND together. The implementation of DVR and PR for *[mc]square* is described in [20]. For all programs, we use the formula *AG true*. This formula does not influence the effect of the abstractions, and therefore enables a fair comparison.

Table 1 presents the outcome of this case study for all programs. The first column shows the name of the program. In the second column it is indicated which abstraction techniques were used (here: *none, DVR & PR, DND*, and *all*). The column *# states stored* represents the number of different states stored in the state space. In contrast, the column *# states created* shows the number of all states created during building of the state space, including revisits. *Size [MB]* gives the size of the state space in main memory, and *Time [s]* shows the total time needed for building the state space including all preparatory steps (e.g., preprocessing, parsing, and static analyses) and model checking the formula *AG true*. Column *Reduction* shows the reduction factor for stored states in % compared to the run using no abstraction technique.

Plant is a program that controls a virtual chemical plant. It consists of 73 lines of C code (225 lines of assembly code) and uses one timer and two interrupts. Without abstraction, 801,616 states are stored. DVR & PR reduce the state space size by 93%. Using DND merely 188,404 states are stored. Here, the state space size is reduced by 76% because only one aspect of DND has an impact. The reduction is effected by the delay of the split up (i.e., split up is performed at another location). The number of successors that are created during a split up cannot be reduced because no values are read from the environment. Hence, DND alone does not reduce the state space size as much as DVR & PR do, but the combination of all three abstraction techniques together (DVR & PR &

DND) reduces the state space size by 99%. That means that DND can even improve the good results obtained when using DVR & PR.

Traffic Light is a program which was developed by our students in a lab course. Its purpose is to control a traffic light. The program has 85 lines of C code (155 lines of assembly code) and uses one timer and two interrupts. The resulting state space comprises 35,613 elements. Using delayed nondeterminism, the size can be reduced by 72% to 10,004 states. As in the *plant* program, only the delay of the split up influences the state space size in this program because input is not read from the environment. Hence, the reduction by DND alone is not as efficient as the reduction obtained by DVR & PR, but again DND can improve the results obtained by using DVR & PR. Using all three abstraction techniques together, the state space size is reduced by 99%.

The last program called *window lift* is an automotive task. Here a controller for a power window lift used in a car had to be implemented. This solution consists of 115 lines of C code (289 assembly code lines) and uses two interrupts and one timer. In this program, both aspects of DND affect the size of the state space because input is read from the environment and split up can be delayed. This can be seen in the results shown in Tab. 1. Using DND, the size of the state space is reduced by 97% from 10,100,400 states to 323,450 states. Again, DVR & PR alone perform better, but this time only by 2%. Using all three techniques together, the state space size is reduced by more than 99%. Again, DND improves the results obtained by using DVR & PR. Moreover, this example shows that this reduction also significantly influences the time and memory needed to conduct model checking. Time drops down from 416 to 7.43 seconds, and memory consumption drops down from 2,049 to 3.26 MB.

Summarizing, it can be seen that DND significantly reduces the state space size. DND alone does not perform as good as DVR & PR, but DND improves the results obtained from DVR & PR. It is important to notice that DVR or PR alone do also not perform that good [20]. In the first two programs only one effect of DND reduced the state space size. In the last program, both effects of DND influenced the state space size. The last program is more realistic than the other two programs as it, for example, reads input from the environment and does not only monitor certain events like the other two programs do. We chose these three small programs because we wanted to build the complete state space without using abstraction techniques to compare the effects of the different abstraction techniques. This would not be possible with bigger programs, as the case study [21] shows. In this case study we checked three out of 23 microcontroller programs. All these programs were written by students in a lab course. The programs had 400–1300 lines of code. Without using all our abstraction techniques, it was not possible to build the state spaces of these programs.

6   Conclusion and Future Work

In this paper, delayed nondeterminism, which is a new abstraction technique implemented in *[mc]square*, was described. It is used to tackle the state-explosion problem. Delayed nondeterminism introduces symbolic abstract states to *[mc]-square*. A single state no longer represents just one concrete state, but may represent a set of states. Nevertheless, all parts of the state (e.g., variables, registers, I/O registers and memory locations) that are accessed by the model checker or the simulator have to be represented explicitly. That means parts of a state may be represented symbolically as long as they are not accessed. In contrast to other abstraction techniques used in *[mc]square* such as path and dead variable reduction, delayed nondeterminism does not require a previous static analysis of the program.

In Sect. 4.4 it was shown that delayed nondeterminism indeed induces a simulation relation between the concrete transition system and the symbolic transition system. Hence, it preserves the validity of ACTL and LTL formulae. However, if the user checks the validity of an ECTL formula, he or she has to inspect whether the witness is also present in the concrete state space. This can be done with the help of the different counterexample/witness representations available in *[mc]square*. Automatic support as described in [22] is difficult here since counterexamples and witnesses usually exhibit nondeterministic choices as timers are modeled nondeterministically.

In the future, we want to investigate if we can establish a bisimulation relation between the concrete and the abstract transition system by taking the compiler behavior into account, and by disabling delayed nondeterminism for certain memory locations.

As seen in Sect. 5, delayed nondeterminism has a significant influence on the state space size of many programs. Together with the other abstraction techniques implemented in *[mc]square*, a reduction of up to 99% was observed.

The delayed nondeterminism technique can be transferred to many other microcontrollers (e.g., Infineon Tricore, Intel MC51 and MC91, all microcontroller that use an ARM7 core) without changing the approach. There are some microcontrollers where a straightforward adoption is not possible, e.g., the Infineon XC167 microcontroller. The problem with this microcontroller is that every instruction changes bits in the status register (e.g., C, Z, N). To change these bits, the values used in the instruction have to be determined, viz even a move instruction has to instantiate values.

However, we think that an adoption of this approach to higher level programming languages is not promising because in higher level programming languages nondeterminism is often evaluated at the location where it first occurs, preventing the delay of the instantiation. Furthermore, rather seldom only single bits of values are evaluated, making a partial instantiation useless.

Summarizing, we think that this is a promising approach to analyze software for embedded systems. *[mc]square* can already handle programs of interesting size. Delayed nondeterminism is an abstraction technique that helps to tackle the state explosion problem. It can be combined with other techniques implemented in *[mc]-square* (e.g., path reduction, dead variable reduction). This technique can also be used for model checking software for many other microcontrollers. As we have experienced with delayed nondeterminism or path reduction (cf. [20]), there are abstraction techniques which perform better when model checking assembly code. Hence, we will focus future research on domain specific abstraction techniques.

References

1. Clarke, E.M., Grumberg, O., Peled, D.A.: Model Checking. MIT Press, Cambridge (1999)
2. Holzmann, G.J.: The Spin Model Checker: Primer and Reference Manual. Addison-Wesley, Reading (2003)
3. Larsen, K.G., Pettersson, P., Yi, W.: UPPAAL in a nutshell. Int. Journal on Software Tools for Technology Transfer 1(1–2), 134–152 (1997)
4. Mehler, T.: Challenges and Applications of Assembly-Level Software Model Checking. PhD thesis, Universität Dortmund (2005)
5. Mercer, E.G., Jones, M.D.: Model checking machine code with the GNU debugger. In: Godefroid, P. (ed.) SPIN 2005. LNCS, vol. 3639, pp. 251–265. Springer, Heidelberg (2005)
6. Schlich, B., Kowalewski, S.: [mc]square: A model checker for microcontroller code. In: Margaria, T., Philippou, A., Steffen, B. (eds.) Proc. 2nd Int'l Symp. Leveraging Applications of Formal Methods, Verification and Validation (IEEE-ISoLA 2006), IEEE proceedings (2006)
7. Schlich, B., Rohrbach, M., Weber, M., Kowalewski, S.: Model checking software for microcontrollers. Technical Report AIB-2006-11, RWTH Aachen University (2006)
8. Balakrishnan, G., Reps, T., Melski, D., Teitelbaum, T.: WYSINWYX: What You See Is Not What You eXecute. In: Verified Software: Theories, Tools, Experiments. Springer, Heidelberg (to appear, 2007)
9. Schlich, B., Kowalewski, S.: An extendable architecture for model checking hardware-specific automotive microcontroller code. In: Schnieder, E., Tarnai, G. (eds.) Proc. 6th Symp. Formal Methods for Automation and Safety in Railway and Automotive Systems (FORMS/FORMAT 2007)GZVB, pp. 202–212 (2007)
10. Meseguer, J., Thati, P.: Symbolic reachability analysis using narrowing and its application to verification of cryptographic protocols. ENTCS 117, 153–182 (2005)
11. Clark, A.: A lazy non–deterministic functional language. (2000) http://www.dcs.kcl.ac.uk/staff/tony/docs/LazyNonDetLanguage.ps
12. Bryant, R.E.: A methodology for hardware verification based on logic simulation. Journal of the ACM 38(2), 299–328 (1991)
13. Godefroid, P., Klarlund, N., Sen, K.: Dart: Directed automated random testing. SIGPLAN Not. 40(6), 213–223 (2005)
14. Sen, K., Marinov, D., Agha, G.: CUTE: A concolic unit testing engine for C. In: ESEC/FSE-13: Proc. 10th European Software Engineering Conference/13th ACM SIGSOFT Int. Symp. on Foundations of Software Engineering, pp. 263–272. ACM Press, New York (2005)
15. Visser, W., Havelund, K., Brat, G., Park, S., Lerda, F.: Model checking programs. Automated Software Engineering Journal 10(2) (2003)
16. Leven, P., Mehler, T., Edelkamp, S.: Directed error detection in C++ with the assembly-level model checker StEAM. In: Graf, S., Mounier, L. (eds.) SPIN 2004. LNCS, vol. 2989, pp. 39–56. Springer, Heidelberg (2004)
17. Heljanko, K.: Model checking the branching time temporal logic CTL. Research Report A45, Helsinki University of Technology (1997)

18. Vergauwen, B., Lewi, J.: A linear local model checking algorithm for CTL. In: Best, E. (ed.) CONCUR 1993. LNCS, vol. 715, pp. 447–461. Springer, Heidelberg (1993)
19. Emerson, E.: Temporal and Modal Logics. In: Handbook of Theoretical Computer Science, vol. B, Elsevier, Amsterdam (1990)
20. Schlich, B., Löll, J., Kowalewski, S.: Application of static analyses for state space reduction to microcontroller assembly code. In: Proc. Formal Methods for Industrial Critical Systems (FMICS 2007). LNCS, Springer, Heidelberg (to appear)
21. Schlich, B., Salewski, F., Kowalewski, S.: Applying model checking to an automotive microcontroller application. In: Proc. IEEE 2nd Int'l Symp. Industrial Embedded Systems (SIES 2007), IEEE Computer Society Press, Los Alamitos (2007)
22. Saidi, H.: Model checking guided abstraction and analysis. In: Palsberg, J. (ed.) SAS 2000. LNCS, vol. 1824, pp. 377–396. Springer, Heidelberg (2000)

A Complete Bounded Model Checking Algorithm for Pushdown Systems

Gérard Basler*, Daniel Kroening, and Georg Weissenbacher**

Computer Systems Institute, ETH Zurich, 8092 Zurich, Switzerland
{firstname.lastname}@inf.ethz.ch

Abstract. Pushdown systems (PDSs) consist of a stack and a finite state machine and are frequently used to model abstractions of software. They correspond to sequential recursive programs with finite-domain variables. This paper presents a novel algorithm for deciding reachability of particular locations of PDSs. We exploit the fact that most PDSs used in practice are *shallow*, and propose to use SAT-based Bounded Model Checking to search for counterexamples. Completeness is achieved by computing *universal summaries* of the procedures in the program.

1 Introduction

Pushdown systems (PDSs) consist of a finite state machine and stack with a finite set of stack symbols. The use of PDSs as abstractions of software was promoted by the SLAM project at Microsoft Research. PDSs are equally expressive as *Boolean Programs* [1]. The finite-state part of the PDS is used to model the global variables and the control location of the Boolean program. The stack can be used to model the call stack of the program, which permits unbounded recursive function calls.

We present a novel algorithm for deciding reachability of particular error locations of PDSs. Our algorithm is tailored to the verification of automatically generated abstractions of commodity software within a program analysis tool such as SLAM or SATABS.

We record two observations about such systems. First of all, most tools that implement an abstraction/refinement framework compute a *conservative abstraction*. If the property holds on the abstract model, it also holds on the original program. As a consequence, the abstraction/refinement loop terminates as soon as an abstraction is built in which the error location is unreachable. In all previous iterations, there exists a path that reaches an error location. It is reported in [2] that the verification of device drivers may require as much as twenty iterations, with an average of 5 iterations. This motivates the need for an algorithm that performs well on models with a counterexample.

---

* Supported by the Swiss National Science Foundation.
** Supported by Microsoft Research through its European PhD Scholarship Programme.

K. Yorav (Ed.): HVC 2007, LNCS 4899, pp. 202–217, 2008.
© Springer-Verlag Berlin Heidelberg 2008

Second, we exploit the fact that pushdown systems generated as abstractions of commodity software are typically very *shallow*. Formally, this means that any node of the Kripke structure that is reachable from an initial state is reachable with a few steps.

Bounded Model Checking (BMC) is a perfect fit for this scenario. In BMC, a transition system is unwound together with a property up to a given bound k to form a propositional formula. The formula is satisfiable if and only if there exists a path of length k that refutes the property. If the formula is unsatisfiable, BMC is inconclusive as longer counterexamples might still exist. SAT-based BMC is therefore known as an effective method to discover shallow bugs.

In order prove the absence of errors, we extend BMC with *procedure summarization* [3]. A procedure summary maps a configuration of a PDS at the entry of a procedure to the set of configurations observable upon exit. As there are only finitely many summaries, saturation can be used to compute the set of reachable states [4,5].

Contribution and Outline. We present preliminaries of PDSs, summarization, and symbolic representations in Sec. 2. This paper extends the concept of *Universal Summaries* [6], which are described in Sec. 3. This paper makes two contributions:

1. We present a novel abstraction-based procedure to obtain universal summaries of non-recursive procedures in Sec. 4. The abstraction is refined on-demand if required by a spurious counterexample.
2. We show how to obtain universal summaries for recursive procedures by means of a head-counting argument in Sec 5.

2   Preliminaries

Definition 1 (Pushdown Systems [7]). *A* pushdown system *(PDS) is a transition system in which each state comprises of a control location and a stack. The set of control locations P as well as the stack alphabet Γ is finite. A state is a pair $\langle p, w \rangle$, where $p \in P$ denotes a control location, and $w \in \Gamma^*$ represents the stack content. We use s_0 to denote the initial state of a PDS. The* head *of a state comprises of the control location and the topmost element of the stack. The state space of a PDS may be infinitely large, since the stack height is not bounded. The number of heads is bounded by $|P| \cdot |\Gamma|$.*

The transition relation is defined in terms of a finite set of rules Δ. These rules determine the successors of a state $\langle p, \gamma w \rangle$ $(w \in \Gamma^*)$ based on the head $\langle p, \gamma \rangle$ of this state. Each rule is of the form $\langle p, \gamma \rangle \hookrightarrow \langle q, w \rangle$, where $|w| \leq 2$ (in particular, w may be ϵ, $|\epsilon| = 0$). Depending on the size of w, we distinguish between expansion *rules,* neutration *rules, and* contraction *rules (see Fig. 1). The transition relation $\rightarrow \subseteq (P \times \Gamma^*) \times (P \times \Gamma^*)$ is defined as follows: If $\langle p, \gamma \rangle \hookrightarrow \langle p', w \rangle \in \Delta$, then $\langle p, \gamma w' \rangle \rightarrow \langle p', ww' \rangle$.*

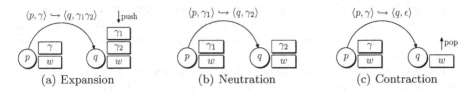

Fig. 1. Transitions of a Pushdown System

We use $\rightarrow^*$ to denote the reflexive transitive closure of $\rightarrow$. A state s_i of a PDS is reachable iff $s_0 \rightarrow^* s_i$. The set of reachable states of a PDS can be represented by means of a finite automaton [8], which may be obtained using a saturation procedure [4,5]. Intuitively, an expansion $\langle p_0, \gamma_0 \rangle \rightarrow \langle p_1, \gamma_1\gamma_2 \rangle$ followed by neutration that yields $\langle p_2, \gamma_3\gamma_2 \rangle$, followed by a contraction $\langle p_2, \gamma_3\gamma_2 \rangle \rightarrow \langle p_3, \gamma_2 \rangle$ can be *summarized*[1] by $\langle p_0, \gamma_0 \rangle \rightarrow^* \langle p_3, \gamma_2 \rangle$. Augmenting the transition relation with this summary may give rise to new summaries. The set of states reachable from s_0 is computed by repeatedly applying summarization until a fixpoint is reached (i.e., no new summaries can be constructed).

The efficiency of these saturation based algorithms can be significantly improved by using a *symbolic* BDD-based representation of the PDS. The notion of symbolic PDSs was introduced by Schwoon [7]:

Definition 2 (Symbolic Pushdown Systems). Symbolic pushdown systems *use a propositional encoding for control locations $p \in P$ and stack elements $\gamma \in \Gamma$. A set of $\lceil \log_2(|P|) \rceil + \lceil \log_2(|\Gamma|) \rceil$ Boolean variables is sufficient to encode all heads of a PDS. The right hand side $\langle q, w \rangle$ (where $|w| \leq 2$) of a rule is represented using a separate set of Boolean variables. We use primed variables to denote elements of the latter set. The symbolic rules Δ_S are expressed in terms of a propositional relation over primed and unprimed variables. We use $R^{\nearrow}$, $R^{\rightarrow}$, and $R^{\searrow}$ to refer to the relation for expansions, neutrations, and contractions, respectively.*

Assume, for instance, that P is represented using $\{a_0, a_1\}$, and Γ using $\{b_0, b_1\}$. One way to encode the neutration rule $\langle p_1, \gamma_1 \rangle \hookrightarrow \langle p_2, \gamma_3 \rangle$ is

$$(\bar{a}_1 \cdot a_0) \cdot (\bar{b}_1 \cdot b_0) \cdot (a_1' \cdot \bar{a}_0') \cdot (b_1' \cdot b_0')$$

i.e., to use the variables to represent a binary encoding of the indices i of $p_i \in P$ and $\gamma_i \in \Gamma$ (where a_0 and b_0 correspond to the lower bits). The set of symbolic relations $\Delta_S = \{R^{\nearrow}, R^{\rightarrow}, R^{\searrow}\}$ is a disjunctive partitioning of symbolic relations corresponding to the union of transition rules.

The same technique is used to represent summaries. The symbolic representation of the summary $\langle p_0, \gamma_0 \rangle \rightarrow^* \langle p_3, \gamma_2 \rangle$ is $\bar{a}_1 \cdot \bar{a}_1 \cdot \bar{b}_1 \cdot \bar{b}_1 \cdot a_1' \cdot a_1' \cdot b_1' \cdot \bar{b}_1'$. The symbolic representation of summaries (and states) is more succinct than the explicit representation used in [5]. The symbolic summary

---

[1] The idea of summarization was introduced by Sharir and Pnueli [3].

$$(\bar{a}_1 + a_0) \cdot (b_1 \cdot b_0) \cdot (a'_1 \cdot (a'_0 = a_1)) \cdot (b'_1 \cdot \vec{b}'_0)$$

stands for the three explicit summaries

$$\langle p_0, \gamma_3 \rangle \rightarrow^* \langle p_2, \gamma_2 \rangle, \langle p_1, \gamma_3 \rangle \rightarrow^* \langle p_2, \gamma_2 \rangle, \text{ and } \langle p_3, \gamma_3 \rangle \rightarrow^* \langle p_3, \gamma_2 \rangle.$$

Ordered BDDs are a suitable data structure to encode such formulas, since the canonical representation enables efficient fixpoint detection [7,1]. An alternative algorithm based on satisfiability solvers for propositional logic (SAT) and quantified Boolean formulas (QBF) is presented in [6].

Symbolic PDSs are a popular formalism to represent abstractions of programs [9,10]. Abstraction mechanisms like predicate abstraction [11] preserve the control flow structure of the original program. In that case, it is convenient to maintain an explicit representation of program locations, i.e., to discriminate the rules in Δ_S by their source and target nodes of the control flow graph (CFG).

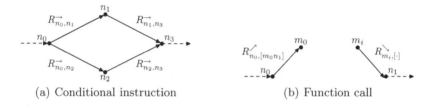

(a) Conditional instruction   (b) Function call

Fig. 2. Symbolic transitions rules with explicit CFG node information

Fig. 2 shows examples for symbolic transitions that are annotated with explicit control flow information (n_i and m_j are control flow nodes two different functions). From these pictures, it becomes intuitively clear how pushdown rules are used to model programs: The neutration rules in Fig. 2(a) model a conditional statement, whereas the expansion and contraction rules in in Fig. 2(b) model a function call and a return statement. A finite number of global (Boolean) variables is modeled by means of the control locations, and the (also finite) local variables of functions are represented using the stack alphabet Γ. For instance, the summary $\langle p_0, \gamma_0 \rangle \rightarrow^* \langle p_3, \gamma_2 \rangle$ modifies the control location (which represents the global variables of a program) and the topmost stack element. Intuitively, the return value of the corresponding function is passed on to the caller via the control location in this example. Throughout this paper, we use the notion of a *function* of a PDS to denote the transition rules associated with a function in the CFG. The correspondence indicates that PDSs are equally expressive as Boolean programs [9].

3   Universal Summaries

The reachability checking algorithms for PDSs presented in [1] and [6] are based on *symbolic simulation*. They determine the *reachability of a given head of a state* (or a program location, respectively). This is sufficient to verify arbitrary safety properties of a PDS, even though it may be necessary to modify the PDS to state more complicated safety specifications. Each sequence of PDS transitions is represented by a propositional formula that is only satisfiable if the corresponding path is feasible.

Starting from s_0, the search algorithm simulates the transition system. It avoids getting caught in an infinite loop by keeping track of the heads it already visited. Whenever the algorithm encounters a contraction rule, it computes a summary for the corresponding expansion that matches head of the "calling context". This summary relates the heads of two states with the same stack height. The sequences of transitions that may form a summary are described by the grammar in Fig. 3.

$$\text{Summary} \quad ::= R^\nearrow \text{ Transitions } R^\searrow ;$$
$$\text{Transitions} ::= \text{Transitions Summary} \mid \text{Transitions } R^\rightarrow \mid \epsilon;$$

Fig. 3. A grammar for summaries

Each new summary is added to a set Σ (using disjunction), such that summaries can be reused whenever the algorithm encounters a head and an expansion which are already covered. Eventually, Σ converges, since there are at most $|P|^2 \cdot |\Gamma|^2$ summaries that are not logically equivalent. The result is the least fixpoint of the set of summaries for the PDS, i.e., Σ contains only summaries for which the corresponding heads are indeed reachable.

An alternative to computing the set of reachable summaries Σ is to use *universal summaries* instead [6]:

Definition 3 (Universal Summary). *A universal summary $\Sigma_\mathcal{U}$ for a PDS $\langle P, \Gamma, \Delta, s_0 \}$ is a relation $\Sigma_\mathcal{U} \subseteq (P \times \Gamma) \times (P \times \Gamma)$ such that*

$$\forall \langle p, \gamma \rangle, \langle p', \gamma' \rangle \in P \times \Gamma. \ (\exists \langle p_1, w_1 \rangle, \dots, \langle p_n, w_n \rangle \in P \times \Gamma^*.$$
$$\langle p, \gamma \rangle \rightarrow \langle p_1, w_1 \rangle \rightarrow \dots \rightarrow \langle p_n, w_n \rangle \rightarrow \langle p', \gamma' \rangle \wedge$$
$$\forall i \in \{1..n\}.|w_i| \geq 2) \Longleftrightarrow \Sigma_\mathcal{U}(\langle p, \gamma \rangle, \langle p', \gamma' \rangle)$$

holds.

Intuitively, for *any* head $\langle p, \gamma \rangle$, a universal summary subsumes *all* paths that "traverse a function" of the PDS, no matter whether there exists a reachable state $\langle p, \gamma w \rangle$ or not. The restriction $|w_i| \geq 2$ guarantees that $\Sigma_\mathcal{U}$ relates expansions to their matching contractions (according to the grammar in Fig. 3). Note that this definition does not rule out *nested* summaries. (A summary is nested if it is entirely contained in another summary according to the grammar in Fig. 3.) In particular, it does not exclude *recursion*, i.e., a summary $\langle p_0, \gamma_0 \rangle \rightarrow^* \langle p'_0, \gamma'_0 \rangle$ may stem from a sequence of transitions that contains a nested summary $\langle p_1, \gamma_1 \rangle \to^* \langle p_1', \gamma_1' \rangle$ such that $p_0 = p_1$, $\gamma_0 = \gamma_1$, $p_0' = p_1'$, and $\gamma_0' = \gamma_1'$.

In the following section, we discuss how symbolic summaries are computed. Based on this, we present an algorithm that computes symbolic universal summaries for recursion-free PDSs in Section 3.

3.1   Computing Symbolic Summaries

A symbolic model checking algorithms for PDSs represents a sequence of transitions by a propositional formula that is only satisfiable if the corresponding path is feasible. For instance, the path

$$\underbrace{\langle p_0, \gamma_0 \rangle}_{s_0} \to \underbrace{\langle p_1, \gamma_1 \gamma_2 \rangle}_{s_1} \to \underbrace{\langle p_2, \gamma_3 \gamma_2 \rangle}_{s_2} \to \underbrace{\langle p_3, \gamma_2 \rangle}_{s_3}$$

is represented by following *path formula*:

$$(\bar{a}_1 \cdot \bar{a}_0) \cdot (\bar{b}_1 \cdot \bar{b}_0) \ \cdot \ (\bar{a}_1' \cdot a_0') \cdot (\bar{b}_1' \cdot b_0') \ \cdot \ (a_1'' \cdot \bar{a}_0'') \cdot (b_1'' \cdot b_0'') \ \cdot \ (a_1''' \cdot a_0''') \cdot (b_1''' \cdot \bar{b}_0''')$$

where the variables $\{a_0, a_1, b_0, b_1\}$ are used for the representation of s_0, the variables $\{a_0', a_1', b_0', b_1'\}$ for s_1, and so on. The parts of the formula that refer to s_1 and s_2 constrain only the topmost element of the stack. The content of the bottom element of the stack (γ_2) is determined by the expansion rule $\langle p_0, \gamma_0 \rangle \hookrightarrow \langle p_1, \gamma_1 \gamma_2 \rangle$, but the neutration rule cannot access this element. It only becomes "visible" to subsequently applied transition rules after the contraction $\langle p_2, \gamma_3 \rangle \hookrightarrow \langle p_3, \epsilon \rangle$.

As discussed in Sec. 2, this sequence of transitions gives rise to the symbolic summary $\bar{a}_1 \cdot \bar{a}_1 \cdot \bar{b}_1 \cdot \bar{b}_1 \ \cdot \ a_1' \cdot a_1' \cdot b_1' \cdot \bar{b}_1'$. The summary is obtained by existentially quantifying the variables that represent the intermediate heads (i.e., $\{a_0', a_1', b_0', b_1'\}$ and $\{a_0'', a_1'', b_0'', b_1''\}$ in our example). Each symbolic summary is a propositional relation over a set of primed and unprimed variables.

Merging Paths. Whenever the algorithm encounters a branch (as illustrated in Fig. 2(a)) it splits the path and constructs a new formula for each branch. To avoid an exponential blowup, path formulas are *merged* (by means of a disjunction) when they agree on their initial and final CFG nodes (see, for instance, [12]). A detailed description of an algorithm that performs aggressive merging by delaying transitions until merging becomes possible is given in [6].

3.2   Using BMC to Compute Universal Summaries

The symbolic algorithms discussed compute the least fixpoint of reachable summaries [1,6]. This fixpoint detection is implemented using either BDDs or a QBF solver. Unfortunately, neither of these approaches scales for a large number of variables. Bounded Model Checking (BMC) addresses this issue by avoiding fixpoint detection altogether: The transition system is simply unrolled up to a bounded path length k. This idea is illustrated in Fig. 4(b) for the cyclic transition system shown in Fig. 4(a) (instead of unrolling each path separately, we merge paths as discussed in Sec. 3.1). The satisfiability of the resulting path formula can be decided using an efficient SAT-solver (e.g., MINISAT [13]).

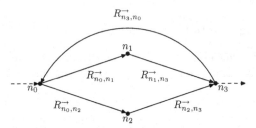

(a) A PDS transition system with a cycle

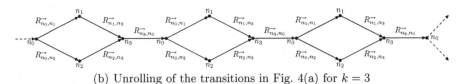

(b) Unrolling of the transitions in Fig. 4(a) for $k = 3$

Fig. 4. Bounded Model Checking for Pushdown Systems

BMC is complete with respect to reachability if (and only if) k is large enough to guarantee that all reachable states of the transition system are considered (the smallest k that has this property is called the *reachability diameter* of a transition system [14]). For a PDS with an infinite state space, there is no such finite k.

However, a function containing only neutrations is a finite state transition system. For a set of neutrations that are represented by $\xrightarrow{R}$ and a symbolic representation $I(s_0)$ of the initial state(s), the constant

$$k = \max\{i \in \mathbb{N} | \exists s_0, \ldots, s_i \in P \times \Gamma^*.I(s_0) \wedge \bigwedge_{j=0}^{i-1} s_j \xrightarrow{R} s_{j+1} \wedge \bigwedge_{j=0}^{i-1} \bigwedge_{l=j+1}^{i} s_j \neq s_l\}$$

is the length of the longest *loop-free* path that contains only neutrations (this corresponds to the *reachability recurrence diameter* of a finite state transition system [14]). Let $\langle p, \gamma \rangle \rightarrow^i \langle p', \gamma' \rangle$ denote the path formula obtained by means of unrolling $\xrightarrow{R}$ exactly i times. Then, the relation

$$R^{\rightarrow^*}(\langle p, \gamma \rangle, \langle p', \gamma' \rangle) \stackrel{\text{def}}{=} \bigvee_{i=1}^{k} \langle p, \gamma \rangle \rightarrow^i \langle p', \gamma' \rangle$$

is sufficient to determine all heads $\langle p', \gamma' \rangle$ that are reachable from $\langle p, \gamma \rangle$ by means of neutrations. Using this technique, we can compute a path formula that represents all heads reachable from an initial state $\langle p, \gamma \rangle \in I(s_0)$ by the loop in Fig. 4(a). In particular, if $I(s_0) = \mathsf{true}$, then the relation $R^{\rightarrow *}$ determines the states reachable from an arbitrary initial state.

Given an explicit representation of the CFG (as suggested in Sec. 2), it is possible to determine the *innermost* function f that contains no expansion/contraction rules (at least as long as f is not a recursive function). Let $R_f^{\rightarrow}$ denote the neutrations of this function, and let $R_f^{\nearrow}$ and $R_f^{\searrow}$ the initial expansion and the final contraction, respectively. Furthermore, let $R_f^{\rightarrow *}$ denote the unrolled path formula for the neutrations $R_f^{\rightarrow}$ and an arbitrary initial state $I(s_0) = \mathsf{true}$. Then, we obtain a universal summary for f by composing $R_f^{\rightarrow *}$ with $R_f^{\nearrow}$ and $R_f^{\searrow}$:

$$\Sigma_{\mathcal{U}}^f(\langle p, \gamma \rangle, \langle p', \gamma' \rangle) \overset{\text{def}}{=}$$
$$R_f^{\nearrow}(\langle p, \gamma \rangle, \langle p_1, \gamma_1 \gamma' \rangle) \ \wedge \ R_f^{\rightarrow *}(\langle p_1, \gamma_1 \rangle, \langle p_2, \gamma_2 \rangle) \ \wedge \ R_f^{\searrow}(\langle p_2, \gamma_2 \rangle, \langle p', \epsilon \rangle)$$

We proceed by finding a function g that calls only f and compute the universal summary for $R_g^{\rightarrow}$ using the universal summary for f. Thus, a universal summary for the whole PDS can be obtained in a top-down manner (assuming that the CFG representation of the PDS does not contain recursive function calls).

Corollary 1. *Let k be the length of the longest loop-free path through a recursion-free function f of a PDS. Then, the summary that subsumes all loop-free paths through f up to length k is a universal summary for the function f.*

Universal summaries have been presented only recently in [6]. The algorithm described there handles recursion by falling back to QBF-based summarization.

4 Abstraction and Refinement with Summaries

The technique discussed in the previous section (and presented in [6]) applies universal summaries in an *eager* manner: Whenever the search algorithm encounters an expansion rule and an appropriate (universal) summary is available, the summary replaces the expansion transition. If we are only interested in the reachability of a given head (or a program location), this approach is wasteful: A subsequence of a path may be sufficient to show that a head is not reachable. In that case, computing and applying the universal summaries for the nested functions in a top-down manner does not contribute to the infeasibility of the resulting path formula.

Therefore, we propose to compute universal summaries for functions *on demand*, and to apply them in a bottom-up manner. Given the transition rules of a function g of the PDS, we obtain an *over-approximation* of the corresponding universal summary $\Sigma_{\mathcal{U}}^g$ by replacing all occurrences of f in g by a non-deterministic summary $\Sigma_{\star}^f$:

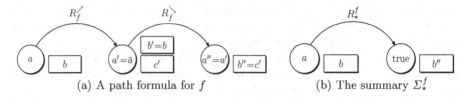

(a) A path formula for f (b) The summary $\Sigma_\star^f$

Fig. 5. Over-approximation of a universal summary

$$\Sigma_\star^f(\langle p, \gamma\rangle, \langle p', \gamma'\rangle) \overset{\text{def}}{=}$$

$$\exists \langle p_1, \gamma_1\rangle, \langle p_2, \gamma_2\rangle. R_f^{\nearrow}(\langle p, \gamma\rangle, \langle p_1, \gamma_1 \gamma'\rangle) \wedge R_f^{\searrow}(\langle p_2, \gamma_2\rangle, \langle p', \epsilon\rangle)$$

The summary $\Sigma_\star^f$ is a conservative over-approximation of $\Sigma_{\mathcal{U}}^f$, since

$$\Sigma_{\mathcal{U}}^f(\langle p, \gamma\rangle, \langle p', \gamma'\rangle) \implies \Sigma_\star^f(\langle p, \gamma\rangle, \langle p', \gamma'\rangle)$$

always holds. A head $\langle p', \gamma'\rangle$ that is *not* reachable via the over-approximated summary for g is also not reachable using $\Sigma_{\mathcal{U}}^g$. The converse does not hold.

Example 1. Consider the following transition rules for a function f:

$$R_f^{\nearrow}(a, b, a', b', c') = (a \cdot b) \cdot (a' = \bar{a}) \cdot (b' = b) \cdot c'$$
$$R_f^{\searrow}(a, b, a') \quad\quad = (a' = a)$$

The composition of $R_f^{\nearrow}$ and $R_f^{\searrow}$ yields the path formula in Fig. 5(a). The corresponding over-approximation of the summary for f is

$$\Sigma_\star^f(a, b, a'', b'') = \exists a' b' a_\star. (a \cdot b) \cdot (a' = \bar{a}) \cdot (b' = b) \cdot b'' \cdot (a'' = a_\star)$$

The summary $\Sigma_\star^f$ does not constrain the value of a'' (see Fig. 5(b)), even though the control state represented by $a'' = 1$ on return contradicts the path formula in Fig. 5(a).

Now consider the transitions of a function g shown in Fig. 6, and assume that the rules $R_g^{\rightarrow}$ require that transitions from n_2 to n_3 are only feasible if $a'' = 1$ holds at n_2 (e.g., $R_g^{\rightarrow}(a, b, a', b') = a \cdot a' \cdot (b' = b)$ for the transition from n_2 to n_3). If we over-approximate the function f as indicated in Fig. 6(a), then there exists a valuation (with $a'' = 1$ at n_2) to the variables of the corresponding path formula that represents a path through n_0, n_1, n_2 and n_3.

Unfortunately, this path is *spurious*, i.e., there is no feasible corresponding path in the original PDS. Therefore, we have to eliminate it from our over-approximated transition system. This can be achieved by computing $\Sigma_{\mathcal{U}}^f$ and using it to constrain the transition from n_1 to n_2 (as illustrated in Fig. 6(b)).

The reachability of a head $\langle p, \gamma\rangle$ at a node n can be determined by repeatedly refining the transition system until either a feasible path is found, or the head

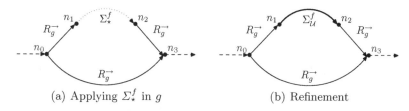

(a) Applying $\Sigma_\star^f$ in g (b) Refinement

Fig. 6. Refining an over-approximated universal summary

becomes unreachable. Fig. 7 shows the pseudo code for this algorithm. Unfortunately, this algorithm does not work if the CFG contains recursive function calls. Therefore, our implementation still uses the QBF-based approach presented in [6] to compute summaries for recursive functions. Universal summaries and the refinement technique are orthogonal to this approach and can be integrated easily. In the following section, we present a theoretical result that eliminates the need for a QBF-solver.

1: **procedure** IsReachable(PDS $\langle P, \Gamma, \Delta, s_0 \rangle$, head $\langle p, \gamma \rangle$, node n)
2:     **for all** functions $f \in$ CFG of PDS $\langle P, \Gamma, \Delta, s_0 \rangle$ **do**
3:         $\Sigma(f) := \Sigma_\star^f$;
4:     **end for**

5:     **while** true **do**
6:         **if** n contained in function f s.t. $\Sigma(f) = \Sigma_\star^f$ **then**
7:             $n' :=$ exit node of f;
8:         **else**
9:             $n' := n$;
10:        **end if**
11:        Use BMC and Σ to construct a path formula φ ending at n';
12:        **if** $\varphi(s_0, \langle p, \gamma \rangle)$ is satisfiable **then**
13:            **if** path does not traverse a function f with $\Sigma(f) = \Sigma_\star^f$ **then**
14:                **return** reachable;
15:            **else**
16:                $\Sigma(f) := \Sigma(f)_\mathcal{U}^f$; $\triangleright$ Use Σ for function calls in f
17:            **end if**
18:        **else**
19:                **return** unreachable;
20:        **end if**
21:     **end while**
22: **end procedure**

Fig. 7. Abstraction/Refinement algorithm for PDS

5   Recursion

In this section, we generalize Cor. 1 and extend the algorithm in Fig. 7 in order to enable the construction of universal summaries for recursive functions.

Given a recursive function f, we can compute an over-approximation Σ_{*1}^{f} of $\Sigma_{\mathcal{U}}^{f}$ by replacing all recursive calls to f with Σ_{*}^{f}. A refined over-approximation Σ_{*2}^{f} can then be obtained by applying Σ_{*1}^{f} for all calls to f. Unfortunately, this technique may fail to eliminate all spurious paths, since any Σ_{*i}^{f} contains a nested summary Σ_{*}^{f} (i.e., nested according to the grammar in Fig. 3).

We can eliminate these spurious paths by "blocking" all paths in Σ_{*i}^{f} that traverse Σ_{*}^{f}, i.e., we can replace the corresponding expansion by false. Unfortunately, this approach may also eliminate feasible paths. The following Theorem states that it is sufficient to consider only paths up to a certain nesting depth:

Theorem 1 (Universal Summaries with Recursion). *Let r be the largest natural number for which both of the following conditions hold:*

1. *There is a feasible path which contains r nested summaries, and*
2. *this path contains no pair of nested summaries $\langle p_0, \gamma_0 \rangle \rightarrow^* \langle p_0', \gamma_0' \rangle$ and $\langle p_1, \gamma_1 \rangle \rightarrow^* \langle p_1', \gamma_1' \rangle$ for which $\langle p_0, \gamma_0 \rangle = \langle p_1, \gamma_1 \rangle$ and $\langle p_0', \gamma_0' \rangle = \langle p_1', \gamma_1' \rangle$ holds.*

We claim that

a) *such a finite r always exists and can be computed, and*
b) *a summary that subsumes all loop-free paths with at most r nested summary applications is a universal summary $\Sigma_{\mathcal{U}}$.*

Proof. The proof of claim a) is simple: Given a summary $\langle p, \gamma \rangle \rightarrow^* \langle p', \gamma' \rangle$, we call $\langle p, \gamma \rangle$ the *entry*-head and $\langle p', \gamma' \rangle$ the *exit*-head. There are at most $|P|^2 \cdot |\Gamma|^2$ different combinations of entry- and exit-heads. After a path reaches a certain recursion depth $r \leq |P|^2 \cdot |\Gamma|^2$, the pairs of heads inevitably start to repeat. Furthermore, if this path exceeds a length l of at most $|P| \cdot \Sigma_{i=1}^{r} |\Gamma|^r$, then there is a state $\langle p, w \rangle$ that is visited twice. Thus, r can be computed by examining all paths up to depth $|P|^2 \cdot |\Gamma|^2$ and length $|P| \cdot \Sigma_{i=1}^{r} |\Gamma|^r$.

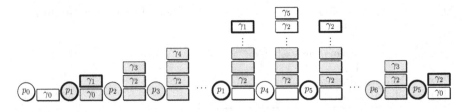

Fig. 8. Nested summaries with repeating entry- and exit-heads

Claim b) follows from the observations made above: Fig. 8 shows a path that contains two nested summaries for which the entry-heads and exit-heads are equal. By eliminating the control states and stack elements that are colored grey in Fig. 8, we obtain a new path with a smaller number of nested summaries. This truncation has no impact on the states reachable from the final state $\langle p_5, \gamma_2 \gamma_0 \rangle$ of the path. Formally, let

$$\langle p_0, \gamma_0 \rangle \rightarrow \langle p_1, \gamma_1 w_1 \rangle \rightarrow \langle p_2, \gamma_2 w_2 \rangle \rightarrow \ldots \rightarrow$$
$$\langle p_i, \gamma_i w_i \rangle \rightarrow \langle p_{i+1}, \gamma_{i+1} w_{i+1} \rangle \rightarrow \ldots \rightarrow \langle p_{j-1}, \gamma_{j-1} w_{j-1} \rangle \rightarrow \langle p_j, \gamma_j w_j \rangle$$
$$\rightarrow \ldots \rightarrow \langle p_{k-1}, \gamma_{k-1} w_{k-1} \rangle \rightarrow \langle p_k, \gamma_k w_k \rangle \rightarrow \langle p_{k+1}, \gamma_{k+1} \rangle$$

be a summary of the PDS, where $|w_1| = |w_k|$, $|w_i| = |w_j|$, $|w_1| < |w_2| < \ldots < |w_i| < |w_{i+1}|$ and $|w_{j-1}| > |w_j| > \ldots > |w_{k-1}| > |w_k|$, i.e., the summaries $\langle p_1, \gamma_1 \rangle \rightarrow^* \langle p_k, \gamma_k \rangle$ and $\langle p_i, \gamma_i \rangle \rightarrow^* \langle p_j, \gamma_j \rangle$ are nested. Furthermore, let $p_1 = p_i$, $\gamma_1 = \gamma_i$, $p_k = p_j$, and $\gamma_k = \gamma_j$. Then, there exists a summary

$$\langle p_0, \gamma_0 \rangle \rightarrow \langle p_i, \gamma_i w_1 \rangle \rightarrow \langle p_{i+1}, \gamma_{i+1} w_r \rangle \rightarrow \ldots \rightarrow$$
$$\langle p_{j-1}, \gamma_{j-1} w_t \rangle \rightarrow \langle p_j, \gamma_j w_k \rangle \rightarrow \langle p_{k+1}, \gamma_{k+1} \rangle$$

that also covers $\langle p_0, \gamma_0 \rangle \rightarrow^* \langle p_{k+1}, \gamma_{k+1} \rangle$, and the nesting depth of this summary is smaller than the nesting depth of the original summary. Thus, any path with a pair of nested summaries can be truncated such that condition 2 holds without changing the set of states reachable via this path. A similar argument can be made for paths that contain a certain state twice (i.e., for paths that are not loop-free). □

The same proof technique has been used by Richard Büchi to show that the set of reachable states of a PDS can be expressed using a finite automaton [8].

There is an obvious similarity between the reachability recurrence diameter presented in Section 3.2 and the bound for the nesting depth introduced in Thm. 1. The reachability recurrence diameter of a PDS is two-dimensional and comprises of a sufficiently large nesting depth r and the length l of the longest loop-free path with a nesting depth at most r. This nesting depth can be computed symbolically using the same SAT-based unrolling technique: The longest loop-free path that contains no nested summaries is of length $|P| \cdot |\Gamma|$. If we increase the depth of the nestings to one, this length increases to $|P| \cdot (|\Gamma| + |\Gamma|^2)$, since each summary in this path may be of length $|P| \cdot |\Gamma|$. For any nesting depth greater than 1, we perform a pairwise comparison of the nested summaries. This can be achieved by means of a SAT-formula that is of quadratic size in the number of nested summaries. By repeatedly increasing the nesting depth r, we can determine the largest r for which the properties in Thm. 1 hold. Note, that if the second condition of Thm. 1 fails for all paths represented by a symbolic path that contains the summary Σ_{*i}^f, then it still fails if we replace Σ_{*i}^f with $\Sigma_{*(i+1)}^f$ (assuming that the first condition still holds after this transformation). In that case, it is not necessary to unroll the summary up to the worst case depth $|P|^2 \cdot |\Gamma|^2$.

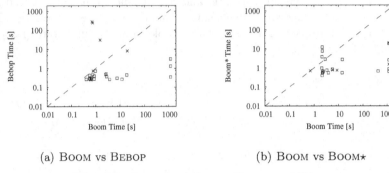

(a) BOOM vs BEBOP   (b) BOOM vs BOOM⋆

Fig. 9. Comparison of BEBOP, BOOM, and BOOM⋆

6   Experiments

We implemented the algorithm in Fig. 7 and evaluated it using 40 PDSs generated by SLAM. In the scatter graphs in Fig. 9 we distinguish between PDSs with
reachable error locations (indicated by ×) and with unreachable error locations
(indicated by □). Fig. 9(a) shows the scatter graph of our comparison of BEBOP
and the version of our tool that applies universal summaries eagerly. We conclude
from these results that our algorithm that applies universal summaries eagerly
(BOOM) tends to perform better than the BDD based model checker BEBOP
when the location in question is reachable in the PDS. It performs worse than
BEBOP when it has to examine the whole state space. Fig. 9(b) compares the effect of the lazy abstraction approach (called BOOM⋆) that we presented in Sec. 4
to the eager algorithm (BOOM). The situation is less obvious than in Fig. 9(a). To
some extent, the algorithm improves the performance for model checking PDSs
with reachable error locations. Unfortunately, this cannot be generalized. We
observed that about a third of the non-deterministic summaries are not replaced
by refined summaries by the algorithm. We believe that we can still improve on
these results, since our tool is in a very early state of development. The most
recent version of BOOM⋆ is available at `http://www.verify.ethz.ch/boom/`.

7   Related Work

The decidability of reachability properties of PDSs was shown by Büchi more
than 40 years ago [8]. Efficient automata-based algorithms to construct the regular set of reachable states are presented by Finkel et al. [4] and Esparza et
al. [5] (see Sec. 2). Schwoon improved the latter approach using a BDD-based
symbolic representation of PDSs [7]. A saturation-based technique for similar
models, namely recursive state machines, is presented in [15].

Summarization was introduced by Sharir and Pnueli as part of a dataflow
analysis algorithm based on iterative fixpoint detection [3]. Ball and Rajamani's
model checker BEBOP is based on this work and uses BDDs to represent states

symbolically [1]. An implementation of their algorithm based on satisfiability solvers for propositional logic (SAT) and quantified Boolean formulas (QBF) is presented in [6] (see Sec. 3.1). Universal summaries are introduced in [6] (see Sec. 3). Kroening's model checker BOPPO uses SAT-based symbolic simulation and QBF-based fixpoint detection, but does not use summarization [16]. BOPPO requires that all function calls can be inlined. Leino combines BDDs and SAT-based techniques in his model checker DIZZY. He does not use summarization and reports that his benchmarks suggest that the approach does not scale [12].

Several attempts have been made to extend the formalism of PDSs with concurrency. In that case, the reachability problem becomes undecidable. Various verification techniques for concurrent PDSs have been proposed, but are either unsound or incomplete: For instance, bounding the number of context switches [17] or bounding communication [18] may miss feasible paths, while over-approximating the set of reachable states [19,20] may report spurious paths. We do not discuss these techniques here, since our approach is inappropriate for asynchronous systems: In general, there is no sufficiently large but finite bound for the sequential depth of concurrent PDSs.

Lal and Reps present a graph-theoretic approach for model checking *weighted* PDSs [21]. Their approach is incomparable to our algorithm, since we do not support weighted PDSs and their approach is not based on satisfiability solving techniques. Boujjani and Esparza survey approaches that use rewriting to solve the reachability problem for sequential as well as for concurrent pushdown systems [22].

BMC was introduced by Biere [23] as a SAT-based alternative to finite-state model checking algorithms that use Binary Decision Diagrams (BDDs). BMC and the recurrence diameter [14] for finite state transition systems is discussed in Sec. 3.2. The SATURN verification tool uses SAT and summarization to detect errors in C programs [24], but handles loops in an unsound manner.

8   Conclusion

BMC is an efficient technique for finding bugs. We showed how it can be applied to PDSs. Our algorithm uses BMC to compute *universal summaries* that relate arbitrary input states to their respective return states according to the transition relation of the function. Universal summaries can be applied in any calling context. We implemented an algorithm that uses SAT to compute universal summaries for functions without recursive calls, and QBF to compute summaries in the presence of recursion. Our benchmarks show that this approach performs better than BDD based algorithms when it comes to detecting bugs, but is less efficient for proving the unreachability of error states. This is a very useful result, since CEGAR-based model checkers generate PDSs with reachable error locations in all but the last iteration. Furthermore, we describe an extension to our algorithm that allows to compute universal summaries for functions with recursion. The implementation and evaluation of this extension is future work.

References

1. Ball, T., Rajamani, S.K.: Bebop: A symbolic model checker for Boolean programs. In: Havelund, K., Penix, J., Visser, W. (eds.) SPIN 2000. LNCS, vol. 1885, pp. 113–130. Springer, Heidelberg (2000)
2. Ball, T., et al.: SLAM and Static Driver Verifier: Technology transfer of formal methods inside Microsoft. In: Boiten, E.A., Derrick, J., Smith, G.P. (eds.) IFM 2004. LNCS, vol. 2999, pp. 1–20. Springer, Heidelberg (2004)
3. Sharir, M., Pnueli, A.: Two approaches to interprocedural dataflow analysis. In: Program Flow Analysis: Theory and Applications, pp. 189–233. Prentice-Hall, Englewood Cliffs (1981)
4. Finkel, A., Willems, B., Wolper, P.: A direct symbolic approach to model checking pushdown systems. In: Workshop on Verification of Infinite State Systems (INFINITY). ENTCS, vol. 9, pp. 27–39 (1997)
5. Esparza, J., Hansel, D., Rossmanith, P., Schwoon, S.: Efficient algorithms for model checking pushdown systems. In: Emerson, E.A., Sistla, A.P. (eds.) CAV 2000. LNCS, vol. 1855, pp. 232–247. Springer, Heidelberg (2000)
6. Basler, G., Kroening, D., Weissenbacher, G.: SAT-based summarisation for Boolean programs. In: Bošnački, D., Edelkamp, S. (eds.) SPIN 2007. LNCS, vol. 4595, pp. 131–148. Springer, Heidelberg (2007)
7. Schwoon, S.: Model-Checking Pushdown Systems. PhD thesis, Technische Universität München (2002)
8. Büchi, J.R.: Regular canonical systems. Archive for Mathematical Logic 6, 91 (1964)
9. Ball, T., Rajamani, S.: Boolean programs: A model and process for software analysis. Technical Report 2000-14, Microsoft Research (2000)
10. Ball, T., Majumdar, R., Millstein, T., Rajamani, S.K.: Automatic predicate abstraction of C programs. In: Programming Language Design and Implementation (PLDI), pp. 203–213. ACM Press, New York (2001)
11. Graf, S., Saïdi, H.: Construction of abstract state graphs with PVS. In: Grumberg, O. (ed.) CAV 1997. LNCS, vol. 1254, pp. 72–83. Springer, Heidelberg (1997)
12. Leino, K.R.M.: A SAT characterization of Boolean-program correctness. In: Ball, T., Rajamani, S.K. (eds.) SPIN 2003. LNCS, vol. 2648, pp. 104–120. Springer, Heidelberg (2003)
13. Eén, N., Sörensson, N.: An extensible SAT-solver. In: Giunchiglia, E., Tacchella, A. (eds.) SAT 2003. LNCS, vol. 2919, pp. 502–518. Springer, Heidelberg (2004)
14. Kroening, D., Strichman, O.: Efficient computation of recurrence diameters. In: Zuck, L.D., Attie, P.C., Cortesi, A., Mukhopadhyay, S. (eds.) VMCAI 2003. LNCS, vol. 2575, pp. 298–309. Springer, Heidelberg (2002)
15. Alur, R., Benedikt, M., Etessami, K., Godefroid, P., Reps, T., Yannakakis, M.: Analysis of recursive state machines. ACM Transactions on Programming Languages and Systems (TOPLAS) 27, 786–818 (2005)
16. Cook, B., Kroening, D., Sharygina, N.: Symbolic model checking for asynchronous Boolean programs. In: Godefroid, P. (ed.) SPIN 2005. LNCS, vol. 3639, pp. 75–90. Springer, Heidelberg (2005)
17. Qadeer, S., Rehof, J.: Context-bounded model checking of concurrent software. In: Halbwachs, N., Zuck, L.D. (eds.) TACAS 2005. LNCS, vol. 3440, pp. 93–107. Springer, Heidelberg (2005)
18. Touili, T., Sighireanu, M.: Bounded communication reachability analysis of process rewrite systems with ordered parallelism. In: Verification of Infinite State Systems (INFINITY). ENTCS, Elsevier, Amsterdam (2006)

19. Cook, B., Kroening, D., Sharygina, N.: Over-Approximating Boolean Programs with unbounded thread creation. In: Formal Methods in Computer-Aided Design FMCAD, pp. 53–59. IEEE Computer Society Press, Los Alamitos (2006)
20. Bouajjani, A., Esparza, J., Touili, T.: A generic approach to the static analysis of concurrent programs with procedures. In: Principles of Programming Languages (POPL), pp. 62–73. ACM Press, New York (2003)
21. Lal, A., Reps, T.: Improving pushdown system model checking. In: Ball, T., Jones, R.B. (eds.) CAV 2006. LNCS, vol. 4144, pp. 343–357. Springer, Heidelberg (2006)
22. Bouajjani, A., Esparza, J.: Rewriting models of Boolean programs. In: Pfenning, F. (ed.) RTA 2006. LNCS, vol. 4098, Springer, Heidelberg (2006)
23. Biere, A., Cimatti, A., Clarke, E.M., Zhu, Y.: Symbolic model checking without BDDs. In: Cleaveland, W.R. (ed.) ETAPS 1999 and TACAS 1999. LNCS, vol. 1579, pp. 193–207. Springer, Heidelberg (1999)
24. Xie, Y., Aiken, A.: Saturn: A scalable framework for error detection using boolean satisfiability. ACM Transactions on Programming Languages and Systems (TOPLAS) 29 (2007)

Locating Regression Bugs

Dor Nir[1], Shmuel Tyszberowicz[2], and Amiram Yehudai[1]

[1] Tel-Aviv University
[2] The Academic College Tel-Aviv Yaffo

Abstract. A regression bug is a bug which causes a feature that worked correctly to stop working after a certain event (system upgrade, system patching, daylight saving time switch, etc.). Very often an encompassed bug fix included in a patch causes the regression bug. Regression bugs are an annoying and painful phenomena in the software development process, requiring a great deal of effort to find. Many tools have been developed in order to find the existence of such bugs. However, a great deal of manual work is still needed to find the exact source-code location that caused a regression bug.

In this paper we present the *CodePsychologist*, a tool which assists the programmer to locate source code segments that caused a given regression bug. The CodePsychologist goes beyond current tools, that identify all the lines of code that changed since the feature in question worked properly (with the help of a Source Control Tool). The CodePsychologist uses various heuristics to select the lines most likely to be the cause of the error, from these often large number of lines of code. This reduces the fixing time of regression bugs. It allows a quick response to field errors that need an immediate correction.

1 Introduction

Various research has been done to study the cost of software maintenance, especially the cost and effort ratio of new development versus maintenance. System maintenance is estimated to comprise at least 50% of the total life cycle costs [16]. According to [4], the proportional maintenance costs range from 49% for a pharmaceutical company to 75% for an automobile company. At the maintenance phase the product is already in the market, and the new versions of the product are due to changes in the code for fixing newly discovered bugs, improving performance, developing new features, or adapting to new environments (IEEE 1219 Standard for Software Maintenance).

While implementing these changes in the maintenance phase, one can accidentally insert regression bugs [2]. Regression bugs occur whenever software functionality that previously worked as desired stops working, or no longer works as planned. Typically regression bugs occur as an unintended consequence of program changes.

To overcome this painful and costly phenomenon, one should check the functionality of the product after each change of the source code. This kind of checking is called a regression test, or a sanity test. Regression testing is any type of software testing which seeks to uncover regression bugs. Those tests are sets of test cases that check the basic

K. Yorav (Ed.): HVC 2007, LNCS 4899, pp. 218–234, 2008.

functionality of the Application Under Test (AUT). A test case consists of commands and checkpoints. Commands describe the steps needed to be performed on the AUT, such as clicking on a specific button, or inserting some text to an edit box. A checkpoint is a verification point that compares the actual value of a specified property with the expected value of that property. Checkpoint examples are checking that a certain edit-box contains some specific text, checking the content of a database, etc. A failure of a checkpoint means that the expected functionality was not met, implying that the application source code contains a bug.

The testing process needs to be comprehensive and accurate, and it may be long and exhausting. Tools for functional testing, that will perform automatic tests on the AUT, are desired. Using both automatic and manual testing finds out whether a regression bug exists. This, however, is not enough. If a regression bug exists in the code, some extra manual work is needed, in order to trace and find the exact location in the source code that has caused this regression bug.

In this paper we present an algorithm for tracing regression bugs. The algorithm's input is:

- The description of the failed checkpoint.
- The version number of the AUT which was the last one to pass the checkpoint (when running the test case on this version the checkpoint passed, whereas the following version failed).

The output is a set of changes in the source code which most likely have caused the bug. Our goal is to reduce the number of locations in the source code that the programmer has to examine in order to fix a bug.

The solution that we present here uses a Source Control Tool (SCT). An SCT is used to manage multiple versions of the same unit of information. It is most commonly used in software development to manage ongoing development of digital documents like the application source code, which contains critical information that may be worked on by a team of people. Changes to these documents are identified by incrementing an associated number or letter code, termed the "version" and associated historically with the person making the change. Some known source control tools are source-safe [17], CVS [3] and ClearCase [11] [1]. We used the SCT to retrieve the source code locations that have changed since the last time the checkpoint passed. After obtaining those changes our solution ranks them according to their likelihood to be the cause for the failure.

In order to implement our algorithm we built a tool named *CodePsychologist*. Like a psychologist, it tries to look for the cause and nature of the problem in the past. Revealing the cause, eases the process of "curing" it.

The rest of the paper is organized as follows. The following section discusses related work, and explains the technical background needed for the rest of the paper. In Section 3, we introduce the CodePsychologist and describe its structure and the techniques it uses. Experiments and evaluations are reported in Section 4, and we conclude and discuss future work in Section 5.

---

[1] In our implementation we used Source-Safe as our source control tool [17].

2   Related Work

Software testing is the process of identifying the completeness, correctness, security, and quality of a software application. The separation of debugging from testing was initially introduced by Myers [7]. He illustrated the desire of the software engineering community to separate fundamental development activities, such as debugging, from that of verification.

Regression tests are software tests whose purpose is to detect bugs which lead the application to a "less developed state", those bugs are called regression bugs. In [14], Leena, Leonard, and Neyaz discuss the importance of regression tests, the goals of those tests, and how to build comprehensive and modular regression tests. In [9], Piziali describes the methodology of regression tests. It introduce two approaches of detecting regression bugs:

- – Classical regression: Tests suite incrementally constructed over period of time. The test suite is composed of directed tests specified by the test plan.
- – Autonomous regression: Hundreds to thousands of copies of different testing environments are dispatched to a regression farm[2] each evening, each differing from the others only by its initial random generation seed.

Ren et-al [12] described a tool for Java programs that statically analyze the impact of each change, and report the affected tests. Using the program's call graph, and set of regression tests, it analyzes two versions of the source code and decomposes their differences into set of atomic changes, then it calculate a partial order of inter-dependencies between the changes. This algorithm is used in order to find which test cases to run after the source code has changed. In the CodePsychologist tool we use a similar algorithm for a different purpose. We use it to rank the likelihood of a change to contain regression bugs (see functions affinity in Section 3.3).

In [5], a bug finding algorithm is described. It uses bug fix memories, project-specific bug and fix knowledge base, developed by analyzing the history of bug fixes. [15] explores how change classification can focus programmer attention on failure-inducing changes, by automatically labeling changes with Red, Yellow, or Green, indicating the likelihood that they have contributed to a test failure. The classification is done by the effect of these changes on a set of tests. Tests whose outcome has improved are marked as green, tests whose outcome has degraded are marked as red, and tests whose outcome has remained unchanged are marked as yellow. The CodePsychologist also tries to rank and classify changes based upon their relevance for the bug. However, it uses only one failing test case.

Another approach for finding regression bugs is by automatic debugging. The Delta Debugging algorithm [19] automates the scientific method of debugging. The algorithm isolates failure causes automatically by systematically narrowing down failure-inducing circumstances until a minimal set of changes remains. Delta Debugging has been applied to isolate failure-inducing program input (e.g. an HTML page that causes a Web browser to fail), failure-inducing user interaction (e.g. the key strokes that make a program crash), or failure-inducing changes to the program code (e.g. after a failing regression test). We are interested in the latter, because it examines changes made to the

---

[2] A Computer farm used for running regression tests.

source code. It uses the Source Control Tool to obtain the changes of the source code, as the CodePsychologist does (cf. Section 3). The algorithm tries to isolate the changes that caused the failure. This is done by binary-search on the changes, running sets of changes at a time. The preeminence of this algorithm is that it is sound and accurate. Its output is the changes in the source code that caused the failure. However, for most of the industrial application it is not applicable, because it needs some automatic tools that are not trivial to implement for every application. For example, in order to examine a change in the source code of a common desktop application, the AUT has to be built with the right source version, then to be installed on a clean machine with the right environment, and then to be automatically tested. This is the motivation for the CodePsychologist tool, which does not demand any build, installation, testing or establishment of special environments. The tool examines the source code statically, without the need of reproducing the bug. It is therefore applicable even for large scale projects.

3   The CodePsychologist

We have built the CodePsychologist to assist the programmer to locate source code segments that caused a given regression bug. The overall structure of the tool is illustrated in Figure 1. The problem that the tool intends to solve is defined as follows:

The AUT has failed at checkpoint C when running a test case. Let V be the last version of the AUT where checkpoint C still passed when running the test case. We want to find in the source code of the AUT the locations $\{p_1, p_2...p_n\}$ that caused C to fail.

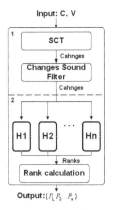

Fig. 1. The CodePsychologist tool

The CodePsychologist obtains as input a checkpoint C, and V – the last version that passed the checkpoint C. The algorithm starts by fetching from the SCT the latest version of the source code, coping it into a temporary folder $TempDir$. Then it receives from the SCT the source-code files one by one, version by version, in a reverse chronological order, i.e., from the newest version to the oldest one, until version V is received.

The algorithm decides if the file is relevant. If not, the file is copied into the $TempDir$ directory, overriding the newer version, and the algorithm continues to the next version from the SCT. If the file is relevant, it is compared to the sequential version (the newer version) that is already in the $TempDir$ directory. The comparison result is the changes between the two versions. Each change is analyzed and ranked. Each ranked change is inserted into a database. After ranking all the changes in the file, the algorithm copies the file to the $TempDir$ directory, overriding the newer version and continuing to the next version from the SCT. After all the changes have been ranked, they are sorted according to their ranks.

As seen, the CodePsychologist algorithm includes two steps.

1. Retrieving the relevant changes between version V and the version where the checkpoint failed. The regression bug has been caused by some of those changes.
2. Ranking the changes.

In the following sections we elaborate these steps.

3.1   Retrieving Relevant Changes

In this step we want to retrieve the changes between V, the last version that we know that had passed checkpoint C tests, and the current version of the AUT, that has failed. The cause of the failure lies in those changes. In order to retrieve versions we use the Source Control Tool (SCT). We assume that the AUT development was done with the assistance of this SCT, which saves all the history and the versions of the AUT during the development. The SCT provides the content of the versions as well as the time the change was submitted (check-in time). The check-in time is used to retrieve all the changes that occurred since the time T of the version V, the last version that passed the checkpoint. We use the check-in time of version V to obtain T. Changes that occurred prior to T are not relevant. There is no way that those changes caused the failure, since at time T the checkpoint C passed. In order to filter out irrelevant changes, we use the *Changes Sound Filter* (CSF) component, that uses the following techniques.

1) A mapping table is used to map checkpoints into locations in the source code. Locations can be coarse grained, e.g. folders or files, or accurate and specific, e.g. lines in the file, classes, or functions. The checkpoints are taken from the test cases (sanity tests). The mapping table is the outcome of a joint effort of the quality assurance people, who know the test cases and the checkpoints they contain, and the development team, which knows the source code and the responsibilities of each module and file. The mapping can also be done at the test case level, which means that the table entry is a test case (instead of a checkpoint) and all the checkpoints of the test case are mapped into the same entry in the mapping table.

The mapping table must be sound. This means that if the lines of code $\{L_1...L_n\}$ of the AUT have been executed during the running of a test case till reaching checkpoint C, then the locations $\{K_1...K_m\}$ in the entry of C in the mapping table contain the locations $\{L_1...L_n\}$. The soundness of the mapping table insures that if the changes $\{P_1...P_n\}$ in locations $\{L_1...L_n\}$ were the cause to the failure of checkpoint C, and the entry of C in the mapping table contains the set of locations $\{K_1...K_m\}$, then $\{K_1...K_m\} \supseteq \{L_1...L_n\}$. The mapping table can be built automatically, by running the test case with some profiling tools. In our implementation, however, we built the mapping table manually. Using the table in the CSF component, we can take only the relevant changes for the checkpoint C. This means that we take only the changes that occurred in the locations taken from the entry of C in the mapping table. For example, suppose that we use the mapping table shown in Table 1, and that the checkpoint *cp1* failed. We go to the *cp1* entry, and retrieve the changes that occurred in the files dialog.cpp, dialog.h, and console.cpp. Since the mapping table is sound, the regression bug is located in the changes we have retrieved. In the example we can also see a mapping from checkpoints *cp2* and *cp3* to the folder c:/project/gui, and a mapping from all the checkpoints in the test case "Sanity test 1" into the folder c:/project. Theoretically, since every change may alter the mapping table, the mapping table should be updated every time there is a change in the source code or in the test cases. Sanity test-cases, however, are rarely changed, and if the mapping is general enough, the updating and maintenance of the mapping table is an easy task.

Table 1. Mapping checkpoints to locations

Checkpoint or test case	Locations
cp1	dialog.cpp, dialog.h, console.cpp
cp2,cp3	c:/project/gui
Sanity test 1	c:/project

2) The filtering of *refactoring-changes*. Refactoring changes are changes that do not affect the functionality of the application. For example, changing variables or functions name, extract common function, comments, function declarations, etc. Those changes do not affect the functionality of the application and therefore can not be the cause of the failure of checkpoint C. Therefore we can remove refactoring changes and still remain sound.

3) When we have profiling information about the failure test case, we can use it in order to remove changes that have not been executed. If a line in the code has not been executed it could not affect the behavior of the application, so it is safe to remove it.

One should bear in mind that the first step of retrieving relevant changes is sound, meaning that it does not filter the changes causing the regression bug. However, after this step we can end up with too many changes that have not been filtered out. This is the main reason for the second step: ranking the changes from the first step.

3.2 Changes Ranking

The second step takes as input the set of changes $\{p_1, p_2...p_n\}$, produced in the first step, and uses various heuristics to rank them based on likelihood of their being the cause of the error. The output of this step, and of the whole CodePsychologist tool, is the set of changes sorted by rank.

The relevance of each change to the checkpoint failure is ranked according to several heuristics we will describe in Section 3.3. The final change-rank Rank(p) is the weighted average of all the heuristic-ranks of change p.

$$\text{Rank}(p) = \sum_{i=1}^{H} \alpha_i \cdot \text{HeuristicRank}_i(p)$$

where α_i is the coefficient of the heuristic i, and H is the number of heuristics the algorithm uses. The coefficients are based on experimental results described in Section 4.

It should be noted that the first step, retrieving relevant changes, is sound. The output includes all the changes between version V (the last version that passed the checkpoint C) and the current version, which contains the regression bug. The second step, ranking changes by heuristics, is not sound, which means that the changes containing the regression bug are not guaranteed to have the highest rank. However, our experiments, reported in Section 4, show that the rank of the change containing the bug the is one of the highest.

At the core of most of the heuristics we use (to be described in the following section), is the concept of **affinity-ranking**. Affinity can be defined as "close connection marked by community of interests or similarity in nature or character" [6].

The affinity between two collections of words A and B, quantifies their similarity. For example, if we look on the following three collections of words: $A = \{car, bicycle\}$, $B = \{train, car, track\}$, $C = \{camel, elephant, monkey, zebra\}$, we can say that the affinity between A and B is higher than the affinity between A and C.

In order to rank the affinity between two collections of words, we have to calculate the affinity between two words. We treat a taxonomy of words as an undirected connected graph, where each node represents a synonym set. A synonym set is a collection of words with similar meaning. This undirected connected graph is created by the WordNet tool [6]. We measure the distance between two words as the distance between their synonyms sets. The shorter the path between the related nodes, the more similar the words are.

The distance of identical words is defined as 1, and the distance between two members of the same synonym set is 2 (synonym relations). The rationale for these numbers is the way we define the affinity formula, as soon explained.

Figure 2, taken from [13], presents an example of the hyponym taxonomy in WordNet [6], used for path-length similarity measurement. Note that the distance between the words 'car' and 'auto' is 2 because they are in the same synonym set. The distance between 'car' and 'bicycle' is 5: distance of 3 between the synonym sets plus 2 for the distance in the same synonym set. The distance between 'car' and 'fork' is 13: distance of 11 between the synonym sets plus 2 for the distance in the same synonym set.

For two words a and b let us define distance(a,b) as the length of the path between a and b in the taxonomy graph plus 2. If the words are located in the same synonym set their distance value is 2. If the two words are identical their distance value is 1. The affinity function WrdAff between a and b is calculated as follows:

$$\text{WrdAff}(a, b) = \frac{1}{\text{distance}(a, b)}$$

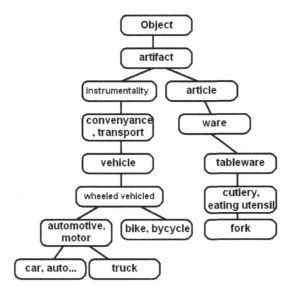

Fig. 2. Wordnet taxonomy example

Hence the affinity is a number in the range (0,1] where a larger affinity means stronger similarity, and 1 means identity.

In order to compare two words, and to determine if they are equal, it is not enough to do a simple string matching comparison. For example, the words 'sort' and 'sorting' are different words, yet we know they are very close in meaning. To overcome this difficulty we use Porter's suffix-stripping algorithm [10], which returns the stem of a word. For the words 'sorting' and 'sorted', the stem is 'sort', hence after removing the suffix the comparison finds them equal.

Another technique to determine if words are equal, that we considered but did not adopt, is to use Makagonov's method for testing word similarity [1]. This method determines words equality by empirical results. The formula relies on the following characteristics of pair of words:

- y: the length of the common initial substring.
- n: the total number of final letters differing in the two words.
- s: the total number of letters in the two words.

In order to determine if two words are equal the following condition need to be satisfied: $\frac{n}{s} \leq 0.53 - 0.029 \cdot y$.

The ranking ignores the semantic of the words. For example, if we have the following two sentences: "We use it to **sort** the items" and "What **sort** of desserts are there?" The affinity-rank between the word 'sort' from the sentence line to the word 'sort' from the second sentence is 1 although they have different meanings.

Given two collections of words: $A = \{a_1, a_2...a_n\}$ and $B = \{b_1, b_2...b_m\}$, we define the affinity function GrpAff(A, B) as follows:

$$\text{AsyGrpAff}(A, B) = \frac{1}{n} \cdot \sum_{i=1}^{n} \max\{\text{WrdAff}(a_i, b_j) \mid 1 \leq j \leq m\},$$

$$\text{GrpAff}(A, B) = \left(\text{AsyGrpAff}(A, B) + \text{AsyGrpAff}(B, A)\right)/2.$$

The $\text{WrdAff}(a_i, b_j)$ (for each j) in the first formula is the affinity function between two words we defined earlier. Like the WrdAff formula, this function range is between (0,1].

The affinity-ranking method is aimed to a spoken language with meaningful words. However, in the CodePsychologist algorithm we sometimes have to use this method on source code, which is written in a formal programming language. Programming languages differ form spoken languages in both grammar and vocabulary. The ranking affinity method does not relate to the order of the words, so the difference in the grammar is not causing any problem. The vocabulary of programming languages however, can cause a problem, because code-items names like methods, variables, and classes can be words without any meaning. However, we assume the programmer is using meaningful words in order to create a readable program. A code-item name can be composed from a concatenation of meaningful words, and some extra characters with special meaning. For example, the class member *m_nClerkSocialNumber* composed from *'m_'* meaning this is a class member, the *'n'* means this is an integer number and the concatenation *'ClerkSocialNumber'* disassembled to 'clerk social number'. In order to disassemble code-item name into meaningful words, we use the code conventions rules. It is widely believed that providing meaningful names to code elements enhances program understandability. We have observed that programmers indeed tend to use meaningful names and to write comments in the source code explaining the code. The test cases and the checkpoints also describe their purpose. Hence we can expect high affinity between those two groups of words (source code and checkpoint description).

Another challenge in finding the affinity between words taken from spoken language (the test-cases) and words taken from a source code is that in some cases the set of terms is different. You can find many application that uses one term in the logical computation of the application while the user interface use different term. For example in the *WinButler* application of the DDS company[18] we used in the experiments, the logical computation uses the word *Waiter* while the user interface use the word *Clerk*. This phenomena add noise to the CodePsychologist results and reduce accuracy. In order to bridge this gap between the test case language and the source code language, we use a translation table that maps one set of terms to another.

3.3   The Heuristics

This section describes the heuristics we used. Most heuristics are based on the affinity-ranking algorithm we previously described in Section 3.2.

The affinity-ranking algorithm ranks the affinity between two collections of words. One collection of words given to the algorithm is the checkpoint-description, containing the set of operations needed for performing the check and testing the AUT. The checkpoint description can also include text from the test case steps that have to be performed prior to the checkpoint. All the heuristics rank are normalized to 1, hence the rank is always in the range (0,1]. As *Heuristic* hints, the rank is not always accurate, and in certain cases might cause ranking errors. In all heuristics we use $\ddot{W}(C)$, as the collection of words in the description of checkpoint C.

Code Lines Affinity: This heuristic ranks the affinity between the checkpoint-description and the source-code lines that have been changed. The heuristic takes into account also code-lines that have not been changed, but are close to the lines that did change. $\ddot{W}(P, l)$ is the collection of source-code words located exactly l lines from the change P. For example, if the lines 5 to 7 have been changed due to change P, $\ddot{W}(P, 2)$ are lines 3 and 9. The ranking formula is:

$$\text{Rank}_1(C, P) = \beta \cdot \text{GrpAff}\left(\ddot{W}(C), \ddot{W}(P, 0)\right) +$$
$$\frac{(1 - \beta)}{L} \cdot \sum_{l=1}^{L} \text{GrpAff}\left(\ddot{W}(C), \ddot{W}(P, l)\right).$$

The coefficient for lines that have changed is β $(\geq \frac{1}{2})$, and $(1 - \beta)$ is the coefficient for unchanged lines at distance up to L lines from the location of the change.

Check-in comment Affinity: Committing a change into the SCT is called a *check-in operation*. Most SCTs demand that programmers will insert a comment describing the changes they made in the source code. The programmer can then describes the change using a free text. The heuristic ranks the affinity between the checkpoint description and the check-in comment that has been inserted by the programmer as follows:

$$\text{Rank}_2(C, P) = \text{GrpAff}\left(\ddot{W}(C), \ddot{W}(\text{checkin}(P))\right).$$

$\ddot{W}(\text{checkin}(p))$ is the collection of words in the check-in comment of change P. Notice that when a programmer performs several changes in the same file, only one check-in comment can be used. This yields the same rank for all the changes made in one file (for a specific version).

File affinity: This heuristic ranks the affinity between the checkpoint description and the file in which the change is located. It requires a words-histogram of the file. The words-histogram is a mapping between a word in the file and the number of occurrences of this word in the file. The purpose of this heuristic is to determine, in a coarse granularity, what are the most relevant files to look for the regression bug. The histogram of the file can be automatically built. We define the histogram affinity function $\text{HstAff}(A, B, map)$, which takes as input two collections of words A and B, and a word-histogram map, and computes the affinity between the two collections according to the given mapping. Let $A = \{a_1, a_2, \ldots, a_n\}$, $B = \{b_1, b_2, \ldots, b_m\}$, and

$$\text{MaxAff}(a, B) = \max\{\text{WrdAff}(a, b_i) \cdot map[b_i] \mid 1 \leq i \leq m\}.$$

The WrdAff function in the first formula is the affinity between two words, describes in Section 3.2. $map[b_i]$ is the number of occurrences of the word b_i in the file F (according to the histogram). The rationality behind this formula, is to increase the rank of affinities between words with a high number of occurrences in the file. We achieve that by multiplying the affinity function $\text{WrdAff}(a, b_i)$ by the number of occurrences of the word in the file $map[b_i]$:

$$\text{HstAff}(A, B, map) = \frac{\sum_{i=1}^{n} \text{MaxAff}(a_i, B)}{n \cdot \max\{map[b_i] \mid 1 \leq i \leq m\}}.$$

In this formula we used the MaxAff function we already defined, in order to calculate the affinity between the collections A and B in respect to the word histogram map. We accumulate all the MaxAff's between the words in A to collection B, and then we normalized it. Now we can use the HstAff function in order to rank a file F with respect to the checkpoint C, according to F histogram $\mathrm{Hstg}(F)$:

$$\mathrm{Rank}_3(C, P) = \mathrm{HstAff}\left(\ddot{W}(C), \ddot{W}(F), \mathrm{Hstg}(F)\right).$$

P is a change in the file F. Like the previous heuristic, changes in the same file will get the same rank.

Functions affinity: This heuristic is based on the affinity between the checkpoint description and the function where the change is located. The calculation is divided into two parts. First we retrieve the function F where the change is located. Then we call the function affinity method FncAff with two parameters: the checkpoint C that failed and the function F. FncAff calculates the affinity between checkpoint C and function F's name, the comment that describes F (if such a comment exists), and F's body. Finally it recursively calls FncAff for each function F_i that F calls:

$$\mathrm{Rank}_4(C, P) = \frac{\alpha}{k + \alpha + \beta} \cdot \mathrm{GrpAff}\left(\ddot{W}(C), \ddot{W}(F)\right) +$$

$$\frac{\beta}{k + \alpha + \beta} \cdot \mathrm{GrpAff}\left(\ddot{W}(C), \mathrm{Bdy}(F)\right) +$$

$$\sum_{i=1}^{k} \frac{1}{k + \alpha + \beta} \cdot \mathrm{FncAff}\left(C, \mathrm{FncCall}(F, i)\right),$$

where

- $\ddot{W}(F)$: The words in the function name of F.
- $\mathrm{Bdy}(F)$: The words in the function body of F.
- $\mathrm{FncCall}(F, i)$: The i-th function that F calls to.
- k: The number of functions F calls to.
- α: A Coefficient for the function name affinity.
- β: A coefficient for the function body affinity.
- F: A function containing the change P.

The coefficients α and β are determined based upon experimental results we performed (see Section 4). We intend to perform more experiments in order to determine the coefficient values that give the best results. This ranking method ignores changes located outside a function, such as functions declarations, include statements, etc. This is acceptable as we are looking for a change in the *functionality* of the application rather than in its *structure*. Nevertheless, this heuristic has some limitations:

- As the heuristics analysis is static, the call graph has a limited accuracy. Calls to virtual functions can not always be resolved, because the dynamic type is not always known. Function calls inside a condition block influence the rank, even when the condition is not met and thus the functions are actually not called. We can resolve those problems if we have some profiling information about the failed run of the test case. Another solution we consider for the next version, is to adopt the heuristic rule of taking the path or the function with the higher rank. For example, if we have two virtual function named *foo*, and both can be called by function F (the function that we currently analyzing), we will calculate the affinity to both functions but we will take into account only the function with the higher rank. The rationality behind this heuristic rule, is that the heuristic search for the possible paths of execution that are closed to the test case, the closest they are the most probable they are relevant for the heuristic rank. One should remember that even if we have some errors in this heuristic, the coefficients α, β and k can reduce the impact of that error.

– We ignore indirect changes of the functionality, such as changes to macros located outside a function, changes of static class members initialization, and changes in include and imports statements. These changes can lead to change in functionality. We intend to refine the algorithm to take those changes into account.

Those limitation can damage the accuracy of the heuristic, However the initial results we present in Section 4 shows that the accuracy of this heuristic is good. This affinity heavily depends on the technology in which the AUT is developed. We need to implement the heuristic differently for each programming language.

Due to lack of space we omit two other heuristics that we have developed but have not yet implemented: **Code complexity** and **Human Factor**. Their description may be found in [8].

4   Experiments

We performed two kinds of experiments: synthetic and real-world. The synthetic experiments were intended to tune CodePsychologist and to get an initial indication about our theory. In the second kind of experiments we tested the CodePsychologist on a real-world regression bug, and analyzed the results.

After ranking each change, we used two modes of views in order to analyze the results.

– *No Grouping*. Each change was ranked separately.
– *File Grouping*. Changes in the AUT, like fixing a bug, or adding new feature, require a change in the source code. This change can spread through many locations in a file. This is the reason to rank the file version according to the ranks of all the changes it contains. The file-version rank is the average of the ranks of all changes located in the specific version of the file[3] (the ranks are taken from the database).

4.1   Synthetic Experiments

In order to tune the CodePsychologist, and test it, we have used a demo project as the AUT. The project, called WinButler developed by the DDS company [18] is a desktop application used to configure electronic cache registers via RS232. It is written in C++, using the Microsoft Foundation Classes library. It contains 891 files in 29 folders and has 3 million lines of code. The number of check-ins is 3984 and the effort is estimated

---

[3] We intend to experiment with other ways to compute the file-version rank, e.g. the maximal rank.

as 6 man-years. We have *planted* regression bugs in the source code, and wrote test-cases that expose those bugs, meaning that the checkpoint in each test case will fail when running the test case on the AUT (containing our planted regression bugs). We tried to imitate as close as we can, common errors done by programmers, such as off by one error in numerical expressions, or a small change in the control flow of the application (e.g. changing a boolean expression in an *if* statement). We examined the CodePsychologist with the failed test-cases and the WinButler source code. Then we used the results of the experiments to tune the CodePsychologist and recalculate the coefficients for each heuristic.

Table 2 and Table 3 summarize the results for the *No Grouping* and *File Grouping* modes, respectively. Each table presents the results of five different changes that we made. Those changes introduce regression bugs. Each change was ranked with respect to all 256 changes that occurred in the code during a real development of the application, for the last 5 months. We show the rank that was obtained using each of the 4 heuristics used. The columns are labeled as follows: (1) Code Lines Affinity, (2) Check-in comment Affinity, (3) File affinity, and (4) Functions affinity. A minus (-) sign, indicates that the change was not ranked among the top 10 changes (except for the file affinity heuristic), which we usually view as a failure of the tool to find the bug. We then present the simple (arithmetic) average of the ranks this change obtained by the different heuristics. The last column of each table presents the weighted average which provides improved results. We will explain shortly how the weights were chosen.

Table 2. No Grouping Results

Bug	Heuristic				Average	
	Code Lines	Check-in	File Affinity	Functions	Simple	Weighted
1	5	3	9	1	1	1
2	-	1	24	-	7	3
3	5	3	3	1	1	1
4	-	-	-	6	6	5
5	2	1	4	1	4	1

Table 3. File Grouping Results

Bug	Heuristic				Average	
	Code Lines	Check-in	File Affinity	Functions	Simple	Weighted
1	1	3	9	1	1	1
2	9	1	24	-	3	2
3	3	3	3	2	1	1
4	-	-	-	3	9	4
5	1	1	4	1	1	1

Looking at the tables, we can observe several things. In both modes, no heuristics was able to find all bugs. In fact, different heuristics did well on different bugs. Consequently, using the simple average, the tool found all bugs in the top 10. Furthermore, in the *No Grouping* two of the five bugs were ranked first among the 256 code changes, and in the *File Grouping* mode, three of the five bugs were ranked first. In some cases the file grouping view gets better results then without grouping, for example bug 4. The reason for those results is that some changes that do not contain the regression bug get a better rank then the change with the regression bug. In the file grouping view the rank is determined for the whole file. The changes with the higher rank are taken along with other changes in the file, usually with a low rank. This might lower the average rank for the changed file.

When we compare the results of the various heuristics, we can observe several phenomena. Analyzing the results together with the source code, we can conclude that the code lines affinity heuristic does well when the changed code contains variables, functions and classes with meaningful names, and comments that explains and elaborating the logic of the code.

The check-in comment heuristic is heavily dependent on the programmers "good will", and the ability of the source control tool to enforce adding comments when committing a check-in operation. Some SCTs enforce entering of detailed comments while other don't enforce anything. The SCT that was used during the development of the AUT was *Visual SourceSafe* [17], which does not enforce the insertion of a comment while check-in, therefore many check-in operations were missing a comment, which results with an affinity rank of 0. Still we can learn from the results that it is possible to find bugs using this heuristic. We conclude that detailed and accurate check-in comments are important in order to find the suspicious changes, therefore SCTs that enforce insertion of detailed check-in comments are likely to give better results for the CodePsychologist. Our experiments were done only on one project with one SCT, this is the reason why we can not conclude much from the results of this heuristic. We intend to perform additional experiments of the check-in comment heuristic on other applications developed using different SCTs.

The file affinity heuristic was developed with the view that it may be used as a coarse grained filter of changes, prior to activation of the other heuristics. It is much faster than the other heuristics, because all the changes located in the same file version gets the same rank. For this heuristic we show the rank even when it is larger than 10. We can see that all the files containing the bugs were found in the top 25 suspicious files. These results encourages us to use this heuristic as a coarse grained filter.

The function affinity heuristic was the only heuristic that analyzes the source code and found bug number four. Change number four has an indirect affinity to the checkpoint, which means that the words in the change have low affinity to the checkpoint, but the functions being called from the changed function (the function containing the change), have high affinity to the checkpoint description. The ability to find indirect affinity is important, because many regression bugs are due to an unintentional flow of the program caused by a "simple" and "naive" change.

For two of the heuristics *File Grouping* and *No Grouping* yield identical results. In general, *File Grouping* usually does better than the *No Grouping*.

After performing the experiments we computed the coefficients of each heuristic, to maximize the weighted average results: $\alpha_1 = \frac{1}{5}$, $\alpha_2 = \frac{2}{5}$, $\alpha_3 = 0$, $\alpha_4 = \frac{2}{5}$. The coefficient α_3 is zero because we want to use 'file affinity heuristic' as a coarse grain filter, instead of a regular ranking heuristic.

We can see that the results are better then the simple average results as expected. The results support our assumption that the algorithm of CodePsychologist works, and have added value to programmers in accelerating the resolution of regression bugs.

4.2   A Real World Regression Bug

We tested CodePsychologist on a real world regression bug. The bug insertion was during the development of a new feature in the application. When running a sanity test on the AUT containing the bug, a warning message box showed, causing the failure of a checkpoint in the sanity test, and exposing the existence of the regression bug. The reason for the warning message was a resource leak. Initializing the new feature which used resource X, caused the incremental of the reference counter for resource X. The new feature did not release resource X, then when X was destroyed it's reference counter was 1, causing the warning message box. In order to find this bug, one should go over all objects in the source code which hold a reference to resource X, and confirm that the reference was released before X is destroyed. This was a hard task. The number of objects holding a reference to X was big, involving many composite modules, with composite relations between them. Finding this bug, without fixing it, took 20 hours of strenuous work of two experienced programmers (fixing it took less then an hour). Using the CodePsychologist to trace this bug, accelerate the time of finding the bug. The results of this experiment are summarized in Table 4. We used the *'File Grouping'* view (described in Section 4), because the changed lines containing the bug were spread in different places in the file. We can see that the 'Code Lines Affinity' heuristic and the 'Functions affinity' heuristic ranked the change with the bug in the top ten suspicious changes, which leads to an overall rank that placed the change in the fourth place. This leaves the programmers to check only four places in the source code, and find the regression bug much faster.

Table 4. A Real World regression bug results

Heuristic	Rank (Group by File)
Code Lines Affinity	7
Check-in Comment Affinity	-
File Affinity	22
Function Affinity	8

5   Future Work

For the next version of the CodePsychologist we want to implement the *Code complexity* and the *Human factor* heuristics described in [8], and test their accuracy. We need to perform more experiments on the *check-in comment* heuristic with several SCTs.

In order to optimize the performance of the algorithm, we consider to use the *File affinity* heuristic as an initial filter heuristic, to filter out changes that we suspect to have a very small probability to be the cause for the checkpoint failure. The algorithm uses the other heuristics only on the remaining changes. We want to give the tool users the ability to insert a short description of the failure, for example "The application crashes" or "The dialog title's color is green", etc. This description is added to the checkpoint description. We think this could add accuracy to the tool.

In addition to the *No Grouping* and *File Grouping* views (Section 4) we want to add the *Group by task* view. Usually a coding task such as adding a new feature, or fixing a bug, involves more then one file. We rank file that are part of the same task according to the ranks of all the changes inside the file. In order to retrieve those task's groups, we assume that files version with the same check-in comment and approximately the same check-in time are part of the same task.

We intend to test the tool on other real world regression bugs, and eventually to find out if it accelerate the process of fixing regression bugs.

References

1. Blanco, X., Alexandrov, M., Gelbukh, A.: Modified Makagonov's method for testing word similarity and its application to constructing word frequency lists. Advances in Natural Language Processing. J. Research in Computing Science, 27–36 (2006)
2. Brooks Jr., F.P.: The Mythical Man-Month: Essays on Software Engineering, 20th Anniversary edn. Addison-Wesley, Reading (1995)
3. CVS: Concurrent versions system (visited June 2007), http://www.nongnu.org/cvs
4. Grubb, P.A., Takang, A.A.: Software Maintenance: Concepts and Practic, 2nd edn. World Scientific Publishing, Singapore (2003)
5. Kim, S., Pan, K., Whitehead Jr., E.E.J.: Memories of bug fixes. In: SIGSOFT 2006/FSE-14: Proceedings of the 14th ACM SIGSOFT international symposium on Foundations of software engineering, pp. 35–45. ACM Press, New York (2006)
6. Miller, G.A., et al.: Wordnet: An electronic lexical database (1998)
7. Myers, G.J., Badgett, T., Thomas, T.M.: The Art of Software Testing, 2nd edn. John Wiley & Sons, Chichester (2004)
8. Nir, D.: Codepsychologist: Locating regression-bugs. Master's thesis, Tel-Aviv University, Israel (in preparation, 2007)
9. Piziali, A.: Functional Verification Coverage Measurement And Analysis. Springer, Heidelberg (2004)
10. Porter, M.F.: An Algorithm for Suffix Stripping, pp. 313–316. Morgan Kaufmann Publishers Inc., San Francisco (1997)
11. Rational ClearCase (2007), http://www-306.ibm.com/software/awdtools/clearcase/support/index.html
12. Ren, X., et al.: Chianti: A tool for change impact analysis of Java programs. In: Object-Oriented Programming Systems, Languages, and Applications (OOPSLA 2004), Vancouver, BC, Canada, pp. 432–448 (October 2004)
13. Simpson, T., Dao, T.: Wordnet-based semantic similarity measurement (2005), http://www.codeproject.com/cs/library/semanticsimilaritywordnet.asp (visited June 2007)
14. Singh, L., Drucker, L., Khan, N.: Advanced Verification Techniques: A SystemC Based Approach for Successful Tapeout. Kluwer Academic Publishers, Dordrecht (2004)
15. Stoerzer, M., et al.: Finding failure-inducing changes in Java programs using change classification. In: Robshaw, M.J.B. (ed.) FSE 2006. LNCS, vol. 4047, pp. 57–68. Springer, Heidelberg (2006)

16. van Vliet, H.: Software Engineering: Principles and Practices, 2nd edn. John Wiley, West Sussex (2000)
17. Visual source safe (2005), `http://msdn2.microsoft.com/en-us/vstudio/aa718670.aspx` (visited June 2007)
18. DDS (visited June 2007), `http://www.dds-daon.de/`
19. Zeller, A.: Automated debugging: Are we close?, IEEE Computer 34(11), 26–31 (2001)

The Advantages of Post-Link Code Coverage

Orna Raz, Moshe Klausner, Nitzan Peleg, Gad Haber, Eitan Farchi,
Shachar Fienblit, Yakov Filiarsky, Shay Gammer, and Sergey Novikov

IBM Haifa Research Lab, Haifa, Israel

Abstract. Code coverage is often defined as a measure of the degree to
which the source code of a program has been tested [19]. Various metrics
for measuring code coverage exist. The vast majority of these metrics require instrumenting the source code to produce coverage data. However,
for certain coverage metrics, it is also possible to instrument object code
to produce coverage data. Traditionally, such instrumentation has been
considered inferior to source level instrumentation because source code
is the focus of code coverage. Our experience shows that object code
instrumentation, specifically post-link instrumentation, can be very useful to users. Moreover, it does not only alleviate certain side-effects of
source-level instrumentation, especially those related to compiler optimizations, but also lends itself to performance optimization that enables
low-overhead instrumentation. Our experiments show an average of less
than 1% overhead for instrumentation at the function level and an average of 4.1% and 0.4% overhead for SPECint2000 and SPECfp2000,
respectively, for instrumentation at the basic block level. This paper
demonstrates the advantages of post-link coverage and describes effective methodology and technology for applying it.

1 Introduction

Code coverage is the practice of measuring how many 'code entities' have been
exercised by a specific test suite. Code entities vary according to the metric used
for coverage. Examples of common coverage metrics are statement coverage and
basic block coverage. Statement coverage reports how many of the potentially-
executable statements in the source code have actually been executed. Basic
block coverage differs from statement coverage only in the entity of code measured. The code entity in basic block coverage is each sequence of non-branching
statements rather than each statement. The vast majority of common coverage
metrics refer directly to the program source code and are typically implemented
at the source code level. This may stem from the fact that code coverage is considered a 'white-box' testing technique, a technique that uses knowledge about
the structure of the source code. In addition, source code is typically relatively
portable (it is usually more portable than object code). However, instrumenting
the source code of languages such as C/C++ often requires tight coupling with
a compiler (e.g., GCOV[9], GNU's coverage tool that works with GNU's GCC
compiler). In general, coverage metrics that map to source line numbers can
be implemented at the object level if source-level debug information is present.

K. Yorav (Ed.): HVC 2007, LNCS 4899, pp. 235–251, 2008.
© Springer-Verlag Berlin Heidelberg 2008

Though object-level implementations and even object-level coverage metrics exist, they seem to be used mainly for certification of critical airborne software (Section 2).

The common practice in code coverage is to look at coverage only at the source code level. Our experience with code coverage disagrees with this common practice. We have found object-level coverage, in particular post-link coverage, very effective. We have had extensive real-world experience with applying code coverage where existing tools, such as GCOV, do not work. There are various reasons for why existing tools might not work. The software that we deal with typically has fault-tolerance requirements and timing constraints. Real-time requirements are one example of timing constraints. Timing constraint imply that any code instrumentation must refrain from adding significant performance overhead or it may cause time-outs to be hit thus interfering with the functional correctness or even with the execution of the software. Moreover, the software that we deal with often works in an environment in which there is no operating system or only a very primitive one. This means for example, that writing coverage data to files is problematic and that the size of the executable and of the data may need to be limited. In addition, dealing with static libraries is a challenge for many coverage solutions. The same is true for dealing with non-terminating code. Naturally, a coverage solution is not expected to deal with all the challenges we have listed above. However, it should have the ability to deal with a subset of these challenges that is of high impact for specific software. We have used both source-level coverage instrumentation and post-link coverage instrumentation. We found that where we were able to apply our post-link technology we had more flexibility in addressing various challenges. In addition, because more information is available at the post-link level than at the source level, the post-link coverage data has additional information that is beneficial for improving testing; coverage measurements are usually taken to provide help in effectively strengthening the existing test suite. These are the main advantages of post-link coverage:

– Obviously, if the source code is not available then post-link instrumentation still allows you to get coverage data. However, this is not the emphasis of this paper. Our claim is stronger: post-link instrumentation is useful also if the source code is available. Moreover, it has advantages that source-level approaches lack.
– Post-link instrumentation causes no interruption to compiler optimizations. Source-level instrumentation may prohibit optimizations that would otherwise be possible. As a result, post-link optimization works on the actual code whereas source-level instrumentation works on a variant of the code. It is better to test the actual code than a variant of the code. An example [1] of the difference between source and post-link code is provided in the following source code fragment that is taken from a login program

```
memset (password, '\0', len);
free (password)
```

A compiler performing dead-code elimination may reason that the program never uses the memset values and therefore might remove the memset call.

This leaves the clear-text password exposed on the heap, creating a security hazard. However, the mere act of adding coverage instrumentation at the source level will prevent this optimization. As a result, tests that verify that no exposed clear-text exists will pass. Unfortunately, the customer gets code that might contain exposed clear-text. Post-link coverage instrumentation will leave the optimization in place and therefore the same tests that passed before rightly fail now.

- Working at the post-link level lends itself more to introducing instrumentation with minimal performance overhead because the actual code to be executed is already in place. Section 4 provides details about our post-link low-overhead technology. Being able to perform coverage instrumentation while incurring only a very low performance overhead makes it possible to take coverage measurements as part of the regular operation of all the verification phases. Coverage as part of the regular operation has a major advantage of being able to test the actual code and not a variation of it. It may even make it possible to take coverage measurements at the customer's site (in places that were not covered during testing, Section 5 discusses this as future work). Taking coverage measurements as part of the regular operation of all phases also makes it possible to accumulate coverage results cross the different phases. Low-overhead instrumentation does not interfere with the regular regression process.

- It is often interesting and informative when improving testing to understand why certain source lines are only partially covered. A single source line may result in multiple basic blocks and therefore may be only partially covered. Our post-link coverage methodology, presented in Section 3, includes a dictionary of compiler transformations and optimizations.

The main contributions of this paper are the insight regarding the usefulness of post-link coverage and the methodology for a practical implementation of the insight. In our experience, this methodology alleviates the major hurdle of post-link coverage, which is the difficulty in understanding the results of post-link coverage. Post-link coverage data needs to be mapped back to the source but the post-link version and the source version may be very different. We provide both a recommended methodology for applying post-link coverage and a description of our post-link coverage technology. Apart from the post-link coverage methodology, we have been developing and following a general coverage methodology which we find very effective. This methodology is also described in the paper.

2   Related Work

Many different coverage metrics exist. Section 2.1 presents some of the common coverage metrics. Section 2.2 discusses existing work on object-level coverage. Section 2.3 discusses work that relies on a similar insight to the one we make in our work; namely, that object code has more information than source code and this can be beneficial for various analyses.

2.1   Coverage Metrics

In general, source-code coverage metrics can be implemented at the post-link level. Different advantages and disadvantages may exist for each metric for source-level implementation vs. post-link implementation. See for example, the discussion about the define-use metric in Section 2.3. The various coverage metrics (e.g., [19], [2]) can roughly be divided into control-flow coverage metrics, data-flow coverage metrics, and functional coverage metrics. Examples of control-flow metrics are statement coverage and basic-block coverage. An example of data-flow metrics is define-use coverage. An example of functional coverage [10] is synchronization coverage. Statement coverage reports how many of the source code executable statements have been executed. Basic block coverage is similar to statement coverage except that it reports on each sequence of non-branching statements. Define-use coverage reports on all the usages of a definition. Synchronization coverage reports on contention on all the synchronization primitives.

Coverage solutions for C/C++ typically work at the source code level. Coverage solutions for Java typically work at the byte-code level (e.g., [5]). Information in Java byte code is similar to source code as it has a one-to-one mapping with the source code. Such a representation is not available for languages such as C/C++. Object code may differ greatly from source code, especially if optimizations were done, for example by the compiler. We claim that it is interesting and useful to measure coverage on the actual code runs, i.e., coverage at the post-link level.

2.2   Object-Level Coverage Metrics

Metrics and tools for object-level coverage exist (e.g., [8]). However, they seem to concentrate mainly on satisfying the FAA RTCA/DO-178B standard [6]. RTCA/DO-178B"Software Considerationsin Airborne Systemsand EquipmentCertification" is an internationally recognized standard required for certifying software used in airborne systems and equipment. It was developed by the non-profit Radio Technical Commission for Aeronautics (RTCA). DO-178B defines five software levels (A through E), with Level A applicable to the most critical aircraft equipment requiring the greatest level of effort to show DO-178 compliance. Objectives 5, 6 and 7 of Table A-7 address statement, decision, and MCDC (Multiple Condition Decision Coverage).

A common recommendation regarding object-level coverage is "You are better off testing the original source code since it relates to program requirements better than the object code" [3]. One of the contributions of our work is that our post-link coverage technology comes with a methodology that enables users to get the most out of the post-link coverage data. We have not come across any such existing methodology.

2.3   Static Analysis

Static analysis is another instance of traditionally working at the source code level. However, recent work [1] demonstrates the disadvantages of this approach compared to working at the post-link level. Balakrishnan et al. demonstrate that for static analysis targeted at the security domain, some bugs and vulnerabilities are only discovered at the post-link level. They argue that it is important to analyze the precise artifact that will be executed. The source code is not the artifact as it may differ significantly from the code to be executed. We make a similar observation: the source code, especially if it is compiled with aggressive optimizations, might bear little resemblance to the code that will be executed. Code coverage differs from static analysis, though, in the sense that the coverage instrumentation itself may disrupt compiler optimizations and cause different code to be generated when compiling with and without coverage instrumentation. This situation is undesirable because testing should be done on the same code that is to be delivered. The difference between source code and object code, in particular post-link object code, is a result of the fact that during post-link more information is available. The same is applicable for post-link coverage. For example, post-link define-use coverage can give, using static analysis, a better estimation of the define-use relationship and as a result a better coverage task list (a baseline for what constitutes 100% coverage).

3   Methodology: Post-Link Coverage

To better understand how to use post-link coverage, one should put it in the general context of the process of coverage data collection and analysis. Section 3.1 describes our general coverage data collection and analysis approach, including our analysis and view tool, FoCuS. The coverage data collection technology that we use in this paper is post-link coverage through enhancements to an existing tool. Section 3.2 describes both the existing tool, FDPR-Pro, and the coverage enhancements we made to it.

Our experience with post-link coverage suggests that while the technology and its ease-of-use are very important, another highly important factor for the applicability of post-link coverage is the user's ability to understand the coverage results. Therefore, our coverage methodology includes:

1. Applying a post-link coverage technique as described in Section 3.3.
2. Following a process that guides the user in understanding the coverage data as Section 3.4 describes
3. Consulting support items that provide concrete examples of compiler optimizations and code translation. Section 3.5 provides such examples.

3.1   General Coverage Approach

Figure 1 outlines the architecture of our general code coverage methodology. A single front-end, FoCuS [7], serves as a user interface for viewing and analyzing coverage data. The coverage data is created by whichever technology works in the specific environment; for example, GCOV or FDPR-Pro. FoCuS is a complete tool for the functional coverage methodology. It is also used for viewing

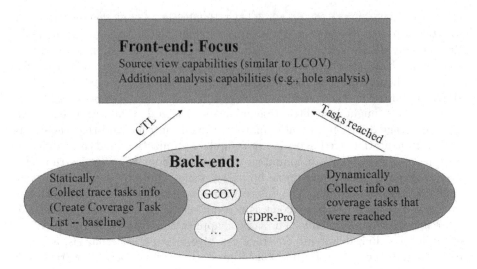

Fig. 1. Our general coverage approach: FoCuS serves as a single front-end to any back-end that works. Examples of back-ends are FDPR-Pro and GCOV.

and analyzing code coverage information. FoCuS also provides a drill-down view, a hierarchical view of the available coverage information (e.g., directories, the files they contain, and the methods in each file) color-coded according to their coverage, and hole analysis support, identifying common names (e.g., files or methods) that are only rarely covered or not covered at all. We recommend a general usage methodology that starts with coarse-grain coverage; for example function-level coverage. The next step is coverage analysis to improve the test suite. The improvement should be a result of identifying major areas of functionality that are not covered and adding new tests to cover the missing parts. It strongly recommended not to write tests only to improve coverage. Tests should be written to improve the ability of the test suite to find potential bugs. Only after improving the test suite as a result of the coarse-grain coverage data analysis, do we recommend doing finer-grain coverage such as basic block coverage. The reason is that it only makes sense to make small improvements to the test suite if no major deficiencies exist.

3.2 Building on an Existing Performance Optimization Technology: FDPR-Pro

FDPR-Pro (Feedback Directed Program Restructuring) [11,13,15,17,12] is a feedback-directed post-link optimization tool. Other post-link optimization tools exist [4,14,16,18]. FDPR-Pro is used extensively for improving performance and memory consumption of large applications and subsystems running on the POWER architecture. It does so by applying a set of aggressive post-link optimizations that help complement compiler optimizations. FDPR-Pro optimizes

the executable image of a program by first collecting information on the behavior of the program while the program executes a typical workload. Then,
it creates a new version of the program that is optimized for that workload.
FDPR-Pro performs global optimizations at the level of the entire executable,
including statically linked library code. Since the executable to be optimized
by FDPR-Pro will not be re-linked, the compiler and linker conventions do not
need to be preserved, thus allowing aggressive optimizations that are not always available to optimizing compilers. The main optimizations of FDPR-Pro
include inter-procedural register re-allocation, improving instruction scheduling,
data prefetching, aggressive function inlining, global data reordering, global code
reordering, and various tuning options for the POWER architecture. FDPR-Pro
operates in three main stages as shown in Figure 2:

1. Program instrumentation stage—Code stubs are injected into a given executable for the purpose of profile gathering. The output of this stage is an
   instrumented executable version along with template of profile file.
2. Program profiling stage—The instrumented executable produced in the previous stage is run with a given input workload. This run fills the profile file
   with execution counters for every executed basic block of code.
3. Program optimization stage—FDPR-Pro is given the original non-
   instrumented executable together with the profile file that was generated
   in the profile stage in order to produce a new optimized executable version.

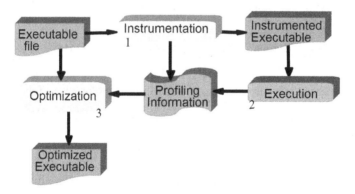

Fig. 2. FDPR-Pro Operation

When using FDPR-Pro for collecting coverage data, only the first two stages
described above are executed. In addition to maintaining program correctness
after optimizing it, FDPR-Pro also maintains the ability to debug the program
after it has been optimized. To enable debugability, FDPR-Pro incorporates the
debug information in its internal structures representing the analyzed program.
This also includes the line number information. To obtain code coverage information with FDPR-Pro we used its regular instrumentation capability with the
ability to map instructions to line-number debug information. We enhanced the

FDPR-Pro disassembly ability to include also line-number information along with the existing basic blocks information and profile information. It should be noted that compilers (e.g. GCC and IBM xlc) can generate line number information and at the same time optimize the code. Figure 3 shows an excerpt of FDPR-Pro's disassembly (taken from SPEC2000 perlbmk benchmark). It includes the dissection into basic blocks of the whole program. For each basic block it includes the basic block count (how many times this basic block was visited), and for each instruction it includes the associated line number information in the form of 'file name':'line number' as it appears in the in the original debug information. The information in the disassembly file is used to create coverage information for FoCuS.

```
.Perl_do_chop { function } ( size = 632 )
safe bb     size = 60    func = .Perl_do_chop ( prolog ) count = 2019
  0x1000b6c8: 0x7c0802a6 mflr   r0           ; doop.c:215
  0x1000b6cc: 0xfb61ffd8 std    r27,-40(r1)  ; doop.c:215
  .......
safe bb     size = 16    func = .Perl_do_chop              count = 0
  0x1000b74c: 0xe8828440 ld  r4,-31680(r2)   ; doop.c:251
  0x1000b750: 0x7f63db78 or  r3,r27,r27       ; doop.c:251
  0x1000b754: 0x38a00000 li  r5,0             ; doop.c:251
  0x1000b758: 0x48076901 bl  0x1007fddc       ; doop.c:251
```

Fig. 3. FDPR-Pro disassembly, annotated with coverage and line number information

3.3   Post-Link Coverage: Getting the Coverage Data

The first stage of coverage analysis is collecting coverage data. The general process of getting coverage measures using our post-link technology is as follows:

1. Make sure you compile your code with a flag to include line-number debug information.
2. Run FDPR-Pro on your executable to instrument it for coverage data collection.
3. Run your test suite on the instrumented executable. The instrumentation will cause profile information to be created.
4. Run FDPR-Pro again to create a disassembly file. Give it as input the profile information gathered in step 3.
5. Run FoCuS on the disassembly file that was created by FDPR-Pro in step 4 to create a coverage model.
6. View the coverage data in FoCuS and analyze the results. We recommend viewing the coverage data using FoCuS's source view. FDPR-Pro produces information that enables FoCuS to map basic block coverage information back to the source code. Figure 6 is one example of what you see in source view. The source code is color-coded according to the coverage of each line.

A single line may map to multiple basic blocks and therefore may be only partially covered. This is an example of having more information per line at the post-link stage. In FoCuS views, green (medium gray in grayscale) indicates locations (e.g., source code statements, files, or functions) that are fully covered, red (dark gray in grayscale) indicates locations that are not covered, and yellow (light gray in grayscale) indicates locations that are partially covered. White source lines lines that are not part of the coverage task list, they are not in the baseline for what constitutes 100% coverage. If the code base size is very large (several hundreds or thousands of files) we recommend starting with FoCuS's drill-down view rather than with FoCuS's source view.

3.4   Post-Link Coverage: Understanding the Coverage Data

Once coverage data is obtained the user can enhance the test suite. We propose a post-link coverage methodology that puts the user at the center. We believe that to get the most from the coverage process, the user needs to understand both what is in the coverage task list, the coverage baseline, and the reasons for only partially covering some of the coverage tasks. This, along with the regular process of coverage analysis (viewing the data in FoCuS and looking for holes), helps the user generate effective tests to strengthen the test suite. Our post-link coverage methodology is as follows:

1. Obtain post-link coverage measurements (process described above) after compiling your code with no optimizations. This has several goals:
   - Understanding better what a basic block is and how it maps to your code (each basic block is mapped to the source code).
   - Better understanding what happens to your source code during the pre-processing stage in the build process.
2. Obtain post-link coverage measurements (process described above) after compiling as for a normal run. We find post-link coverage especially useful on code that went through aggressive compiler optimizations.
3. Consult the dictionary of compiler optimizations and transformations (see examples below) if it is unclear to you why a certain code statement is not part of the coverage task list (as indicated by no coloring of the statement), or why a certain code statement is considered as partially covered (as indicated by yellow coloring).

3.5   Post-Link Coverage: User Support Items

To support the user's comprehension of post-link coverage data, we find it necessary to incrementally create a dictionary of compiler transformations and optimizations. A user may want to consult this dictionary when the coverage information provided is unclear. There are two main cases where coverage information may be unclear:

1. When there is unexplained source code that is not part of the coverage task list.
2. When there is partial coverage of source code.

In general, a source line that is not part of the coverage task list is due to compiler optimizations that optimized this line out. Partial coverage is usually due to a source being compiled into several basic blocks. This is true especially in lines that include control blocks. Following are examples of entries in the compiler transformation dictionary.

Macros. A macro may include a complicated control flow. Such a macro may result in partial coverage on the line that uses it. For example, the source code in Figure 4(a) uses the macro SvTIED_mg (line 398). The SvTIED_mg macro, shown in Figure 4(b), uses the ? operator which is equivalent to If-Then-Else control block. In addition, this macro uses other Macros as well. A partial coverage of the SvTIED_mg macro could be due to the condition in line 398 never being true in any of the tests. In that case, line 398 is partially covered and the body of the If statement is not covered.

```
398  if (mg = SvTIED_mg((SV*)av, 'P')) {
399  dSP;
...  ...
410  return;
411 }
```
(a) Source code using the SvTIED_mg macro

```
#define SvTIED_mg(sv,how) (SvRMAGICAL(sv) ? mg_find((sv),(how)) : Null(MAGIC*))
```
(b) The SvTIED_mg macro which uses the ? operator and calls other macros

Fig. 4. Partial code coverage of macro usage

If Statement An If statement that includes several Boolean sub-expressions is translated into several basic-blocks where each basic-block checks one Boolean part. In Figure 5(a) (taken from SPEC doio.c) the If statement is partially covered and the body is never visited. This means that the last Boolean expression was not evaluated (and possibly also the second one was not evaluated). This is due to the short circuit evaluation of Boolean expressions. To verify, the user may want to create explicit nested If statements for each Boolean expression, as shown in Figure 5(b). Running the test on the nested If code reveals which Boolean expression was not evaluated. This information is helpful in properly extending the existing test suite.

Inlining In compiler inlining a function call is replaced with the code of that function. In addition to eliminating the call sequence, inlining enables the compiler to further optimize the inlined code to be tailored to the replaced call

```
176   if (*name == '+' && len>1 && name[len-1] != '\|') { /* scary */
177     mode[1] = *name++;
178     –len;
179   writing = 1;
180 }
```

(a) The original If statement

```
176-1   if (*name == '+') {
176-2     if (len>1) {
176-3       if (name[len-1] != '\|') { /* scary */
177           mode[1] = *name++;
178           –len;
179           writing = 1;
180-1     }
180-2   }
180-3 }
```

(b) A nested If statement for code coverage analysis

Fig. 5. Partial code coverage of If statement

location. Inlining may be viewed as eliminating the call statement. Therefore, the call statement does not appear in the coverage task list (as indicated by white coloring). Figure 6 shows an example of partial coverage due to compiler inlining (the code is from hv.c in perlbmk). hv_magic_check() was inlined at line 293. The prolog and epilog of the inlined function (lines 260-261 and 276, respectively) are not part of the coverage task list and the body of the function is partially covered. All the calls to this function were optimized via inlining. Since some of these calls were not executed (e.g., the call at line 444), the body of the function is only partially covered.

4   Low-Overhead Instrumentation Method

The overhead of the code instrumentation for basic block coverage is significant. The common implementation of basic block instrumentation counts the number of times each basic block has been visited and has an overhead of at least one hundred percent. In this section we present a method that minimizes the coverage instrumentation overhead. Basic block instrumentation collects extra data that is not usually needed for code coverage which only needs an indication that the basic block has been visited. Therefore, there is an opportunity to reduce the overhead. One might think that it is possible to reduce the overhead by testing the counter before setting it. Unfortunately, the counter fetch operation itself requires bringing the counter to a register and causes a significant overhead. Another approach that can reduce the overhead is to modify the instrumentation code after it is executed once. Code that changes itself is called self-modified

```
260  hv_magic_check (HV *hv, bool *needs_copy, bool *needs_store)
261  {
262      MAGIC *mg = SvMAGIC(hv);
263    *needs_copy = FALSE;
264    *needs_store = TRUE;
265     while (mg) {
266       if (isUPPER(mg->mg_type)) {
267        *needs_copy = TRUE;
268         switch (mg->mg_type) {
269         case 'P':
270         case 'S':
271           *needs_store = FALSE;
272       }
273     }
274      mg = mg->mg_moremagic;
275   }
276  }
...
289  xhv = (XPVHV*)SvANY(hv);
290  if (SvMAGICAL(hv)) {
291    bool needs_copy;
292    bool needs_store;
293    hv_magic_check (hv, &needs_copy, &needs_store);
294    if (needs_copy) {
295      mg_copy((SV*)hv, val, key, klen);
296      if (!xhv->xhv_array && !needs_store)
...
441  if (SvRMAGICAL(hv)) {
442    bool needs_copy;
443    bool needs_store;
444    hv_magic_check (hv, &needs_copy, &needs_store); }
445
446      if (needs_copy && (svp = hv_fetch(hv, key, klen, TRUE))) {
...
```

Fig. 6. Code coverage of inlined function

code. Self-modified code can be used to skip or run on the instrumentation code after the first visit is recorded. For example, one way to modify the code is to replace the first instruction in the instrumentation code with a branch to the first instruction after the instrumentation. However, we claim that using self-modified code is not enough to ensure minimal overhead. For example, in a RISC architecture the instrumentation code itself requires a large number of instructions due to operations executing on registers, so we need to free registers and move the data to the register before operating on it. Since the average basic block size is five instructions a naive implementation of basic block instrumentation with self-modified code may lead to a very bad utilization of the instruction cache wherein most of the instructions in the cache are redundant. We analyze the causes for overhead in code coverage instrumentation and divide them into two instruction groups based on timing. The first group includes delays that are caused by the instrumentation and self-modified code in the first visit to the basic block. The second group includes delays that remain in the code after the first visit and affect the performance throughout the entire run. We assume that the delays in the first visit have a negligible effect on performance since they happen only once. The experiments in Section 4.1 prove this assumption. Following the assumption, our approach minimizes the delays in performance that have a performance effect after the first visit by moving most of the overhead to the instruction group that executes only once. To achieve that we pack the instrumentation and self-modified code in general procedures that are called from the original code. Appendix A provides details regarding the implementation of low-overhead instrumentation on POWER architecture.

4.1   Experimental Results

To evaluate the overhead of the suggested method for code coverage we used SPEC2000 using Linux on POWER. We choose Linux since we can make the needed changes in the access permission of the program header to allow self-modifying code. We used the gcc 4.1 compiler and optimized all programs with -O3 optimization level. First, we tried to evaluated the long run overhead after replacing the function call instruction (BL instruction on POWER) with NOP. This was done by instrumenting every basic block with a single NOP. The results on SPEC2000 are shown in Figure 7. Note that the overhead for additional NOP execution at the function level is negligible (for FP it even improved performance) and for the basic block level is 3.9% and 1% for INT and FP respectively. It is interesting to note that in several cases, and even for the average for FP at the function level, performance was improved (designated with negative percentage) by the NOP insertion. This is because the inserted code caused a better alignment of the hot portions of the code, which affected the overall performance. Note that we see more such cases for programs with a small number of hot functions as is the case for the FP benchmarks. The conclusion is that overhead can be consciously reduced by further optimizing the code in a way that does not affect the code coverage results. Such optimizations can include improving alignment, reducing specific stalls by inserting NOP instructions (for example Load After Store in the case of POWER architecture), and even global code reordering. The guideline for applying optimizations on the instrumented code is that we can map the coverage information of the instrumented/optimized program faithfully back to the source code.

As expected, the results of real instrumentation, shown in Figure 8, indicate that the additional one-time code insertion did not have much effect on performance.

	bzip2	crafty	eon	gap	gcc	gzip	mcf	parser	perlbmk	twolf	vpr	Average
Functions level	4.37	-1.41	2.3	-3.81	4.48	2.47	-2.74	-0.46	-0.5	0.61	2.21	0.7
Basic blocks level	5.52	5.02	1.2	-6.6	12.66	7.65	0.26	3.58	2.4	3.67	7.42	3.9

(a) SPECint2000

	ammp	applu	apsi	art	equake	mesa	mgrid	sixtrack	swim	wupwise	Average
Functions level	3.8	0.8	0.2	0.1	-2.7	-8.7	0.8	-0.4	-5.1	-8.1	-1.9
Basic blocks level	7.1	3.6	0.3	0.8	0.3	-7.2	-0.8	3.3	1.0	1.7	1.0

(b) SPECfp2000

Fig. 7. Overhead of NOP insertion (percent over base) for SPEC2000

	bzip2	crafty	eon	gap	gcc	gzip	mcf	parser	perlbmk	twolf	vpr	Average
Functions Level	2.2	1.3	1.8	-1.4	0.4	1.8	-4.2	2.1	-0.6	3.0	3.3	0.9
Basic Blocks Level	3.1	7.7	0.8	3.4	1.3	4.1	-3.9	13.4	3.6	5.1	5.9	4.1

(a) SPECint2000

	ammp	applu	apsi	art	equake	mesa	mgrid	sixtrack	swim	wupwise	Average
Functions level	1.2	0.4	-0.5	-0.3	-1.5	-12.2	0.9	-0.1	-1.6	-1.3	-1.5
Basic blocks level	1.4	4.5	1.8	2.6	1.0	-6.8	0.4	-0.3	-3.1	2.8	0.4

(b) SPECfp2000

Fig. 8. Overhead of code coverage instrumentation (percent over base) for SPEC2000

5   Conclusions and Future Work

We have been working with various development groups at IBM on testing actual code. Our experience indicates that post-link coverage has significant advantages when compared to source-level coverage. Two major advantages on which we elaborated in this paper are the ability to work even with highly optimized code and the ability to introduce coverage instrumentation with very low performance overhead. Without these abilities, coverage cannot be part of the regular testing process. Moreover, coverage measurements are taken over a (less-optimized) variation of the code rather than on the code that the customers get. This is highly undesirable, especially in systems that have high quality requirements. Usually, such systems also have system-level test suites that run for days. Adding significant performance overhead to the already heavy system test process might be unacceptable.

We showed examples of coverage over optimized code and of mapping back post-link code to the source code. We demonstrated that the performance overhead of our technology is expected to be no more than 4.1% on average. Moreover, it is often expected to be less than 1%. Simple optimizations such as controlled alignment may significantly reduce this overhead and even improve the overall performance. An example is the function level overhead on SPECfp2000 in Figure 8 (1.5% improvement in performance on average).

We provided a methodology that enables users to better understand post-link coverage data. This methodology relies on a dictionary of compiler optimizations and transformations. We believe that one of the major hurdles to date in applying object-level coverage has been the inability of users to understand how to map the coverage data to improvements they need to do to their test suite. Our methodology helps in better understanding what was not covered and why that was the case. This is a major step toward improving the user's test suite.

Once a very low performance overhead instrumentation is in place, together with the ability to measure coverage on optimized code, we envision having coverage throughout the development process. We believe coverage should be present not only in all the stages of the development process, but even at the customer site. We are developing a process in which each stage of testing only keeps coverage instrumentation in places that were never hit during the past stages. This partial instrumentation, combined with very low overhead instrumentation in places where the instrumentation is kept, may enable us to even keep the coverage instrumentation in production code. It can be very useful for the owner of the code to know that a customer is executing the software in ways that were never covered during testing. This is probably an early indication of a forthcoming bug report.

In this paper, we concentrated on basic block coverage at the post-link level. However, we believe that our conclusions are applicable to post-link coverage in general, regardless of the coverage metric. For some metrics, however, it may be difficult to map the post-link information back to the source code thus making it harder to understand.

A   Low Overhead Instrumentation on POWER Architecture

Each location that we want to test for coverage (typically a basic block) is augmented with a branch and link (BL) instruction that jumps to the instrumentation function that is added to the code. The instrumentation function simply replaces the inserted BL instruction with a NOP instruction and then return back to the instruction following the inserted BL instruction. The instrumentation function uses the value in the link register (LR) which is set by the BL to gain access to the location of the BL. This replacement achieves two goals:

1. Having an indication that the code of the calling basic block was visited and should be considered covered.
2. 'Closing the door' so that the function executes only once for every tested location, thereby avoiding extra overhead.

It is important to branch to the instrumentation function with a single instruction. This ensures the atomicity of the operation of 'closing the door', and prevents getting partial, incorrect code by other threads. Each thread that reaches the BL location executes either the branch instruction or a NOP.

```
1 BB-04:   b  BB_STUB  // branch to the intermediate stub
2 BB:        ...           // first instruction of instrumented basic block
```
(a) Instrumentation location

```
0 BB_STUB-8:    .long BB       // holds the address of BB
1 BB_STUB:      st    r0,ZZ(r1) // save ro to stack
2 BB_STUB+4:    mflr  r0        // save Link Register in r0
3 BB_STUB+8:    bl    IS        // after execution the link register will hold address BB_STUB+12
4 BB_STUB+12:   mtlr  r0        // restore Link register value from r0
5 BB_STUB+16:   ld    r0,ZZ(r1) // restore r0 from stack
6 BB_STUB+20:   b     BB        // branch back to the original BB
```
(b) Intermediate stub per instrumentation location

```
 1 IS:       std   r28,YY(r1)    // save r28 at offset YY from stack pointer r1
 2 IS+04     std   r29,XX(r1)    // save r29 at offset XX from stack pointer r1
 3 IS+12     mflr  r29           // move LR (address BB_STUB+12) to r29
 4 IS+16     lds   r29,-20(r29)  // load address of BB from BB_STUB-8
 5 IS+16     addis r28,r0,0x6000 // set NOP opcode in r28
 6 IS+20     stw   r28, -4(r29)  // overwrite b instruction at BB-4 with NOP
 7 IS+24     addi  r28, r29, -4  // place the address BB-4 r28
 8 IS+28     dcbf  r0, r28, 0    // flush block containing address BB-4 from Dcache
 9 IS+32     sync                // wait for flush completion on Dcache
10 IS+36     icbi  r0, r28       // invalidate block containing instruction at BB-4 from Icache
11 IS+40     isync               // wait for invalidation completion on Icache
12 IS+48     ld    r28,YY(r1)    // restore r28
13 IS+52     ld    r29,XX(r1)    // restore r29
14 IS+56     blr                 // return (to BB)
```
(c) Instrumentation function

Fig. 9. Instrumentation location when the link register (LR) needs to be freed

To enable the insertion of the BL instruction in the instrumentation location the LR must be available for use at the instrumentation location so its contents can be overwritten by the link operation of the branch. If the LR is not free, a register spill code needs to be added. Figure 9 shows the instrumentation function (A) and how we branch to it using a single branch instruction (9(a) and an intermediate stub (9(b)). The intermediate stub includes the store/restore of LR and holds a pointer (at BB_STUB-8) to the instrumentation location to enable the instrumentation function overwrite the branch instruction with a NOP. Althouhg we add an intermediate stub for each instrumentation location and thus increase the code size, these stubs are executed only once so they do not pollute the caches.

Note that the instrumentation function includes cache invalidation instructions. Although these instructions introduce many cycles, they are executed only once and ensure that the modified code is used on the next execution cycle. During the off-line instrumentation phases, all the locations that are instrumented with a BL instruction are recorded to create a mapping between the location of the BL instruction and tested locations. After completing the tests, the recorded locations in the image are examined by going over all the locations that were instrumented by the BL and if the BL was replaced with a NOP the location is marked as 'visited'. The use of the NOP as indication of coverage reduces the need for external bookkeeping of visited locations and thus reduces the space needed for recording visited locations.

References

1. Balakrishnan, G., Reps, T., Melski, D., Teitelbaum, T.: Wysinwyx: What you see is not what you execute. In: Verified Software: Theories, Tools, Experiments. Springer, Heidelberg (to appear), http://citeseer.ist.psu.edu/ 762389.html
2. Code coverage metrics (accessed June 2007), http://www.bullseye.com/ coverage.html
3. Object coverage. (accessed June 2007), http://www.bullseye.com/coverage. html#other_object
4. Cohn, R., Goodwin, D., Lowney, P.G.: Optimizing alpha executables on windows nt with spike. In: Digital Technical Journal (1997)
5. Contest concurrent testing tool (accessed June 2007), http://w3.haifa.ibm.com/ softwaretesting/ConTest-Java/index.html
6. Do-178b software considerations in airborne systems and equipment certification (accessed June 2007), http://en.wikipedia.org/wiki/DO-178B
7. Focus functional and code coverage visuals and analysis (accessed June 2007) http://w3.haifa.ibm.com/softwaretesting/FoCuS/index.html
8. G-cover object level coverage analysis (accessed June 2007), http://www.ghs.com/ products/safety_critical/gcover.html
9. Gcov coverage with gnu compiler gcc (accessed June 2007), http://gcc.gnu.org/ onlinedocs/gcc/Gcov.html
10. Grinwald, R., Harel, E., Orgad, M., S. U.S., Ziv, A.: User defined coverage - a tool supported methodology for design verification. In: DAC (June 1998)
11. Haber, G., Henis, E., Eisenberg, V.: Reliable post-link optimizations based on partial information. In: 3rd Workshop on Feedback Directed and Dynamic Optimizations (December 2000)
12. Haber, G., Klausner, M., Eisnebreg, V., Mendelson, B., Gurevich, M.: Optimization opportunities created by global data reordering. In: 1st International Symposium on Code Generation and Optimization (March 2003)
13. Henis, E.A., Haber, G., Klausner, M., Warshavsky, A.: Feedback based post-link optimization for large subsystems. In: 2nd Workshop on Feedback Directed Optimization (November 1999)
14. Muth, R., Debray, S., Watterson, S.: Alto: A link-time optimizer for the compaq alpha. Technical Report, 98-14, Dept. of Computer Science, The University of Arizona (December 1998)
15. Nahshon, I., Bernstein, D.: Fdpr - a post-pass object code optimization tool. In: Poster Session of the International Conference on Compiler Construction (April 1996)
16. Romer, T., Voelker, G., Lee, D., Wolman, A., Wong, W., Levy, H., Bershad, B., Chen, B.: Instrumentation and optimization of win32/intel executables using etch. In: USENIX Windows NT Workshop (August 1997)
17. Schmidt, W.J., Roediger, R.R., Mestad, C.S., Mendelson, B., Shavitt-Lottem, I., Bortnikov-Sitnitsky, V.: Profile-directed restructuring of operating system code. In: IBM Systems Journal (1998)
18. Schwarz, B., Debray, S., Andrews, G., Legendre, M.: Plto: A link-time optimizer for the intel ia-32 architecture. In: Workshop on Binary Rewriting (September 2001)
19. Wikipedia: Code coverage (accessed June 2007), http://en.wikipedia.org/ wiki/Code_coverage

GenUTest: A Unit Test and
Mock Aspect Generation Tool

Benny Pasternak[1], Shmuel Tyszberowicz[2], and Amiram Yehudai[1]

[1] Tel-Aviv University
[2] The Academic College Tel-Aviv Yaffo

Abstract. Unit testing plays a major role in the software development process. It enables the immediate detection of bugs introduced into a unit whenever code changes occur. Hence, unit tests provide a safety net of regression tests and validation tests which encourage developers to refactor existing code. Nevertheless, not all software systems contain unit tests. When changes to such software are needed, writing unit tests from scratch might not be cost effective.

In this paper we propose a technique which automatically generates unit tests for software that does not have such tests. We have implemented GenUTest, a tool which captures and logs inter-object interactions occurring during the execution of Java programs. These interactions are used to generate JUnit tests. They also serve in generating mock aspects – mock object like entities, which assist the testing process. The interactions are captured using the aspect oriented language AspectJ.

1 Introduction

Unit testing plays a major role in the software development process. A unit is the smallest testable part of an application; in the object oriented paradigm it is a class. A unit test consists of a fixed sequence of method invocations with fixed arguments. It explores a particular aspect of the behavior of the Class Under Test, hereafter CUT. Testing a unit in isolation is one of the most important principles of unit testing. However, the CUT usually depends on other classes, which might even not exist yet. *Mock objects* [9] are used to solve this problem by helping the developer break those dependencies during testing, thus testing the unit in isolation.

Extreme Programming (XP) [23] adopts an approach that requires that *all* the software classes have unit tests; code without unit tests may not be released. Whenever code changes introduce a bug into a unit, it is immediately detected. Hence, unit tests provide a safety net of regression tests and validation tests. This encourages developers to refactor working code, i.e., change its internal structure without altering the external behavior [6].

The number of unit tests for a given project might be very large. For instance, Microsoft reported that the code for unit tests is often larger than the code of the project [4]. In order to effectively manage unit tests, execute them frequently, and analyze their results, a unit testing framework should be used [23]. The framework automatically executes all unit tests and reports their results. One of the most popular unit testing

K. Yorav (Ed.): HVC 2007, LNCS 4899, pp. 252–266, 2008.

frameworks is *JUnit* [25, 7], which helps to standardize the way unit tests are written and executed.

The maintenance phase is estimated to comprise at least 50% of the software's total life cycle [15]. At this phase, the software is already being used, and future versions of the software, which include new features as well as bug fixes, continue to be developed. Unit tests can assist developers during the maintenance phase. Nevertheless, not all developed software contains unit tests. Writing effective tests is a hard and tedious process, and developing them from scratch at the maintenance phase might not be cost effective. In this case they are usually not written, and maintenance continues to be a difficult process.

We propose a technique which automatically generates unit tests for systems that do not have such tests. This is achieved by capturing and recording the execution of the software in order to obtain test cases. The recorded data can then be used to construct unit tests for the software.

We have implemented GenUTest, a tool which captures and logs inter-object interactions occurring during the execution of Java programs. The recorded interactions are then used to generate JUnit tests that assist in the testing process.

Figure 1 presents a high level view of GenUTest's architecture and highlights the steps in each of the three phases of GenUTest: *capture phase*, *generation phase*, and *test phase*. In the capture phase the program is modified to include functionality to capture its execution. When the modified program executes, inter-object interactions are captured and logged. The generation phase utilizes the log to generate unit tests and *mock aspects*, mock object like entities. In the test phase, the unit tests are used by the developer to test the code of the program.

The interactions are captured by utilizing *AspectJ*, the most popular *Aspect Oriented Programming* (AOP) extension for the Java language [20, 8]. AOP has been proposed as a powerful programming paradigm that helps to modularize crosscutting concerns, behavior that cuts across the typical divisions of responsibility, such as logging. AOP captures crosscutting concerns and encapsulates them in a single module – the *aspect*. An aspect contains *advices*, which are code fragments that are inserted into other modules using a weaving mechanism. An advice modifies the behavior of the code or adds new behavior. It can be applied to *join points*, points of interest in the flow of a program, such as object instantiation, method-call, variable access, etc. An advice code can be specified to be executed *before* or *after* the locations specified by a join point, or it can even replace it completely. Finally, a pointcut is an expression that specifies the collection of join points where an advice is to be executed.

We are not aware of any other tool which utilizes aspects for the capturing process. Compared to conventional instrumentation techniques, aspects provide a clean and structured way to implement the capture functionality. One advantage of our approach is that it makes it is easy to implement the tool for other aspect oriented programming languages. In addition, GenUTest automatically generates mock aspects, which assist in testing units in isolation. The mocks aspects, which use AspectJ, can easily be combined with the unit tests in an almost seamless manner.

The rest of the paper is organized as follows. In Section 2 we describe the capture phase, and Section 3 explains how unit tests are generated from the captured data.

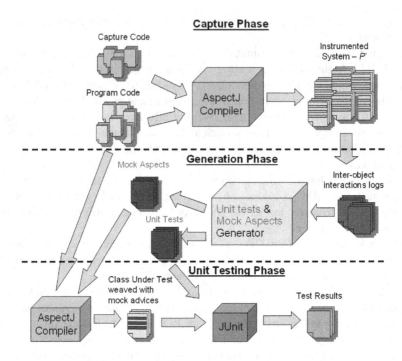

Fig. 1. GenUTest architecture

Section 4 elaborates on the creation of mock aspects. Section 5 discusses related work, and we conclude with Section 6 which describes initial experiments performed and discusses future plans.

2   The Capture Phase

This section describes how interactions between objects are captured and logged. To illustrate our ideas we employ a simple example which we use throughout the paper. This is an integer stack implemented using a linked list. In addition to the conventional stack operations, the stack also supports a *reverse* operation, which reverses the order of the items in the stack. Figure 2 presents a UML sequence diagram which describes a possible scenario of the stack behavior [1].

In order to perform the capture phase for a given program P, specific capture functionality has to be added to P. The functionality is added by instrumenting P with the capture code. Instrumentation is a technique which changes a program in order to modify or to extend its behavior. The AspectJ compiler does the instrumentation using a weaving mechanism. This mechanism enables code modifications defined in *advices* to

---

[1] The numbers in *italic* are used to denote method intervals which are explained in Section 3. Note that in order to make it easier for the reader to follow the example, we use dashed lines to denote return from a call even for the constructor.

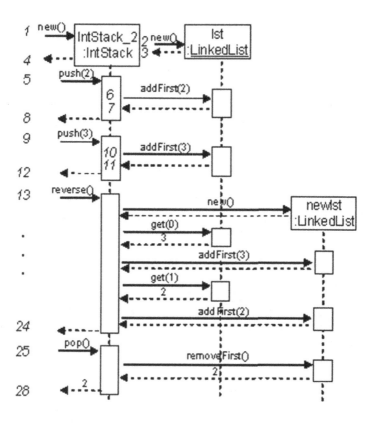

Fig. 2. A sequence diagram describing a scenario of the stack behavior

be performed at specific *join points*, which specify well defined locations in the control flow of the program. A pointcut is an expression that specifies the collection of join points where an advice is to be executed. We show parts of the AspectJ code used, with explanations aimed at the reader not familiar with AspectJ.

The *call(signature)* join point refers to the location where a call to a method with a given *signature* is invoked. For example, `call(public void IntStack.push(int))` specifies all the locations that call the method push of the IntStack class, with a single integer argument.

In GenUTest, we need to match all constructor-calls, all method-calls, and all read/write field-accesses in P. The pointcut is defined as follows:

```
pointcut all_calls(): call(* *(..))   || call(new *(..)) ||
                      call(get *..*)  || call(set *..*) &&
                      !within(GenUTest.*);
```

The first two `calls` match all method-calls and all constructor-calls, respectively. The other two match all read/write field-accesses. The `!within(GenUTest.*)` join point ensures that only designated join points within P are matched. The two wildcards

('*' and '..') enable matching a set of signatures. Constructor-calls and field-accesses can also be viewed as method-calls, and will be considered as such for the rest of the paper.

Capturing a method-call involves recording the method's signature and the target object of the call. Returned values and thrown exceptions are recorded as well. The type of the arguments and the return value can be one of the following: primitive, object, or array. For instance, the attributes of the `IntStack_2.push(3)` (cf. Figure 2) are: the AspectJ signature, which consists of full name (`IntStack_2.push()`), arguments type (`int`), access modifier (`public`), and the return type (`void`); the target object (`IntStack_2`); the arguments values (`3`); the return value (none); and the exception thrown by the method (none).

The instrumented program P' is executed and the actual capturing begins. The capture code, which is specified by the advice, is responsible for obtaining the above mentioned attributes. This is achieved using an AspectJ reflective construct (*thisJoinPoint*). After the attributes of the method-calls are obtained, they are serialized and logged using a library which supports the serialization of complex nested objects (this is especially important for arrays) [28].

The capturing process ends after all method-calls have been logged. The log is used in the generation phase to create unit tests. Due to lack of space, we have simplified the description of the capture phase. The full discussion consists of a lot of implementation details, and can be found in [13].

3   The Unit Test Generation Phase

After the method-calls have been captured, unit tests can be generated. The generation process is described in this section.

Unit tests are created only for those methods that can be examined, i.e., methods that either return a value or throw an exception. In the example, when `IntStack` serves as the CUT, GenUTest generates a unit test only for the `pop()` method-call (cf. Figure 3).

```
1   @Test public void testpop1()
2   {
3           // test execution statements
4           IntStack IntStack_2 = new IntStack();   // mi [1,4]
5           IntStack_2.push(2);                     // mi [5,8]
6           IntStack_2.push(3);                     // mi [9,12]
7           IntStack_2.reverse();                   // mi [13,24]
8           int intRetVal6 = IntStack_2.pop();      // mi [25,28]
9
10          // test assertion statements
11          assertEquals(intRetVal6,2);
12  }
```

Fig. 3. Unit test generated for pop() method-call

Test generation is a two step operation. In the first step GenUTest generates the Java statements that execute the test. In the second step GenUTest generates assertion statements that determine whether the test has passed.

3.1   Step I: Test Generation

The Java statements generation algorithm contains two mutually recursive procedures, *restoreObjectState* and *generateStatement*. The procedure *restoreObjectState* selects the method-calls which are needed to execute the test, whereas *generateStatement* generates Java statements that execute those method-calls. In the stack example, the method-calls `new IntStack()`, `push(2)`, `push(3)`, `reverse()`, and `pop()` are selected by *restoreObjectState*, and their corresponding test statements (lines 4 to 8 in Figure 3) are generated by *generateStatement*.

1. **The restoreObjectState procedure:** This procedure obtains as input an object id *objid* (which represents the object *obj*) and a time stamp T. The *concrete state* of the object at a given point of time T is defined by the values of its state variables at that time. We represent an object state using *method-sequences* [17]. In GenUTest this representation consists of the sequence of captured method-calls that had been invoked on the object till T. Time is represented by a global sequence number which is incremented in the capture phase *before* a method begins execution and *after* it finishes execution. The interval [before, after] is called the *method interval*. This interval is recorded, during the capture phase, together with the attributes of the method-call (cf. Section 2). Using the *before* value of the method interval, an order relation can be applied to method-calls.

   In order to test *obj* at its correct state, all method-calls invoked on *obj* prior to T need to be reinvoked. Suppose that the method $m()$ had been invoked at time T. Using the method intervals, *restoreObjectState* reconstructs all method-calls that had been invoked prior to that specific invocation. For example, let us refer to the object `IntStack_2` in Figure 2. To invoke the `reverse()` method which occurred at time stamp 13 on the object `IntStack_2`, the methods `new IntStack()`, `push(2)`, and `push(3)`, which had occurred before time stamp 13, must be reinvoked.

2. **The generateStatement procedure:** This procedure generates a Java method-call statement with the following form:

   ```
   <return variable>=(<return type>)<object reference>.
                      <method name>(<arg #1,..., arg #n>);
   ```

   The *object reference* is a string representation of the target object. It is formed by concatenating the object type (obtained from the method signature) with the object id. For example, an IntStack object with the object id 2 is represented as "`IntStack_2`". The *return variable* name is formed by creating a unique string representation. The arguments' array is traversed by the procedure to obtain the values of the arguments. The representation depends on the argument's type:

   (a) A primitive value is represented according to Java rules. For instance, float values are suffixed with the character '`f`'. Character strings are handled according to Java String rules (e.g., newlines and tabs are replaced with '\n' and '\t', respectively) and then are surrounded by a pair of quotes.

(b) An objects is represented by an object reference. To ensure that the object is in the correct state when it is used, *restoreObjectState* must be invoked with the relevant arguments, which in turn leads to the invocation of *generateStatement*.

(c) An array is represented by the following code fragment:

```
new <ArrayType> { <elem #1>, ..., <elem #n> },
```

where elements are represented according to their type.

In the following example we demonstrate how both procedures work on a more complicated example involving objects. Figure 4 presents the method-calls occurring at consecutive method intervals for three different objects: obj1, obj2, and obj3.

Method Interval	obj1	obj2	obj3	...
[1,2]	obj1 = new Type1()			
[3,4]			obj3 = new Type3()	
[5,8]		obj2 = new Type2()		
[9,20]			obj3.initialize()	
[21,30]		obj2.goo1(obj3)		
[31,50]	**obj1.foo1(obj2)**			
[51,64]		obj2.goo2()		
[65,80]	obj1.foo2()			
...				

Fig. 4. Method-calls invoked on the objects obj1, obj2, and obj3

Suppose GenUTest encounters the method-call obj1.foo1(obj2) which had occurred at time stamp 31. In order to invoke the method-call, GenUTest must restore obj1, the target object, to its correct state at time stamp 31. This is achieved by the procedure *restoreObjectState* which selects the constructor-call obj1 = new Type1() that had occurred at time stamp 1. Then the procedure *generateStatement* is invoked in order to generate the Java statement for the method-call obj1.foo1(obj2). During the execution of the generation procedure, it encounters the argument obj2 and in order to restore this object to its correct state at time stamp 31, the procedure invokes *restoreObjectState*. Then, *restoreObjectState* selects the constructor-call obj2 = new Type2() and the method-call obj2.goo1(obj3) which had occurred at time stamps 5 and 21, respectively. For the latter method-call, *generateStatement* is invoked in order to generate its corresponding Java statements. It encounters the argument obj3, and invokes *restoreObjectState* in order to restore the argument to

```
1  Type1 obj1 = new Type1();
2  Type3 obj3 = new Type3();
3  Type2 obj2 = new Type2();
4  obj3.initialize();
5  obj2.goo1(obj3);
6  obj1.foo1(obj2);
```

Fig. 5. Statements generated to restore the correct state of obj1 and obj2.

its correct state at time stamp 21. Eventually, the algorithm generates the statements as shown in Figure 5.

After generating the statements, the algorithm performs some post processing tasks. One of those tasks is the removal of redundant statements. For example, when replacing the method-call obj1.foo1(obj2) in the previous example with the call obj1.foo1(obj2,obj3), then the statements at lines 2 and 4 in Figure 5 would be generated twice. This leads to an incorrect sequence of statements which in some cases might affect the state of the objects. The post processing task detects and disposes of such redundant statements.

3.2 Step II: Test Assertion

The assertion statements generated by GenUTest determine whether the test has passed. There are two cases to handle: 1) the method returns a value and, 2) the method throws an exception.

For the first case, GenUTest generates statements which compare the value returned by the test ($value_{test}$) with the captured return value ($value_{captured}$). Primitive values can be directly compared using one of JUnit's asserts statements. In the example, intRetVal6 ($value_{test}$) is compared to 2 ($value_{captured}$) (cf. Figure. 3, line 11).

When the returned values are objects or arrays, the comparison is more complicated. First, GenUTest generates the statements that restore the state of $value_{captured}$ (as described in Section 3.1). Then, GenUTest checks whether an equals method had been implemented for the objects being compared. If equals exists, GenUTest generates a JUnit assertTrue statement which simply checks equality by invoking the equals method. Otherwise, special statements are generated to compare the concrete state of the two objects. This is achieved using the Java reflection mechanism, which enables to discern information about the fields of the objects. Then, the discovered fields are compared according to their types.

For the second case, when a method throws an exception, GenUTest generates a statement that informs JUnit that an exception of a specific kind is to be thrown. The exception kind is obtained from the captured attributes of the method-call. For example, suppose the method pop() is invoked on a newly created object IntStack_3. This is an attempt to remove an item from an empty stack. Thus, an exception of type NoSuchElementException is thrown. GenUTest informs JUnit to expect an exception of this type. Figure 6 presents the generated code for this scenario.

```
1  @Test(expected= NoSuchElementException.class)
2  public void testpop2() {
3          // test execution statements
4          IntStack IntStack_3 = new IntStack();
5          IntStack_3.pop();
6  }
```

Fig. 6. Unit test generated for exception throwing pop() method-call

4   The Mock Aspect Generation Phase

In this section we describe what mock objects are and what virtual mocks are. We then introduce a new concept, namely mock aspect, explain its advantages, and describe how it is generated.

Testing a unit in isolation is one of the most important principles of unit testing. However, most units are not isolated, and the dependencies between units complicate the test process. Moreover, the developer's intervention is required. One of the common approaches to deal with this issue is the use of mock objects [9].

A mock object is a simulated object which mimics the behavior of a real object in a controlled way. It is specifically customized to the Class Under Test (CUT). It can be programmed to expect a specific sequence of method-calls with specific arguments, and to return a specific value for each method-call. A mock object has the same interface as the real object it mimics. The references of a CUT to real objects can be replaced with references to mock objects, leaving the CUT unaware of which objects are addressed. In order to support the creation of mock objects, the CUT's code must be modified. *Virtual mocks* [27] utilize aspects to enable units to use mock objects, without having to modify the code of the CUT. This is achieved by defining pointcuts that match real object method-calls. The associated advices which are performed at those pointcuts redirect the method-calls to the mock objects.

Developing mock objects is a hard and tedious process. This involves activities such as declaring new classes, implementing methods, and adding lots of bookkeeping code. The process can be simplified using mock object frameworks. Such frameworks (e.g., EasyMock [21]) do the job for us. This is achieved by instructing the framework to expect a certain sequence of method calls and to return specific values.

We make use of the advantages of both mock objects and virtual mocks. We have defined a new concept, the *mock aspect*. A mock aspect is an aspect which intervenes in the execution of the CUT. Being an aspect, it has pointcuts and advices. The pointcuts match method-calls invoked by the CUT on real objects. The advices directly mimic the behavior of the real object, as opposed to virtual mocks, which act as mediators to the mock objects. GenUTest automatically generates mock aspects. Once created, the mock aspects can easily be integrated with the CUT to enable testing it in isolation.

Figure 7 illustrates two kinds of method calls. An **invocation** of a CUT method from within the unit test is called an *incoming method-call*. An *outgoing method-call* is an **invocation** of a method in some other class from within the CUT. In the example (cf. Figure 2), the incoming method-calls of IntStack are: new IntStack(), push(2), push(3), reverse(), and pop(),

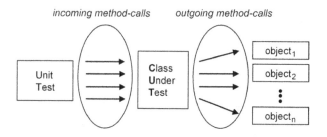

incoming method-calls   outgoing method-calls

Fig. 7. A Class Under Test (CUT) and its incoming and outgoing method-calls

whereas its outgoing method calls are: `addFirst(2)`, `addFirst(3)`, `get(0)`, `get(1)`, etc.

The mock aspect has pointcuts which match outgoing method-calls. For each method in $object_i$, $1 \leq i \leq n$, there exists a different pointcut. Each pointcut matches all the outgoing method-calls to a specific method. For example, all outgoing method-calls to the method `addFirst()` are matched by a single pointcut declaration, and are handled by a single advice. This advice mimics the effect of all these outgoing method-calls. Thus, it needs to know which particular outgoing method-call to mimic.

Before continuing, we provide some definitions and observations.

Definition 1. $mi\big(A()\big)$ is the method interval of method-call $A()$, i.e., $[before_A, after_A]$.

Definition 2. Method-call $A()$ **contains** method-call $B()$ if $mi\big(A()\big)$ contains $mi\big(B()\big)$, i.e., $[before_A, after_A] \supset [before_B, after_B]$.

Following these definitions, we observe that:

1. Method-call $B()$ resides within the control flow of method-call $A()$ iff method-call $A()$ contains method-call $B()$.
2. An outgoing method-call of the CUT is contained in **exactly one** incoming method-call. An incoming method-call, on the other hand, may contain several outgoing method-calls. For example, the outgoing method-calls `get(0)` and `get(1)` are contained in the one incoming method-call `reverse()`, while `reverse()` contains several other outgoing method-calls, besides those two.

Definition 3. $Outgoing\big(I()\big)$ is the sequence $< Io_1(), Io_2(), ..., Io_n() >$, where $I()$ is an incoming method-call and $Io_1(), Io_2(), ..., Io_n()$ are all the outgoing method-calls contained in $I()$.

Suppose the outgoing method-call $o()$ is contained in the incoming method-call $I()$, and suppose that it is the jth element in $outgoing\big(I()\big)$. Then, $o()$ is uniquely identified by the pair $\big(mi(I()), j\big)$.

In Figure 2 there are four outgoing method-calls to the method `addFirst()`. The first outgoing method-call, `addFirst(2)`, is contained in the incoming method-call `push(2)`. Hence, $mi\big(push(2)\big)$ is [5, 8], $outgoing\big(push(2)\big)$ is $< addFirst(2) >$, and addFirst(2) is uniquely identified by the pair ([5, 8], 1). Similarly, the second outgoing method-call addFirst(3) is uniquely identified by the pair ([9, 12], 1). Both the third and fourth outgoing method-calls, addFirst(3) and addFirst(2), are contained in the incoming method-call reverse(). Thus, $mi(reverse())$ is [13, 24] and $outgoing(reverse())$ is $< new, get(0), addFirst(3), get(1), addFirst(2) >$. The outgoing method-calls, addFirst(3) and addFirst(2), are uniquely identified by the pairs ([13, 24], 1) and ([13, 24], 2), respectively.

In order to identify a specific outgoing method-call, the advice needs to:

1. Know all the incoming method-calls of the CUT.
2. Keep track of the outgoing method-calls sequence for each incoming method-call.

The mock aspect generation algorithm works as follows:

1. For each incoming method-call $I()$ of the CUT, $outgoing(I())$ is calculated.
2. Each outgoing method-call is uniquely identified.
3. The mock aspect code is created.
   This requires generating the following: aspect headers, pointcuts, bookkeeping statements, and statements that mimic the outgoing method-call. The bookkeeping statements are responsible for uniquely identifying the outgoing method-calls. These statements include matching method intervals of the incoming method-calls and maintaining inner counters to keep track of sequence of outgoing method-calls. For an outgoing method-call that returns a primitive value, the statement mimicking its behavior is one that returns the value. When an object is returned, it needs to be in the correct state. This is achieved by using the procedure $restoreObjectState$ described in Section 3.

Figure 8 shows a code snippet of the mock aspect for the CUT IntStack. This code mimics outgoing method-calls to the method get().

5 Related Work

There exist various tools that automatically generate unit tests. Unit test creation in those tools requires generating test inputs, i.e., method-call sequences, and providing test assertions which determine whether a test passes.

There are several techniques to generate test inputs. Tools such as [3, 12, 10, 1], categorized as *random execution tools*, generate a random sequence of method calls with random arguments. *Symbolic execution* tools, such as [18, 16, 2], generate a sequence of method calls with symbolic arguments. By statically analyzing the CUT's code they provide real values for the arguments. *Capture and replay* tools, e.g. [19, 14, 11, 5], capture and record method sequences, argument values, and return values observed in the real, or test, executions of software. The recorded data can be replayed for testing purposes.

The capture and replay tools can also serve the creation of test assertions. This is done by employing the recorded values. In order to provide test assertions other techniques can be used as well. Tools such as [3] analyze exceptions thrown by the CUT and determine whether they uncover faults in the CUT. Some tools, e.g. [12, 4, 2], infer an operational

```
 1   // ensure that only CUT outgoing methods
 2   // are intercepted and prevent advices
 3   // from intercepting themselves
 4   pointcut restriction(): !adviceexecution() &&
 5       && this(testedClass) && !target(testedClass);
 6
 7   int around(): restriction() &&
 8       call (Object java.util.LinkedList.get(int))
 9   {
10     // match current incoming method interval [before,after]
11     // to associated incoming interval [13,24]
12     if (before == 13 && after == 24)  {
13         // match inner counter
14         if (innerCounter == 1)  {
15             innerCounter++;
16             return 3;
17         }
18         // match inner counter
19         if (innerCounter == 2)  {
20             innerCounter++;
21             return 2;
22         }
23     }
24   }
```

Fig. 8. A code snippet of the mock aspect generated for IntStack

model from manual tests or from user specifications. Violations of pre-conditions, post-conditions, or invariants may suggest faulty behavior of the code under test.

GenUTest generates both method calls and test assertions based on the method-call sequences and the values captured in real executions. Thus, it is related to capture and replay tools. In [19, 14, 11, 5] the capture process of Java programs is implemented by applying complicated instrumentation techniques on the target's bytecode. These may include renaming interfaces, adding members and methods to existing classes, handling language specific constructs, and even modifying Java runtime libraries. The instrumentation technique used in GenUTest is quite simple and relies on weaving aspects. This is sufficient to effectively implement the capture mechanism in a natural and elegant manner. Furthermore, it is easy to implement the tool for other aspect oriented programming languages. Saff et al. [14], in their work on automatic test factoring, partition the system into two parts, a tested component T and its environment E. They limit the capturing and recording process to the interactions that occur between T and E only. These interactions are used to generate mock objects that comprise E', the mimicked environment. During testing, T is tested with E', and E' can only be used for this particular partition. In addition, it is required that T will be instrumented to enable the use of mock objects. Similar techniques are used in SCARPE [11], where the replay scaffolding technique can also be used to mock the behavior of the environment.

GenUTest captures and record interactions between all objects in the system. Besides the creation of mock aspects, GenUTest also generates unit tests. Each unit test is in an independent entity, thus the developer can execute any subset of them. Moreover, their use does not require the instrumentation of the CUT.

The techniques employed in our work, in [11], and in [14], are based on method sequence object representation. In the works described in [19] and in [5], the concrete state of an invoked object prior and after each method-call is captured and recorded as well. In Substra [19], the captured object states are used to infer constraints on the order of invoked method-calls. Based on these constraints new method-call sequences are generated with random values for arguments. In [5] the object states and sequences are used to create entities called differential unit test cases. Their motivation and goals are similar to those discussed in our paper. However, the use of concrete object states incurs a heavy price on the performance and storage requirements of their framework. Also, since concrete object state representation is composed of all the fields of an object, it is more sensitive to changes introduced into the unit as compared to the method sequence representation comprised of public method invocations. Thus, method sequence representation seems to be more suitable for unit testing, which perform black box testing of the unit, and for refactoring.

6   Conclusion

GenUTest is a tool that captures the execution of Java programs and automatically generates unit tests and corresponding mock aspects.

We have employed GenUTest in several open source projects. One is a small sized project called NanoXML [26]. It is an XML parser consisting of 24 classes and about 7,700 lines of code. Another project that we have used to test GenUTest is JODE (Java Optimize and Decompile Environment) [24], a medium sized Java project which consists of approximately 160 classes and about 35,000 lines of code. GenUTest effectively captured interactions and generated unit tests and mock objects. We intend to examine GenUTest also with larger examples.

The unit tests generated by GenUTest depend on the specific run of the CUTs. In order to examine code coverage of a given run, we have used the EclEmma code coverage tool [22]. It turned out that the execution of the generated unit tests achieve less code coverage than the execution of the system test from which they are derived.

In the future, we intend to increase the code coverage obtained by the generated unit tests. We will also improve the tool, for example by better handling inner classes, supporting multi-threaded programs, performance, etc.

References

1. Andrews, J.H., Haldar, S., Lei, Y., Li, F.C.H.: Tool support for randomized unit testing. In: Proceedings of the 1st International Workshop on Random Testing, pp. 36–45 (2006)
2. Boshernitsan, M., Doong, R., Savoia, A.: From Daikon to Agitator: Lessons and challenges in building a commercial tool for developer testing. In: Proceedings of the 2006 International Symposium on Software Testing and Analysis, pp. 169–180 (2006)

3. Csallner, C., Smaragdakis, Y.: JCrasher: An automatic robustness tester for Java. Software Practice and Experience 34(11), 1025–1050 (2004)
4. d'Amorim, M., Pacheco, C., Xie, T., Marinov, D., Ernst, M.: An empirical comparison of automated generation and classification techniques for object-oriented unit testing. In: Proceedings 21st IEEE/ACM International Conference on Automated Software Engineering (ASE 2006), pp. 59–68 (September 2006)
5. Elbaum, S., Chin, H.N., Dwyer, M.B., Dokulil, J.: Carving differential unit test cases from system test cases. In: Proceedings of the 14th ACM SIGSOFT International Symposium on Foundations of Software Engineering, pp. 253–264 (2006)
6. Fowler, M.: Refactoring: Improving the Design of Existing Code. Addison-Wesley, Reading (2000)
7. Husted, T., Massol, V.: JUnit in Action. Manning Publications Co. (2003)
8. Laddad, R.: AspectJ in Action: Practical Aspect-Oriented Programming. Manning, (2003)
9. Mackinnon, T., Freeman, S., Craig, P.: Endo-testing: unit testing with mock objects. In: Extreme Programming Examined, pp. 287–301. Addison-Wesley, Reading (2001)
10. Oriat, C.: Jartege: A tool for random generation of unit tests for Java classes. In: Reussner, R., et al. (eds.) QoSA 2005 and SOQUA 2005. LNCS, vol. 3712, pp. 242–256. Springer, Heidelberg (2005)
11. Orso, A., Kennedy, B.: Selective capture and replay of program executions. In: Proceedings of the 2005 Workshop on Dynamic Analysis, pp. 1–7 (2005)
12. Pacheco, C., Ernst, M.: Eclat: Automatic generation and classification of test inputs. In: Black, A.P. (ed.) ECOOP 2005. LNCS, vol. 3586, pp. 504–527. Springer, Heidelberg (July 25–29, 2005)
13. Pasternak, B.: GenUTest: A unit test and mock aspect generation tool. Master's thesis, Tel-Aviv University (in preparation, 2007)
14. Saff, D., Artzi, S., Perkins, J., Ernst, M.: Automated test factoring for Java. In: Conference of Automated Software Engineering (ASE), pp. 114–123 (2005)
15. van Vliet, H.: Software Engineering: Principles and Practice, 2nd edn. John Wiley & Sons, Inc., New York (2000)
16. Visser, W., Păsăreanu, C.S., Khurshid, S.: Test input generation with Java PathFinder. In: Proceedings of the 2004 ACM SIGSOFT International Symposium on Software Testing and Analysis, pp. 97–107 (2004)
17. Xie, T., Marinov, D., Notkin, D.: Rostra: A framework for detecting redundant object-oriented unit tests. In: Proceedings of the 19th IEEE International Conference on Automated Software Engineering (ASE), pp. 196–205 (September 2004)
18. Xie, T., Marinov, D., Schulte, W., Notkin, D.: Symstra: A framework for generating object-oriented unit tests using symbolic execution. In: Halbwachs, N., Zuck, L.D. (eds.) TACAS 2005. LNCS, vol. 3440, Springer, Heidelberg (2005)
19. Yuan, H., Xie, T.: Substra: A framework for automatic generation of integration tests. In: Proceedings of the 2006 International Workshop on Automation of Software Test, pp. 64–70 (2006)
20. The AspectJ Project. (Visited July 2007), http://www.eclipse.org/aspectj
21. Easy Mock (Visited July 2007), http://www.easymock.org
22. EclEmma (Visited November 2007), http://www.eclemma.org
23. Extreme Programming (Visited July 2007), http://www.extremeprogramming.org
24. JODE (Java Optimize and Decompile Environment) (Visited November 2007), http://jode.sourceforge.net

25. JUnit (Visited July 2007), http://www.junit.org
26. NanoXML (Visited July 2007), http://nanoxml.cyberelf.be
27. Virtual Mock Objects using AspectJ with JUnit (Visited July 2007), http://www.xprogramming.com/xpmag/virtualMockObjects.htm
28. XStream 1.2.1 (Visited July 2007), http://xstream.codehaus.org

Author Index

Lecture Notes in Computer Science

Sublibrary 2: Programming and Software Engineering

For information about Vols. 1– 4260
please contact your bookseller or Springer